THE
ULTIMATE
PALEO
DIET

Get Healthy, Lose Weight, and Feel Great by Eating the Foods You Were Designed to Eat

LOREN CORDAIN, PhD

— Exclusive Edition featuring —
The Paleo Diet and *The Paleo Answer*

RODALE.

Previously published as *The Paleo Diet* in 2011 and *The Paleo Answer* in 2012 © Loren Cordain and reprinted by permission of John Wiley & Sons, Inc., Hoboken, New Jersey.
This exclusive direct mail edition published in March 2015 by Rodale Inc.

Printed in the United States of America
Rodale Inc. makes every effort to use acid-free ∞, recycled paper ♻.

Library of Congress Cataloging-in-Publication Data is on file with the publisher.

ISBN 978–1–62336–576–9   direct mail hardcover

4   6   8   10   9   7   5   3   direct mail hardcover

We inspire and enable people to improve their lives and the world around them.
rodalestore.com

To Lorrie, Kyle, Kevin, and Kenny
for making it all worthwhile

Contents

Part 1

The Paleo
Answer

Chapter 1

The Ground Rules for the Paleo Diet

With the Paleo Diet, you'll be restoring the diet you are genetically programmed to eat. You'll be following the diet that every single person on the planet ate only 333 generations ago. It is the diet the modern world has completely forgotten.

The Paleo Diet is simplicity itself. Here are the ground rules:

1. All the meats, fish, and seafood you can eat
2. All the fruits and nonstarchy vegetables you can eat
3. No cereals
4. No legumes
5. No dairy products
6. No processed foods

The Paleo Diet is not a fat-free diet, it's a "bad fat"–free diet. It contains few of the artery-clogging fats found in the typical Western diet, but plenty of protein and good fats—such as those found in salmon and other cold-water fish, as well as in nuts and olive oil. It is not a fanatically strict diet, either.

There are three levels of adherence that make it easy to follow the diet's principles. Each level contains a limited number of Open Meals—meals in which you can still eat your favorite foods. If you enjoy an occasional glass of wine or beer, that's fine—it's allowed here. Because the Paleo Diet is a lifetime program of eating—and not a quick-fix weight-loss diet—it has built-in flexibility to accommodate a little cheating and your own individuality.

Try it, and from the beginning your appetite will be reduced and your metabolism will be increased. This means you'll lose weight without the hunger pangs that accompany so many diets—and ultimately doom these diets to fail. There's no need to count carbohydrate grams on this diet. You can eat as much carbohydrate as you want, as long as it's the good kind—the kind that comes from low-glycemic fruits and vegetables (which don't cause blood sugar to spike; see page 85). There is no need to count calories. This is how our diet was meant to be: Eat until you're full. Enjoy nature's bounty. Lose weight, and be healthy while you're doing it.

Here's how the Paleo Diet compares to the faddish low-carbohydrate diets.

Item	The Paleo Diet	Fad Low-Carb Diets
Protein	High	Moderate
Carbohydrate	Moderate	Low
Total fat	Moderate	High
Saturated fat	Moderate	High
Monounsaturated fat	High	Moderate
Polyunsaturated fat	Moderate	Moderate
Omega-3 fat	High	Low
Total fiber	High	Low
Fruits and vegetables	High	Low
Nuts and seeds	Moderate	Low
Salt	Low	High
Refined sugars	Low	Low
Dairy foods	None	High

The Fundamentals of the Paleo Diet

The Paleo Diet is based on the bedrock of Stone Age diets—eat lots of fresh, grass-produced meats, fresh fruits, and vegetables. From the work my research team and I have done in analyzing the daily food intake of hunter-gatherer societies, we have found the ideal dietary ratio. Although you don't need to count calories with the Paleo Diet, if you did you'd find that a little more than half—55 percent—comes from fresh meats, organ meats, fish, and seafood. The balance comes from fresh fruits and vegetables, some nuts, and healthful oils.

My research team and I have spent years analyzing what Paleolithic humans ate—running hundreds of computerized analyses exploring every conceivable dietary component, varying the amounts and types of plant and animal foods that were available to our ancient ancestors. No matter how we mixed up the ingredients, seven dietary characteristics consistently emerged. They are the Seven Keys of the Paleo Diet—your guidelines to weight loss and good health.

The Seven Keys of the Paleo Diet

1. Eat a relatively high amount of animal protein compared to that in the typical American diet.
2. Eat fewer carbohydrates than most modern diets recommend, but eat lots of good carbohydrates—from fruits and vegetables, not from grains, starchy tubers, and refined sugars.
3. Eat a large amount of fiber from nonstarchy fruits and vegetables.
4. Eat a moderate amount of fat, with more good (monounsaturated and polyunsaturated) fats than bad (trans and certain saturated) fats, and nearly equal amounts of omega-3 and omega-6 fats.
5. Eat foods with a high potassium content and a low sodium content.
6. Eat a diet with a net alkaline load.
7. Eat foods rich in plant phytochemicals, vitamins, minerals, and antioxidants.

The Seven Keys optimize health, minimize the risk of chronic disease, and cause excess weight to melt away. This is the way we're genetically programmed to eat.

Just the Foods You Can Hunt and Gather at Your Supermarket

You don't have to eat wild game meat (unless you want to) to achieve the same health benefits that kept the world's hunter-gatherers free from the chronic diseases of civilization. The mainstays of the Paleo Diet are the fresh meats, organ meats, and fish and seafood that are available at your local supermarket (and some health food stores).

Here are some high-protein foods that are part of the Paleo Diet.

- Turkey breast (94 percent protein)
- Shrimp (90 percent protein)
- Red snapper (87 percent protein)
- Crab (86 percent protein)
- Halibut (80 percent protein)
- Beef sweetbreads (77 percent protein)
- Steamed clams (73 percent protein)
- Lean pork tenderloin (72 percent protein)
- Beef heart (69 percent protein)
- Tuna steak (68 percent protein)
- Veal steak (68 percent protein)
- Sirloin beef steak (65 percent protein)
- Chicken livers (65 percent protein)
- Chicken breasts (63 percent protein)
- Beef liver (63 percent protein)
- Beef flank steak (62 percent protein)
- Pork chops (62 percent protein)
- Mussels (58 percent protein)

Although you may think of ground beef, eggs, cheese, milk, and legumes as high-protein foods, think again. None of these foods can hold a candle to lean meats and fish when it comes to protein content, and they are much lower in protein than you might expect. Check out the percentage of protein in each food, then compare it to the higher-protein foods above.

- Eggs (34 percent protein)
- Cheeses (28 percent protein)
- Legumes (27 percent protein)
- Lamb chops (25 percent protein)
- Fatty ground beef (24 percent protein)
- Dry salami (23 percent protein)
- Link pork sausage (22 percent protein)
- Bacon (21 percent protein)

- Whole milk (21 percent protein)
- Liverwurst sausage (18 percent protein)
- Bologna (15 percent protein)
- Hot dogs (14 percent protein)
- Cereal grains (12 percent protein)
- Nuts (10 percent protein)

You don't have to eat bone marrow (a favorite food of hunter-gatherers) on the Paleo Diet, either, but here's why it was good for our Paleolithic ancestors: Marrow is a major source of monounsaturated fat—another good fat. Monounsaturated fats lower your cholesterol level and reduce your risk of breast cancer and heart disease. You can find monounsaturated fats in nuts, avocados, and olive oil.

Nor do you have to eat brains (another delicacy for hunter-gatherers) to get omega-3 fats—one of the good fats that's quite important in preventing many chronic diseases. You can get plenty of health-sustaining omega-3 fats from many foods found in the supermarket, such as:

- Fish and seafood, particularly cold-water fish such as salmon, mackerel, herring, and halibut
- Flaxseed oil, which can be used in several ways—as an ingredient in salad dressings, poured over steamed vegetables, or taken as a supplement
- Liver
- Game meat
- Free-range chicken
- Pasture-fed beef
- Free ranging or cage-free eggs
- Salt-free walnuts and macadamia nuts (which are also tasty in salads)
- Leafy green vegetables
- Fish oil capsules

Meal Preparation and Typical Meals

Eating unadulterated, healthful fresh meats, seafood, fruits, and veggies at every meal requires a little bit of planning and foresight, but once you get into the swing of things, it will become second nature. Even working people who must eat away from home can easily incorporate real foods into their busy schedules; so can people who travel often or who must frequently dine out.

One of the keys to becoming a successful Paleo dieter is to prepare some of your food at home and bring it with you to work either as a snack or as a meal. For lunch, nothing could be simpler than to brown-bag a few slices of last night's roast beef or chicken breasts along with some fresh tomato wedges, a few carrot sticks, and an apple or a fresh peach.

Eating Paleo style while dining out is also quite easy if you follow a few simple guidelines. Order a tossed green salad with shrimp, but hold the croutons and dress it with olive oil and lemon juice. For breakfast out, try two poached eggs and half a cantaloupe, skip the toast, and treat yourself to a cup of decaffeinated coffee or herbal tea. Although you will be eliminating grains, dairy products, refined sugars, and processed foods from your daily fare, you will soon discover the incredible bounty and diversity of delicious and healthful foods that the Paleo Diet has to offer. How about a breakfast omelet made with cage free, free ranging eggs and stuffed with crab and avocado and covered with peach salsa? A filet of sole simmered in wine sauce accompanied by spinach salad and gazpacho soup for lunch? For dinner, does roast pork loin, a tossed green salad dressed with flaxseed oil, steamed broccoli, a glass of Merlot, and a bowl of fresh blackberries sprinkled with almond slices sound tempting? These are just a few examples from the 6 weeks' worth of meal plans and dozens of Paleo recipes I provide for you.

The Paleo Diet: A Nutritional Bonanza

Many registered dietitians and knowledgeable nutritionists would predict that any diet that excludes all cereal grains, dairy products, and legumes would lack many important nutrients and would require extremely careful planning to make it work. Just the opposite is true with the Paleo Diet—which confirms yet again that this is exactly the type of diet human beings were meant to thrive on, as they have for all but the last 10,000 years. The Paleo Diet provides 100 percent of our nutrient requirements. My research team has analyzed the nutrient composition of hundreds of varying combinations of the Paleo Diet, altering the percentages as well as the types of plant and animal foods in those combinations. In virtually every dietary permutation, the levels of vitamins and minerals exceed governmental recommended daily allowances (RDAs). The Paleo Diet even surpasses modern cereal- and dairy-based diets in many nutritional elements that protect against heart disease and cancer, including:

- Vitamin C
- Vitamin B_{12}
- Vitamin B_6
- Folic acid
- Magnesium
- Chromium
- Potassium
- Selenium
- Soluble fiber
- Omega-3 and monounsaturated fats
- Beta-carotene and other plant phytochemicals

In fact, the Paleo Diet is packed with much higher levels of many nutrients that are deficient in both vegetarian and average American diets, such as iron, zinc, vitamin B_{12}, vitamin B_6, and omega-3 fats.

Let's take a quick look at the daily nutrient intake of a 25-year-old woman on the Paleo Diet. Out of a typical 2,200 calories, half come from animal foods and half from plant foods—all available at the supermarket.

For breakfast, she eats half a cantaloupe and a 12-ounce portion of broiled Atlantic salmon. Lunch is a shrimp, spinach, and vegetable salad (seven large boiled shrimp, 3 cups of raw spinach leaves, one shredded carrot, one sliced cucumber, two diced tomatoes, and a dressing made from lemon juice, olive oil, and spices). For dinner, she has two lean pork chops, 2 cups of steamed broccoli, and a tossed green salad (2 cups of romaine lettuce, $\frac{1}{2}$ cup of diced tomatoes, $\frac{1}{4}$ cup of sliced purple onions, and half an avocado, dressed with lemon juice). She tops it all off with $\frac{1}{2}$ cup of fresh or frozen blueberries and $\frac{1}{4}$ cup of slivered almonds. For a snack, she has $\frac{1}{4}$ cup of slivered almonds and a cold pork chop.

Nutritional Analysis for One Day on the Paleo Diet

Nutrient	Daily Intake	RDA
Calories	2,200	100%
Protein	190.0 g	379%
Carbohydrate	142.0 g	—
Fat	108.0 g	—
Saturated fat	21.0 g	—
Monounsaturated fat	54.0 g	—
Polyunsaturated fat	21.0 g	—
Omega-3 fats	6.7 g	—
WATER-SOLUBLE VITAMINS		
Thiamin (B$_1$)	4.6 mg	417%
Riboflavin (B$_2$)	3.6 mg	281%
Niacin (B$_3$)	56.2 mg	374%
Pyridoxine (B$_6$)	5.9 mg	369%
Cobalamin (B$_{12}$)	10.3 mcg	513%
Biotin	113.0 mcg	174%
Folate	911.0 mcg	506%
Pantothenic acid	11.5 mg	209%
Vitamin C	559.0 mg	932%
FAT-SOLUBLE VITAMINS		
Vitamin A	6,861.0 RE	858%
Vitamin D	0.0 mcg	0%
Vitamin E	26.5 mg	331%
Vitamin K	945.0 mcg	1,454%
MACRO MINERALS		
Sodium	813.0 mg	—
Potassium	8,555.0 mg	—
Calcium	890.0 mg	111%
Phosphorus	2,308.0 mg	289%
Magnesium	685.0 mg	245%

TRACE MINERALS

Iron	21.5 mg	143%
Zinc	19.8 mg	165%
Copper	3.5 mg	155%
Manganese	6.4 mg	181%
Selenium	0.147 mg	267%
Dietary fiber	47.0 g	—
Beta-carotene	3,583.0 mcg	—

As you can see, the Paleo Diet is extremely nutritious. The macronutrient breakdown for this sample 2,200-calorie diet is 33 percent protein, 25 percent carbohydrate, and 42 percent fat. Note that for every nutrient except vitamin D, the daily nutrient intake ranges from 100% to more than 10 times the governmentally suggested RDA. Even "healthful" vegetarian diets don't reach these nutrient levels. The Paleo Diet is rich in antioxidant vitamins (A, C, and E), minerals (selenium), and plant phytochemicals, such as beta-carotene, which can help prevent the development of heart disease and cancer. In addition, the high levels of B vitamins (B_6, B_{12}, and folate) prevent elevated levels of blood homocysteine, a potent risk factor for atherosclerosis, and also have been associated with a reduced risk of colon cancer and spina bifida, a neural tube birth defect.

Even though the fat content (42 percent of total calories) is higher than that in the average American diet (31 percent of total calories), these are good fats—healthful, cholesterol-lowering monounsaturated and polyunsaturated fats. Actually, the monounsaturated fat intake is twice that of saturated fat. The high levels of omega-3 fats also help protect against heart disease because they thin the blood, prevent fatal heartbeat irregularities, and lower blood triglycerides.

Not only does the Paleo Diet provide you with an abundance of nutrients, it's also extremely high in fiber. This, too, can lower blood cholesterol. It promotes normal bowel function and prevents constipation as well.

Finally, because extra salt and processed salty foods are not part of the Paleo Diet, the sodium (and chloride) content here is very low, while the potassium content is quite high. This high-potassium/low-sodium balance helps prevent high blood pressure, kidney stones, asthma, osteoporosis, certain types of cancer, and other chronic diseases known to be associated with high-salt diets.

The amount of vitamin D you'll get on the Paleo Diet is negligible, because vitamin D is found only in trace quantities in all naturally occurring foods, except for fish liver oils. But we don't *need* to eat that much vitamin D—we can get all we need from the sun. (When we're exposed to ultraviolet radiation from sunlight, our bodies synthesize vitamin D from the cholesterol in our skin.) Our Paleolithic ancestors spent much of their time outdoors, and they manufactured all the vitamin D they needed from the sun's natural rays. Today, many of us get insufficient sunlight exposure to synthesize optimal levels of vitamin D. This is why milk, margarine, and other processed foods are fortified with vitamin D. We would all do well to incorporate some of the Stone Age lifestyle and make sure to get some daily sunshine. However, if your busy lifestyle doesn't allow it, particularly during short winter days, I recommend that you take a vitamin D supplement (at least 2,000 international units per day).

Perhaps the most important element of the Paleo Diet is its high protein intake— nearly four times higher than the DRI.* As I've discussed, this high level of protein helps you lose weight by increasing your metabolism and reducing your appetite. A 1999 clinical report in the *International Journal of Obesity* by my friend Dr. Soren Toubro and colleagues from the Royal Veterinary and Agricultural University in Copenhagen, Denmark, has shown that when it comes to weight loss, high-protein, low-calorie diets are much more effective than low-calorie, high-carbohydrate diets. In the ensuing 11 years, hundreds of scientific papers have confirmed these seminal results. Also, high levels of protein lower your cholesterol, reduce triglycerides, increase good HDL cholesterol, and reduce your risk of high blood pressure, stroke, and certain forms of cancer. When accompanied by sufficient amounts of alkaline fruit and vegetables, high-protein diets do not promote osteoporosis. Instead, they protect you from it. See "The Osteoporosis Connection" below.

The Osteoporosis Connection

One of the greatest—and least recognized—benefits of fruits and vegetables is their ability to slow or prevent the loss of bone density, called osteoporosis. But what about calcium? Surely eating a lot of cheese can help prevent osteoporosis. The answer is a bit more complicated. Nutrition scientists use the term "calcium balance" to describe the difference between how much calcium you take in and how much you

---

Beginning in 1997, the Food and Nutrition Board of the Institute of Medicine replaced RDA values with updated Dietary Reference Intake (DRI) numbers.

excrete. Most of us have gotten the message about consuming calcium. But the other part of the equation—how much calcium you excrete—is just as important. It is quite possible for you to be in calcium balance on a low-calcium intake if your calcium excretion is also low. On the other hand, it's easy for you to fall out of calcium balance—even if you load up on cheese at every meal—if you lose more calcium than you take in.

The main factor that determines calcium loss is balance of another type—the acid-base balance. If your diet has high levels of acid, you'll lose more calcium in your urine; if you eat more alkaline food, you'll retain more calcium. A study in the *New England Journal of Medicine* by my colleague Dr. Anthony Sebastian and his research group at the University of California at San Francisco showed that simply taking potassium bicarbonate (an alkaline base) neutralized the body's internal acid production, reduced urinary calcium losses, and increased the rate of bone formation. In a follow-up report in the *New England Journal of Medicine,* Dr. Lawrence Appel at Johns Hopkins University reported that diets rich in fruits and vegetables (these are alkaline foods) significantly reduced urinary calcium loss in 459 men and women.

Cereals, most dairy products, legumes, meat, fish, salty processed foods, and eggs produce net acid loads in the body. By far, the worst offenders on this list are the hard cheeses, which are rich sources of calcium. Again, unless you get enough fruits and vegetables, eating these acid-rich foods will actually promote bone loss and osteoporosis.

Virtually all fruits and vegetables produce alkaline loads. When you adopt the Paleo Diet, you won't have to worry about excessive dietary acid causing bone loss because you'll be getting 35 percent or more of your daily calories as healthful alkaline fruits and vegetables that will neutralize the dietary acid you get when you eat meat and seafood.

The Typical American Diet: A Nutritional Nightmare

Now let's take a look at this same 2,200-calorie diet for our sample 25-year-old woman—but let's replace most of the real foods (lean meats and fruits and vegetables) with processed foods, cereal grains, and dairy products. The nutrient breakdown depicted on page 14 closely resembles that of the average American diet. This is the same diet that has produced a nation in which 68 percent of all American men over age 25 and 64 percent of women over age 25 are either overweight or obese.

For breakfast, our 25-year-old woman eats a Danish pastry and 2 cups of cornflakes with 8 ounces of whole milk, topped off with a teaspoon of sugar, and she drinks a cup of coffee with a tablespoon of cream and a teaspoon of sugar. Because of the large amounts of refined carbohydrates consumed for breakfast, her blood sugar level soon plummets and she is hungry again by midmorning, so she eats a glazed doughnut and drinks another cup of coffee with cream and sugar. By noon, she's hungry again. She goes to the McDonald's near her office and orders a Quarter Pounder, a small portion of French fries, and a 12-ounce cola drink. For dinner, she eats two slices of cheese pizza and a small iceberg lettuce salad with half a tomato, covered with 2 tablespoons of Thousand Island dressing. She washes it all down with 12 ounces of lemon-lime soda. Let's examine the nutrient breakdown of this dietary disaster.

Nutritional Analysis for One Day on the Typical American Diet

Nutrient	Daily Intake	RDA
Calories	2,200	100%
Protein	62.0 g	57%
Carbohydrate	309.0 g	—
Fat	83.0 g	—
Saturated fat	29.0 g	—
Monounsaturated fat	19.0 g	—
Polyunsaturated fat	10.0 g	—
Omega-3 fats	1.0 g	—
WATER-SOLUBLE VITAMINS		
Thiamin (B_1)	1.0 mg	95%
Riboflavin (B_2)	1.1 mg	87%
Niacin (B_3)	11.0 mg	73%
Pyridoxine (B_6)	0.3 mg	20%
Cobalamin (B_{12})	1.8 mcg	88%
Biotin	11.8 mcg	18%
Folate	148.0 mcg	82%
Pantothenic acid	1.8 mg	32%
Vitamin C	30.0 mg	51%

FAT-SOLUBLE VITAMINS		
Vitamin A	425.0 RE	53%
Vitamin D	3.1 mcg	63%
Vitamin E	2.7 mg	34%
Vitamin K	52.0 mcg	80%
MACRO MINERALS		
Sodium	2,943.0 mg	—
Potassium	2,121.0 mg	—
Calcium	887.0 mg	111%
Phosphorus	918.0 mg	115%
Magnesium	128.0 mg	46%
TRACE MINERALS		
Iron	10.2 mg	68%
Zinc	3.9 mg	33%
Copper	0.4 mg	19%
Manganese	0.9 mg	28%
Selenium	0.040 mg	73%
Dietary fiber	8.0 g	—
Beta-carotene	87.0 mcg	—

This diet typifies everything that's wrong with the way most of us eat today—the modern, processed food–based diet. It violates all of the Seven Keys of the Paleo Diet—the ones we're genetically programmed to follow. Almost every nutrient falls below the RDA. The protein intake on the standard American diet is a paltry 62 grams compared to that of the Paleo Diet (a mighty 190 grams). Remember, protein is your ally in weight loss and good health. It lowers your cholesterol, improves your insulin sensitivity, speeds up your metabolism, satisfies your appetite, and helps you lose weight.

Even though there is very little meat in the typical American diet of this woman, the saturated fat content (29 grams) is 38 percent higher than that of the Paleo Diet. Worse still is the mix of fats. Healthful, cholesterol-lowering polyunsaturated and monounsaturated fats total a meager 29 grams. (In contrast, they add up to 75 grams on the Paleo Diet.) There is only 1 gram of heart-healthy

omega-3 fats for the whole day in the typical American diet, compared to a bountiful 6.7 grams in the sample Paleo Diet. Is it any wonder that the cereal-based,
processed food–laden American diet promotes heart disease?

Now take a look at vitamin B_6 (20 percent of the RDA), vitamin B_{12} (88 percent of the RDA), and folate (82 percent of the RDA). This woman's diet is deficient in all three of the vitamins that prevent toxic buildup of homocysteine, the
substance that damages the arteries and further predisposes you to heart disease. Inadequate amounts of folate also increase the risk of colon cancer and the
birth defect spina bifida.

It's also worth noting that this sample American diet has three times more
sodium—but only a quarter of the potassium—found in the Paleo Diet. This
mineral imbalance promotes or aggravates conditions and diseases caused by an
acid-base imbalance, including high blood pressure, osteoporosis, kidney stones,
asthma, stroke, and certain forms of cancer. The daily intake of magnesium is
also quite low here (46 percent of the RDA). Numerous scientific studies have
shown that having a low magnesium level puts you at risk for heart disease by
elevating your blood pressure, increasing your cholesterol level, and predisposing
your heart to beat irregularly. A low intake of magnesium also promotes the formation of kidney stones.

A high intake of antioxidant vitamins and phytochemicals from fresh fruits
and vegetables is one of the best dietary strategies you can adopt to reduce the
risk of cancer and heart disease. Unfortunately, when cereals, dairy products,
processed foods, and fatty meats displace fruits and vegetables, they automatically lower your intake of health-giving antioxidants and phytochemicals from
fruits and veggies. There is no comparison between the RDA percentages of
vitamin A (53 percent), vitamin C (51 percent), vitamin E (34 percent), and selenium (73 percent) in the example above and those in the Paleo Diet: vitamin A
(858 percent), vitamin C (932 percent), vitamin E (331 percent), and selenium
(267 percent). The Paleo Diet contains 41 times more beta-carotene (a natural
plant antioxidant) than the average American diet.

The average American diet is also deficient in zinc (33 percent of the RDA)
and iron (68 percent of the RDA)—which, along with a low intake of vitamins A
and C, can impair your immune system and open the door to colds and
infections.

Because the average American diet is loaded with refined cereal grains (six
servings in our example) and sugars (123 grams or about ¼ pound in our example), it increases blood sugar and insulin levels in many people. If insulin remains

constantly elevated, it causes a condition known as hyperinsulinemia, which increases the risk of a collection of diseases called metabolic syndrome—type 2 diabetes, high blood pressure, high cholesterol, obesity, and harmful changes in blood chemistry. But refined cereals and sugars are not part of the Paleo Diet, which means that your dietary insulin level will be naturally low and you will automatically reduce your risk of metabolic syndrome diseases. Last but not least is fiber. The average American diet contains a measly 8 grams, compared to 47 grams on the Paleo Diet.

Many nutritionists would say that the example diet is healthful because it contains large amounts of carbohydrate (55 percent of total calories) and low total fat (34 percent of total calories). This is also the message that most Americans have heard loud and clear—that healthful diets should be high in carbohydrate and low in fat. Unfortunately, when it comes to actual practice, most high-carbohydrate, low-fat diets look pretty much like our example of the typical American diet—a nutritional nightmare that promotes obesity, heart disease, cancer, and a host of other chronic illnesses.

Losing 45 Pounds and Healing Crohn's Disease
Sally's Story

Sally is a manager for a large telecommunications company in Illinois. Her reasons for adopting the diet were primarily health related. However, she also benefited from the diet's remarkable ability to normalize excess body weight.

In fall of 1986, I became severely ill. It started with several months of unshakable diarrhea, followed by gut-wrenching pain. It became so bad that I could not keep any food down. I lost 70 pounds in 3 months, and I was only 13 years old. I barely made it through my classes at school, and then I'd go home and sleep. My best friends no longer came over, my mother was sick with worry, and my father thought I was anorexic. When my symptoms began, doctors could not find anything wrong except for "perhaps some allergies." And when my symptoms grew worse, I was shuffled back and forth between doctors and specialists, each speculating on tumors, liver disease, and other life-threatening conditions. I was subjected to every conceivable test: MRIs (magnetic resonance imaging), ultrasounds, upper/lower GIs (gastrointestinal studies), blood tests, stool samples, urine tests, X-rays, throat scopes, and others. It took almost 9 months to reach the diagnosis of Crohn's disease.

I was given large doses of prednisone (a steroid drug) and scheduled to have a portion of my bowels surgically removed if I didn't respond to the medication. Within days of taking the steroids, I felt much better. Within weeks I was outside mowing the lawn and eating more in a day than I had eaten previously in a month. At the time, my medications were a miracle.

For most of my life I have been cycling between steroids, anti-inflammatory drugs, and immune suppressors. All of these medications alleviated the symptoms, but none treated the underlying disease. My overall health slowly deteriorated. I was severely depressed and powerless to stop my life from slowly wasting away. When questioning doctors, I was given unhelpful speculations: "Crohn's disease is genetic; it runs in families. It may be caused by a virus or bacterium, it is not contagious, and we do not know what causes this disease." Every specialist I saw agreed that Crohn's is not diet-related.

By the time I graduated from college, I became determined to do something. I enrolled in graduate school to learn more about scientific research so that one day I might help find a cure. While in graduate school, I discovered literature about diet-related treatments for a whole range of degenerative illnesses, including Crohn's disease. All of the diets used to treat Crohn's disease are very similar to a Paleolithic diet. It became my turn to become responsible for my own health, and I started eating a strict Paleolithic diet. The results were amazing. Within a month I was 90 percent symptom-free. I felt like I had been reborn.

I have been on the diet for almost 2 years now. I've lost 45 pounds and am near my optimal weight. I am 100 percent symptom-free of Crohn's disease and haven't seen a doctor in over a year. I've started running 4 miles a day, something that I could never have achieved before. This diet is anything but a quick fix. It takes time to heal the wounds of disease and medication. However, to anyone looking for control over their disease or their weight, I urge them to give it a try. It might just save your life as it saved mine.

Why the Paleo Diet Discourages Overeating

Most of the foods we crave—and that make us fat if we eat enough of them—contain some combination of sugar, starch, fat, and salt in a highly concentrated form. (If you think about it, sugar, starch, fat, and salt are pretty much the recipe for *all* the foods people tend to overeat.)

In nature, a sweet taste is almost always associated with fruit. This is what drew our ancestors to strawberries, for instance—the desire for a "sweet." However, as a bonus, they got much more than the sweet taste—fiber, vitamins, minerals, phytochemicals, and other healthful substances that improved their chances of survival. Similarly, our Paleolithic ancestors sought foods with a salty taste. Salt is absolutely essential for your health—but you don't need much of it. The trace amounts of salt found in fresh fruits, vegetables, and meats were just right for our ancient ancestors—who also got a hefty dose of potassium along with the sodium. Today, however, almost all processed foods are grossly overloaded with salt.

Real Food versus Fake Food

Today, much of our food is also fake. What does this mean? It's created, not natural, food. See for yourself. How about a snack of dry white flour? Of course not; by itself, flour is bland and tasteless—you'd choke on it. However, if you add water, yeast, salt, vegetable oil, and sugar and then bake the result, suddenly you've got white bread. If you take this same mixture, deep-fry it in hydrogenated fats, and then glaze it with sugar, it becomes tastier still—a glazed doughnut. Or you could add bananas and walnuts to the original dough, bake it, and coat it with sugar and margarine, and you've got banana nut bread with frosting.

If you want to feel more virtuous about the whole thing, you can substitute whole wheat flour and honey and call it "health food." But the bottom line is that none of these highly palatable food mixtures even remotely resemble the foods that nourished all human beings until very recently. In Paleolithic times, starchy foods weren't *also salty*; now we have potato chips and corn chips. Sweet foods were never *also fat*. Now we have ice cream and chocolates. Fatty foods were almost never *also starchy*. Now we have doughnuts that are not only fatty and starchy, but sugary as well.

It is extremely easy to overeat processed foods made with starch, fats, sugars, and salt. There is always room after dinner for pie, ice cream, or chocolates. But how about another stalk of celery or another broiled chicken breast? Many over-weight people can easily polish off a quart of ice cream after a full dinner. How many could—or would—eat an additional quart of steamed broccoli? The point here is that it's very difficult to overeat real foods—fruits, vegetables, and lean meats. Fruits and vegetables provide us with natural bulk and fiber to fill up our stomachs. Because they are low-glycemic, they also normalize our blood sugar and reduce our appetites. The protein in lean meats satisfies our hunger pangs rapidly and lets us know when we are full. Two chicken breasts for dinner may be filling—and two more might be impossible. Can we say the same for pizza slices?

Fake foods distort our appetites, allowing us to eat more than we really need. The most insidious—doughnuts, corn chips, vanilla wafers, croissants, wheat crackers—have a terrible one-two punch: high fats plus high-glycemic carbohydrates.

Normally, purely high-fat foods allow our appetites to self-regulate. For example, you can only eat a certain amount of pure butter before your body says "Ugh" and you become full and stop eating. However, when a high-glycemic carbohydrate sneaks in along with fat, you can continue eating the fat long after you would normally be full. The carbohydrate makes the fat taste better than it would alone (particularly if some salt and sugar are added), so you eat more. But the high-glycemic carbohydrate also may fool your body into thinking that it's still hungry.

When you eat a doughnut, for example, the high-glycemic carbohydrates cause your blood insulin level to shoot up. At the same time, your blood level of a hormone called glucagon tends to fall. These chemical changes cause a cascade of events that may result in impaired metabolism by limiting the body's access to its two major metabolic fuels—fat and glucose. The other important result of these chemical changes is hypoglycemia—low blood sugar, which paradoxically stimulates your appetite, making you feel hungry even though you've just eaten. These high-fat, high-glycemic carbohydrate foods perpetuate a vicious cycle of being hungry and eating and never being satisfied. They cause excessive rises in your blood sugar and insulin levels and promote rapid weight gain.

High-fructose corn syrup can make this bad situation even worse. Fructose powerfully promotes insulin resistance. It's added to almost every processed food imaginable; we get most of it from soft drinks, sweets, and baked items. But it's also an ingredient in most low-fat or nonfat salad dressings—foods many of us buy in an attempt to be more responsible, to count calories, and to limit as many unwholesome ingredients as possible. The best approach is to stay away from these foods. Stick with humanity's original fare: fruits, vegetables, and meats.

What to Expect on the Paleo Diet

The key to the Paleo Diet is to stay with this wonderful way of eating. I can guarantee that you will immediately feel better. Your energy level will increase; you won't have to endure that late afternoon tiredness or "blah" feeling. In the morning, you'll wake up charged and ready to greet the new day. You'll feel better with each passing day, and as the weeks go by, you'll notice that your clothes feel a bit loose. Your weight will gradually drop—week by week—until your normal, healthy body weight is restored. For some people, this may only take 1 or 2 months; for others, 6 months to a year; and for those with severe weight and health problems, a year or more. But the bottom line is that *it will happen.*

Many people also experience clearing of their sinuses, less stiffness of their joints in the morning, and normalization of bowel function. Indigestion, heartburn, and acid stomach are reduced and may even vanish completely within a few weeks of adopting this diet.

People with high cholesterol and abnormal blood chemistry can expect to see improvements within 2 weeks of starting the diet. Blood triglyceride levels will drop within days, and good HDL cholesterol will rise rapidly as well. In addition, for most people on the Paleo Diet, total blood cholesterol and LDL cholesterol drop within the first 2 weeks.

The Paleo Diet is particularly helpful for people with type 2 diabetes, cardiovascular disease, high blood pressure, kidney stones, asthma, acne, and osteoporosis. There is also a significant body of evidence suggesting that the Paleo Diet may help treat certain autoimmune diseases such as celiac disease, dermatitis herpetiformis, rheumatoid arthritis, multiple sclerosis, and Sjögren's syndrome. It even reduces your risk of many types of cancer. So eat well, lose weight, and be healthy with the Paleo Diet.

Chapter 2

How Our Diet Went Wrong and What You Can Do About It

The blink of an eye. That's how long, in the grand scheme of human history, we have grown food and domesticated livestock. It's been only 333 generations since this change—known as the Agricultural Revolution—happened, and yet we have almost completely lost track of the foods our ancient ancestors ate. The so-called new foods that agriculture gave us so completely displaced the old foods that most of us are unaware that these foods were ever new. Many people assume that cereals, dairy products, salted foods, legumes, domesticated meats, and refined sugars have always been part of our diet. Not true! We need to rediscover the foods that brought our Paleolithic ancestors vibrant health, lean bodies, and freedom from chronic disease. The foods that agreed nicely with their genetic blueprints are the same foods that agree nicely with our genetic blueprints.

But what are these foods? How can we possibly know what our Paleolithic ancestors ate? My research team and I have been asking these same questions for the past decade. I am happy to tell you that we have found answers to these questions by carefully piecing together information from four sources.

- The fossil record
- Contemporary hunter-gatherer diets
- Chimpanzee diets
- Nutrients in wild animals and plants

The Paleolithic (Old Stone Age) era began some 2.5 million years ago in Africa when the first crude stone tools were developed. It ended about 10,000 years ago in the Middle East, with the first ancient farms. (Perhaps 20 different species of ancient humans lived in the Paleolithic era. However, for the purposes of this book, we'll cover only the diets of our direct ancestors.) We can trace the evidence showing the dominance of lean meat in human diets from our origins 2.5 million years ago until the beginnings of agriculture 10,000 years ago.

Animal Food Is Brain Food

The notion that human beings were meant to be vegetarians runs contrary to every shred of evolutionary evidence from the fossil and anthropological record. We owe a huge debt to animal food. In fact, scientific evidence overwhelmingly suggests that if our ancient ancestors had eaten a meatless diet, we wouldn't be where we are today. I wouldn't have become a scientist, you wouldn't be reading this book, and we would all look a lot more like our nearest animal relative—the chimpanzee.

How can this be? Chimps are hairy, and they have a big gut. They swing from trees. Well, yes, but about 5 to 7 million years ago, so did our prehuman ancestors. The evidence is that the family tree forks—and humans moved into a category all their own. But genetically speaking, we are only about 1.7 percent different from the chimp.

Chimps are mostly vegetarians (although they do eat a few insects, bird eggs, and the occasional small animal), and they have the big, protruding belly characteristic of vegetarian animals (horses and cows, for example, have big bellies, too). Apes need large, active guts to extract the nutrients from their fiber-filled, plant-based diet.

About 2.5 million years ago, our ancestors began trading in their big guts for bigger brains—to the point where today our bellies are about 40 percent smaller than those of chimps and our brains are about three times larger. The turning point came when our ancestors figured out that eating animal food (meat and organs) gave them much more energy. Over the years, their bellies began to shrink—because they didn't need the extra room to process all that roughage. All the energy formerly needed by the gut was diverted to the brain, which doubled and then tripled in size. Without nutrient-dense animal foods in the diet, the large brains that make us human never would have had the chance to develop. Meat and animal foods literally shaped our genome.

Interestingly, just before the same period when human brains began to expand, something new came on the scene: tools—crude stone weapons, and knives that our ancestors used to butcher animal carcasses and later, to hunt. We know this because of telltale cut marks that have been found on the bones of fossilized animals and from evidence compiled at thousands of archaeological sites worldwide. (A classic example is the 125,000-year-old spear crafted from a yew tree found embedded between the ribs of an extinct straight-tusked elephant in Germany.)

At first, humans were not terribly good hunters. They started out as scavengers who trailed behind predators such as lions and ate the leftovers remaining on abandoned carcasses. The pickings were slim; ravenous lions don't leave much behind, except for bones. But with their handy tools (stone anvils and hammers), our early ancestors could crack the skulls and bones and still find something to eat—brains and fatty marrow.

Marrow fat was the main concentrated energy source that enabled the early human gut to shrink, while the scavenged brains contained a specific type of omega-3 fat called docosahexaenoic acid (DHA), which allowed the brain to expand. Docosahexaenoic acid is the building block of our brain tissue.

Without a dietary source of DHA, the huge expansion of our brain capacity could never have happened. Without meat, marrow, and brains, our human ancestors never would have been able to walk out of tropical Africa and colonize the colder areas of the world. If these people had depended on finding plant foods in cold Europe, they would have starved. In a landmark series of studies, my colleague Mike Richards, at Oxford University, studied the bones of Paleolithic people who lived in England some 12,000 years ago. Their diet, Richards confirmed, was almost identical to that of top-level carnivores, such as wolves and bears.

Hunting Big Game

Why would any sane person get close enough to poke a spear into a sharp-hoofed, kicking, and snorting 600-pound horse—much less a raging 5-ton mammoth? Why didn't Paleolithic people play it safe, gathering berries and nuts and snaring rabbits, rodents, and small birds? Again, the wisdom of the old ways becomes clear.

The basic idea of foraging for food—whether you're a human, a wolf, or even a house cat chasing a mouse—is simple. You've got to receive more energy from the food you capture than you use in trying to capture it. If you run around all day and use up 1,000 calories, but you come home with only 10 apples worth a grand total of 800 calories, you're going to be very hungry. So when Paleolithic people went looking for food, they tried to get the most bang for the buck. The best way to do this, they found, was with a large animal. It takes a lot more energy to run down and capture 1,600 one-ounce mice than it does to kill a single deer weighing 100 pounds (1,600 ounces). But there's a much more important reason why larger animals were preferred. It's called "protein toxicity."

We can only tolerate a certain amount of protein at a time– about 200 to 300 grams a day. Too much protein makes us nauseated, causes diarrhea, and eventually can kill us. This is why our Paleolithic ancestors couldn't just eat lean muscle meat. They needed to eat fat along with the lean meat, or they needed to supplement the lean meat with carbohydrates from plant foods. Early explorers and frontiersmen in North America knew this, too. They were painfully aware of the toxic effect of too much lean protein; they called the illness "rabbit starvation."

On average, large animals like deer and cows (or, for Paleolithic people, mammoths and wild horses) contain more fat and less protein than smaller animals like rabbits and squirrels. The squirrel's body is 83 percent protein and 17 percent fat; the mule deer's body is 40 percent protein and 60 percent fat. If you ate nothing but squirrel, you would rapidly exceed the body's protein ceiling, and like those early pioneers, you'd end up with rabbit starvation. On the other hand, if you only had deer to eat, you'd be doing fine. You would not develop protein toxicity because you'd be protected by the deer's higher fat content. This is why Paleolithic hunters risked their lives hunting larger animals.

In the Paleo Diet, you're protected from protein toxicity, too—by unlimited access to fresh fruits and vegetables. You're also protected by the good cholesterol–lowering monounsaturated fats and by our most powerful deterrent to heart disease—omega-3 fatty acids. With these safeguards in place, protein is your friend. High levels of protein speed up your metabolism, reduce your appetite, and lower your cholesterol. You will benefit from eating lean protein at every meal. I can assure you that as long as you eat plenty of fresh fruits and vegetables, there is no such thing as too much protein.

Restoring the Balance in Your Diet

My research team and I have found that, ideally, a little more than half—55 percent—of your calories should come fresh meats, organ meats, fish, and seafood. The balance should come from fresh fruits and vegetables, some nuts, and healthful oils.

In the average American diet, not only is the balance of plant to animal food off-kilter, it's almost exactly the opposite of what we are genetically programmed to eat. In the typical American diet, 24 percent of the calories come from cereals, 11 percent from dairy products, 18 percent from refined sugars, and 18 percent from refined oils. These foods represent 71 percent of the energy consumed in the typical American diet—yet virtually none of them are to be found on the Paleo menu of fresh meats, fresh fruits, and vegetables. In the American diet, about 38 percent of the calories come from animal foods, most of them unhealthy meats (hot dogs, fatty ground beef, bacon, lunch meats, etc.)—a far cry from the Paleo Diet.

Vegetarian Isn't Better

Ann's Story

After high school graduation, Ann Woods left her home for a summer waitressing job in Alaska. She had a great time living away from her parents and partying with her friends, but the continual stream of on-the-job glazed doughnuts, burgers, and fries, along with evening treats of M&Ms and Baskin-Robbins ice cream, eventually caused her waistline to balloon. When she came back home to start college in the fall, her weight had jumped from 110 to 135 pounds. She was still not fat but was much heavier than she had ever been. After a bit of friendly razzing from her boyfriend, she managed to lose all the weight by adopting a near-vegetarian diet that emphasized grains, potatoes, lots of starch, and very little fat or meat. At the time, this seemed a prudent thing to do. After all, this type of diet was supposed to be the healthiest.

Ann also began to jog, an activity that soon blossomed into a lifetime interest in running and fitness. Her weight stabilized, and she became lean and fit. Her blood pressure and cholesterol levels were low, but after almost 7 years of running, she noticed that her energy began to wane. She was continually tired and wanted nothing more than to sleep after long runs. Ann recovered from one running-related injury only to find herself injured again within weeks. Dark circles formed underneath her eyes, and she caught colds more frequently than ever. She finally discovered that she had iron-deficiency anemia caused by her "healthful" staples of oatmeal, brown rice, beans, pasta, and low-fat yogurt.

Ann discovered the Paleo dietary principles in *The Complete Book of Alternative Nutrition,* which featured my research. It made a lot of sense to her, and she gave it a try. She replaced her former vegetarian staples with lean meat, chicken, and seafood at almost every meal. Fruits and veggies were no problem—she had eaten a lot of these before her switch. Within a week, Ann noticed that her energy level was stable throughout the day. She no longer had late-afternoon slumps. Her stamina increased, and she was less tired after her runs. After 3 months on the diet she dropped 5 additional pounds to her present weight of 106, her stomach was now totally flat, and her muscle tone and strength were better than ever. On top of this, her iron-deficiency anemia disappeared, and the dark circles underneath her eyes vanished.

How "Progress" Has Hurt Us

The Agricultural Revolution changed the world and allowed civilization—cities, culture, technological and medical achievements, and scientific knowledge—to develop. These were all good things. And yet, there was a huge downside. The Agricultural Revolution is also responsible for much of today's obesity and chronic disease. The foods that agriculture brought us—cereals, dairy products, processed meats, salted foods, and refined sugars and oils—proved disastrous for our Paleolithic bodies.

Nobody could have anticipated this revolution or its consequences. The early farmers didn't have some great plan to overthrow the old system. They were just looking for better ways to feed their families in the face of a rising population and dwindling food resources. It all started in the Middle East about 10,000 years ago, when some enterprising people started to sow and harvest wild wheat seeds. Later, they domesticated barley and a few legumes and then livestock—sheep, goats, and pigs. They still picked wild fruits and vegetables and still hunted wild game, but the die was cast; the diet had changed dramatically.

Hello Grains, Hello Health Problems

The archaeological record clearly shows that whenever and wherever ancient humans sowed seeds (and replaced the old animal-dominated diets), part of the harvest included health problems. One physical ramification of the new diet was immediately obvious: Early farmers were markedly shorter than their ancestors. In Turkey and Greece, for example, preagricultural men stood 5 feet 9 inches tall and women 5 feet 5 inches. By 3000 BC, the average man had shrunk to 5 feet 3 inches and the average woman to 5 feet. But getting shorter—not in itself a health problem—was the least of the changes in these early farmers. Studies of their bones and teeth have revealed that these people were basically a mess: They had more infectious diseases than their ancestors, more childhood mortality, and shorter life spans in general. They also had more osteoporosis, rickets, and other bone mineral disorders, thanks to the cereal-based diets. For the first time, humans were plagued with vitamin- and mineral-deficiency diseases, such as scurvy, beriberi, and pellagra; vitamin A and zinc deficiencies; and iron-deficiency anemia. Instead of the well-formed, strong teeth their ancestors had, there were now cavities. Their jaws, which were formerly square and roomy, were suddenly too small for their teeth, which overlapped each other.

What had gone wrong? How could the benign practice of agriculture—harnessing nature's bounty—have caused so many health problems? We now know that although the population was soaring, the quality of life—as well as the average life span—was in a nosedive. The new staples, cereals and starches, provided calories but not the vital nutrients of the old diet of lean meats, fruits, and vegetables. The result—ill health and disease.

The health picture got worse over the years with the arrival of salt, fatty cheeses, and butter. Our ancestors learned to ferment grains, make beer, and eventually distill spirits. Selective breeding—and the innovation of feeding grain to livestock—steadily produced fatter pigs, cows, and sheep. Most meat wasn't eaten fresh—fewer people hunted—but instead was pickled, salted, or smoked. Fruits and vegetables became luxuries—rare seasonal additions to the monotony of cereal and starch.

More recently—just 200 years ago—the Industrial Revolution brought refined sugar, canned foods, and refined white flour to the average family's table. Food was processed in earnest by the mid-20th century with the invention of trans fatty acids, margarine, shortening, and combinations of these fats mixed with sugar, salt, other starches, high omega-6 vegetable oils, high-fructose corn syrup, and countless additives, preservatives, coloring agents, and emulsifiers.

Imagine a Paleolithic human confronted with a Twinkie or even a pizza. He or she wouldn't even recognize these modern-day treats as food.

Big Mistakes in the 1950s

In many ways, the 1950s were a simpler time. Part of the mind-set then seemed to be to find simple solutions for complicated problems. In the early 1950s, when scientists were unraveling the links between diet and heart disease, they found that *saturated fat* (the kind found in butter, cheese, and fatty meats) raised total blood cholesterol; it also raised the LDL (the bad kind) cholesterol level and increased the risk of heart disease. More recent research has shown that not all saturated fats raise total and LDL cholesterol. Stearic acid actually lowers blood cholesterol similar to the way that monounsaturated fats do. Unfortunately, red meat became the scapegoat; all of a sudden, it was the chief artery clogger and cause of heart attacks. Even many nutritionists and physicians jumped to the conclusion that red meat was an unhealthy food that promoted heart disease and bowel cancer.

The food industry responded to the message that saturated fats were bad by creating all sorts of "healthy alternatives"—highly polyunsaturated vegetable oils (corn, safflower, sunflower, and cottonseed, to name a few). They also gave us all kinds of products made from these oils, such as margarines, shortening, spreads, and dressings. And almost overnight, these vegetable oils and their spin-offs were incorporated into virtually all processed foods and baked goods.

Unfortunately, as we now know, this was a very bad move. The indiscriminate infusion of vegetable oils into the American diet gave us far too many omega-6 polyunsaturated fats at the expense of the good omega-3 polyunsaturated fats. And the increased use of margarine and spreads caused the widespread introduction of still another kind of fat, called trans fatty acids, into our meals and snacks.

The next plan the nutritional masterminds came up with—like the anti–red meat campaign, it was not well thought out and was inadequately tested before being put into practice—was to replace saturated fats with carbohydrates, primarily starchy carbohydrates, like those found in bread, potatoes, and cereals. By the early 1990s, this recommendation had become so entrenched that it was the official policy of the USDA, with the former Food Pyramid showing 6 to 11 servings of cereal grains as the foundation for a healthy diet. We now know, from scientific studies examining something called the glycemic index of certain foods, that this is 6 to 11 servings too many.

Part of the confusion here is that all carbohydrates are not created equal. Some of them are good for us. But others promote ill health and disease, and this brings us to the glycemic index. Good carbohydrates have a low glycemic index. This means they cause a minimal or slow rise in our blood glucose (sugar) level. The glycemic load is the glycemic index of a food times its carbohydrate content. It is this high glycemic load that elevates blood insulin levels in many people. High-glycemic carbohydrates cause large and rapid rises in blood glucose and have been implicated in a wide variety of chronic diseases—adult-onset diabetes, high blood pressure, heart disease, obesity, elevated blood uric acid levels, elevated blood triglycerides (the building blocks of fat, which float around in the bloodstream), elevated small-dense LDL cholesterol, and reduced HDL cholesterol. This cluster of diseases is known to cardiologists as the metabolic syndrome. Regrettably, the architects of the Food Pyramid did not distinguish between high- and low-glycemic carbohydrates when they started this carbomania.

Let's see how our modern way of eating has deviated from the Seven Keys to nutrition I laid out in Chapter 1 and how this has affected our health.

The Seven Major Problems in the Typical American Diet

1. Not Enough Protein

Protein makes up 15 percent of the calories that most Americans (and people in other Western countries) eat every day. But it should be much higher—between 19 and 35 percent—to give us more energy and help us burn off extra calories. Look at the numbers: For every 100 calories, cereals average only about 12 percent protein—compared to 83 percent protein for game meats. Legumes like lentils, peas, and beans average 27 percent protein.

As for dairy products, the phenomenon of the "milk cow" (or goat or sheep) happened roughly 9,000 years ago. Milk contains 21 percent protein, cheese averages 28 percent protein, and butter has absolutely no protein—but a lot of fat.

The bottom line: Most of us are getting only half of the protein we need. Why is this bad? I'll show how a low protein intake contributes to weight gain and a high blood cholesterol level and increases your risk of many chronic diseases.

2. Too Much of the Wrong Carbohydrates

We're a nation of starch and sugar eaters. Carbohydrates often make up about half of the typical Western diet—a considerable difference from the Paleo Diet. For our ancient ancestors, carbohydrates accounted for 22 to 40 percent of daily calories—but these were good carbohydrates, from wild fruits and vegetables. These low-glycemic foods—which don't cause blood sugar to spike—are digested and absorbed slowly.

With nonstarchy fruits and vegetables, it's very hard to get more than about 35 percent of your calories from carbohydrates. For example: There are 26 calories in the average tomato. To get 35 percent of your daily calories as carbohydrates from tomatoes only, you'd have to eat 30 tomatoes. And this is why, with the Paleo Diet, you can indulge yourself by eating all the nonstarchy fruits and vegetables you want. When you eat the right foods, getting too many carbohydrates—or eating too many high-glycemic carbohydrates, which can cause a dangerous rise in your blood sugar and insulin levels—is simply not something you have to worry about. The average carbohydrate content of fruits is only about 13 percent per 100 grams, about 4 percent for nonstarchy vegetables—and zero for meats, fish, and seafood. In stark contrast, the average carbohydrate content of cereal grains is 72 percent per 100 grams.

Why are many carbohydrates bad? Many whole grains and legumes don't have a lot of vitamins and minerals. They're poor dietary sources of these important nutrients. So a diet that's tilted too heavily toward grains and legumes—at the expense of meats, fruits, and vegetables—can lead to vitamin and mineral deficiencies. This is why so many of our breads and cereals are fortified with extra nutrients. Food shouldn't need to be supplemented with vitamins, and if you're getting the right balance of meats, fruits, and vegetables, neither should you.

Worse, cereal grains and legumes even contain "antinutrients"—chemicals that actually *prevent* your body from absorbing the proper nutrients and can damage the gastrointestinal and immune systems. Too many grains and legumes can disrupt the acid balance in the kidneys as well, and can contribute to the loss of muscle mass and bone mineral content that occurs with aging.

Finally, if you eat more carbohydrates, you're eating less protein. Protein is the dieter's friend: It reduces your appetite and increases your metabolism—and this translates rapidly into weight loss.

One of the great dietary myths in the Western world is that whole grains and legumes are healthful. The truth is that these foods are marginal at best. But what about the "healthy" breads? At best, they're *less bad* than the overprocessed, superrefined white breads you could be buying. But they're still not part of the Paleo Diet. Formerly (before "progress" brought refined milling technology to bread making), almost all cereal grains either were eaten whole or were so crudely milled that nearly the entire grain—bran, germ, and fiber—remained intact, and flour was much less refined than the kind we buy today. Our great-great-grandparents ate cracked wheat breads and baked goods with a moderate glycemic index—which meant a more moderate rise in blood sugar level.

Does this mean that whole grains are good for you? Not necessarily. It just means that an extra bad characteristic—a high glycemic index—wasn't incorporated into them yet. That unfortunate addition happened about 130 years ago, when steel roller mills came on the flour-making scene. They smashed all the fiber out of the grains and left the wimpy white, high-glycemic powder most of us think of as flour. Today, almost all baked goods made with this stuff frequently cause the blood sugar level to rise excessively.

Even "whole wheat" bread made from flour ground by these steel roller mills does the same thing to your blood sugar, because the flour particle size is uniformly small—so it's virtually no different from white flour. About 80 percent of all the cereal products Americans eat come from refined white flour with a high glycemic index.

Compounding the Problem: Sugar and Sweeteners. Our Paleolithic ancestors loved honey. But it was a rare treat because it was only available seasonally and in limited quantities (and they had to outmaneuver bees to get it). So for the most part, refined sugars—another source of carbohydrates—simply were not part of humanity's diet for 2.5 million years. In fact, until about the last 200 years or so, they weren't part of anybody's diet.

Sugar is another of those side effects of technological "progress," and its rise to prominence in our daily life has been rapid. In England in 1815, the average person used about 15 pounds of table sugar a year; in 1970, the average person used 120 pounds. How much sugar do you buy a year? Do you buy another 5-pound bag every time you go to the grocery store? You're not alone.

Yet sugar, like refined cereal grains, is not good for us. Sure, it causes cavities—most of us hear that message every time we go to the dentist. But it's also becoming evident that sugar poses more serious health problems. It promotes insulin resistance and metabolic syndrome diseases almost as much as high-glycemic breads and starchy potatoes do.

The chemical name for table sugar is sucrose. Although sucrose has nearly the same high glycemic index (65) as white bread (70), it has two additional characteristics that make it particularly harmful for insulin metabolism. First, it is 100 percent carbohydrate, meaning that its glycemic load is very high.

Second, when your body digests sucrose, it is broken down into two simple sugars—high-glycemic glucose (with a glycemic index of 97) and low-glycemic fructose (with a glycemic index of 23). Scientists used to think that fructose was not harmful because of its low glycemic index. But recent laboratory studies by Dr. Mike Pagliassotti and colleagues at Arizona State University have revealed that fructose is actually the main culprit in table sugar that causes insulin resistance. Dr. Pagliassotti's findings were bolstered by research at the University of Lausanne Medical School in Switzerland, by Dr. Luc Tappy and colleagues, showing that fructose can cause insulin resistance in humans. Insulin resistance, in turn, often promotes obesity and chronic metabolic syndrome diseases, including hypertension, heart disease, and diabetes.

High-Fructose Corn Syrup: A Really Bad Idea. The steady increase in table sugar use was an unfortunate development that increased the carbohydrate content of our diet. But in the 1970s, the food-processing industry made a discovery: High-fructose corn syrup could save them a lot of money. Because fructose is so much sweeter than sucrose, less of it is needed to sweeten any processed food. Today, corn syrup is the food-processing industry's sweetener of choice. Imagine the financial incentive here: With fructose, millions of tons of sugar are saved each year.

What does this mean to average Americans? It means we are getting grossly disproportionate amounts of sweetener in our diets. There are about *10 teaspoons of high-fructose corn syrup in a single 12-ounce can of soda*. The average American now eats 66 pounds of corn syrup a year, plus 64 pounds of sucrose, and an appalling total of 131 pounds of refined sugars. When you begin the Paleo Diet and gradually wean yourself off processed foods, your daily sugar intake will drastically shrink—and, better still, the sugar you get will come from healthful fruits and vegetables.

3. Not Enough Fiber

Fiber intake began to go down the day our ancient ancestors started harvesting cereal grains. How can this be? Don't whole grains equal fiber? When our doctors tell us to add more fiber to our diet, don't they mean for us to eat more oatmeal? The truth is that calorie for calorie, whole grains can't hold a candle to fruits and vegetables. Fruits on average contain *almost twice as much* fiber as whole grains. Compared to whole grains, nonstarchy vegetables have *eight times more fiber.* Sugars have absolutely no fiber.

And yet we know that dietary fiber is absolutely essential for good health. Not having enough fiber raises our risk of developing scores of diseases and health problems. A comprehensive medical text edited by Drs. Hugh Trowell, Denis Burkitt, and Kenneth Heaton has implicated low dietary fiber in the following diseases and health problems: constipation, diverticulitis, colon cancer, appendicitis, Crohn's disease, ulcerative colitis, irritable bowel syndrome, duodenal ulcer, hiatal hernia, gastroesophageal reflux, obesity, type 2 diabetes, gallstones, high blood cholesterol, varicose veins, hemorrhoids, deep vein thrombosis, and kidney stones.

4. Too Much Fat and Too Many Bad Fats

Cut the fat! If the nutritional experts have had an overriding message over the last decades, this is it.

The thing is, this dictum is flat-out wrong. We now know that it's not *how much* fat you eat that raises your blood cholesterol levels and increases your risk of heart disease, cancer, and diabetes—it's the *kind* of fat you eat. We consume too many omega-6 polyunsaturated fats at the expense of the healthful omega-3 kind. And we get plenty of those cholesterol-raising, artery-clogging trans fatty acids found in margarine, shortening, and many processed foods.

All of those kinds of fat are bad and need to go. But in removing all fats from our diet, we are doing more harm than good. This problem is easy to solve: With the Paleo Diet—which contains healthful fats—you will automatically reestablish the proper balance of fats in your diet. You'll also lower your blood cholesterol and reduce your risk of heart disease, cancer, and other chronic illnesses.

From our analyses of the fats in wild animals, my research team and I have found that even though ancient humans ate meat at nearly every meal, they consumed about half of the palmitic acid found in the average Western diet. (Wild game meat is low in total fat and palmitic acid and high in healthful, cholesterol-lowering monounsaturated fat and stearic acid.) They also ate lots of omega-3 polyunsaturated fats.

The ratio of omega-6 to omega-3 fats in Paleo diets was about 2 to 1; for the average American, the ratio is much too high—about 10 to 1. Eating too many omega-6 fats instead of omega-3 fats increases your risk of heart disease and certain forms of cancer; it also aggravates inflammatory and autoimmune diseases. The meats, fish, fruits, vegetables, and oils found in the Paleo Diet guarantee that you will have the proper ratio of omega-6 and omega-3 fats—and of all other fats.

Cereal Doesn't Help. Cereal grains are low in fat. But the little fat they do have is unbalanced—tilted heavily toward omega-6. For example, in game and organ meat, the average ratio of omega-6 to omega-3 is 2 or 3 to 1. In eight of the world's most commonly consumed cereals, this ratio is a staggering 22 to 1.

Cereal grains also have contributed to generations of blubbery cows that bear little resemblance to the lean wild animals our ancestors ate. Grain-fed cows have become loaded down with palmitic acid; worse, the fats in their meat have taken on the same high omega-6 to omega-3 ratio that's in their grain.

Milk Doesn't Help, Either. Dairy foods have taken a further toll on humanity's health over the last 9,000 years or so. Milk, cream, cheese, butter, fermented milk products (including yogurt), ice cream, and the many processed dairy products of the 20th century are some of the richest sources of certain saturated fats in the typical Western diet. In particular, fatty dairy foods contain palmitic and myristic fatty acids—two substances that elevate blood cholesterol. When you evaluate dairy products for fat percentage by calories, butter is the worst at 100 percent fat. Cream is 89 percent fat, cheeses average about 74 percent fat, and whole milk is about 49 percent fat. And most of the fats in these dairy products—about 40 percent—are the bad saturated fatty acids. Despite their wholesome image, whole milk and fatty dairy products are some of the least healthful foods in our diets. Their fatty acids (palmitic acid and myristic acid) raise your blood cholesterol; they also raise your risk of developing heart disease and other chronic illnesses.

The Trouble with Unbalanced Vegetable Oils. The next major misstep in food innovation happened just a few decades ago, when vegetable oils became part of our diet.

In the 1940s and 1950s, when most of these vegetable oils were introduced, nobody realized that the *ratio* of omega-6 to omega-3 fats was terribly important to health. What food scientists knew at that point was pretty simple—that polyunsaturated fats lowered blood cholesterol. And it was with this limited piece of the total picture that they happily created a great variety of cooking and salad oils that were highly polyunsaturated—but regrettably also extremely high in omega-6 fats. The worst offenders are safflower oil and peanut oil (with extremely high omega-6 to omega-3 ratios), cottonseed oil, sunflower oil, sesame oil, and corn oil. Walnut oil is more balanced. And flaxseed oil is better still— low in omega-6 fats and high in omega-3s.

Trans Fats Are Terrible. Cooking and salad oils are just part of the high omega-6 problem. Nearly all processed foods—breads, cookies, cakes, crackers, chips, doughnuts, muffins, cereals, and candies—and all fast foods are cooked with some form of high omega-6 vegetable oil. Worse, many of these foods are still made with hydrogenated vegetable oils that contain harmful trans fatty acids. Trans fats raise blood cholesterol and increase your risk of developing heart disease. A study published in the *American Journal of Public Health* concluded that consumption of trans fats by Americans was responsible for more than 30,000 deaths annually from heart disease. Trans fats are found in margarine, shortening, and some peanut butters—foods that definitely were not part of humanity's original diet.

5. Too Much Salt, Not Enough Potassium

Paleo diets were exceptionally rich in potassium and low in sodium. Just about everything Paleolithic people ate—meats, fish, fruits, vegetables, nuts, and seeds—contained five to ten times more potassium than sodium. This means that when you eat only fresh, unprocessed food, it's impossible to consume more sodium than potassium.

We don't know exactly when farmers began to include salt in their diets, but we can guess why. Salt performed a great service, in the centuries before refrigeration, in preserving meats and other foods. It helped make foods like olives edible; it added flavor to bland cereals and other foods. At least 5,600 years ago, archaeological evidence shows us, salt was mined and traded in Europe. It remains a staple today; in fact, the average American consumes about twice as much sodium as potassium. And that's not healthy.

6. An Acid-Base Imbalance

Very few people—including nutritionists and dietitians—are aware that the acid-base content of your food can affect your health. Basically, this is what happens: Everything you digest eventually reports to the kidneys as either an acid or an alkaline base. Acid-producing foods are meats, fish, grains, legumes, dairy products, and salt. Alkaline-producing foods are fruits and vegetables. You need both kinds—acid and alkaline. Fats are generally neutral.

The average American diet is slightly acidic—which means that our kidneys must handle a net acid load. For example: Suppose you have a typical "light" lunch, probably available at a dozen places near your home or office, of pepperoni pizza and a small salad with Caesar dressing. This meal is a disaster for the body's acid-base balance: The pizza's white-flour crust, melted cheeses, and salty pepperoni are all highly acidic. Add salt, and you make it even more acidic. Any alkaline remnant available in the tiny salad is neutralized by the salt and cheese in the Caesar salad dressing.

In the long run, eating too many acid foods and not enough alkaline foods can contribute to bone and muscle loss that occurs with aging. There are more immediate dangers, too: Excessive dietary acid can raise blood pressure and increase your risk of developing kidney stones. It can also aggravate asthma and exercise-induced asthma.

7. Not Enough Plant Phytochemicals, Vitamins, Minerals, and Antioxidants

The Paleo Diet is rich in vitamins and minerals. One of the best ways to prove how healthy our diet used to be is to show what happened when our ancestors fiddled with it.

Vitamin C deficiency, a disease unknown to Paleolithic people, causes scurvy. Paleolithic people didn't have this problem; their diets were extremely high in vitamin C (around 500 milligrams per day) because they ate so many fresh fruits and vegetables. But even Eskimo groups—who for thousands of years have eaten virtually no plant foods for most of the year—didn't get scurvy. How can this be? They got their vitamin C from other natural sources—raw fish, seal, and caribou meat.

But as our ancestors began eating more cereal grains and fewer meats, fresh fruits, and vegetables, they lost much of the vitamin C in their diets. Cereal grains have no vitamin C, which is one of the body's most powerful antioxidants. Vitamin C helps lower cholesterol, reduces the risk of heart disease and cancer, boosts the immune system, and helps ward off infections and colds.

Vitamin A deficiency, like scurvy, could only have emerged after the coming of agriculture. Paleo diets were always rich in fruits and vegetables—excellent sources of beta-carotene, a nutrient that can be converted to vitamin A by the liver. (Our ancient ancestors also ate the entire carcasses of the animals they hunted and killed, including the vitamin A–rich liver.) Again, trouble happened when cereals took over and fresh fruits, vegetables, and organ meats were pushed aside. Vitamin A is essential for all of the body's mucous membranes. Vitamin A deficiency results in a condition called xerophthalmia (dry eyes), which can lead to blindness; in fact, this is the leading cause of blindness in children worldwide. Vitamin A deficiency also impairs the body's ability to fight infection and disease.

Vitamin B deficiency is another problem. Many people believe that whole-grain cereals are rich sources of B vitamins. They're mistaken. Compared to meats, fruits, and vegetables, calorie for calorie, cereals are vitamin B lightweights. Even worse, as I mentioned earlier, whole grains and legumes contain antinutrients that block the absorption of B vitamins in the intestines. For instance, antinutrients called pyridoxine glucosides can prevent your body from getting as much as two-thirds of the vitamin B_6 you eat. In a study of vegetarian women from Nepal, Dr. Robert Reynolds, of the USDA Human Nutrition Research Center, linked the low vitamin B_6 levels in these women to the high levels of pyridoxine glucosides in their grain- and legume-heavy diets. In contrast, the availability of vitamin B_6 in meats is nearly 100 percent.

Another B vitamin that's poorly absorbed when you eat whole grains is biotin. Experiments by my colleague Dr. Bruce Watkins from Purdue University have shown that wheat and other whole grains impair the body's ability to get enough biotin. Biotin deficiencies result in dry, brittle fingernails and hair. Research by Dr. Richard K. Scher and colleagues at Columbia University has shown that biotin supplements reduce fingernail brittleness and vertical "ridging" in nails. But you won't need to supplement your diet if you get enough biotin (or any other vitamin or mineral) the old-fashioned way—by eating the right foods. The availability of biotin from animal foods is almost 100 percent.

Pellagra and beriberi are two of the most devastating and widespread B vitamin–deficiency diseases that have ever plagued humankind. They are caused exclusively by excessive consumption of cereals. Pellagra is a serious, often fatal, disease caused by a lack of the B vitamin niacin and the essential amino acid tryptophan. In a sad chapter of US history, between 1906 and 1940 there was an epidemic of pellagra in the South. An estimated 3 million people developed it, and at least 100,000 of them died. Similar outbreaks have occurred in Europe and India, and pellagra is still common in parts of Africa.

Underlying every worldwide pellagra epidemic was excessive consumption of corn. Corn has low levels of both niacin and tryptophan, and the tiny amounts of niacin that are present are poorly absorbed. Pellagra could never have happened in the Paleolithic era, because meats are excellent sources of both niacin and tryptophan. Invariably, whenever we stray from the meats, fruits, and vegetables that we are genetically adapted to eat, ill health is the result.

Beriberi, caused by a deficiency of vitamin B_1 (thiamin), ultimately causes paralysis of the leg muscles. This disease was virtually unknown until the introduction of polished rice in the late 1800s. In parts of Japan and Southeast Asia, where rice was the staple food, beriberi became epidemic as people replaced their traditional brown rice with white rice. Eventually, scientists discovered that removing the thiamin-containing bran during the polishing process was largely responsible for this disease. Beriberi has been mostly eliminated with the introduction of "enriched" rice, to which vitamin B_1 is added. However, the message should be clear: If we have to add a vitamin to a food to prevent it from causing ill health and disease, we shouldn't be eating it in the first place.

Vitamin B Deficiency and Heart Disease. In North America, we enrich our refined cereal grains with vitamin B_1 and niacin—which means you will never have to worry about pellagra or beriberi. But it doesn't mean that these foods are good for you. Far from it. Within the past 20 years, a major risk factor for heart disease has surfaced. It has been found that low dietary intakes of three B vitamins—B_6, B_{12}, and folate—increase your blood level of an amino acid called homocysteine. A high blood level of homocysteine, in turn, increases your risk of heart disease. Whole grain cereals have no vitamin B_{12}, their vitamin B_6 is poorly absorbed, and they are at best a meager source of folate. So excessive consumption of whole grain cereals instead of meats, fruits, and vegetables is a formula for disaster for your heart. Again, meats are rich sources of vitamins B_6 and B_{12}, and fresh fruits and vegetables are our best food sources of folate. By eating the foods nature intended, you will never have to worry about your B vitamin status, homocysteine level, and heart disease.

Folate Deficiency. Since most Americans don't eat enough fresh fruits and vegetables, our dietary intake of folate is often marginal or low. Folate not only protects us from heart disease, it also reduces our risk of colon cancer. Taken by pregnant women, it prevents spina bifida in their babies.

The bottom line is that grains are an inferior food. No matter how you slice your bread (whole or refined), grains are not good for you. Even when they're artificially pumped full of vitamins and minerals, they cannot measure up to meats, fruits, and vegetables.

Nutritionist Loses 30 Pounds

Melissa's Story

Melissa Diane Smith, a nutritionist and a health journalist based in Tucson, Arizona, is the coauthor of *Syndrome X: The Complete Nutritional Program to Prevent and Reverse Insulin Resistance* and is the author of *Going against the Grain: How Reducing and Avoiding Grains Can Revitalize Your Health.* This is her story.

In 1986, I began a job at a health spa and naturally emphasized foods in my diet that I thought were healthy—bagels, muffins, chicken-pasta dishes, chicken-rice dishes, and turkey sandwiches. This type of diet was disastrous for me. During the next year and a half, I gained 30 pounds and developed a whole host of health problems, including a very severe flulike illness that I could not shake, which was much later diagnosed as chronic fatigue syndrome.

In an effort to regain my health, I tried several popular and recommended vegetarian, macrobiotic, and high-carbohydrate diets but grew weaker and sicker on each one. I continued to experiment and eventually stumbled upon the diet that turned my health around. It was based on lean animal protein and lots of nonstarchy vegetables and was entirely free of wheat or other gluten grains, dairy, legumes, processed fats, and sugar.

When I ate this way, the difference in my health was dramatic. I quickly felt more energetic, mentally focused, and less sick. I also began to effortlessly lose the excess weight I had put on. Within about 6 months, I lost all the weight I had gained and was back to 115 pounds—size 6 for me. It was hard to turn against established nutritional wisdom, but I kept eating this way and totally recovered from chronic fatigue syndrome. The diet was the answer to regaining my health, and it's kept me trim and healthy ever since.

Minerals

On paper, whole grains appear to be a fairly good source of many important minerals, such as iron, zinc, copper, and calcium. Actually, cereals are lousy sources of these nutritionally important minerals.

Iron

Remember the antinutrients that block our absorption of B vitamins? Other antinutrients, called phytates, chemically bind iron, zinc, copper, and calcium within grains and block their absorption during digestion. Phytates do their job so well that the worldwide epidemic of iron-deficiency anemia—which affects 1.2 billion people—is universally attributed to the poor availability of iron in cereal- and legume-based diets. Iron-deficiency anemia weakens you and hinders your ability to work; it also makes you more susceptible to infection and more likely to develop a severe infection. It increases a mother's risk of dying during childbirth. It can permanently impair a child's learning ability. Iron-deficiency anemia—like the other deficiency diseases caused by agriculture's new foods— would not have been possible with Paleo diets. Meats and animal foods are rich sources of iron. More important, the type of iron found in meats and animal foods is easily assimilated by the body.

Zinc

Zinc deficiency is another disaster caused by whole grain cereals. In much of the Middle East, a whole wheat flat bread called tanok contributes more than half of the total daily calories. Studies done by Dr. John Reinhold and colleagues have shown that tanok causes a zinc deficiency that stunts growth and delays puberty in children. We need zinc to help us fight infection and colds, to sustain our strength, and to enable us to work. Once again, meats are excellent sources of zinc. In fact, the "bioavailability" (the amount you receive of a particular nutrient) of zinc from meat is four times greater than from grains.

Calcium

Most American women, and many men, have gotten the message about calcium: Insufficient dietary calcium can eventually lead to bone loss and osteoporosis. Few realize that cereal grains and legumes are a catastrophe for your bone health. As with iron and zinc, the little calcium that's present in whole grains is bound to phytates—which means that most of it never gets absorbed by the body. Cereals also contain high levels of phosphorus. We know that an unfavorable calcium-to-phosphorus ratio can speed up bone loss. Also, cereals produce a net acid load to the kidneys—and this, too, increases calcium loss in the urine.

Whole grains are even known to disrupt vitamin D metabolism in the body. Vitamin D increases calcium absorption and prevents rickets, a disease that causes bone deformities. In fact, scientists who want to study rickets in laboratory animals know exactly how to produce it—by feeding the animals whole grains. In many of the world's undeveloped countries, where whole grains and legumes are the main sources of calories, rickets, osteoporosis, and other bone-mineral diseases are common.

From the fossil record, we know that these same bone-mineral problems were also common among the first farmers. Not surprisingly, the hunter-gatherers who came before them didn't have these diseases. Hunter-gatherers never drank milk. They did not have bone-mineral problems because they ate lots of fruits and vegetables—which gave them enough calcium to build strong bones. Fruits and veggies also gave them an abundant source of alkaline base that prevented excessive losses of calcium in the urine. When you adopt the Paleo Diet, you won't have to worry about your calcium intake. You'll get all you need from the fruits and vegetables. But more important, you'll be in calcium balance. You will be taking in more calcium than you lose, and this is essential for bone health.

By restoring meats, fruits, and veggies to your diet and eliminating agriculture's new foods, you will lose weight, feel better, and reduce your risk of developing the diseases of civilization that plague us all.

Chapter 3

Losing Weight the Paleo Diet Way

Here are four reasons why you should make animal protein a major part of your diet:

- It can't be overeaten.
- It raises your metabolism, causing you to burn more calories.
- It satisfies your appetite, causing you to feel less hungry between meals.
- It improves insulin sensitivity.

Determining Whether You Need to Lose Weight

How do you know if you're overweight? Scientists have devised a simple measure based on your height and weight that allows you to know exactly how much extra weight you may be toting. This measure system is called the "body mass index" (BMI), and here are the categories:

BMI	Classification
Below 18.5	Underweight
18.5–24.9	Normal
25.0–29.9	Overweight
Above 30.0	Obese

The BMI is easy to calculate. It is simply your weight in kilograms (kg) divided by your height in meters (m) squared. You can calculate your weight in kilograms by dividing your weight in pounds by 2.2. You can change your height to meters by multiplying your height in inches by 0.0254. So a 5-foot, 4-inch (64 inches) tall woman who weighs 154 pounds would weigh 70 kilograms (154 / 2.2 = 70 kg), and her height in meters would be 1.63 meters (64 x 0.0254 = 1.63 m). Her height in square meters would be 2.66 (1.63 x 1.63 = 2.66). Her BMI would be 26.3 (70 / 2.66 = 26.3). This would put her in the overweight category. If your BMI is greater than 27, this may be a sign that you are insulin resistant and have (or are at high risk of developing) one or more of the diseases of metabolic syndrome.

A Doctor Loses 30 Pounds

Ben's Story

Here is what Dr. Ben Balzer, a general family physician from Sydney, Australia, has to say about the Paleo Diet.

In April this year, I reached the end of my tether with my weight. I'd tipped the scales at 222 pounds. My weight for my height should be under 172 pounds. In fact, I'd been too frightened to get on the scales for some weeks, as I knew what they would tell me. I'm sure I hit 225 pounds during this time. I'd been following the standard dietary advice of low-fat dieting reasonably well for 7 years. Although it worked well at first, it stopped, and my weight had gradually increased.

As a doctor, I knew exactly what I was in for. I have a strong family history of diabetes, hypertension, and stroke. I was 37 years old. Medically, I knew it was inevitable that I would be affected if I didn't act. I was feeling tired, bloated, and sluggish. It seemed harder to get through each day. I tried to exercise but had trouble finding the time and could swim only 500 meters with difficulty. My feet were also hurting badly. I had had heel pain syndrome (heel spur) for 2½ years, despite cortisone shots and physical therapy. I had headaches at least 5 days a week.

Fortunately, 10 years earlier I'd heard a noted Australian professor of medicine mention the Paleolithic diet. That sounds like a logical idea, I thought, and filed it away for future reference; there was no Internet then. In my time of need, I searched the Internet for Paleolithic diet and immediately found Don Wiss's Paleofood.com site. Also, a local dietitian recommended a scientific paper by Eaton, Eaton, and Konner, and I was off.

The first thing that I noticed on the diet was a feeling of a surge in my vitality. Within 2 weeks, my heel pain syndrome disappeared—a totally unexpected effect.

My headaches soon reduced to once each 2 weeks and after 8 months are down to once each 6 weeks or so, and very mild at that—another unexpected effect.

The weight fell off very quickly—15 pounds in the first month, and now 29 pounds altogether. If that wasn't enough, I've had an increase in my muscle bulk, despite having little chance to exercise. The end result was that my trousers were almost falling off me, but my shirts were getting tight across the shoulders. The effect on my fitness was immediate. The first time I went swimming on the diet, I clocked up 1,000 meters and was hardly puffing afterward. I can run around better than I can ever remember.

My mental clarity has improved and is sharper than it has ever been before in my life. Everyone who knows me tells me how well I look. Interestingly, when I socialize, I'll often break the diet to be sociable. If I eat bread twice in one weekend, I'll always get up on Monday morning with sore heels again.

Since then, I've studied the diet intensively. I am totally convinced that far more illnesses than were previously suspected are related to factors in the modern diet. In addition to the usual illnesses listed as dietary (hypertension, diabetes, hypercholesterolemia, cardiovascular disease, stroke), we can add many forms of arthritis, throat infection, peptic ulcer, acne, and many others.

I plan to stay on the Paleolithic diet (as well as one can in this modern age) for the rest of my life. I think it's obvious from the above that I would be silly if I didn't!

A lean and healthy body is your birthright. The Paleo Diet is not a quick-fix solution. It is not a temporary, gimmicky diet. It's a way of eating that will gradually normalize your body weight to its ideal level and keep the pounds off permanently.

There's one very simple concept that you must understand when it comes to losing weight—the First Law of Thermodynamics, which states that energy is neither created nor destroyed. This means that the energy—calories—you put into your body must equal the energy you expend. Otherwise, you'll either gain or lose weight. If you eat more calories than you burn off, you'll gain weight. If you burn more than you take in, you'll lose weight.

Why Protein Helps Burn Calories

When it comes to human metabolism, this basic law of physics is a bit more complicated: *All calories are not created equal.* Protein is different from carbohydrates and fats.

How do you burn calories? Some you burn at a very low level all the time as part of your "resting metabolism"—for basic, unconscious functions such as beating of the heart, breathing, and digestion. You burn more calories when you move and still more when you exercise.

The common wisdom is that there are only two ways to burn more calories than you eat: Eat less or move around—exercise—more.

But there's another way to burn calories—a subtle process that can work wonders over weeks and months to create a substantial, long-term caloric deficit. Best of all, you don't even have to get out of bed to reap the benefits. This amazing phenomenon is called the thermic effect, and the key to making it work is protein.

This is how it works: During the digestive process, your body breaks down food into its basic components—carbohydrates, fats, and proteins—and turns them into energy it can use. There's a trade-off: To get the energy from the food, the body must spend some of its own energy. There's a scientific name for this use of energy to digest and metabolize food—dietary-induced thermogenesis (DIT). Carbohydrates and fats generate about the same low DIT. Protein's DIT is huge in comparison—more than 2½ to 3 times greater. So, in order for the body to obtain energy from dietary protein, it must give up almost 3 times more energy than it needs for either fat or carbohydrates.

What this means is that *protein boosts your metabolism and causes you to lose weight* more rapidly than the same caloric amounts of fat or carbohydrates. A study carried out at the Dunn Clinical Nutrition Center in Cambridge, England, by Dr. M. J. Dauncey and colleagues showed that during a 24-hour period, a high-protein diet increased total energy expenditures by 12 percent (220 calories) compared to a calorically matched high-carbohydrate diet.

Think about it. You don't have to cut calories one bit. You can lose 20 to 30 pounds in a year with utterly no change in the quantity of food you eat or even any change in your exercise habits. Or a lot more than that if you exercise more or eat less. That's just what happened with Dean (see opposite).

Over 6 months—with absolutely no increase in exercise or decrease in caloric intake—a high-protein diet could cause you to lose 10 to 15 pounds. Over those same 6 months—with increased exercise and a somewhat decreased caloric intake—a high-protein diet could cause you to lose 30 to 75 pounds!

Losing 75 Pounds in 6 Months

Dean's Story

In April 1999, *Dateline NBC* ran a feature story on my research into Paleo diets and interviewed Dean Stankovic, age 32. Dean's weight had fluctuated wildly on his 6-foot, 3-inch frame since his graduation from high school, at one point reaching a high of 280 pounds. Before he adopted the Paleo Diet, Dean had tried dozens of diets. Although Dean was very determined to lose weight, he just couldn't seem to stick to traditional low-calorie diets like the one created by Weight Watchers. They made him feel hungry all the time. Worse, on all of these diets, his weight dropped at first—but the longer he stayed with them, the slower the weight loss became. This is because the body's metabolic rate slows down to conserve body stores during periods of starvation—which is exactly what low-calorie diets are. Eventually, after a few months of starvation with these low-calorie diets, no matter how strong his willpower and resolve, Dean always went back to his normal way of eating—basically, the standard American diet.

Dean had tried the high-fat, low-carbohydrate diets advocated by Dr. Atkins and others. He lost weight with these diets but complained of a low energy level, lethargy, and constant fatigue. He also believed that all of those fatty, salty, bacon-and-egg breakfasts; greasy sausages and salami; and fatty cheeses just couldn't be good for his body. And these diets became boring. It was fun at first to trade in one evil (sweets and starches) for another (fats). But after a while he craved apples, peaches, and strawberries—any fresh fruit. Dean just couldn't imagine going through the rest of his life eating only tiny amounts of fruits and veggies. This was not a lifelong way of eating! Life was not worth living when all he had to look forward to was fatty meats and cheeses, cream, and butter. Dean's mind and body rebelled, and he found himself once again down in the dumps—back to his old diet and back to his old weight.

In fall of 1998, Dean met a young woman who had been eating in the Paleo manner for a number of years. She gave Dean some of my writings and dietary recommendations. After a few false starts, Dean began the Paleo Diet in earnest and started to lose weight steadily. By spring of 1999, after 6 months on the Paleo Diet, he had lost 70 pounds and was down to a svelte 185 pounds. Dean's opening remark on *Dateline NBC*—"It is a very satisfying diet; I don't feel hungry"—is a characteristic comment, echoed by almost everyone who gives this way of eating a try. Two years later, Dean has kept the weight off and sums up his feelings this way: "I consider it more than just a diet; it's more of a lifestyle. I think it is one of the greatest diets ever created. I have no plans to go back to my old ways."

Protein Satisfies Your Appetite

Protein's high DIT is not the only reason you lose weight when you start eating more lean animal protein. Protein also affects your appetite. Protein satisfies hunger far more effectively than either carbohydrate or fat. Dr. Marisa Porrini's research group at the University of Milan in Italy has found that high-protein meals are much more effective than high-fat meals in satisfying the appetite.

High-protein meats also do a much better job of reducing hunger *between meals* than do high-carbohydrate vegetarian meals. Dr. Britta Barkeling and colleagues at the Karolinska Hospital in Stockholm served 20 healthy women lunches of identical caloric value; the women ate either a high-protein meat casserole or a high-carbohydrate vegetarian casserole. The researchers then measured how much food the women ate at dinner. The women who had eaten the meat casserole ate 12 percent fewer calories during their evening meal. As this study illustrates, protein's powerful capacity to satisfy hunger not only influences how much you eat at the very next meal but also how much you'll eat all day long.

At the Rowett Research Institute in Great Britain, Dr. R. James Stubbs and colleagues fed six men a high-protein, high-fat, or high-carbohydrate meal at breakfast and then monitored their feeling of hunger for the next 24 hours. The high-protein breakfast suppressed hunger much more effectively than the other two breakfast meals did—even more than the high-fat breakfast. These experiments and many others have convincingly shown that if you want to feel less hungry and stay less hungry, lean animal protein is your best line of attack.

Theoretically, any leftover calories—whether they're from protein, carbohydrates, or fats—would count as a calorie "surplus" and result in weight gain. In reality, the body doesn't work that way. It is very difficult and inefficient for the body's metabolic machinery to store excess protein calories as fat. The surplus almost always comes from extra fats or carbohydrates—and these are the foods that most frequently make you fat.

It is impossible to overeat pure protein. In fact, you couldn't gain weight just on lean, low-fat protein if your life depended on it. The body has clear limits, determined by the liver's inability to handle excess dietary nitrogen (released when the body breaks down protein). For most people, this limit is about 35 percent of your normal daily caloric intake. If you exceed this limit for a prolonged stretch of time, your body will protest—with nausea, diarrhea, abrupt weight loss, and other symptoms of protein toxicity.

But remember, protein is your best ally in waging the battle of the bulge—and when it is accompanied by plenty of fruits and veggies and good fats and oils, you will never have to worry about getting too much protein. Now let's take a look at the next major reason why the Paleo Diet causes you to lose weight without nagging hunger.

Promoting Weight Loss by Improving Your Insulin Sensitivity

The Paleo Diet promotes weight loss not only because of its high protein level that simultaneously revs up your metabolism and reduces appetite, but also because it improves your insulin metabolism.

Insulin resistance is a serious problem, and most people who are overweight have it. In insulin resistance, the pancreas (the gland that makes insulin) must make extra insulin to clear blood sugar—glucose—from the bloodstream. There's a bit of a "chicken and egg" argument as to which event happens first. Does being overweight cause insulin resistance or vice versa? Scientists aren't entirely sure. However, once insulin resistance starts, it prompts a domino effect of metabolic changes that encourage weight gain. The body frequently stores more fat, for one thing. For another, excessive insulin in the bloodstream can cause low blood sugar (a condition called hypoglycemia). The body's response to low blood sugar is: "Hey—we're in trouble. We'd better eat something fast!" Low blood sugar stimulates the appetite, and this can be deceptive: It causes you to feel hungry even if you've just eaten.

The good news is that what you choose to eat—protein, fats, or carbohydrates—can influence the progression of insulin resistance. Dr. Gerald Reaven's research at Stanford University has shown that low-fat, high-carbohydrate foods hinder insulin metabolism. But *high-protein diets are known to improve insulin metabolism.* Dr. P. M. Piatti and colleagues at the University of Milan put 25 overweight women on one of two diets. The first contained 45 percent protein, 35 percent carbohydrate, and 20 percent fat. The second contained 60 percent carbohydrate, 20 percent protein, and 20 percent fat. After 21 days the women on the high-protein diet had significantly improved insulin metabolism, but those on the high-carbohydrate diet actually got worse.

With all these benefits, it seems obvious that lean protein should be the starting point for all weight-loss diets. Prior to 2002, only three clinical trials of high-protein diets had been conducted. All three investigations found high-protein diets to be excellent—far better than low-fat, high-carbohydrate diets—at promoting weight loss.

Dr. Arne Astrup's nutritional research group at the Royal Veterinary and Agricultural University in Copenhagen, Denmark, studied weight loss in 65 people placed on either high-protein or high-carbohydrate, reduced-calorie diets. After 6 months, those in the high-protein group had lost an average of 19.6 pounds—and 35 percent of the participants in this group had lost more than 22 pounds. The people in the high-carbohydrate group, however, lost only an average of 11.2 pounds; only 9 percent of the people in this group lost 22 pounds.

Dr. Hwalla Baba and colleagues at the American University of Beirut demonstrated almost identical results when they put 13 overweight men on high- and low-protein, reduced-calorie diets. After only a month the average weight loss for men on the high-protein diet was 18.3 pounds compared to only 13.2 pounds for the high-carbohydrate group.

Dr. Donald Layman, a professor of nutrition at the University of Illinois, studied 24 overweight women who for 10 weeks were on 1,700-calorie-a-day diets. Half of the women followed the USDA guidelines that were current at the time, with a diet of 55 percent carbohydrate, 15 percent protein (68 grams per day), and 30 percent fat. The other half had a diet of 40 percent carbohydrate, 30 percent protein (125 grams a day), and 30 percent fat. The average weight loss for both groups was about 16 pounds, but the high-protein group lost 12.3 pounds of body fat and just 1.7 pounds of muscle compared to 10.4 pounds of body fat and 3 pounds of muscle for the group following the diet using the USDA guidelines. Interestingly, the study also found that women on the higher-protein diet had higher levels of thyroid hormone, which indicates that they had a faster metabolic rate. The higher-protein diet also resulted in a noticeable drop in triglyceride levels and a slight increase in the good HDL cholesterol. In the 8 years since I wrote the first edition of *The Paleo Diet*, numerous human clinical trials have conclusively demonstrated the superiority of high-protein diets in producing weight loss and benefiting overall health.

What You Can Expect to Lose on the Paleo Diet

When you start the Paleo Diet, you'll probably realize—perhaps with a shock— just how much of your diet has been built around cereal grains, legumes, dairy products, and processed foods. Even most vegetarians must eat large amounts of grains and legumes to make their plant-based diets work, because it's very difficult to get enough calories just from eating fruits and vegetables. Except for the 2,000 or fewer hunter-gatherers still remaining on the planet, none of the world's people obtain their daily sustenance just from fruits, vegetables, meats, and sea-food. When you start the Paleo Diet, you may choose to count yourself among the dietary elite—knowing that about 6 billion people on the planet aren't eating this way. And yet just 10,000 years ago—a mere drop in the bucket of geological time—there wasn't a single person who did *not* follow the Paleo Diet.

Everything I'm telling you about how the Paleo Diet will affect your body weight, health, and well-being is based on scientifically validated information that has been published in high-quality, peer-reviewed scientific and medical journals.

If you're overweight, the Paleo Diet will normalize your weight. This means that you will steadily lose pounds, as long as you continue to follow the diet, until your weight approaches its ideal. Most people experience rapid weight loss within the first 3 to 5 days. This is mainly water loss, and it stabilizes fairly quickly. After that, how much weight you lose will depend on two things—how overweight you are to begin with and how many total "deficit" calories you accumulate. After the initial water loss, it takes a deficit of 3,500 calories to lose a pound of fat. It is not unusual for people who are obese (medically, this means people who have a body mass index [BMI] of greater than 30) to lose between 10 and 15 pounds each month.

Losing Weight the Right Way

With the Paleo Diet, weight loss is a continuous, deliberate decline that occurs gradually, over a period of a few to many months. There are no quick fixes here—but then again, quick fixes don't work. Most people who try such diets are unable to stick with them over the long haul.

You won't feel hungry on this diet. Protein is a great satisfier. The low carbohydrate content of the diet combined with its low glycemic load will normalize your insulin and blood sugar levels and will also help keep you from overeating. The weight that you will lose will stay off if you just stick to the diet—all the lean meats, fish, seafood, fresh fruits, and vegetables (except starchy vegetables) you can eat. Isn't it time to get started and give your body what it is genetically programmed to eat?

Chapter 4

Metabolic Syndrome: Diseases of Civilization

It requires a very unusual mind to undertake the
analysis of the obvious.

—ALFRED NORTH WHITEHEAD

Metabolic syndrome diseases—the diseases of insulin resistance—are the main health problems of Western countries, affecting as many as half of all adults and children. There are four major metabolic syndrome diseases:

- Type 2 diabetes
- High blood pressure
- Heart disease
- Dyslipidemia (low HDL cholesterol, elevated triglycerides, and high small-dense LDL cholesterol)

Gout and blood-clotting abnormalities are usually grouped with metabolic syndrome diseases, too, and so is obesity.

When people become insulin-resistant, the pancreas must secrete more insulin than normal to clear sugar (glucose) from the bloodstream. This creates a state in which the blood insulin level is elevated all the time.

Insulin is a major hormone that affects nearly every cell. A chronically high blood-insulin level is thought to be the underlying culprit in all metabolic syndrome diseases, which are all complicated and with many contributory factors.

Some scientists believe that high-saturated-fat diets make insulin metabolism less efficient. Others, including Dr. Gerald Reaven at Stanford University, believe that high-carbohydrate diets—both low- and high-glycemic foods—are to blame. Still others single out high-glycemic carbohydrates. However, the obvious has been ignored: Most people who develop obesity and diseases of insulin resistance do it with *mixtures* of high-fat and high-glycemic carbohydrates. Some examples of these bad food combinations: Baked potato and sour cream. Bread with butter. Eggs with toast and hash browns. Pizza with cheese. Ice cream, candies, cookies, chips. These and all of the other processed foods we eat contain both a high-fat component and high-glycemic carbohydrates.

With the Paleo Diet, it doesn't matter which of these kinds of foods ultimately cause insulin resistance—because these unnatural food combinations aren't part of the picture (except as Open Meal treats). Your meals won't suffer—in fact, they'll be richer, more varied, and more delicious than ever. Instead of fatty gourmet ice cream, treat yourself to a bowl of fresh blueberries or half a cantaloupe filled with diced strawberries and walnuts. Instead of fish sticks, how about peel-and-eat shrimp or a lean grilled steak? We'll get to specific recipes and meal plans later in Chapters 9 and 10.

Healing Metabolic Syndrome

Jack's Story

Jack Challem, known worldwide as the "Nutrition Reporter," is a leading health journalist with more than 25 years of experience reporting on nutrition research. He is a contributing editor for *Let's Live* and *Natural Health* magazines and the coauthor of a number of popular nutrition books.

When I started writing my book *Syndrome X: The Complete Nutritional Program to Prevent and Reverse Insulin Resistance,* I was in denial about having the early stages of Syndrome X. I was 48 years old, weighed 170 pounds, and I had a 38-inch waist and a fasting glucose of 111 mg/dL. I should have known better. I made a point of getting back to the very diet I advocate in my book, *Syndrome X.* I also stopped eating all pasta and virtually all bread. Basically, I was following a Paleo Diet with lean meats and a lot of veggies.

In 3 months, I lost 20 pounds and 4 inches from my waist. My fasting blood sugar was 85 mg/dL. My blood cholesterol and triglyceride values also improved. It has been extremely easy to maintain these improvements. Eating the Paleo Diet is simple and tasty.

How Insulin Resistance
Increases Your Risk of Heart Disease

High-glycemic carbohydrates cause an increase in your blood triglycerides and a decrease in your good HDL cholesterol. They also cause an increase in a special type of cholesterol in your bloodstream called small-dense LDL cholesterol. All of these changes in blood chemistry severely increase your risk of death from heart disease.

Small-Dense LDL Cholesterol

In recent years, small-dense LDL cholesterol has emerged as one of the most potent risks for atherosclerosis, the artery-clogging process. The study of atherosclerosis has become increasingly specific. First, we had cholesterol, then HDL and LDL (good and bad) cholesterol, and now a particularly bad kind of LDL cholesterol whose small, dense particles are ideal for artery blockage.

Even if you have normal total and LDL blood cholesterol levels, you still may be at risk for developing heart disease if your small-dense LDL cholesterol level is elevated.

Although low-fat, high-carbohydrate diets may reduce total and LDL cholesterol, they are useless in lowering small-dense LDL cholesterol. In fact, they make it worse. Dr. Darlene Dreon and colleagues at the University of California–Berkeley have shown repeatedly that high-carbohydrate diets increase small-dense LDL cholesterol particles in men, women, and children. High-glycemic foods increase our blood triglycerides, which make small-dense LDL cholesterol. When we lower triglycerides—by cutting out the starch and the high-glycemic carbohydrates—we automatically lower our small-dense LDL cholesterol.

The Keys to Greater Insulin Sensitivity

The Paleo Diet improves insulin sensitivity in many ways. First, because it's humanity's original low-glycemic-carbohydrate, low-sugar diet, you won't have to worry about triglycerides, HDL cholesterol, or small-dense LDL cholesterol. All of these blood values will rapidly normalize as your insulin level becomes reduced and stabilized.

The Paleo Diet's high fiber, high protein, and omega-3 fat content all improve insulin sensitivity as well. Unlike starchy carbohydrates, protein causes only small changes in your blood levels of glucose and insulin. By itself, a single meal of pure fat doesn't change these blood levels, either. The omega-3 fats that are integral to the Paleo Diet actually *improve* insulin metabolism and cause a rapid drop in blood triglycerides. The high fiber content in nonstarchy vegetables and fruits found in the Paleo Diet slows the passage of carbohydrates through your intestines; this slows blood sugar rises and ultimately also improves insulin sensitivity.

Other Diseases Related to Insulin Resistance

Scientists are expanding the scope of insulin resistance research. In research worldwide, this condition is being linked to many other chronic diseases and health problems. Scientists are exploring the role of insulin resistance in certain types of cancer, nearsightedness, polycystic ovary syndrome, and even acne— although in all of these, as in heart disease, many causative factors are believed to be involved. It is premature to establish a direct cause-and-effect relationship. But if these diseases ultimately do turn out to have insulin resistance as their underlying cause, you'll be protected—because the Paleo Diet contains all of the dietary elements known to stop insulin resistance.

Breast, Prostate, and Colon Cancers and Insulin Resistance

Over the last 5 years, scientists have discovered through a chain reaction of metabolic events that elevated levels of insulin in the bloodstream increase blood levels of a hormone called insulinlike growth factor one (IGF-1) and decrease the hormone called insulinlike growth factor binding protein three (IGFBP-3). The decrease in IGFBP-3 causes tissues to be less sensitive to one of the body's natural chemical signals (retinoic acid) that normally limits tissue growth. In addition, IGF-1, a potent hormone in all tissues, is a major regulator of growth: Increased levels of IGF-1 encourage growth, and reduced levels slow growth. Children who are below normal height have low levels of IGF-1. When IGF-1 is injected into these children, they immediately start to grow taller. As you might expect, tall children have higher levels of IGF-1. Studies of growing children by Dr. William Wong and colleagues at the Children's Nutrition Research Center in Houston found that girls who were taller and heavier and who matured earlier had higher blood levels of both insulin and IGF-1 and lower levels of IGFBP-3. Diets that cause insulin resistance—particularly high-glycemic-carbohydrate diets—increase IGF-1 levels, lower IGFBP-3 levels, and decrease tissue sensitivity to retinoic acid. These hormonal changes, in turn, accelerate growth in developing children.

What does this have to do with adult health? It's been found that IGF-1 is a powerful stimulator of cell division—growth—in *all* cells during *all* phases of life. In fact, scientists suspect that IGF-1 may be one of the primary promoters of all unregulated and tissue growth in the body. But IGFBP-3 prevents unregulated cell growth by causing cancer cells to die naturally through a process called apoptosis. Over the last decade, numerous scientific papers have shown a strong association between elevated levels of IGF-1, lowered levels of IGFBP-3, and breast cancer in premenopausal women, prostate cancer in men, and colorectal cancer in all adults. In animal models of many types of cancer, scientists can promote cancer by adding a key ingredient—IGF-1; conversely, adding IGFBP-3 slows cancer. Synthetic derivatives of the body's natural retinoic acid powerfully inhibit the cancer process in cell cultures. So, the whole chain of hormonal events initiated by elevated blood levels of insulin tends to promote the cancer process.

Two risk factors for breast cancer are early onset of puberty and above-average height. It is entirely possible that the same high insulin levels that elevate IGF-1 and lower IGFBP-3 (in other words, the levels that make children taller and make puberty happen sooner during childhood) also increase susceptibility to cancer during adulthood.

Many women, worried about breast cancer, have adopted vegetarian diets in an attempt to reduce their risk. Unfortunately, it may be that these grain- and starch-based diets actually increase the risk of breast cancer, because they elevate insulin—which, in turn, increases IGF-1 and lowers IGFBP-3. A large epidemiological study of Italian women, led by Dr. Silvia Franceschi, has shown that eating large amounts of pasta and refined bread raises the risk of developing both breast and colorectal cancer.

Most vegetarian diets are based on starchy grains and legumes. Sadly—despite continuing perceptions of these as healthy foods—vegetarian diets don't reduce the risk of cancer. In the largest-ever study comparing the causes of death in more than 76,000 people, it was decisively shown that there were no differences in death rates from breast, prostate, colorectal, stomach, or lung cancer between vegetarians and meat eaters.

Cancer is a complex process involving many genetic and environmental factors. It is almost certain that no single dietary element is responsible for all cancers. However, with the low-glycemic Paleo Diet, which is also high in lean protein and health-promoting fruits and vegetables, your risk of developing many types of cancer may be very much reduced.

Myopia and Insulin Resistance

Because insulin resistance changes the hormonal profile of the blood to one that facilitates tissue growth, scientists have good reason to suspect that insulin resistance lies at the root of any disease in which abnormal tissue growth occurs. One extremely common such disease is myopia—nearsightedness—which affects an estimated one-third of all Americans. Myopia results from excessive growth of the eyeball. Although the eye looks normal from the outside, inside it's too long for the eye to focus properly. Myopia typically develops during the childhood growth years and usually stabilizes by the time people reach their early twenties. New evidence that implicates insulin resistance in the childhood development of myopia may be useful in preventing nearsightedness in young children.

Eye doctors generally agree that nearsightedness results from an interaction between excessive reading and your genes. If you spent your youth with your nose in a book and if nearsightedness runs in your family, chances are good that you're now wearing glasses or contact lenses. Myopia is thought to stem from a slightly blurred image on the back of your eye (the retina) that's produced as you focus on the written page. This blurred image causes the retina to send out a hormonal signal telling the eyeball to grow longer. Experiments in laboratory animals suggest that the hormonal signal is produced by retinoic acid. Excessive reading slows the retina's production of retinoic acid, a substance that normally checks or prevents the eyeball from growing too long. Additionally, recent research shows that elevated insulin also directly contributes to the excessive growth of the eyeball. This may mean that if your children's diet prevents insulin resistance during growth and development, their risk of developing myopia may be lower.

Polycystic Ovary Syndrome

Polycystic ovary syndrome (PCOS) affects 5 to 10 percent of all North American women. Women with PCOS ovulate irregularly or not at all, and their ovaries produce high levels of male hormones such as testosterone. Women with PCOS are prone to obesity, excessive body hair, acne, high blood pressure, and type 2 diabetes. They also have a seven times greater risk of heart disease and heart attack than other women do. Almost 60 percent of all women with PCOS are insulin resistant, and most of these women have elevated levels of IGF-1. Numerous clinical studies have shown that simply changing the diet—eating foods that improve insulin metabolism—can reduce many of the symptoms of PCOS. The

Paleo Diet, which normalizes insulin metabolism, can greatly help women with this problem.

Acne

For years, many dermatologists believed that diet had absolutely nothing to do with acne. But very new scientific evidence has linked insulin resistance to acne. Diets loaded with sugar, fructose, and high-glycemic carbohydrates may contribute to this problem, which can be devastating. Between 40 and 50 million American teens and adults have acne.

Some striking information to support the link between acne and diet comes from Dr. Otto Schaefer, who spent his entire professional career in the wilderness of the Canadian Far North, working with Inuit natives who literally were transferred from the Stone Age to the Space Age in a single generation during the 1950s and 1960s. Dr. Schaefer reported that in those Eskimos who ate their traditional foods, acne was absent. Only when they adopted Western foods laced with refined sugars and starches and dairy products did acne appear.

Four things happen when acne develops: First, there's accelerated growth of the skin surrounding the hair follicle (called follicular hyperkeratosis). Second, oil (sebum) production speeds up within the follicle. Third, the cells in the follicle abnormally stick together as they are being shed, thus plugging the follicle. And, finally, the plugged-up follicle gets infected. Until recently, dermatologists didn't know why the accelerated growth occurred, why these cells became excessively cohesive, or what caused the boost in oil production. But growing evidence suggests that elevated insulin and IGF-1 are directly responsible for the increased follicular skin growth, along with reductions in circulating blood levels of IGFBP-3. Remember that high-glycemic foods raise your blood level of IGF-1 while lowering IGFBP-3. This is why low-glycemic-load, high-protein diets are so effective at eliminating acne. They put the brakes on excessive follicular skin growth.

Besides causing increases in IGF-1 and reductions in IGFBP-3, elevated insulin levels from eating high-glycemic carbohydrates cause a rise in the male hormone testosterone. It is these increases in IGF-1 and testosterone that promote the discharge of oil. This means that insulin resistance caused by high-glycemic diets may be directly responsible for the first three steps in acne development. In the last 5 years, dietary intervention studies and a series of epidemiological studies from the Harvard School of Public Health have conclusively demonstrated that high-protein, low-glycemic diets like the Paleo Diet improve insulin metabolism and can help prevent acne. It is now safe to say that the Paleo Diet will improve your insulin metabolism—and if you have acne, this lifetime program of healthy eating will help it disappear.

As you can see, the Paleo Diet can be a very effective tool in fighting virtually all the diseases of metabolic syndrome.

Chapter 5

Food as Medicine:
How Paleo Diets Improve
Health and Well-Being

*We never used to be so sick. The white man's
food is not good for us.*

—MALAYA KULUJUK, A BAFFIN ISLAND ESKIMO

The Diet-Disease Connection

Many of the chronic illnesses that plague the Western world—the "diseases of civilization"—can be attributed to dietary missteps. Diet and disease are obviously linked. And when we stray from the Seven Keys of the Paleo Diet, which stood firm for 2.5 million years, we not only develop metabolic syndrome diseases, but we also increase our susceptibility to a host of other diseases.

How can we know whether a particular food, or the lack of it, in our diet is actually the factor responsible for a particular disease—or the absence of it? If you have a milk allergy or lactose intolerance, the cause and effect of your symptoms are probably painfully clear. But it's much harder—if not impossible—to foresee whether the pat of margarine (containing trans fatty acids) you put on your toast yesterday morning will have anything to do with causing a heart attack 40 years later. .

Scientists and physicians use a variety of research procedures to determine whether diet and disease are linked, including dietary interventions, epidemiological studies, animal experiments, and cultured tissue studies. When the results of all four procedures are in agreement, it is quite likely that a certain food may cause a certain disease. However, in most cases the link between diet and disease is usually not this clear-cut; often, genetic susceptibility to disease further clouds the issue. In many of the diseases that we will be examining, the diet-disease connection has only been partially unraveled. Nonetheless, by adhering to the dietary guidelines of your Paleolithic ancestors, you will reduce your risk of developing these illnesses, and if you are currently suffering from one of these illnesses, your symptoms may improve with the Paleo Diet.

Metabolic Syndrome Diseases

I've already talked about the metabolic syndrome diseases (type 2 diabetes, heart disease, hypertension, dyslipidemia, obesity, PCOS, myopia, acne, and breast, prostate, and colon cancers) and how they are linked to elevated levels of insulin in the bloodstream. But all of these diseases also have other known contributing dietary factors. For example, salt is connected to high blood pressure—but so is a lack of fresh fruits and vegetables. Too much omega-6 fat in your diet at the expense of omega-3 fat can also cause your blood pressure to rise. Even a low protein intake has been linked to rising blood pressure.

Breast, prostate, and colon cancers are known to develop more often in people who don't eat enough fresh fruits and vegetables. Fruits and veggies hit cancer with a one-two punch: They're excellent sources of antioxidant vitamins and minerals that may impede the cancer process, and they also contain a variety of special substances called phytochemicals, nutrients that are lethal to cancer cells. The study of most phytochemicals is fairly new; scientists are only beginning to understand how they work. But here are a few examples.

- Broccoli contains sulforaphanes, which chase cancer-causing elements out of cells.

- Broccoli is also loaded with cancer-fighting folic acid, vitamin C, beta-carotene, and a substance called indole-3-carbinol, which helps improve the body's estrogens.

- Strawberries, tomatoes, pineapples, and green bell peppers contain *p*-coumaric acid and chlorogenic acid, compounds known to be powerful anticancer agents.

• Garlic and onions not only contain substances that will lower your cholesterol but are also rich sources of allylic sulfides, which seem to protect
against stomach cancer.

As is the case with high blood pressure, eating too many omega-6 and too few
omega-3 fats further increases your risk of developing breast, prostate, and colon
cancers.

We may not know precisely how dietary factors cause each and every metabolic syndrome disease, but one thing's certain: When you adopt the Paleo Diet,
you will be putting all known dietary factors on your side to prevent these
illnesses.

Cardiovascular Diseases

The number one killer in the United States is cardiovascular disease. A staggering 35 percent of all deaths in this country result from heart attacks, stroke, high
blood pressure, and other illnesses of the heart and blood vessels. Cardiovascular disease, like cancer, is a complex illness, and no single dietary element is
solely responsible. However, once again, by following the nutritional principles
of humanity's original diet, you will put the odds in your favor of not developing
this deadly disease.

Good Fats Help Prevent Cardiovascular Disease

Good fats are what doctors call "cardioprotective." They protect the heart and
the blood vessels from disease. With the Paleo Diet—unlike the average American diet—at least half of your fats are healthful monounsaturated fats. The
other half is evenly split between saturated and polyunsaturated fats. There are
no synthetic trans fats. And the crucial omega-6 to omega-3 fat ratio is about 2
to 1—which greatly reduces your risk of dying from heart disease.

Monounsaturated Fats

Monounsaturated fats reduce your overall risk of heart disease by lowering your
level of total cholesterol—but not your beneficial HDL cholesterol—in the
blood. These healthful fats—found in abundance in the Paleo Diet—also help
prevent LDL cholesterol from oxidizing (breaking down) and contributing to the
artery-clogging process. Monounsaturated fats also may reduce your risk of
breast cancer.

Omega-3 Fats

I've already talked about the beneficial effects of omega-3 fats on insulin metabolism and how they lower blood triglycerides. Omega-3 fats are also exceptionally potent agents in preventing the irregular heartbeats that can make a heart attack fatal. They help prevent blood clotting and ease tension in clogged arteries, as well.

In a landmark dietary intervention study, French physicians Serg Renaud and Michel de Lorgeril evaluated the effect of a diet rich in omega-3 fats in 600 patients who had previously survived a heart attack. In this investigation, known as the Lyon Diet Heart Study, half of the patients were assigned to the American Heart Association reduced-fat diet, in which 30 percent of calories come from fat. The rest followed a 35 percent fat traditional Mediterranean diet that was rich in omega-3 and monounsaturated fats and fruits and vegetables.

The results were striking: Compared to the patients who followed the American Heart Association Diet, those who were on the Mediterranean diet had a 76 percent lower risk of dying from another heart attack, a stroke, or another cardiovascular disease. This remarkable protection from heart disease can be yours, too. Like the Mediterranean diet, humankind's original diet is also high in cardioprotective omega-3 fats, fiber, monounsaturated fats, and the beneficial phytochemicals and antioxidant vitamins that are found in fruits and vegetables.

Diseases of Acid-Base Balance and Excessive Sodium

The average cereal-based, salt-laden, cheese-filled American diet—which is nearly devoid of fresh fruits and vegetables—tilts your body's acid-base balance in favor of acid. As we discussed earlier, grains, cheeses, meats, and salty foods yield a net acid load to the kidneys, while fruits and vegetables always generate an alkaline load. An overload of acid foods—at the expense of alkaline foods—can cause numerous health problems, particularly as you age and your kidneys become less adept at handling dietary acid.

Of the four major acid-producing foods, three—grains, cheeses, and salt—were eaten rarely or never by our Paleolithic ancestors. Instead, they ate huge amounts (by modern standards) of alkaline fruits and vegetables, which buffered the acid from their meat-rich diets.

Many chronic diseases prevalent in Western countries develop because of a dietary acid-base imbalance. These include:

- Osteoporosis
- High blood pressure
- Stroke
- Kidney stones
- Asthma

- Exercise-induced asthma
- Ménière's syndrome
- Stomach cancer
- Insomnia
- Air and motion sickness

The realization that such diverse problems could be linked to acid-base imbalance is fairly recent. Not so long ago, scientists connected many of these illnesses to too much sodium, or salt. But the chemical recipe for salt has two ingredients—sodium and chloride. It's the chloride part of salt that makes it acidic—not the sodium. Chloride may also be more to blame than sodium as a dietary cause of high blood pressure.

Osteoporosis

People who eat a lot of salt excrete more calcium in their urine than do people who avoid salt. In turn, this calcium loss contributes to bone loss and osteoporosis, because the acidic chloride in salt must be buffered in the kidneys by alkaline base—and the body's largest reservoir of alkaline base is the calcium in our bones. When we eat salty potato chips or a pepperoni pizza, we are leaching calcium from our bones. When we do it over the course of a lifetime, we may well develop osteoporosis.

Asthma and Exercise-Induced Asthma

But salt is not just bad for the bones. Although it has not been shown to cause asthma or exercise-induced asthma, it can aggravate both conditions. Studies in humans and animals have shown that salt can constrict the muscles surrounding the small airways in the lungs. My research team demonstrated that salt (both the sodium and the chloride components) increases the severity of exercise-induced asthma. We also showed that low-salt diets can reduce many symptoms of exercise-induced asthma.

Other Problems Caused by Salt

Maybe you don't salt your food. Good for you—but you should be aware that despite your good intentions, there's probably more salt in your diet than you think. The average American eats 10 to 12 grams of salt every day. Almost 80 percent of this comes from processed foods—even those considered healthful.

Two slices of whole wheat bread, for instance, give you 1.5 grams of salt. So automatically there's salt in any sandwich you make—even before you add salty meats like ham, salami, or bologna.

A high-salt diet increases your risk of kidney stones, stroke, and stomach cancer. It also impairs sleep—this is one of the least-recognized benefits of low-salt diets. When you cut the salt out of your diet, you will sleep better almost immediately. Low-salt diets also have been shown to reduce motion and air sickness.

Many other foods are acidic and able to disrupt the body's acid-base balance. Every time you eat cereals, peanuts, peanut butter, bread, muffins, cheese, sandwiches, pizza, doughnuts, cookies—basically, any processed food—you are overloading your body with dietary acid. Unless you balance these foods with healthful alkaline fruits and vegetables, you will be out of acid-base balance—and at increased risk for many chronic diseases.

Potassium

Another crucial chemical balance in the body is that of potassium and sodium. Paleo diets contained about ten times as much potassium as sodium. The average American eats about five times as much sodium as potassium every day. The beauty of the Paleo Diet is that it swiftly returns your body to humanity's original high intake of potassium and low intake of sodium.

Digestive Diseases

Fiber is absolutely essential to your health—and at least 13 illnesses can result when you don't get enough fiber in your diet. Some of the most common digestive diseases that develop when you eat the standard American diet with its overload of refined grains, sugars, dairy, and processed foods are:

- Constipation
- Varicose veins
- Hemorrhoids
- Heartburn
- Indigestion
- Appendicitis
- Diverticular disease of the colon
- Crohn's disease
- Ulcerative colitis
- Irritable bowel syndrome
- Duodenal ulcer
- Hiatal hernia
- Gallstones

The Paleo Diet is naturally high in fiber because of its abundance of fruits and vegetables—about three to five times as much fiber each day as there is in the average American diet.

Some people worry that meat-based diets are constipating. This is not true. Meat, fish, and seafood are not constipating at all. The famous Arctic explorer Vilhjalmur Stefansson spent years mapping and exploring the Far North at the turn of the 20th century. During his expeditions on dogsleds, he frequently lived off the land for more than a year at a time. He and his men were entirely dependent on the all-animal food diet that could be obtained from hunting and fishing. Amazingly, he reported in his journal that men who had suffered from constipation on their former rations of flour, corn biscuits, rice, and breads were almost completely cured of their problem within a week of adopting the all-meat (high in protein, but with enough fat to avoid the risk of protein toxicity) menu of the Eskimos.

Years later, when Stefansson returned to civilization, he and another explorer were put on an all-meat diet for an entire year, under controlled hospital conditions, by the most respected scientists and physicians of the day. The clinical evaluations at the end of the year showed bowel function to be normal. Just like Stefansson and the Eskimos, you will not suffer from constipation when meat, fish, and seafood dominate your diet. In fact, you will find that most of your digestive problems will disappear.

Crohn's Disease and Ulcerative Colitis

As with every other disease of civilization, it is not the soluble fiber from fruits and vegetables that will reduce your digestive problems, but rather the entire diet. Dairy products, cereals, and yeast have been implicated time and again in the development of Crohn's disease, an inflammatory disease of the gastrointestinal tract. Elemental diets (special liquid formulas without dairy, cereal, or yeast proteins) are the first line of defense physicians use in treating these patients. Amazingly, almost 80 percent of patients achieve complete remission while on elemental diets with absolutely no drug therapy. But there is a big problem here: Hardly anyone can stay on a liquid diet forever. What would you rather do, drink a liquid diet or eat humanity's real foods—fruits, veggies, and meats?

One of our most powerful therapies to calm down the inflammation of both Crohn's disease and ulcerative colitis (an inflammatory disease of the colon) is to prescribe fish oil capsules—an excellent source of omega-3 fats. Once again, we find that multiple elements in humanity's original diet complement one another to eliminate or prevent chronic illness. And it is our deviation from the three simple foods (fruits, vegetables, and meats) we are genetically adapted to eat that invariably causes us trouble and ill health.

Inflammatory Diseases

Omega-3 fats are powerful weapons in other wars, as well. Perhaps because of their anti-inflammatory properties, they may prevent cancer from developing. They are also extremely effective in calming down virtually all inflammatory diseases—illnesses that end in "itis," such as rheumatoid arthritis, ulcerative colitis, and gingivitis. These amazingly healthful fats can even reduce symptoms of certain autoimmune diseases: The combination of supplementing your diet with omega-3 fats and eliminating grains, dairy foods, legumes, potatoes, and yeast may substantially reduce the severity of symptoms of these diseases.

Autoimmune Diseases

Autoimmune diseases such as rheumatoid arthritis, multiple sclerosis, and type 1 (juvenile) diabetes develop when the body's immune system can't tell the difference between its own tissues and those of foreign invaders. The result: The body attacks itself. The type of disease depends on the nature of the body's assault: When the immune system invades and destroys nerve tissue, multiple sclerosis and other neurological diseases develop. When the pancreas is the target, type 1 diabetes occurs. When joint tissues are attacked and destroyed, the result is rheumatoid arthritis.

All autoimmune diseases develop because of interactions between the genes and one or more environmental factors, such as a viral or bacterial infection or exposure to a certain food. No one knows exactly how viruses, bacteria, and foods can spark the disease in genetically susceptible people, but research from our laboratory increasingly implicates recently introduced Neolithic foods such as grains, legumes, dairy foods, potatoes, and other members of the nightshade family.

Many environmental agents have been suspected in the development of autoimmune diseases. But only one of these types has proved capable of causing a disease. Cereal grains—such as wheat, rye, and barley—are responsible for celiac disease and dermatitis herpetiformis. In celiac disease, the immune system attacks and destroys cells in the intestine, leading to diarrhea and many nutritional problems. In dermatitis herpetiformis, the skin is attacked.

Withdrawal of all gluten-containing cereals causes complete remission of both diseases. Cereal grains, dairy products, and legumes are suspected in other autoimmune diseases, such as type 1 diabetes, multiple sclerosis, and rheumatoid arthritis. To date, no dietary intervention studies have been conducted to see whether Paleo diets—free of grains, dairy products, and legumes—can reduce the symptoms of these diseases. However, anecdotal reports from Canada show improvement in symptoms of multiple sclerosis patients following the Paleo Diet.

Lectins and Autoimmune Disease

My research group and I have published a paper in the *British Journal of Nutrition* describing our theory that dairy foods, grains, legumes, and yeast may be partly to blame for rheumatoid arthritis and other autoimmune diseases in genetically susceptible people. Legumes and grains contain substances called lectins. These substances are proteins that plants have evolved to ward off insect predators. Lectins can bind with almost any tissue in our bodies and wreak havoc—if they can enter the body, that is.

Normally, when we eat food, all proteins are broken down into basic amino acid building blocks and then absorbed in the small intestine. Lectins are different. They are not digested and broken down; instead, they attach themselves to cells in our intestines, where nutrient absorption takes place. The lectins in wheat (WGA), kidney beans (PHA), soybeans (SBA), and peanuts (PNA) are known to increase intestinal permeability and allow partially digested food proteins and remnants of resident gut bacteria to spill into the bloodstream. (Alcohol and hot chile peppers also increase intestinal permeability.) Usually, special immune cells immediately gobble up these wayward bacteria and food proteins. But lectins are cellular Trojan horses. They make the intestines easier to penetrate, and they impair the immune system's ability to fight off food and bacterial fragments that leak into the bloodstream.

Surprisingly, we have found that many common gut bacteria fragments are made up of the same molecular building blocks as those found in certain immune system proteins and in the tissues under attack by the immune system. This matchup—of gut bacteria or food protein, immune system protein, and body tissue protein—may confuse the immune system, causing it to attack the body's own tissues. A number of research groups worldwide have found that milk, grain, legume, and nightshade proteins can also trick the immune system into attacking the body's own tissues by this process of molecular mimicry.

If you have an autoimmune disease, there is no guarantee that diet will cure it or even reduce your symptoms, but there is virtually no risk, and there are many other great benefits from the Paleo Diet that will improve your health.

Psychological Disorders

One of the least-known benefits of grain-free diets is their ability to improve mental well-being. My colleague Dr. Klaus Lorenz of Colorado State University has extensively studied how cereals may influence the development and progression of schizophrenia. In a wide-ranging review study, Dr. Lorenz concluded that in "populations eating little or no wheat, rye, and barley, the prevalence of schizophrenia is quite low." Dr. Lorenz's analysis included the clinical studies by Dr. F. Curtis Dohan of the Eastern Pennsylvania Psychiatric Institute. In studies spanning almost 25 years, Dr. Dohan reported time and again that the symptoms of schizophrenia were reduced in patients on grain- and dairy-free diets but worsened when these foods were returned to the diet. Exactly why cereals may alter mood and mental well-being is not entirely clear. But several studies have shown that when wheat is digested, it contains a narcotic-like substance that may affect certain areas in the brain that influence behavior. Similar substances called casomorphins have been isolated from cow's milk; however, no one knows whether they can alter mood or behavior.

My colleague Joe Hibbeln at the National Institutes of Health has demonstrated that omega-3 fats may be effective in reducing depression, hostility, schizophrenia, and other mental disorders. His finding was confirmed in a 4-month study of 30 manic-depressive patients by Dr. Andrew Stoll of the Brigham and Women's Hospital in Boston. Dr. Stoll used medicine's most powerful study tool, a double-blind, placebo-controlled trial, to compare the efficacy of omega-3 fats versus olive oil for treatment of manic-depressive illness. According to Dr. Stoll and his colleagues, "for nearly every outcome measure, the omega-3 fatty acid group performed better than the placebo group." This work lends credence to a number of recent studies demonstrating that the symptoms of depression are much lower in people who eat a lot of fish (an excellent source of omega-3 fats).

The Paleo Diet will also improve your mental outlook because it normalizes your insulin level. Almost everyone knows that a low blood sugar level can make you feel tired, irritable, and tense. When you normalize your insulin level with low-glycemic carbohydrates and plenty of lean protein, your blood sugar level will be more even throughout the day and so will your mood.

Vitamin-Deficiency Diseases

In the United States the common vitamin deficiency diseases (beriberi, pellagra, and rickets) were wiped out after World War II with the wide-scale fortification of our white flour and white rice with B vitamins and our milk and margarine with vitamin D. However, people living in less-developed nations are not so lucky; these diseases still run rampant wherever diets are heavily based on cereals and legumes. It goes without saying that the world's primary vitamin deficiency diseases, including scurvy from a lack of vitamin C, are completely a result of agriculture's new foods. When you eat the way nature intended, you will protect yourself from all illnesses that develop from vitamin deficiencies.

Dental Cavities

Nearly all archaeological studies of Paleolithic people's teeth show them to be almost completely free of cavities. How can this be when they never brushed, gargled with mouthwash, or flossed? The answer is simple: With their diet of lean meats, fruits, and veggies, cavities simply couldn't get a foothold. Historically speaking, cavities and tooth decay didn't start until the coming of agriculture and its starchy, sugary foods. Cavities are caused when acid produced by certain bacteria eats away part of the enamel of your tooth. These bacteria can't set up shop in your teeth unless there is a constant source of sugar or starch that fuels their acid production.

We can learn a lot from our teeth because any food that does so much damage to our teeth can't be very good for the rest of our bodies, either. Refined sugars and starches are foreign substances to our Paleolithic bodies. We simply haven't had time to adapt to agriculture's new foods. We are best designed to run on the foods nature provided: meats, fruits, and veggies.

Alcoholism

Alcohol—and its enormous potential for abuse—was not part of the preagricultural equation. No alcoholic beverage has ever been linked to Paleolithic people, although it would have been possible to make alcoholic drinks from gathered honey (mead) or berries (wine) by natural fermentation. It wasn't until the Agricultural Revolution, with its abundance of starchy grains, that the first beers were brewed on a regular basis. Quite a bit later came wine, made from fermented grapes. (Because beer and wine are yeast fermentation by-products, they do not contain more than 6 to 13 percent alcohol; the alcohol-producing yeast organisms die when the alcohol concentration rises above this level.) Hard liquor didn't come on the scene until about AD 800, with the invention of distillation.

In most Western countries, moderate consumption (5 to 10 drinks per week) of alcohol is not considered detrimental to health; in fact, it has been associated with a reduced risk of dying from all combined causes of death. Moderate alcohol consumption also may improve your insulin sensitivity and is associated with a reduced risk of other chronic diseases.

Does this mean you should take up drinking to improve your health? Absolutely not. You don't need alcohol to obtain the health and weight-loss benefits of the Paleo Diet. However, if you currently enjoy an occasional glass of wine, there is no need to forgo this pleasure. Consumption of alcoholic beverages a few times a week won't hurt your health, nor will it slow your weight loss. However, if you suffer from an autoimmune disease or another serious health problem, alcoholic beverages should not be part of your dietary equation.

Skin Cancers

Skin cancers come in three basic varieties:

- Squamous cell cancers, which form on the top layers of the skin

- Basal cell cancers, which form on the bottom layers of the skin

- Melanomas, which form within the skin's pigment-producing cells, the melanocytes

The American Cancer Society estimated that 2 million Americans would develop the first two types of skin cancer in the year 2010. These cancers grow slowly, rarely spread to other areas of the body, and are easily curable by early removal. An estimated 69,000 Americans were expected to develop melanoma in 2009. If detected early and surgically removed before they spread to other parts of the body, melanomas are highly curable, with 95 out of 100 people alive 5 years after diagnosis. But if melanomas spread to the rest of the body, they can be deadly; the 5-year survival rate drops drastically, to 16 out of 100.

Scientists know that excessive sunlight exposure is linked to all three cancers. But this does not mean you should avoid sunlight in any amount. Here
again, the experience of our hunter-gatherer ancestors proves helpful. Ironically,
many studies have shown that people with high lifetime sunlight exposure (similar to that of hunter-gatherers) have lower rates of melanoma than those with
low sunlight exposure. Also, indoor workers have a greater risk of developing
melanoma than outdoor workers do. Even more puzzling, melanomas often arise
in body areas that are infrequently or intermittently exposed to the sun. These
unexpected findings have led researchers to believe that severe sunburn during
childhood, or intense burns in body areas that are infrequently or intermittently
exposed to the sun, may be more important in the development of melanoma
than cumulative exposure during adulthood.

When your exposure to sunlight is gradual, moderate, and continuous—if
you don't get excessive sunburn—your body responds in a manner guided by
evolutionary wisdom. The skin begins to tan from increased production of melanin, and the darkened skin provides protection from the sunlight's damaging
ultraviolet rays. Also, vitamin D levels in the blood begin to rise as ultraviolet
light strikes the skin, causing it to convert cholesterol into vitamin D.

Vitamin D is a potent inhibitor of the cancer-causing process. In fact, vitamin
D has been shown to prevent the growth of melanomas in experimental animals
and cultured tissue lines.

An unexpected bonus of vitamin D is that it may also be one of our most
important allies in the war against prostate, breast, and colon cancers. Evidence
from population studies confirms that people with the greatest lifetime sun
exposures have the lowest rates of these cancers.

Skin cancer is a complex disease, with several factors influencing its ultimate
course. In laboratory animals, scientists have found that excessive omega-6 fats
promote the development of skin cancer—but omega-3 fats slow it down. Furthermore, antioxidants like beta-carotene, vitamin C, and vitamin E tend to
prevent the sun's ultraviolet damage to the skin. You can get these same dietary
advantages when you adopt the dietary principles I have laid out in the Paleo
Diet. (Note: As with many of the diseases we have discussed, proper diet reduces
your risk of developing some types of skin cancer, but it cannot completely prevent it.)

Exposure to sunlight is natural for human beings. It is part of our evolutionary heritage. Without sunlight, it is virtually impossible to achieve an adequate
intake of vitamin D from the natural foods that were available to our hunter-

gatherer ancestors. Our food supply has been a significant source of vitamin D for a very short time—less than a century, when dairy producers began adding it to milk and later, margarine. Sunlight exposure is healthy as long as it occurs in a slow, gradual, and limited dose over the course of a lifetime.

As you have seen, the Paleo Diet will not only help you get thin; it will also help prevent and treat a broad range of diseases. The Paleo Diet is good medicine!

Part 2

The Paleo Diet Program

Chapter 6

Eating Great:
What to Eat, What to Avoid

Now that I've talked about why the Paleo Diet is the diet nature intended, let's get down to specifics: how do you get started?

This is the best part—it's so easy. You don't have to balance food blocks, weigh portions, keep a food log, or count calories. As I've shown, the basic guidelines of the Paleo Diet are very simple: all the meats, poultry, fish, seafood, fruits (except dried fruits), and vegetables (except starchy tubers—primarily, potatoes) you can eat. Because the mainstay of the Paleo Diet is high-quality protein, you won't need to feel guilty about eating meat, fish, or seafood at every meal. This is exactly what you *should* be doing, along with as many low-glycemic fruits and veggies as you want.

You're about to embark on a diet of enormous and bountiful diversity, fully backed by thousands of clinical nutrition trials and—most important—by 2.5 million years of evolutionary experience. What do you get in return? If you follow the simple nutritional guidelines laid out in this chapter and the tempting meal plans and delicious, easy recipes in Chapters 9 and 10, you will lose weight; reduce your risk of heart disease, cancer, diabetes, and other chronic diseases; and feel energized all day long. And unlike with almost every other diet you can think of, *you won't feel hungry all the time*. You will feel good on this diet, *because this is the only diet that is consistent with your genetic makeup*.

By imitating the diets of our Paleolithic ancestors with foods you can buy at the supermarket or grow in your own garden, you'll be able to reap the health benefits that are your genetic heritage—freedom from obesity, a high energy level, and excellent health.

It is not possible for us to duplicate precisely all the foods that our ancient ancestors ate. Many of these foods no longer exist—such as the mammoth—or they're unavailable commercially, or they just aren't palatable, given our modern tastes and cultural traditions. However, most of the advantages and benefits of the Paleo Diet can easily be obtained from common foods following the general nutritional guidelines observed by our Paleolithic ancestors.

Making the Diet Work for You

It isn't easy to change the habits of a lifetime, and you don't have to do it overnight. You can ease the transition by adopting the three levels of the Paleo Diet. The levels are based on the concept that what you do occasionally won't harm the overall good of what you do most of the time. Does this mean you can cheat? Yes—sometimes. Occasional cheating and digressions may be just what you need to help you stick to the diet the rest of the time, and they won't sidetrack the weight loss and health effects of this diet.

Getting Enough of the Right Foods

As I discussed earlier, there was no single Paleo diet. Our ancient ancestors made the most of their environment wherever they happened to be. For example, the Inuit people were able to live healthy lives, free of chronic diseases, on a diet that derived at least 97 percent of its energy from animal foods. At the other end of the spectrum were groups like the !Kung in Africa, who obtained 65 percent of their daily calories from plant foods (chiefly the mongongo nut). However, most Paleolithic groups fell somewhere in between, with animal foods generally making up around 55 to 60 percent of the daily caloric intake. On the Paleo Diet, you should attempt to get a little more than half of your calories from meats, organ meats, fish, shellfish, and poultry and the rest from plant foods.

Let's take a look at the wonderful, diverse foods that you can eat in unlimited quantities.

Meats

The key word here is "fresh." Of course, this includes chicken and fish. But many people are surprised to find that red meat—beef and pork—organ meats, and game meats are also on the list. How can this be? Because, as I discussed earlier, *the Paleo Diet is not a fat-free diet, it's a bad fat–free diet.* As long as the meat is fresh and not processed, you can eat your fill. Another noteworthy aspect of the meats available on this diet is their great variety. This is a common response as people begin this diet: "I was in a rut before—hamburgers, hot dogs, and pizza. Now I'm planning my meals around all kinds of meats—some I had never tried before, some I'd never even heard of."

In order to get enough protein and calories, you should eat animal food at almost every meal. You can't just eat animal food, however. You must eat fruits and vegetables, too. Here's why: If protein-dense, extremely lean meats and seafood are your main sources of calories, you will get sick—with nausea, diarrhea, and weakness—because your body can't handle this much undiluted protein without something else, either fat or carbohydrates. Early Arctic explorers, trappers, and frontiersmen who had no choice but to eat the fat-depleted meat of game animals in the dregs of winter rapidly developed these same symptoms, frequently referred to as "rabbit starvation" or protein toxicity.

The problem, as shown in Dr. Daniel Rudman's laboratory at Emory University in Atlanta, is that the liver can't effectively eliminate the nitrogen caused by the protein overload. For most people, the dietary protein ceiling is 200 to 300 grams a day, or about 30 to 40 percent of the normal daily caloric intake.

On the other hand, eating too many processed meats can wipe out any health benefits that eating high levels of protein will help you achieve. Paleolithic people couldn't eat processed meats if they tried—they had nothing like the grain-fed animals that produce our steaks today. Wild game meat contains 15 to 20 percent of its calories as fat. A lean cut of beef trimmed of all visible fat contains more than double this amount (35 to 40 percent fat).

FAT AND PROTEIN CONTENT
(PERCENTAGE OF TOTAL CALORIES OF MEAT AND FISH)

Meats/Seafood You Can Eat	% Protein	% Fat
Turkey breasts	94	5
Boiled shrimp	90	10
Orange roughy	90	10
Pollock	90	10
Broiled lobster	89	5
Red snapper	87	13

Meats/Seafood You Can Eat	% Protein	% Fat
Dungeness crab	86	10
Alaskan king crab legs	85	15
Buffalo roast	84	16
Broiled mackerel	82	18
Roast venison	81	19
Broiled halibut	80	20
Beef sweetbreads	77	23
Steamed clams	73	12
Pork tenderloin	72	28
Beef heart	69	30
Broiled tuna	68	32
Veal steak	68	32
Sirloin beef steak	65	35
Chicken livers	65	32
Chicken breasts	63	37
Beef liver	63	28
Lean beef flank steak	62	38
Broiled salmon	62	38
Lean pork chops	62	38
Mussels	58	24
Fat pork chops	49	51
Lean lamb chops	49	51
Pork shoulder roast	45	55
T-bone steak	36	64
Chicken thigh/leg	36	63
Ground beef (15% fat)	35	63
Eggs	34	62
Lamb shoulder roast	32	68
Pork ribs	27	73

Meats/Seafood You Can Eat	% Protein	% Fat
Beef ribs	26	74
Fat lamb chops	25	75
Meats to Avoid	**% Protein**	**% Fat**
Ham lunch meat	39	54
Dry salami	23	75
Link pork sausage	22	77
Bacon	21	78
Liverwurst	18	79
Bologna	15	81
Hot dog	14	83

Not only is the total amount of fat higher in commonly consumed grain-produced meats—such as ground beef, T-bone steak, hot dogs, and pork chops—than that found in fish and game meat, but the *types* of fat are also quite different. Because most commercially available beef has been feedlot-fattened (mainly with corn and sorghum), it contains low levels of omega-3 fats and high levels of omega-6 fats. This is the wrong mix. When eaten in excess, omega-6 fats are harmful, while omega-3 fats are greatly beneficial. The average Western diet is burdened by high levels of omega-6 fats— which can promote the development of heart disease in many ways. The meats, fish, and seafood you'll be eating on the Paleo Diet are generally high in protein, and they contain the correct balance of omega-3 and omega-6 fats.

What about eggs? Eggs are a relatively high-fat food (62 percent fat, 34 percent protein). Eating eggs doesn't promote weight gain and has little effect on blood cholesterol levels. There is no doubt that Paleolithic people would have eaten wild bird eggs whenever they found them. Wild eggs always would have been a seasonal food and would not have been eaten every day. Also, wild bird eggs are nutritionally different from domesticated chicken eggs; they have higher levels of beneficial omega-3 fats and lower levels of certain saturated fats. You should also buy free ranging eggs or eggs enriched with omega-3 fats.

The high protein of the Paleo Diet is the key to many of its weight-loss benefits. Protein helps you lose weight faster by boosting your metabolism while simultaneously blunting your hunger. And while this is happening, low-fat protein is improving your blood lipid and cholesterol levels, as studies from Dr. Bernard Wolfe's laboratory at the

University of Western Ontario have confirmed. Low-fat protein also prevents blood sugar swings and reduces the risk of hypertension, stroke, heart disease, and certain cancers.

Salmon for breakfast? Breakfast is one part of the Paleo Diet that may seem a bit strange at first. In Western countries, breakfast is usually a high-carbohydrate affair, featuring a cereal product (bagel, sweet roll, buttered bread, packaged cereal with milk, oatmeal), coffee or fruit juice, and a piece of fruit. The other common option frequently includes high-fat, grain-produced processed meats such as bacon, sausage, and ham, along with cheese-filled omelets.

Salmon steak and chicken breast aren't on very many breakfast menus. And yet studies indicate that for Paleolithic people, the morning meal was high in protein, low in carbohydrates, and probably contained "leftovers" from the animal that was killed the day before. A common breakfast on the Paleo Diet, then, might be a cold salmon steak or cold crab (left over from last night's supper) and half a cantaloupe. So go ahead—try fish or meat first thing in the morning. You'll soon find yourself looking trimmer and feeling fitter right at the start of the day.

What to Eat?

Here are the specifics of the Paleo Diet. We'll start with domestic meats. Eat as much as you want for breakfast, lunch, and dinner. Cook the meats simply—broiling, baking, roasting, sautéing, browning, or stir-frying over high heat with a little olive oil (but never deep-fat frying).

Meats

Beef

- Flank steak
- Top sirloin steak
- Ground beef
- London broil
- Chuck steak
- Veal
- Any other cut

Lean pork (trimmed of visible fat)

- Pork loin
- Pork chops
- Any other lean cut

Poultry

- Chicken breast
- Turkey breast
- Game hen breast

Eggs

- Chicken (go for the enriched omega-3 variety)
- Duck
- Goose

Other meats

- Rabbit meat (any cut)
- Goat meat (any cut)

Organ meats

- Beef, lamb, pork, and chicken livers
- Beef, pork, and lamb tongues
- Beef, lamb, and pork marrow
- Beef, lamb, and pork sweetbreads

Next, more exotic fare. You may hunt your own or buy locally or via mail order. For a list of exotic-meat suppliers, see Resources on page 313.

Game meat

- Alligator
- Bear
- Bison (buffalo)
- Caribou
- Elk
- Emu
- Goose
- Kangaroo
- Muscovy duck
- New Zealand cervena deer
- Ostrich
- Pheasant
- Quail
- Rattlesnake
- Reindeer
- Squab
- Turtle
- Venison
- Wild boar
- Wild turkey

Fish

- Bass
- Bluefish
- Cod
- Drum
- Eel
- Flatfish
- Grouper
- Haddock
- Halibut
- Herring
- Mackerel
- Monkfish
- Mullet
- Northern pike
- Orange roughy
- Perch
- Red snapper
- Rockfish
- Salmon
- Scrod
- Shark
- Striped bass
- Sunfish
- Tilapia

- Trout
- Tuna

- Turbot
- Walleye

- Any other commercially available fish

Shellfish

- Abalone
- Clams
- Crab

- Crayfish
- Lobster
- Mussels

- Oysters
- Scallops
- Shrimp

Fruits and Vegetables

It's not easy to get 50 percent of your daily calories from fruits and vegetables because of the high bulk and low caloric density of fruits and salad vegetables. On an average 2,200-calorie diet, you'd have to eat more than 5 pounds of fruits and vegetables a day. Most people are simply unwilling or physiologically unable to consume this much plant food; there is a limit to how much fiber the human gut can hold. However, some plant foods, such as avocados, nuts, seeds, and olive oil, are rich in healthful fats. Eating these in moderate amounts will help you get the calories you need for a balanced diet.

Unless you are severely overweight or obese, you should not worry about how many fresh fruits you eat on the Paleo Diet. Only people with signs and symptoms of metabolic syndrome need to limit consumption of fresh fruits. High-sugar fruits like grapes, bananas, cherries, and mangos should be limited for obese patients or those with signs and symptoms of metabolic syndrome. Low-sugar fruits like berries and melons present no problems.

Nuts are rich in calories. If you are trying to lose weight, you should eat only about 4 ounces of them a day. Also, except for walnuts, almost all nuts have high levels of omega-6 fats, and if eaten excessively, they can unbalance the ratio of omega-6 to omega-3 fats in your diet.

For ideal health, then, you should eat fruits and vegetables with every meal, along with moderate amounts of nuts, avocados, seeds, and healthful oils (flaxseed and olive). However, just because it's a vegetable doesn't mean it's good—or that it's on the list on the opposite page. High-carbohydrate starchy tubers like potatoes are restricted on the Paleo Diet. Also, dried fruit should be eaten only in small amounts because it, too, can produce a high glycemic load (causing a rapid increase in the blood glucose level), particularly when you eat too much of it. When you're hungry or in doubt, start with a high-protein food. Remember, lean protein is the most effective nutrient in reducing your appetite and boosting your metabolism to help you burn stored fat.

Fruits

- Apple
- Apricot
- Avocado
- Banana
- Blackberries
- Blueberries
- Boysenberries
- Cantaloupe
- Carambola
- Cassava melon
- Cherimoya
- Cherries
- Cranberries
- Figs
- Gooseberries
- Grapefruit
- Guava
- Grapes
- Honeydew melon
- Kiwi
- Lemon
- Lime
- Lychee
- Mango
- Nectarine
- Orange
- Papaya
- Passion fruit
- Peach
- Pear
- Persimmon
- Pineapple
- Plums
- Pomegranate
- Raspberries
- Rhubarb
- Star fruit
- Strawberries
- Tangerine
- Watermelon
- All other fruits

Vegetables*

- Artichoke
- Asparagus
- Beet greens
- Beets
- Bell peppers
- Broccoli
- Brussels sprouts
- Cabbage
- Carrots
- Cauliflower
- Celery
- Collards
- Cucumber
- Dandelion
- Eggplant
- Endive
- Green onions
- Kale
- Kohlrabi
- Lettuce
- Mushrooms
- Mustard greens
- Onions
- Parsley
- Parsnip
- Peppers (all kinds)
- Pumpkin
- Purslane
- Radish
- Rutabaga
- Seaweed
- Spinach
- Squash (all kinds)
- Swiss chard
- Tomatillos
- Tomato (actually a fruit, but most people think of it as a vegetable)
- Turnip greens
- Turnips
- Watercress

* All, except for starchy tubers like potatoes. Remember, peas and green beans are legumes, and these foods were rarely on Paleo menus.

Nuts and Seeds

Nuts are rich sources of monounsaturated fats. Monounsaturated fats tend to lower cholesterol and reduce the risk of heart disease and may also reduce the risk of certain cancers, including breast cancer. However, because nuts and seeds are such concentrated sources of fat, they have the potential to slow down weight loss, particularly if you're overweight. Again, if you are actively losing weight, you should eat no more than 4 ounces of nuts and seeds a day. Once your metabolism has increased and you've reached your desired weight, you can eat more nuts, particularly walnuts, which have a favorable omega-6 to omega-3 ratio. Note: *Peanuts are legumes, not nuts, and are not on the list.*

- Almonds
- Brazil nuts
- Cashews
- Chestnuts
- Hazelnuts (filberts)

- Macadamia nuts
- Pecans
- Pine nuts
- Pistachios (unsalted)

- Pumpkin seeds
- Sesame seeds
- Sunflower seeds
- Walnuts

Foods You Can Eat in Moderation

Some people are surprised to find alcohol in this next category. There is no evidence to suggest that our Paleolithic ancestors drank any form of alcoholic beverage. And it's abundantly clear, in our own day, that abuse of alcohol—in addition to causing a host of serious behavioral and social problems—can impair your health, damage your liver, and increase your risk of developing many cancers. However, if you currently drink in moderation— if you enjoy an occasional glass of wine—there's no need to give up this pleasure on the Paleo Diet. In fact, numerous scientific studies suggest that moderate alcohol consumption significantly reduces the risk of dying from heart disease and other illnesses. Wine in particular, when consumed in moderation, has been shown to have many beneficial health effects. A glass of wine before or during dinner may help improve your insulin sensitivity and reduce your appetite. Wine is also an appetizing, salt-free ingredient that adds flavor to many meat and vegetable dishes. Note: If you have an autoimmune disease, you should avoid alcoholic beverages and other yeast-containing foods.

Oils

- Olive, avocado, walnut, coconut, macadamia nut, and flaxseed oils (use in moderation—4 tablespoons or less a day when weight loss is of primary importance)

Beverages

- Diet sodas (I no longer recommend consuming any diet beverage because recent evidence shows artificial sweeteners to cause insulin resistance and hence obesity by altering the gut flora.)

- Coffee

- Tea

- Wine (two 4-ounce glasses) (Note: Don't buy "cooking wine," which is loaded with salt.)

- Beer (one 12 ounce serving; gluten free beers are preferable)

- Spirits (4 ounces)

Paleo sweets

- Dried fruits (no more than 2 ounces a day, particularly if you are trying to lose weight)

- Nuts mixed with dried and fresh fruits (no more than 4 ounces of nuts and 2 ounces of dried fruit a day, particularly if you are trying to lose weight)

Foods You Should Avoid

I've spent a lot of time talking about why the foods in this next category should not be part of your diet. Except for honey, refined sugars were nonexistent in Paleo diets; so were dairy products and excess salt. Almost all processed food is a mix of three or four of the following: sugar, some form of starch (wheat, potatoes, corn, rice), fat or oil, dairy products, salt, and flavorings. Because most processed foods are made with refined grains, starches, and sugars, they are high-glycemic items and can cause large swings in blood sugar levels. Most modern cereal- and sugar-based processed foods adversely affect insulin metabolism and are associated with a greater risk of obesity, heart disease, diabetes, high blood pressure, and other chronic health problems.

Just because these foods are not part of the diet, you don't have to banish them from your life forever. But you should try to avoid them most of the time.

Dairy foods

- All processed foods made with any dairy products
- Cheese
- Cream
- Dairy spreads
- Frozen yogurt
- Ice cream
- Ice milk
- Low-fat milk
- Nonfat dairy creamer
- Powdered milk
- Skim milk
- Whole milk
- Yogurt

Cereal grains

- Barley (barley soup, barley bread, and all processed foods made with barley)
- Corn (corn on the cob, corn tortillas, corn chips, cornstarch, corn syrup)
- Millet
- Oats (steel-cut oats, rolled oats, and all processed foods made with oats)
- Rice (brown rice, white rice, ramen, rice noodles, basmati rice, rice cakes, rice flour, and all processed foods made with rice)
- Rye (rye bread, rye crackers, and all processed foods made with rye)
- Sorghum
- Wheat (bread, rolls, muffins, noodles, crackers, cookies, cake, doughnuts, pancakes, waffles, pasta, spaghetti, lasagna, wheat tortillas, pizza, pita bread, flat bread, and all processed foods made with wheat or wheat flour)
- Wild rice

Cereal-grainlike seeds

- Amaranth
- Buckwheat
- Quinoa

Legumes

- All beans (adzuki, black, broad, fava, field, garbanzo, horse, kidney, lima, mung, navy, pinto, red, string, white)
- Black-eyed peas
- Chickpeas
- Lentils
- Peanut butter
- Peanuts
- Peas
- Snow peas
- Sugar snap peas
- Soybeans and all soybean products, including tofu

Starchy vegetables

- Starchy tubers
- Cassava root
- Manioc

- Potatoes and all potato products (French fries, potato chips, etc.)

- Sweet potatoes
- Tapioca pudding
- Yams

Salt-containing foods

- Almost all commercial salad dressings and condiments
- Bacon
- Catsup
- Cheese
- Deli meats
- Frankfurters
- Ham

- Hot dogs
- Olives
- Pickled foods
- Pork rinds
- Processed meats
- Salami
- Salted nuts
- Salted spices

- Sausages
- Smoked, dried, and salted fish and meat
- Virtually all canned meats and fish (unless they are unsalted or unless you soak and drain them)

Meats

- Bacon
- Bacon bits
- Bologna

- Breakfast sausage
- Deli meats
- Pepperoni

- Pork sausage
- Salami
- Spam

Soft drinks and fruit juices

- All sugary soft drinks
- Canned, bottled, and freshly squeezed fruit drinks (which lack the fiber of fresh fruit and have a much higher glycemic index)
- All artificially sweetened diet drinks

Sweets

- Candy
- Honey
- Sugars

As you can see, there's a bounty of wonderful foods you can eat on the Paleo Diet, so you'll never get bored. Use your imagination and have fun with these delicious foods.

Chapter 7

The Paleo Diet User's Manual

Stocking Your Refrigerator and Pantry

You know those diets where you have to buy *their food,* in *their packaging,* at *their stores*? This is different. You don't need to buy any special foods to follow the Paleo Diet. Just about everything you need is right in your local supermarket—particularly if it has a health food section. Even if you live in a rural area, the basics of the diet—fresh meats, fish, fresh fruits, and vegetables—can be found in small grocery stores. If you choose, you can order specialty oils and game meats through the mail (some suppliers are listed on page 313). But you don't need anything out of the ordinary to get started.

Look for Fresh Meats

The mainstay of the Paleo Diet is lean animal foods. Always choose the leanest cut of meat you can find.

Beef

If you can get it—it might be at the butcher's counter, not out in the main meat aisle—range-fed is better than grain-fed beef because it's leaner, and it has a better ratio of omega-6 to omega-3 fatty acids. Note: The words "natural beef" are no guarantee that the animal hasn't been fattened with grains (or pumped full of antibiotics, for that matter); check with your butcher. A simple visual inspection of the fat on any cut of meat lets you know if the animal was raised on pasture or on grains. Pasture-produced meat has fat that is orange to dark yellow in color, whereas grain-produced meat has fat that appears white.

Poultry

Free-range chickens are almost always better than broiler chickens, because—like range-fed beef—they're not as fat. Here, too, the natural foraging diet (of insects, worms, and wild plants) guarantees a healthful ratio of omega-6 to omega-3 fatty acids. Free-range chickens can be found in many upscale or health-oriented supermarkets.

Turkey

Turkey breast is one of the best and cheapest sources of very lean meat—it's even leaner than most game meat—and fortunately, it's available almost everywhere. Tip: Before you cook very lean domestic meats, rub them with olive oil. This will add flavor and help keep them moist during cooking.

Pork

Some pork is *even leaner than chicken*. Pork tenderloin, for instance, has 28 percent fat compared to chicken breasts, which have 37 percent. Naturally grown pork—similar to free-range chicken—maintains a more favorable ratio of omega-6 to omega-3 fats compared to grain-produced versions of these meats.

Other Choices

What about organ meats? Organ meats are low in fat and rich sources of vitamins, minerals, and omega-3 fats. Bone marrow is another overlooked food that's seldom eaten in the United States but is considered a delicacy in Europe. Even though it contains about 80 percent fat by weight, almost 75 percent of the fat is monounsaturated—which means that marrow is a good fat that won't raise your cholesterol.

As for lamb, if you can find grass-fed, free-range meat, go for it. The type of lamb produced in Australia and New Zealand is leaner than American grain-fed lamb and contains more healthful omega-3 fats. Remember, grass-produced meat is the key to making this lifelong nutrition plan work for you.

One of the best online resources for locating healthy, naturally produced, grass-fed meats is my friend and colleague Jo Robinson's Eatwild Web site: eatwild.com. Jo's Web site is an incredible cornucopia of information that will help you locate a reliable producer of grass-fed, natural meat in your local region. Eatwild's

Directory of Farms lists more than 1,300 pasture-based farms, with more farms being added regularly. It is the most comprehensive source for grass-fed meat in the United States and Canada. For your convenience, Jo provides customers with contact information of suppliers who will ship their products to you.

Wild Game Meat—at a Gourmet Store Near You

In the United States, it's illegal to harvest wild game meat for commercial use. This means that the game meat you can buy from specialty suppliers (see Resources on page 361) didn't come from the wild, but from a ranch or a farm—where these animals graze freely in large fenced or open areas. Most game animals are raised in free-range conditions. Like its wild counterpart, this game meat is quite low in fat and maintains a healthful balance of omega-6 and omega-3 fatty acids.

You can find buffalo and sometimes rabbit meat in many supermarkets—especially the upscale or health-oriented ones—and more exotic fare in specialty meat and butcher shops. Your local butcher may be able to order game meat as well, but be prepared—it isn't cheap. If you are a hunter (or if you know someone who is, who would be willing to help out), you can save a lot of money by acquiring wild meat yourself.

Like all very lean meat, game meat is a bit tricky to cook. It's also easy to ruin so that it loses its texture and appeal.

It also helps to rub the meat thoroughly with olive oil before cooking and to keep basting it as it cooks. If you grill game meat, keep it on the rare side, baste it often with olive oil or marinades, and it will be tender.

If you've never tasted game meat, you may be in for a big surprise. Some game meats, like buffalo and elk, taste a lot like beef, but with a sweeter, richer flavor. Others, like antelope or sage hen, can have a distinctively pungent flavor—the telltale "gamey" taste. This gamey flavor is actually a good sign; it results from the increased levels of omega-3 fats in the meat, plus various wild plants in the animal's diet. It also indicates that the game meat you're eating is healthy, with a good balance of omega-6 and omega-3 fats. If you're not used to game meat's distinctive flavors—or if you never want to get used to it—overnight marinating can do wonders. You'll find mail-order suppliers that specialize in the sale of game meat in Resources on page 313.

Fish and Seafood

Nutritionally speaking, fish and seafood are a lot like humanity's original staple food—lean game meat. They're high in protein, low in total fat, and typically high in omega-3 fats. Many scientific studies have shown that regular fish consumption reduces bad LDL cholesterol and triglycerides while simultaneously increasing the good HDL cholesterol. The omega-3 fats in fish also prevent the heart from going into irregular, uncontrolled beating patterns called arrhythmias, which can be fatal. *Fish is just plain good for you.* It lowers your risk of heart attack, stroke, and type 2 diabetes. By eating fish and seafood regularly, you can significantly reduce your risk of dying from the number one killer of all Americans—heart disease.

Unfortunately, there's a downside, and it has nothing to do with fish and seafood, but with our own environment. Fish and seafood are often contaminated with heavy metals, particularly mercury; by polychlorinated biphenyls (PCBs); and by pesticides such as DDT and dieldrin. The places where fish live—oceans, rivers, lakes, and streams—are also the dumping grounds for many of these potentially harmful chemicals. Once in the water, these toxins seep into the sediments and then into the plants. They're ingested by the tiny animals that form the base of the food chain. Little fish eat plants and tiny animals, and bigger fish eat little fish. Heavy metals and fat-soluble pesticides can become concentrated in older fish, in predatory fish, and in fatty species of fish.

Mercury finds its way into our waterways as a by-product of fuel-burning and through household and industrial wastes. Bacteria in the water convert mercury into the toxic compound methylmercury. When we eat mercury-contaminated fish, we can develop mercury poisoning, which can damage the brain and the nervous system. The good news is that most of the time, the amount of mercury we get from fish is quite small. And the amount of mercury that you can potentially accumulate by eating fish three or four times a week is tiny compared to how much you could get by industrial or occupational exposure.

For healthy people, regular fish consumption poses virtually no risk to brain or nervous system function. It's safe even for pregnant women and very young children, concludes a comprehensive study conducted by Dr. Philip Davidson and colleagues at the University of Rochester School of Medicine and Dentistry in New York. Their findings, published in the *Journal of the American Medical Association,* come from a 9-year study conducted in the Republic of the Seychelles, an island nation in the Indian Ocean, where most people eat fish nearly a dozen times a week and have mercury levels *about 10 times higher* than those of most Americans. In fact, no harmful effects were seen in the nervous systems and behavior of children at mercury levels *up to 20 times* the average American level.

It is a worrisome fact that we live in a polluted world, and most of us are exposed to a host of toxic compounds. However, the greatest risk to your health is not from environmental pollutants, but from heart disease, diabetes, obesity, stroke, and the associated health disorders of metabolic syndrome. *Eating fish protects you not only from these diseases but also from all causes of death, including cancer.* Because fish is one of our greatest sources of omega-3 fats, it can also help prevent depression and improve your mood, as my friend and colleague Dr. Joseph Hibbeln of the National Institutes of Health has shown. In short, fish should be part of your diet.

You should still be prudent when you shop for fish and seafood. Here are a few ways you can minimize your risk of eating contaminated fish.

- Avoid freshwater fish taken from lakes and rivers—particularly the Great Lakes and other polluted, industrialized areas.

- Choose fish that come from cleaner waters, such as the Pacific Ocean and those in Alaska.

- Eat mainly smaller, nonpredatory species such as flounder, herring, sardines, sole, pollock, catfish, halibut, and clams.

- Eat big fish—swordfish, shark, and tuna—sparingly. These long-lived predatory fish tend to accumulate more mercury.

Fortunately, over the long run, the Paleo Diet's many fruits and vegetables—and their disease-fighting antioxidants—can help prevent cancers and health problems that are a direct result of our environmentally polluted world.

How to Be a Savvy Shopper for Fish

Yet the possibility of environmental contamination isn't the only thing you have to worry about when you eat fresh fish and seafood. Another, much bigger concern is simply whether the fish has gone bad. Improper handling and warm temperatures offer great potential for bacterial contamination and spoilage as fish makes its way from wherever it was caught to its eventual place of sale. The freshness clock begins to tick immediately: Most fish have a shelf life of 7 to 12 days once they're out of the water. But fish often remain on a boat for 5 to 6 days after they're caught. They may spend another day or two in transit from the processor or wholesaler to the marketplace—and then may sit on a retailer's display counter for several days more before they are sold. If the fish get too warm during any stage of transport, they'll spoil even faster. Bacteria are the main culprits in the spoilage process, but enzymes in the fish tissue and even atmospheric oxygen can contribute. Fortunately, spoiled fish release a pungent warning—a compound called trimethylamine, which causes the telltale fishy odor associated with bad fish.

Fresh fish is practically odorless. If a fish smells, spoilage is most likely well under way—so stay away from smelly fish. Here are some other tips.

- If you're buying whole fish—and it passes the odor test—check the gills. If they're bright red and moist, the fish is probably fine. If the gills are brown or clumped together, the fish has been on the shelf too long.

- Buy fish last. If you're making a prolonged excursion to the grocery store, don't get the fish first and then let it sit in the cart for an hour while you get everything else on the list. Select it, pay for it, go home—and immediately refrigerate the fish *in its original package in the coldest part of your refrigerator.* Try to eat the fish no more than a day after you buy it.

- To protect yourself from bacterial contamination, wash the fish in cold water and then cook it thoroughly, until it's opaque and flakes easily with a fork. This is important: Bacteria and parasites sometimes live in raw fish. But if you cook the fish completely, you'll minimize your chances of getting sick—even if you inadvertently eat fish that has partially spoiled.

- Avoid eating raw fish of any kind for the reasons above.

- If you can't eat fresh fish within a day or two of buying it, freeze it. Freezing completely stops bacterial growth. However, once the fish thaws, the same deterioration process starts again.

- Be careful when you buy fish labeled "previously frozen." This may be once-fresh fish that wasn't bought, went past its expiration date, was frozen by the retailer, and was thawed again for quick sale.

- Look for light-colored, cottony spots on the fish—they're freezer burns. Sometimes frozen fish is allowed to thaw and then is refrozen, sometimes several times. Also look for ice crystal coatings—and walk away if you find them. These are fish you don't want to buy. The highest-quality frozen fish are caught at sea and then quick-frozen individually on board the ship. (Often there's a label to this effect saying that the fish was "frozen at sea.")

What about Farm-Raised Fish?

It's called aquaculture. Many species of fish and shellfish—including salmon, trout, catfish, tilapia, carp, eels, shrimp, and crayfish—are produced in closed waters and ponds and fed soy and cereal-based chows. This is similar to the situation of feedlot-fed cattle. What they eat causes their own meat to be low or deficient in the beneficial omega-3 fatty acids that help make fish so good for us. Numerous scientific studies have demonstrated the omega-3 fatty acid inferiority of farmed fish compared to wild fish.

Farmed fish are usually cheaper to bring to market than wild fish. In the United States, trout—unless you have caught it yourself in the wild—is almost always farmed. Fresh, wild salmon has a marvelous flavor; most farmed salmon is bland-tasting. Decide for yourself. Note: Some farmed fish is labeled as such; most is not. If you don't know, ask your grocer.

Should You Eat Canned Fish?

Canned tuna is America's favorite fish by far. But the canning process causes a number of problems, the least of which is a loss of fresh flavor. This is what happens: The tuna is cooked at high temperatures and then sealed in a can containing salt, vegetable oil, water, or a combination of these three ingredients. The canning process removes 99 percent of the vitamin A found in fresh tuna, 97 percent of the vitamin B_1, 86 percent of the vitamin B_2, 45 percent of the niacin, and 59 percent of the vitamin B_6. It also increases the level of oxidized cholesterol in the fish, specifically a molecule called 25-hydroxycholesterol that is extremely destructive to the linings of arterial blood vessels—so destructive that oxidized cholesterol is routinely fed to laboratory animals to accelerate artery clogging in order to test theories of heart disease. In animal models of atherosclerosis and heart disease, only 0.3 percent of the dietary cholesterol needs to be in the form of oxidized cholesterol to cause premature damage to the arterial linings.

To complete the degradation of this formerly healthy food, the tuna is packed with salt water or vegetable oils, which usually are high in omega-6 fatty acids. If you have the choice, always choose fresh or frozen fish over canned fish. If you do eat canned tuna, try to find brands that are packed in water only (no salt) or in more healthful oils, such as olive. (Most water-packed tuna contains added salt, but this can be removed by soaking the tuna in a shallow pan filled with tap water and then rinsing the fish in a colander under running water.)

Eggs: Good or Bad?

Eggs are healthful foods; our Paleolithic ancestors ate them seasonally, because they just weren't available all the time. Several recent studies have shown that eating one egg a day has no discernible effect on your blood cholesterol level and does not increase your risk of heart disease. So go ahead—enjoy a couple of eggs for breakfast every few days.

There's more good news on the egg front: You can buy chicken eggs that, like the wild bird eggs our ancestors ate, have high levels of omega-3 fatty acids. These enriched eggs—produced when chickens are fed omega-3–enriched feeds—are nutritionally superior and are available at many supermarkets and health food stores.

Because eggs are one of our richest dietary sources of cholesterol, the way they're cooked influences the level of oxidized cholesterol—which can damage the cells lining your arteries and increase your risk of developing atherosclerosis and heart disease. High heat—like that of a griddle—produces more oxidized cholesterol than slow cooking: poaching, hard-boiling, or baking. When you have the choice, avoid fried eggs.

A recent study demonstrated that eggs from free-range hens had up to one-third less cholesterol, one-quarter less saturated fat, two-thirds more vitamin A, two times more omega-3 fatty acids, three times more vitamin E, and seven times more beta-carotene than battery-cage eggs.

Similar to the situation with grass-fed, free-range meats, eggs produced from chickens allowed to live and forage freely are more nutritious and healthful than are their factory-produced counterparts. One of the first poultry farmers to recognize the superiority of free-range eggs was my friend George Bass. You can sample George's eggs at his Web site for the Country Hen (see Resources on page 313). I also recommend that you visit Jo Robinson's Web site, eatwild.com, to find a local producer of free-range eggs near your home.

How to Make the Most of Fruits and Vegetables

One of the first changes you'll notice when you start the Paleo Diet is the large amounts of fresh fruits and veggies that you will need to keep on hand. Note: To help produce stay fresh longer, keep fruits and vegetables covered in plastic bags in your refrigerator.

The constant need to replenish your fresh produce supply gives you a good excuse to explore new venues. Try going to local farmers' markets in your area. They're wonderful sources of wholesome, fresh, and delicious fruits and vegetables. They may even inspire you to try growing your own vegetables at home. Also, take this opportunity to try out-of-the-ordinary fruits and vegetables. (Many are included in the recipes and meal plans in this book.) You may want to look for exotic produce in Asian, Far Eastern, and ethnic markets, if there are any in your community. As you gradually wean yourself from salty, sugary, and starchy foods, your taste buds will become attuned to the subtle flavors and textures of wonderful real foods.

To be on the safe side, be sure to wash all produce before you eat it (even if it comes in a bag that says it's been washed). Like fish, fresh produce can contain trace residues of pesticides, heavy metals, or other pollutants. The Food and Drug Administration has monitored the levels of contaminants in the US food supply for almost 40 years in a program called the Total Diet Study. (You can read about it on the Web at fda.gov/Food/FoodScienceResearch/TotalDietStudy /default.htm.) The study, which began in 1961, periodically examines more than 230 foods from eight regional metropolitan areas to determine which hidden ingredients—and how much of them—we're getting in our food. Since its inception, the study has found that our average daily intake of all toxic contaminants—including pesticides, industrial chemicals, heavy metals, and radioactive materials—is well below acceptable limits. Of course, it would be even better if our average daily intake of contaminants were zero and we could rest assured that our food was completely free of any pollution—but it's pretty safe to say that this will not happen any time soon.

The bottom line is that fruits and vegetables have much to offer—antioxidants, vitamins, minerals, and all the healing benefits we've discussed in this book. We can't do without them; more than that, they need to play a starring role in our diet.

Nuts and Seeds

Nuts and seeds are a good adjunct to the Paleo Diet, but they've got a lot of fat, so you need to eat them in moderation. Too many fatty foods—even beneficial nuts and seeds—can rapidly upset your balance of essential dietary fats and derail your weight-loss progress. Throughout the book, we've talked about the omegas—omega-6 and omega-3. One kind—omega-6 fats—is not good for you when eaten in excess. The other kind—omega-3 fats—can make you healthier in many ways. The ideal ratio of omega-6 to omega-3 fats should be between 2 and 3 to 1. For most Americans, unfortunately, it's between 10 and 15 to 1. All nuts and seeds—except for walnuts and possibly macadamia nuts—have unacceptably high omega-6 to omega-3 ratios. This is why you must eat them in small amounts.

Omega-6 to Omega-3 Fat Ratio in Nuts and Seeds

Nut or Seed	Omega-6 to Omega-3 Ratio
Walnuts	4.2
Macadamia nuts	6.3
Pecans	20.9
Pine nuts	31.6
Cashews	47.6
Pistachio nuts	51.9
Hazelnuts (filberts)	90.0
Pumpkin seeds	114.4
Brazil nuts	377.9
Sunflower seeds	472.9
Almonds	Extremely high (no detectable omega-3 fats)
Peanuts (not a nut but a legume)	Extremely high (no detectable omega-3 fats)

But nuts are part of the Paleo Diet. They're high in monounsaturated fats and have been shown in numerous clinical trials to lower cholesterol. This is why they're on the diet *in moderate amounts,* so that you can benefit from the good things nuts have to offer. But the high quantities of omega-6 fats in these nuts can also predispose you to heart disease—because they displace the omega-3 fats, which are known to prevent fatal heartbeat irregularities, decrease blood clotting, lower blood triglyceride levels, and reduce the inflammatory profile of prostaglandins and leukotrienes (hormonelike substances that control the inflammation process). Omega-3 fats have also been shown to lessen the symptoms of many inflammatory and autoimmune diseases, including arthritis and inflammatory bowel disease.

Peanuts are forbidden. As mentioned, they are not nuts at all; they're legumes—and legumes contain lectins and other antinutrients that can adversely affect your health, particularly if you are suffering from an autoimmune disorder.

Important note: Many people are allergic to nuts, and pine nuts can be particularly troublesome for some people. Listen to your body carefully as you begin the Paleo Diet and fine-tune the diet to your specific health needs. Although nuts and seeds are true Paleo foods—and were certainly part of the diets of our ancient ancestors—they were not the staples.

When you shop for nuts:

- Try to buy raw, unsalted nuts. You can find them in their natural state at most supermarkets in late summer and early fall, when they come into season.

- If you don't like cracking nuts, you can find packaged, hulled nuts at some supermarkets and most health food stores. However, read the package label. Hulled nuts are sometimes coated with trans fat–containing oils to increase their shelf life.

- When in doubt, go for walnuts. They have the best omega-6 to omega-3 ratio and are your healthiest choice for a snack food or to use in other dishes. Other nuts should be considered garnishes in salads and other dishes, rather than eaten in quantity.

Purchasing Oils

Vegetable oils were obviously not a component of any preagricultural or hunter-gatherer diet, simply because the technology to produce them did not exist. Oils made from walnuts, almonds, olives, sesame seeds, and flaxseeds were first produced using crude presses between 5,000 and 6,000 years ago. However, except for olive oil, most early oil use was for nonfood purposes, such as illumination, lubrication, and medicine. It wasn't until the beginning of the 20th century, with the advent of mechanically driven steel expellers and hexane extraction processes, that vegetable oils started to contribute significantly to the caloric content of the Western diet. Today, vegetable oils used in cooking, salad oils, margarine, shortening, and processed foods supply 17.6 percent of the total daily energy intake in the US diet. The enormous infusion of vegetable oils into the Western diet, starting in the early 1900s, represents the greatest single factor responsible for elevating the dietary omega-6 to omega-3 ratio to its current and unhealthful value of 10 to 1. In hunter-gatherer diets, the omega-6 to omega-3 ratio was closer to 2 to 1. If we use the evolutionary template exclusively, vegetable oils should probably constitute a minimal part of modern-day Paleo diets.

So, if this is the case, why should we not eliminate all vegetable oils from our diet?

I still believe that certain oils can be used to cook with and add flavor when making condiments, dressings, and marinades. Simply stated, there are four oils (flaxseed, walnut, olive, and avocado) that can promote health and facilitate your getting the correct balance of good fats into your diet. Because hunter-gatherers ate the entire carcasses of wild animals (tongue, eyes, brains, marrow, liver, gonads, intestines, kidneys, and so on) and relished fatty plant foods (nuts and seeds), they did not have to worry about the correct balance of fatty acids in their diet. It came out in the wash.

For most of us, the thought of eating organs is not only repulsive, but it is also not practical, as we simply do not have access to wild game. Consequently, by eating grass-produced meats, fish, and seafood, along with healthful oils, nuts, and seeds, you can get the correct balance of fatty acids in your diet.

As you can see from the table on page 104, only three vegetable oils have omega-6 to omega-3 ratios of less than 3. These are flaxseed (0.24), canola (2.00), and mustard seed (2.60). Although I originally recommended mustard seed oil in the first edition of *The Paleo Diet*, I can no longer make this recommendation because of its high erucic acid (a long-chain monounsaturated fatty acid) concentration of 41.2 percent. Consumption of large quantities of erucic acid in laboratory animals causes adverse changes in their heart structure and function and other organs.

This leaves only two vegetable oils (canola and flaxseed) that do not contribute to an elevated intake of omega-6 fatty acids. A number of epidemiological (population) studies have shown a higher risk of developing prostate cancer with an increased consumption of alpha linolenic acid (ALA), a major fatty acid found in both canola and flaxseed oil. However, epidemiological studies are notorious for their conflicting results. For every six studies that support one nutritional concept, you can often find half a dozen more that conclude precisely the opposite. Such is the case linking ALA and flaxseed oil to an increased prostate cancer risk. A series of the most recent epidemiological studies was unable to statistically show that ALA consumption increased prostate cancer risk. More important, in experiments in which animals were fed flaxseed oil, the flaxseed actually inhibited the growth and development of prostate cancer. The case supporting flaxseed oil as a promoter of prostate cancer is currently based solely on epidemiological evidence and therefore remains inconclusive because of the total lack of confirming experimental evidence. Because the majority of epidemiological studies support the notion that ALA is protective against cardiovascular disease, flaxseed oil should still be viewed as healthful.

Since the original publication of *The Paleo Diet* in 2002, I have reversed my view of canola oil and can no longer support its consumption or use. Let me explain why. Canola oil comes from the seeds of the rape plant (*Brassica rapa* or *Brassica campestris*), which is a close relative of broccoli, cabbage, Brussels sprouts, and kale. Clearly, humans have eaten cabbage and its relatives since prior to historical times, and I still strongly support the consumption of these health-promoting vegetables. The concentrated oil from the seeds of *Brassica* plants is another story.

In its original form, rape plants produced a seed oil that contained high concentrations (20 to 50 percent) of erucic acid (a monounsaturated fatty acid), which I have previously explained is toxic and which causes a wide variety of pathological changes in laboratory animals. In the early 1970s, plant breeders from Canada developed a strain of rape plant that produced a seed with less than 2 percent erucic acid (hence the name canola oil). The erucic acid content of commercially available canola oil averages 0.6 percent. Despite its low erucic acid content, however, a number of experiments in the 1970s showed that even at low concentrations (2.0 percent and 0.88 percent), canola oil fed to rats could still produce minor heart scarring that was considered "pathological."

A series of rat studies of low-erucic canola oil conducted by Dr. Ohara and colleagues at the Hatano Research Institute in Japan reported kidney injuries as well as increases in blood sodium levels and abnormal changes to a hormone, aldosterone, that regulates blood pressure. Other negative effects of canola oil consumption in animals at 10 percent of calories include decreased litter sizes, behavioral changes, and liver injury. A number of recent human studies of canola or rapeseed oil by Dr. Poikonen and colleagues at the University of Tampere in Finland have shown it to be a potent allergen in adults and children and indicate that it may cause allergic cross-reactions from other environmental allergens in children with atopic dermatitis (skin rashes).

Based on these up-to-date studies in both humans and animals, I prefer to be on the safe side and can no longer recommend canola oil.

Both olive oil and avocado oil are high (72.5 and 67.9 percent, respectively) in cholesterol-lowering monounsaturated fatty acids but have less than favorable omega-6 to omega-3 ratios of 11.6 and 13.5. Consequently, excessive consumption of both of these oils without adequate intake of long-chain omega-3 fatty acids (EPA plus DHA) will derail an otherwise healthy diet. I recommend that you get 1.0 to 2.0 grams of EPA and DHA per day in your diet from either fish or fish oil capsules. Because avocado oil is difficult to find and expensive, that pretty much leaves olive oil as the staple for cooking, salad dressings, and marinades.

If you can afford it, I recommend that you always choose extra-virgin olive oil, because this grade of oil is produced by physical means only, without chemical treatment, and it contains the highest concentrations of polyphenolic compounds, which protect against cancer, heart disease, and inflammation.

Although peanut oil has been promoted as a healthy, cholesterol-lowering oil because of its high monounsaturated fat content (46.2 percent of total fat), it has turned out to be one of the most atherogenic (artery-clogging) of all oils. In fact, it is routinely used to induce coronary artery atherosclerosis in monkeys and other laboratory animals. It's not clear exactly why this happens. Some scientific evidence suggests that peanut lectins (proteins that bind to carbohydrates) may be responsible for this effect.

Because soybean oil also contains residual lectin activity (SBA) and maintains a marginal (7.5) omega-6 to omega-3 ratio, it can't be recommended as a staple oil, either. A similar argument can be made for wheat germ oil, which has a marginal omega-6 to omega-3 ratio of 7.9 but also contains large quantities of the lectin WGA, one of the most widely studied and potentially most damaging of all the dietary lectins.

Coconut meat, oil, and milk are traditional foods of indigenous people who live in the tropics. These foods have high amounts of a saturated fat called lauric acid, which is known to elevate blood cholesterol concentrations—a risk factor for cardiovascular disease in modern Westernized populations. Paradoxically, traditional cultures that consume coconut foods have a minimal or nonexistent incidence of heart disease, stroke, or cardiovascular complications normally associated with eating high levels of saturated fats, such as the lauric acid found in coconut food products.

Lauric acid apparently exerts a protective effect in our bodies by eliminating gut bacteria that increase intestinal permeability, a risk factor for cardiovascular disease via heightened chronic low-level inflammation. Based on the evidence of traditional Pacific Islanders who consume coconut, it appears that this food does not present a risk for cardiovascular disease when included as a component of modern Paleo Diets. Let your palate go back to the islands and enjoy the delicious health benefits of this traditional plant food.

SALAD AND COOKING OILS

	Omega-6 to Omega-3	% MUFA	% PUFA	% SAT
Flaxseed oil	0.24	20.2	66.0	9.4
Canola oil	2.00	58.9	29.6	7.1
Mustard seed oil	2.60	59.2	21.2	11.6
Walnut oil	5.08	22.8	63.3	9.1
Olive oil	13.1	72.5	8.4	13.5
Avocado oil	13.0	67.9	13.5	11.6
Almond oil	No omega-3	69.9	17.4	8.2
Apricot kernel oil	No omega-3	60.0	29.3	6.3
Coconut oil	No omega-3	5.8	1.8	86.5
Corn oil	83	24.2	58.7	12.7
Cottonseed oil	258	17.8	51.9	25.9
Grapeseed oil	696	16.1	69.9	9.6
Hazelnut oil	No omega-3	78.0	10.2	7.4
Oat oil	21.9	35.1	40.9	19.6
Palm oil	45.5	37.0	9.3	49.3
Peanut oil	No omega-3	46.2	32.0	16.9
Rice bran oil	20.9	39.3	35.0	19.7
Safflower oil	No omega-3	14.4	74.6	6.2
Sesame oil	137	39.7	41.7	14.1
Soybean oil	7.5	23.3	57.9	14.4
Sunflower oil	No omega-3	19.5	65.7	10.3
Tomato seed oil	22.1	22.8	53.1	19.7
Wheat germ oil	7.9	15.1	61.7	18.8

MUFA = monounsaturated fat, PUFA = polyunsaturated fat, SAT = saturated fat.

Spices

One of the key elements of the Paleo Diet is to cut way down on your use of salt—or, better yet, cut it out entirely. This doesn't mean you need to eat bland, tasteless food—far from it. If you haven't already plunged into the wonderful world of spices, now's your chance.

Lemon crystals and lemon pepper are good replacements for salt, and they give food a mouthwatering zing. There are also several good salt substitutes, commercially available spice mixes designed to take the place of salt. Note: Check the labels; sometimes spice mixes contain cornstarch, hydrolyzed wheat proteins, or other grain and legume products. Some people—particularly if they are suffering from an autoimmune disease—should stay away from spices made from chile peppers (cayenne pepper and paprika). This botanical family of spices contains a substance called capsaicin. Studies by Dr. Erika Jensen-Jarolim and colleagues at University Hospital in Vienna, Austria, have shown that capsaicin increases intestinal permeability and may play a role in the development and progression of certain autoimmune diseases. Again, let your body serve as your guide: If a spice seems to be irritating your system or causing problems, don't use it.

The good news is that most spices are easily digestible and well tolerated and add subtle flavors and overtones to almost all dishes. They'll make your food come alive.

Individualizing Your Diet

The starting point for the optimal Paleo Diet lies in our genes. In some respects, we're all the same. We've all got the basic human genome, shaped by more than 2 million years of evolution and adapted to eat wild animal meats and uncultivated fruits and vegetables. But we're all different, too. Our own genetic differences ultimately influence how we react to certain foods or food types, or how much of a particular nutrient, vitamin, or mineral we need to maintain good health. Even though seafood should be a central part of the Paleo Diet, for example, it's clearly out of the question for people who are allergic to it. If you have a nut, shellfish, or other food allergy, then obviously these foods cannot be part of your individualized program.

The National Academy of Sciences has provided DRIs (Dietary Reference Intakes) for vitamins and minerals. However, these one-size-fits-all guidelines aren't necessarily perfect for everyone. For example, people who are exposed to extra environmental pollutants (say, cigarette smoke) have been shown to require extra antioxidant vitamins. Certain diseases and disorders are known to impair the body's ability to absorb nutrients; pregnant women and breastfeeding mothers need more nutrients than other women do.

No universal dietary recommendations apply to everybody, even though we all have the same starting point—our evolutionary past.

Many people don't even know that some foods—particularly grains, dairy products, legumes, and yeast—are to blame for some of their health problems. They may not make the diet/health connection until they eliminate these foods and then reintroduce them. Listen to your body as you gradually return to the diet nature intended for us all. Find out what works for you and be sensible; alter your diet so that you can live with it—but remember, the further you stray from the basic principles of the diet (animal protein, fresh fruits, and vegetables), the less likely you'll be able to reap its health benefits.

Vitamins, Minerals, and Supplements

When we eat the foods that we're genetically programmed to eat, we won't develop nutritional deficiency diseases. Pellagra (niacin deficiency) and beriberi (vitamin B_1 deficiency) have never been found in hunter-gatherers—modern or Paleolithic. I showed how the vitamins and the minerals eaten every day on the Paleo Diet—a modern Paleo diet—far exceed the RDAs in almost every category. This diet is nutrient-rich by any standard, and it provides us with everything we need to be healthy.

This does not mean that people on the Paleo Diet don't need supplements. You may choose to bolster your diet with certain supplements, including those discussed next.

Vitamin D

Except for fatty ocean fish, there is very little vitamin D in any commonly consumed natural (that is, not artificially fortified) foods. This wasn't a major problem for our Paleolithic ancestors, who spent much of their time outdoors and got all the vitamin D they needed from sunlight. Today, for most of us, sunlight exposure is a hit-or-miss proposition. This is why, to prevent rickets and other vitamin D–deficiency diseases, processed foods such as milk and margarine are fortified with vitamin D.

Do you get enough sun? ("Enough" means about 15 minutes a day.) If you don't, and you've stopped eating margarine and milk, you should supplement your diet with this nutrient. The Dietary Reference Intake for vitamin D is 200 to 600 international units (IU). Because many studies have suggested a link between low vitamin D levels in the blood and a number of cancers—including breast, prostate, and colon cancers—you may want to boost your daily supplementation to 2,000 IU. However, this is not one of those "more is better" nutrients. Vitamin D is fat-soluble, which means it can accumulate in your tissues and eventually become toxic if you take too much of it. The tolerable upper limit for vitamin D in adults is 2,000 IU daily, although recent studies have challenged this value and suggest that a more accurate limit is 10,000 IU.

Here are the keys to healthy sun exposure:

- Build up sun time gradually (15 minutes or less at first, depending on your skin color and ability to tan).
- Never let your skin burn.
- Where it is possible, take the sun year-round.
- Use sunscreens at first to prevent burning; look for sunscreens that block both ultraviolet A and ultraviolet B sunlight.
- However, because sunscreens also impair vitamin D and melanin production, as your tan develops, you can gradually reduce the level of sunscreen protection.

Antioxidants

Although our bodies are basically the same as those of our ancient ancestors, we live in a vastly different world. The pristine, unpolluted Paleolithic environment no longer exists; we are regularly exposed to numerous toxic substances that didn't exist 100 years ago. The food we eat, the air we breathe, and the water we drink all contain minuscule residues of pesticides and chemical and industrial contaminants. These pollutants are inescapable; they're even found in remote parts of Antarctica and Greenland.

Nobody knows the effects of a lifetime of exposure to these noxious agents. However, it's clear that a well-functioning immune system may help protect you from a variety of environmentally dependent cancers and diseases.

The Paleo Diet is exceptionally rich in antioxidants—even with no supplementation. It contains, on average, more than 500 milligrams of vitamin C (more than 9 times the RDA), more than 25 IU of vitamin E (more than 3 times the RDA), and more than 140 micrograms of selenium (more than 2.5 times the RDA). Also, because this diet is loaded with fresh fruits and vegetables, it's high in beta-carotene and many other plant substances (phytochemicals) that protect against many types of cancer.

Fish Oil Capsules

Some people just don't like fish or shellfish, no matter how it's prepared. If you're one of them, I recommend that you take daily fish oil capsules. There are two active ingredients, both fatty acids, in fish oil that produce its many beneficial effects—eicosapentaenoic acid (EPA) and docosahexaenoic acid (DHA). You should try to take 1 to 2 grams of EPA and DHA daily. Depending on the brand and the size of the capsules, you will need to take four to eight capsules per day to get sufficient EPA and DHA. Regular fish oil supplementation will decrease your risk of cancer and heart disease and may reduce certain symptoms of autoimmune diseases and inflammatory disorders.

Food Availability and Preparation Issues

One of the keys to making this diet work is ensuring that your modern Paleo food is always available. Many of us have schedules that keep us away from home or at our jobs, where it is impossible to prepare or buy fresh, unadulterated fruits, veggies, and fresh meats. This means you will need to prepare some of your food at home and bring it with you. But this isn't a problem. For most people, lunch is the most common meal away from home, and "brown-bagging" lunch is the norm for many working people.

You don't have to prepare three separate Paleo meals from scratch every single day. What works best for most people is to simply double or triple the size of the evening meal and then bring the leftovers for lunch. Put parts of your salad and main dish in a sealed container at night and take them with you the next morning. Toss in a piece of fresh fruit, and you've got a terrific lunch! You can also cook two or more main dishes in the evening, use one, and immediately refrigerate the other for use later in the week.

This same principle works for your condiments (salad dressings, salsas, marinades, dips, etc.). Mix up a big batch on the weekend or in the evening, put it in a container, and store it in the refrigerator until you need it. Nothing could be simpler.

Most supermarkets now stock precut, washed salad vegetables and mixes of lettuces. Completely mixed salads (spinach, Caesar, etc.) in sealed plastic bags without added dressing are also commonly available. These packaged veggies are great for people on the go who want to eat fresh foods but don't have time to prepare them. So if time is of the essence, you can make a wonderful, healthful salad by simply opening a bag of cut, washed, and mixed salad greens. Try tossing in some cold shrimp, shredded crabmeat, and olive oil or dressing that you have made beforehand, and you've got another instant Paleo lunch.

Dining Out, Travel, and Peer Pressure

You're invited over to a close friend's house for dinner, and it's spaghetti and meatballs. That's okay, just this once. Your daughter baked you a triple-chocolate birthday cake and would be devastated if you didn't eat at least one piece. That's okay, just this once. Things happen—and a few occasional and minor dietary indiscretions won't make much difference to your overall health if you follow the diet the rest of the time. However, if these indiscretions become the rule and not the exception, you will increasingly lose the healthful benefits and weight-loss effects of the Paleo Diet.

Dining Out

How can you make the Paleo Diet work in the real world? Do the best you can. When you dine out, it can be a challenge—or downright impossible—to follow the Paleo Diet to a T. In the real world, many restaurants build their menus around most of the foods you're trying not to eat. Even though many restaurants now offer low-fat or vegetarian meals, few restaurants sponsor Paleo cuisine. In the best situations, you'll be able to stick pretty close to the Paleo Diet; in the worst cases, you may have to throw in the towel.

However, most of the time, you should be able to pull it off with just a few transgressions. The key is "triage." Assign your priorities based on urgency.

1. Your number one concern is to *get a main dish that is not a starch-based food*. Avoid pancakes for breakfast, for example, sandwiches for lunch, and pasta for dinner.
2. Try to choose fresh meat or seafood, cooked in a simple manner—by baking, broiling, sautéing, roasting, poaching, or steaming—without added starches and fats.
3. Always try to get some fresh fruit or a nonstarchy vegetable at every meal.
4. Keep the meal as simple as you can; the fewer ingredients, the better.

Breakfast

Most breakfast restaurants serve fresh fruit and some form of eggs. Because fried and scrambled eggs are usually cooked with trans fat–containing margarine or shortening, order your eggs poached or hard-boiled. Or have an omelet filled with veggies—hold the cheese and skip the toast. A cup of coffee is okay. Sometimes you can find smoked salmon or fish for breakfast or shrimp-stuffed omelets; try to include healthful omega-3 fats whenever possible. A ham slice or pork chop or a breakfast steak is another option—but make sure that you also get a big bowl of fruit to balance the acid-producing protein load. Try to keep salt to a minimum. (This is probably the most difficult aspect of dining out.)

Lunch

Lunches are usually pretty easy, now that most restaurants offer salads, fresh meats, and fish as entrées. If your salad comes with croutons, ignore them, and try to get an olive oil–based dressing. For dessert, order fresh fruit.

Dinner

Dinners out are usually fairly easy, too. Even pasta-heavy Italian restaurants usually have seafood or meat entrées. You can ask to have these dishes prepared without added flour or breading, skip the potatoes, and get a side order of steamed vegetables. Treat yourself to an occasional glass of wine with dinner. Japanese restaurants are a breeze. They almost always have fish, shellfish, or beef and plenty of steamed veggies; just skip the rice and the soy sauce. (It's far too salty, and most soy sauces are made with wheat.) Chinese restaurants can also be dealt with deftly by avoiding dishes that are rich in sugary, salty sauces, such as sweet-and-sour pork and deep-fried "crispy" dishes. Go with stir-fried chicken dishes or, better yet, steamed crab or fish. Use the same strategy in ordering Chinese vegetable side dishes; ask your waiter or waitress to omit any sauces and just bring fresh steamed veggies. Mexican restaurants are a bit of a challenge, but again, with careful selections you can stick pretty closely to the Paleo Diet. (Order fajitas without the tortillas or browse the seafood and meat selections.) Once in a while, there will be no choice; you'll have to accept whatever food is available. In those cases, limit your portions.

When You Travel

You may choose to dine out, buy food and take it with you in a cooler, or buy it in supermarkets, grocery stores, and even roadside markets along the way. Fresh fruits and veggies are universally available, and they travel well in an ice-filled cooler. Try making your own beef jerky (see Chapter 10); it's delicious and filling, and it tastes great with fresh fruit. Hard-boiled eggs, cooked beforehand and stored in the cooler, can be indispensable for breakfasts on the road.

Instead of stopping where most traveling Americans do—at the first exit with a fast-food restaurant that looks fairly clean—drive a mile or two from the highway and find a supermarket. Most food stores have deli sections with premade salads, and many offer a salad bar. Apply the triage principle and do the best you can. For example, precooked chicken (roasted or rotisserie-cooked) is available at most supermarket deli counters and is an option in a pinch. If you didn't bring any paper plates and plastic utensils, pick some up while you're at the store. Water-packed tuna isn't ideal, either, but it will do while you're on the road.

Ask Your Friends and Family for Support

The support of your spouse, immediate family, and friends can make a world of difference in any big life change. Tell them what you're doing and why—whether it's to lose weight or to improve your health. Explain the logic and rationale of the Paleo Diet and share your successes with them. You don't necessarily have to put the entire family on the diet, and many of the meals that you'll be eating on this lifetime program of nutrition are not very different from the types of foods you ate before. You can always include bread, rolls, or potatoes with your family meals and give family members the option of eating them. In nearly all public settings, unless you call it to their attention, most people won't even realize that your diet has changed—until they notice your weight loss, increase in energy level, and improvement in health. Who knows? They may see the healthful changes you're experiencing and want to join you.

The Paleo Diet is humanity's *normal* diet. The abnormal diet, the odd diet, the out-of-the-ordinary diet is actually the grain-, dairy-, and processed food–based diet that currently pervades the Western world. It's time for a change.

Chapter 8

The 7-Day Quick-Start Plan

To help kick-start your journey (or as a reminder for Paleo Diet veterans), I want to summarize my practical dietary advice by giving you a 1-week quick-start prescriptive plan, and I'll add a few tidbits of wisdom involving health and lifestyle issues.

Meal Plans

In general, three daily meals plus snacks are included in this prescriptive plan. Keep in mind, though, that hunter-gatherers typically did not eat three meals per day. After nearly 20 years of personal experience with contemporary Stone Age diets, I find that lunch is unnecessary for me, and I rarely eat it. On the other hand, my wife, Lorrie, seldom misses it. Some Paleo Dieters fast for a few days each month—others don't. As always, the bottom line is to listen to your body when it comes to the number of daily meals and snacks you require and their timing.

Supplements

Supplements other than vitamin D_3 and fish oils are unnecessary because meats, fish, fruits, and veggies are such nutrient-dense foods. On days that you don't eat fatty fish (salmon, mackerel, sardines, herring, and so on), I recommend that you take fish oil capsules or bottled fish oil. Try to consume at least 500 to 1,800 milligrams of EPA + DHA per day. If you have cardiovascular disease, you should include at least 1 gram (1,000 milligrams) of DHA + EPA in your supplement.

I personally prefer bottled fish oil because it goes down easier and you can smell whether it has spoiled. Except for an increased susceptibility to nose bleeds, no adverse health effects have ever been identified with fish oil supplementation—even at extremely high doses. If you are currently not eating fatty fish on a regular basis or are not supplementing your diet with fish oil capsules, perhaps the best overall health strategy you can take is to do so.

Knowledge Gained, Pounds Lost

Jennifer's Story

I strictly followed your diet, and in the first 2 weeks, I lost 10 pounds! I did not exercise during this time, and I felt rather light-headed at times, but I was never hungry. I imagine that it was quite a shock for my body to stop living on sugar. I started to feel energized as my body began to learn to live on protein without sugar, and during the course of the next 3 months, I lost another 15 pounds. I'm now down to a normal weight of 125 pounds. (I'm 5 feet, 6 inches tall.) Not only am I happy with how I look, I'm ecstatic about how I feel. I'm no longer tired in the afternoons, I have a new energy, and I don't catch every head cold that goes around.

I have relaxed my eating habits a bit in the last few months, and I watch the scale carefully, so that if I start to gain weight, I can tighten the reins on my eating habits. What you have given me and countless others is not a diet but new knowledge of how our bodies function and what we can do to lay down habits that are essential for good health for the rest of our lives.

Thank you, thank you, thank you!

Most of us have indoor jobs and don't get regular daily sun exposure. If this is your situation, I recommend supplementing your diet with at least 2,000 IU of vitamin D_3 per day. In the summertime, 15 to 20 minutes of sunshine exposure during midday on your face and arms will give most of you sufficient and healthful vitamin D levels in your bloodstream. If you live above 40 degrees north latitude (in cities such as Boston, New York, and elsewhere), 15 to 20 minutes of sunlight on your face and arms during the winter months will have little or no positive effect on your blood concentrations of vitamin D. Consequently, daily supplementation with at least 2,000 IU of vitamin D_3 becomes a necessity for most of us, except for during the summer months.

I am a university professor, and my wife, Lorrie, is an elementary school teacher, so we both are pretty much locked into indoor jobs from September until June. Accordingly, our sunlight exposure is minimal for 9 months, making vitamin D_3 supplementation essential for us throughout most of the year. During our summer beach vacations at Tahoe, we completely forget about vitamin D_3 capsules. It is ironic that in our modern world, these three simple environmental elements—the outdoors, sunshine, and fresh air—which were originally the birthright of all human beings, have increasingly become either a luxury of the privileged or, alternatively, an obligation of the disadvantaged.

Exercise

As with sunlight and fresh air, exercise is also a luxury in our modern world. Most of us have occupations in which little strenuous physical activity is required to get through the day. Consequently, as a modern-day Paleo dieter, try to take every opportunity to get into the open air to partake in physical activity outdoors. It may only be walking or gardening a few times a week—even eating lunch or walking outdoors at noon will help.

Any exercise is better than no exercise. Standing is better than sitting. Walking is better than standing. Uphill walking is better than horizontal walking. You get the picture—whenever you have the opportunity to use your muscles or move—do it. Take the stairs—always! Park your car a half mile from the office, and walk the rest of the way. View physical work not as labor, but rather as an escape from your sedentary prison in front of the computer or your stationary workplace. Any time and every time you can stretch your legs, walk, climb stairs, or go outside—do it!

Unfortunately, as good as these job-related efforts are to help you become more active, you will still have to do much more to catch up with the activity patterns of our hunter-gatherer ancestors. Our scientific analysis of forager-movement behavior shows that a hunter-gatherer mom normally hiked 4 miles with a child on her hip or shoulder. Double this distance, and we get into the activity levels of hunter-gatherer men when they left camp for a hunt and returned. Few of us have 2 to 6 hours per day to hike for 4 to 10 miles with a load on our backs. Nevertheless, these kinds of activity patterns and energy outputs are typical for our species and tend to improve almost all health parameters, particularly if we observe a Paleo diet.

Exercise alone is a powerful panacea to restore health. A few years back, one of my departmental co-workers applied for a sabbatical leave to hike along the Appalachian Trail for the fall semester. Forty-nine-year-old Dale started out weighing a flabby 188 pounds, but after 118 days of trekking from dawn until dusk—typically, 10-hour days—with a 40-pound pack, he ended up at a lean and fit 163 pounds. More important, his total blood cholesterol fell from 276 to 196 and his triglycerides dropped from 319 to an amazing 79 (a 75 percent reduction). I barely recognized Dale when this former fat man walked into the office as a slim, fit man restored to his high school weight.

During Dale's 118-day hike, he didn't eat Paleo but rather consumed hikers' dried and concentrated trail foods (gorp, refined sugars, dried fruit, nuts, and processed dehydrated foods). Notable changes in body weight (a 25-pound loss) and health occurred despite eating a diet consisting mainly of processed trail foods. Had he the chance to eat real foods (fresh meats, fresh fish, and fresh fruits and veggies) during his 118-day journey, I suspect that his weight loss and health would have improved even more.

You don't have to walk 10 hours a day for 118 days with a 40-pound pack, as Dale did, to lose weight or experience dramatic improvements in your health. Rather, the Paleo Diet allows you to produce these therapeutic body and blood chemistry changes almost entirely through diet alone. Clearly, any regular exercise program on top of a modern-day Paleo diet will accelerate your fitness and health gains.

Your conditioning program should include all types of exercise. Try to regularly mix aerobic and strength-training activities, along with stretching. If we heed the example of our hunter-gatherer ancestors, hard workouts should be followed by easy or rest days. I also support the nationwide CrossFit movement and know that it dovetails nicely with the Paleo Diet. You may want to visit the owners of your local CrossFit gym and see the type of fitness program they have to offer.

The 7-Day Quick-Start Plan

Sunday

MEAL PLAN

Breakfast:

Free-range or omega-3–enriched eggs scrambled in olive oil with chopped parsley

Grapefruit

Herbal tea

Snack:

Sliced beef

Fresh apricots or seasonal fruit

Lunch:

Caesar salad with chicken (olive oil and lemon dressing)

Herbal tea

Snack:

Apple slices

Raw walnuts

Dinner:

Tomato and avocado slices

Grilled turkey breast

Steamed broccoli, carrots, and artichoke

Bowl of fresh blueberries, raisins, and almonds

1 glass mineral water or white wine

QUICK-START IDEAS

Supplements: Fish oil and 2,000 IU of vitamin D_3 (if you don't get sufficient sun exposure)

Exercise and Relaxation: If you have a sandy beach nearby, try walking or running barefoot at an intensity and duration that are appropriate for your fitness level. Get your feet wet, and let the sand naturally massage your soles.

Health Tip: Peaceful sleep is absolutely essential to our health and well-being. Two dietary elements that can impair restful sleep are alcohol and salt. Try eliminating both of these substances for a few days and see how you do.

Beverage Note: Clearly, wine would never have been available to our ancestors, but don't forget the 85-15 rule (see page 126), which allows you to consume three non-Paleo meals per week.)

Monday

MEAL PLAN

Breakfast:

Strawberry-Blueberry Horizon*

Hard-boiled, free-range or omega-3–enriched eggs

Snack:

Apple with ¼ cup raw walnuts

Lunch:

Grilled halibut steak on a bed of spinach with mandarin orange slices and slivered almonds

Herbal tea

Snack:

Sliced flank steak

Melon balls

Dinner:

Cucumber with avocado dip

Cold boiled shrimp

Steamed carrot and celery slices with parsley

Bowl of fresh boysenberries, raisins, and hazelnuts

Mineral water

QUICK-START IDEAS

Supplements: Fish oil and vitamin D_3 (if you don't get sufficient sun exposure). Try to eat your lunch outside, if the weather permits.

Exercise and Relaxation: Try to give yourself a least an hour a day alone for relaxation (meditation, quiet reading, listening to music, walking the dog, sewing, woodworking, or fishing).

Health Tip: Following a hot shower, turn the water to cold and stand under the spray for about a minute. The invigorating cold water will improve your circulation and increase substances called heat shock proteins, which improve long-term health and resistance to chronic disease.

*Please note: All meal suggestions with an * are recipes featured in Chapter 10.

Tuesday

Breakfast:
Scrambled Basil Eggs Topped with Salsa*

Kiwifruit

Herbal tea

Snack:
Steamed broccoli, drizzled with olive oil, topped with shredded chicken

Lunch:
Turkey breast on mache lettuce, drizzled with flaxseed oil and lemon

Fresh pear slices

Snack:
Mixed fresh berries

Lean beef jerky

Celery sticks

Dinner:
Spinach Salad with Crabmeat*

Steamed cauliflower

1 cup red or green grapes

Baked Walnut-Cinnamon Apples*

Herbal tea

Supplements: Fish oil and vitamin D_3 (if you don't get sufficient sun exposure)

Exercise and Relaxation: Improvements in long-term physical fitness occur due to three variables: exercise intensity, frequency, and duration. Of these three, the intensity of the exercise is the most important to fitness improvement. Whether you are a novice or a seasoned athlete, try to step up the intensity of your workout as you become more fit. You will find that brief, intense bouts of exercise will ultimately make you stronger and fitter more rapidly than will lower-intensity exercise of a longer duration.

Health Tip: If you have recently adopted the Paleo Diet, you may want to take 2 tablespoons of psyllium (such as Metamucil) once or twice a week to help normalize bowel function and reduce intestinal permeability as you transition from a typical low-fiber Western diet to a high-fiber Paleo diet. After a few months on the Paleo Diet, psyllium supplementation will no longer be needed, as you gradually change your intestinal flora to a healthier, less inflammatory pattern.

Wednesday

MEAL PLAN

Breakfast:

Bowl of diced apples, shredded carrots, and raisins

Poached omega-3–enriched or cage-free eggs

Cup of decaffeinated coffee

Snack:

Cucumber, carrot, and apple, chopped and tossed in olive oil, lemon juice, and mint leaves

Dinner:

Steamed broccoli

Salmon Steaks in Curry Sauce*

Sliced tomatoes and cucumbers with olive oil and freshly ground pepper

Half a cantaloupe stuffed with sliced strawberries and mint

1 glass red wine or mineral water

QUICK-START IDEAS

Supplements: Cage-free or omega-3–enriched eggs and salmon are moderate sources of the healthy omega-3 fatty acids (EPA and DHA). To obtain sufficient amounts of these healthy nutrients, you need to either eat other fatty fish (mackerel, sardines, herring, and so on) or supplement with fish oil. If you didn't get into the sun today, you will also need to take vitamin D_3 capsules. Your body stores the vitamin D it makes from sunlight, so if you were able to sunbathe for a while on the weekend, then you wouldn't require supplements during the week.

Exercise and Relaxation: I favor exercise in which we minimize machines and maximize our bodies' natural movements. Lifting free weights appears to have certain advantages over machine-generated workloads, because it stresses muscles more naturally throughout their entire range of motion and prevents overuse injuries. Lifting free weights, climbing rope, doing pullups and pushups, and tossing medicine balls around sounds archaic in this day and age of computerized ergometers and stair-step and lifting machines, but it is precisely these tried-and-true exercises that are being successfully used in CrossFit gyms throughout the country.

Health Tip: In dry climates, some otherwise very healthy people experience recurrent nose bleeds that are difficult to stop—even following cauterization by their physicians. A surefire cure, known to few health professionals, is to coat the inside of the nostrils with zinc oxide ointment (I recommend Desitin) for a few days. The healing power of this ointment stems from zinc, which potently stimulates the growth of new tissues.

*Please note: All meal suggestions with an * are recipes featured in Chapter 10.*

Thursday

MEAL PLAN

Breakfast:
Salmon, green onion, and mushroom omelet

Tangerine segments

Herbal tea

Snack:
Apple slices mixed with raw almonds

Lunch:
Mixed green salad with Omega-3 Russian Salad Dressing*

Sliced beef, topped with blueberries

Steamed artichoke

Herbal tea

Snack:
Spicy Beef Jerky*

Sliced avocado drizzled with lime juice and cilantro

Dinner:
Carrot Salad*

Baked haddock

Steamed asparagus

Almonds, raisins, and peaches

1 glass white wine or mineral water

QUICK-START IDEAS

Supplements: Because salmon was on the menu today, no fish oil supplementation is necessary. If you were unable to get a minimum of 15 to 20 minutes of sunlight exposure during the day or an extended bout of sunbathing earlier in the week, supplement with vitamin D_3.

Exercise and Relaxation: One of the most recent developments in footwear is more natural shoes that mimic bare feet and let our feet do the walking without fancy "scientific" insoles, stiff uppers, computer-designed heel cups, and other fallible human-designed tweaks. Our feet are incredible engineering feats designed by the wisdom of evolution through natural selection over millions of years. We are perfectly suited to walk and run barefoot across all terrains that our ancestors crossed without protective foot gear. No human beings wore shoes until perhaps 50,000 years ago, and those primitive soft leather pieces, similar to modern shoes that were designed to simulate being barefoot, provided only warmth and slight protection from injury.

Our modern, style-conscious shoes force our toes, ankles, and legs into unnatural positions and don't allow our feet to have natural contact with the earth. Because of these features, our feet are forced to become narrower and weaker; our toes grow shorter, and we lack the foot sensitivity our hunter-gatherer ancestors had through-out their lives. When we come home from a long day at work, our first response it to kick off our shoes and relax. If we take just a little bit of time to examine our suffering shod feet, they are hot, red, and swollen, and they smell bad.

The elixir for our feet is restoring them to the environment for which they were designed. We need to walk barefoot whenever possible. I am on board with modern shoe designs that allow our feet the freedom to support our bodies with their liga-ments, tendons, bones, and muscles as they were naturally designed to do.

Health Tip: As you adopt a milk-, grain-, potato-, and legume-free diet, most of you will notice that your sinuses become remarkably clear. You will wake up in the morn-ing clear-headed, with little phlegm or nasal stuffiness, and your joints will be loose, pain free, and ready for the day.

As with my recommendation for psyllium and gastrointestinal tract health, you can accelerate nasal clearances by sniffing salt water. Put a tablespoon or less of salt into a cup or neti pot of tap water, stir well, pinch off a nostril, and sniff the solution into your nose. Hold it, and then release. Repeat a few times, and you have effectively cleansed your nostrils because of the hypertonic effect of salt water. This measure will clear your nostrils of all obstructions that may impair your breathing. After a few weeks on the Paleo Diet, this practice will become unnecessary.

*Please note: All meal suggestions with an * are recipes featured in Chapter 10.

Friday

MEAL PLAN

Breakfast:

Roast turkey breast, drizzled with olive oil and basil

Sliced apples

Water with freshly squeezed lemon juice

Snack:

Cold boiled shrimp

Fresh orange

Lunch:

Spinach salad with tomatoes, walnuts, olive oil, and lemon juice

Paleo-Correct Meat Loaf*

Raspberries

Snack:

Pear slices

Raw pecans

Dinner:

Tossed green salad with purple onions, tomatoes, and parsley, dressed with olive oil and lemon juice

Steamed crab legs

Spicy Stuffed Squash*

Iced herbal tea

QUICK-START IDEAS

Supplements: Note that this menu is rich in shrimp and crab (which contain moderate to high concentrations of omega-3 fatty acids), but it still does not contain sufficient long-chain (> 20 carbon) omega-3 fatty acids to completely protect you from cancer or cardiovascular or autoimmune disease. I recommend that you supplement with either fish oil capsules or liquid fish oil.

Supplement with vitamin D_3 (if you don't get sufficient sunlight exposure).

Exercise and Relaxation: Although clearly not an option available to our ancestors, modern technology has given our bodies an incredible relaxation tool. It's called a sauna, and followed by a cooling bath or shower, you can almost guarantee yourself a long and restful night's sleep.

Health Tip: One of the most therapeutic nonpharmacological remedies you can treat yourself to is a full-body massage lasting for 30 to 60 minutes. Do this weekly, and you will feel like a million dollars.

Saturday

MEAL PLAN

Breakfast:

Cantaloupe Stuffed with Blackberries and Pecans*

Cold broiled halibut

Snack:

Shredded kale, tossed with lime juice, olive oil, and minced red onion, topped with chopped turkey breast

Lunch:

Shrimp-Stuffed Avocados*

Sliced tomatoes

Fresh pineapple

Water with freshly squeezed lemon juice

Snack:

Grapes

Cold steamed oysters

Dinner:

Carrot-Mushroom Stir-Fry*

Grilled lamb chops

Sliced peaches covered with chopped walnuts and liqueur (optional)

Fresh Cinnamon Applesauce*

1 glass red wine or mineral water

QUICK-START IDEAS

Supplements: If you eat Paleo (fresh fruits, veggies, meats, seafood, nuts, and healthful oils), the only supplements you will need are fish oil and possibly vitamin D_3. If you eat fatty fish (salmon, mackerel, sardines, or herring) a few times a week and get out into the summer sun, fish oil and vitamin D_3 supplementation are unnecessary.

Exercise and Relaxation: I have one recommendation—whenever and wherever you can use your body instead of machines to get the job done, do it! Preferably, exercise outdoors and in the sunshine—this is our species' genetic heritage and represents the conditions under which our health flourishes.

*Please note: All meal suggestions with an * are recipes featured in Chapter 10.

Chapter 9

The Meal Plans for the Three Levels of the Paleo Diet

The Paleo Diet is a lifelong way of eating that will gradually restore your normal body weight, health, and well-being. If you follow the dietary guidelines and principles I have laid out, you will reap all the benefits that humanity's original diet has to offer. Your health will immediately improve, and you will definitely begin to lose weight.

In this chapter, you'll find three 2-week meal plans to use after following the 7-Day Quick-Start Plan in Chapter 8. Any of them will work for you; the only difference is in the number of Open Meals. Just use the appropriate number of Open Meals for your level of the diet, and you're set. Use these guidelines and the recipes in Chapter 10 to help you embrace the diet that nature designed for us all.

Here's the recap:

• Level I: three Open Meals per week

• Level II: two Open Meals per week

• Level III: one Open Meal per week

If you are a beginner, you may want to adhere to Level I for 2 to 4 weeks before you move to Levels II and III—or, if you're happy there, you may want to stay at this level of the diet. Note: You should try to include no more than one Open Meal on any given day. Use them as a safety net as you get used to humanity's *real* foods: fresh meats, seafood, and fruits and vegetables.

Should you definitely plan to move up to Levels II and III? Not necessarily. Depending on your nutritional and weight-loss goals, you may be happy with the results you achieve at Level I, particularly if you limit your consumption of non-Paleo foods while consuming your Open Meals.

If you decide to jump into the Paleo Diet more rapidly by advancing to Level II, then you may substitute two Open Meals a week for any of the meals in the meal plans.

If you are one of those people who can make long-term behavioral changes abruptly and want to go cold turkey to the Stone Age, or if it is absolutely essential that you maximize the weight loss and health benefits of this program, then you should adopt Level III. On Level III, you should substitute one Open Meal a week for any of the meal plans.

However, most people do quite well at Level II, and this is the level that I recommend for maintenance, except for dieters with chronic diseases, who may do better with long-term adherence to Level III.

Snacks

When our ancient ancestors were out foraging for food, they often snacked on some of the food they gathered, or they took portions of a previous meal along on their journey. The snacks on the Paleo Diet—like those of our Paleo ancestors—are healthy, wholesome, and made of real food. Most of them are easily portable, so you may want to bring some of them along on your own daily journeys. You may eat snacks between meals whenever you become hungry.

- Fresh fruit of any kind

- Homemade beef jerky (without salt)

- Homemade dried salmon strips (without salt)

- Raw vegetables: carrots, celery sticks, cherry tomatoes, mushrooms, broccoli, cucumbers, cauliflower (with homemade guacamole or salsa dip)

- Cold broiled chicken breast

- Avocado or tomato slices

- Nuts: almonds, pecans, walnuts, filberts (limit to 4 ounces a day if you're trying to lose weight)

- Dried fruit (limit to 2 ounces a day)

- Hard-boiled eggs
- Cold slices of beef
- Cold boiled shrimp
- Unsalted sunflower seeds (limit to 4 ounces a day if you're trying to lose weight)

Level I: Entry Level

The key to Level I is the 85-15 rule and here's how it works: Most people eat about 20 meals a week, plus snacks. On this beginning level, 3 of your meals—15 percent of the meals you eat all week—can be "open." This way, you don't have to give up your favorite foods. Again, the flexibility of the Paleo Diet allows you to cheat occasionally without losing the overall benefits of the diet. The 3 Open Meals provide a good opportunity to taste some of the foods you may miss the most.

There is great potential for abuse here, and you should do your best to avoid it. Do not consider these Open Meals as your chance to pig out on forbidden foods. For example, having 2 pints of Ben & Jerry's Chunky Monkey ice cream for lunch would be a bad move and self-defeating. But if you're invited to a party or go out to eat with friends, the Open Meal is your chance to indulge a bit. A single scoop of Chunky Monkey won't hurt, particularly if you've been on the diet all week. Or eat a slice of toast with your breakfast or have some potatoes with your dinner entrée. But again, don't eat six slices of toast or a pound of mashed potatoes. The basic idea is to ease the feeling of deprivation that generally accompanies the start of any change in diet. If you handle these Open Meals wisely—treating yourself, but not to excess—you'll soon find that you don't need to take advantage of the Open Meals as "cheats."

At first, many people find it difficult to give up bread, cereals, and dairy products. But when you cut down on these foods gradually, you'll eventually be able to replace them with more healthful fruits and vegetables. With Level I, you may want to use some "transitional" condiments. These contain sugar and salt but are low in fat. As you become accustomed to your new eating plan, you'll want to reduce or eliminate them. Transitional condiments include:

- Low-fat salad dressings. Use these in moderation and read the labels. Stay away from brands that contain large amounts of corn syrup or salt.

- Commercial sauces. Mustard, hot sauces, prepared salsa. Note: *No catsup* (except for the Paleo version, the recipe for which is included in Chapter 10); regular catsup is too high in salt and fructose.

- If you are a coffee, beer, or wine drinker, you may continue to enjoy these non-Paleo beverages in moderation, working toward cutting back on them as you become accustomed to the Paleo Diet. Transitional beverages include:

  - Sugar-free soft drinks. I can no longer recommend these beverages because all of them contain artificial sweeteners that alter the gut's flora causing insulin resistance—a condition underlying obesity and the metabolic syndrome.

  - Alcoholic beverages. Use these in moderation.

  - Coffee. Use it in moderation. Excessive caffeine is associated with a number of illnesses and health problems; decaffeinated is preferable.

Sample 2-Week Meal Plan for Level I

WEEK 1 FOR LEVEL I

SUNDAY

Breakfast: Open

Lunch:
- Almond Chicken Salad*
- Herbal tea

Dinner:
- Tomato and avocado slices
- Grilled turkey breast
- Steamed broccoli, carrots, and artichoke
- Bowl of fresh blueberries, raisins, and almonds

Water with lemon slice

Snack:[†] Basic Beef Jerky,* celery sticks

MONDAY

Breakfast:
- Bowl of diced apples, shredded carrots, and raisins
- Poached eggs
- Cup of decaffeinated coffee

Lunch:
- Brockway Tuna Salad*
- Handful of almonds
- Mineral water

Dinner:
- Steamed clams
- Tossed green salad
- Broiled halibut steak with lemon juice and dill
- Steamed asparagus
- Sliced kiwifruit and tangerine wedges
- Glass of dry white wine

Snack:[†] cold beef slices, carrot sticks

TUESDAY

Breakfast:
- Cantaloupe and strawberries
- Broiled pork chops
- Herbal tea

Lunch:
- Spinach salad with choice of Paleo dressing
- Broiled orange roughy with fresh orange juice and oregano
- Steamed cauliflower
- Apple
- Mineral water

Dinner:
- Paleo Zucchini Soup*
- Slow-Cooked Veal with Salsa*
- Figs
- Iced tea

Snack:[†] hard-boiled eggs. walnuts, raisins

WEDNESDAY

Breakfast:
- Grapefruit
- Strawberries with blackberries
- Cold leftover Slow-Cooked Veal with Salsa*
- Cup of decaffeinated coffee

Lunch: Open

Dinner:
- Avocado and tomato slices
- Oysters on the half shell
- Altamira Stuffed Chicken*
- Ratatouille*
- Fresh boysenberries, raisins, and almonds
- Cup of decaffeinated coffee

Snack:† mango, unsalted macadamia nuts, Dried Salmon*

THURSDAY

Breakfast:
- Raspberries with walnuts
- Scrambled eggs with a small beefsteak
- Herbal tea

Lunch:
- Lime and Dill Crab*
- Figs and fresh nectarines
- Iced tea

Dinner:
- Spicy Tomato Soup*
- Green salad with black olives (rinsed of salt)
- Burgundy Beef Roast*
- Steamed cauliflower with lemon juice and paprika
- Fresh peaches
- Glass of red wine

Snack:† cold chicken breast, cherry tomatoes, celery sticks

*Please note: All meal suggestions with an * are recipes featured in Chapter 10.

†Snacks are permitted anytime.

FRIDAY

Breakfast:
- Blueberries and cantaloupe
- Cold crab legs
- Water with lemon slice

Lunch:
- Gingery Chicken and Veggies*

- Tomatoes and black olives (rinsed of salt) on a green salad with Anaheim Cilantro Salsa*
- Iced tea

Dinner: Open

Snack:† hard-boiled eggs, cold broiled salmon steak

SATURDAY

Breakfast:
- Casaba melon
- Cold chicken breasts
- Herbal tea

Lunch:
- Tahoe Shrimp Salad*
- Melon slices and strawberries

Dinner:
- Cold mackerel
- Tomato and cucumber wedges with olive oil and lemon juice
- Auroch Beef Cabbage Rolls*
- Chopped pecans, raspberries, and Medjool dates
- Water with lemon slice

Snack:† Basic Beef Jerky,* apple slices

WEEK 2 FOR LEVEL I

SUNDAY

Breakfast:
- Bowl of sliced bananas, strawberries, and walnuts
- Cup of decaffeinated coffee

Lunch:
- Waldorf Salad*

- Tangerine slices
- Water and lemon slice

Dinner: Open

Snack:[†] guava, dried apricots without sulfur, and kiwifruit, Dried Salmon*

MONDAY

Breakfast:
- Cantaloupe Stuffed with Blackberries and Pecans*
- Herbal tea

Lunch:
- Spinach Salad à la Cordani*
- Orange sections
- Mineral water

Dinner:
- Chicken Vegetable Soup*
- Marinated Mushrooms*
- Omega Meatballs*
- Baked Walnut-Cinnamon Apples*
- Iced tea

Snack:[†] Spicy Beef Jerky,* dried apricots without sulfur

TUESDAY

Breakfast:
- Fresh or frozen blackberries and raspberries
- Trout sautéed in olive oil and lemon juice
- Water with lemon slice

Lunch:
- Turkey burgers
- Tossed green salad with olive oil and lemon juice
- Apple slices with lemon juice and mint leaves
- Iced tea

Dinner:
- Tossed green salad with flaxseed oil and lemon juice
- Paleo Zucchini Soup*
- Baked Tomatoes*
- Savory Steamed Mussels*
- Fresh melon
- Mineral water

Snack:[†] fresh peaches, cold boiled shrimp, walnuts

*Please note: All meal suggestions with an * are recipes featured in Chapter 10.

[†]Snacks are permitted anytime.

WEDNESDAY

Breakfast:
- Fresh or frozen strawberries and/or blueberries
- Grilled venison sausage
- Herbal tea

Lunch: Open

Dinner:
- Celery and carrot sticks dipped in Guacamole Fiesta*
- Spicy Tomato Soup*
- Steamed asparagus
- Sautéed Rocky Mountain Chicken Livers*
- Pomegranate
- Cup of decaffeinated coffee

Snack:[†] hard-boiled egg, unsalted macadamia nuts

THURSDAY

Breakfast:
- Fresh plums
- Small lean beefsteak covered with Peach Salsa*
- Cup of decaffeinated coffee

Lunch:
- Gazpacho*
- Shrimp-Stuffed Avocados*
- Apple
- Iced tea

Dinner:
- Tomato, cucumber, and red onion salad with olive oil
- Red Snapper in Snappy Sauce*
- Carrot-Mushroom Stir-Fry*
- Peach-Almond Delight*
- Glass of wine or mineral water

Snack:[†] cold crab legs, tomato quarters

FRIDAY

Breakfast:

- Grapefruit
- Scrambled Basil Eggs Topped with Salsa*
- Herbal tea

Lunch:

- Tossed green salad with olive oil and lemon juice
- Paleo-Correct Meat Loaf*
- Water with lemon slice

Dinner:

- Marinated Mushrooms*
- Altamira Stuffed Chicken*
- Spicy Stuffed Squash*
- Baked Walnut-Cinnamon Apples*
- Mineral water

Snack:[†] sliced cold turkey breasts, sunflower seeds, hard-boiled eggs

SATURDAY

Breakfast: Open

Lunch:

- Broiled Tenderloin of Pork with Spicy Rub*
- Honeydew melon
- Herbal tea

Dinner:

- Waldorf Salad*
- Chicken Cacciatore*
- Steamed broccoli with lemon juice
- 2 or 3 Medjool dates

Snack:[†] carrot and celery sticks, dried pears, walnuts

---

*Please note: All meal suggestions with an * are recipes featured in Chapter 10.

[†]Snacks are permitted anytime.

Level II: Maintenance Level

Level II of the Paleo Diet is structured around the 90-10 split. Two Open Meals are permitted each week; the rest of your meals are made up of modern Paleo foods. At this level, you should restrict or eliminate all of the transitional foods, except during your two Open Meals. As in Level I, all snacks should be chosen from the list of Paleo snacks (see "Snacks" on page 125). Many people do quite well at this level and find that there's no need to move to the next level unless weight loss or health considerations are paramount.

Sample 2-Week Meal Plan for Level II

WEEK 1 FOR LEVEL II

SUNDAY

Breakfast: Open

Lunch:
- Beef and Spinach Scramble*
- Herbal tea

Dinner:
- Tomato wedges and cucumber slices dipped in flaxseed oil
- Salmon Steaks in Curry Sauce*
- Steamed brussels sprouts
- Tangerines
- Mineral water

Snack:† apple, Spicy Beef Jerky*

MONDAY

Breakfast:
- Half a cantaloupe with strawberries
- Cold halibut steak
- Herbal tea

Lunch:
- Brockway Tuna Salad*
- Tangerine
- Water with lemon slice

Dinner:
- Tomato and cucumber slices with Veggie Dip*
- Omega Meatballs*
- Steamed carrots and cauliflower with dill and paprika
- Kiwifruit and strawberries with walnut pieces
- Iced herbal tea

Snack:† Spicy Beef Jerky,* celery sticks

TUESDAY

Breakfast:
- Grapefruit
- Two-egg (cage-free) omelet with avocado, scallion, and tomato filling cooked in olive oil
- Herbal tea

Lunch:
- Gingery Chicken and Veggies*
- Apple and walnuts

Dinner:
- Tomato wedges
- Artichoke leaves dipped in Omega-3 Mayonnaise*
- Tossed green salad with flaxseed oil and lemon juice
- Salmon Steaks in Curry Sauce*
- Fresh or frozen berries
- Glass of nonalcoholic wine

Snack:[†] carrot sticks, sliced zucchini, cold boiled shrimp

WEDNESDAY

Breakfast: Open

Lunch:
- Gazpacho*
- Cajun Catfish Bake*
- Fresh peaches
- Herbal tea

Dinner:
- Chicken Vegetable Soup*
- Ambrosia Salad*
- Barbecued Alaskan Shrimp*
- Fresh blackberries
- Water with lemon slice

Snack:[†] walnuts and raisins, hard-boiled egg

THURSDAY

Breakfast:
- Fresh pineapple slices
- Broiled small breakfast steak covered with Anaheim Cilantro Salsa*
- Herbal tea

Lunch:
- Spinach Salad with Crabmeat*
- Fresh oranges
- Mineral water

Dinner:
- Butter Leaf Avocado Salad*
- Baked Haddock Italiano*
- Steamed summer squash with lemon pepper and paprika
- Fresh Cinnamon Applesauce*
- Water with lemon slice

Snack:[†] cold chicken breasts, celery and carrot sticks

*Please note: All meal suggestions with an * are recipes featured in Chapter 10.*

[†]*Snacks are permitted anytime.*

FRIDAY

Breakfast:

Pink grapefruit

Chilled steamed shrimp

Cup of decaffeinated coffee

Lunch:

- Tossed green salad with Omega-3 Russian Salad Dressing*
- Grilled pork chops covered with Raspberry Barbecue Sauce*
- Mineral water

Dinner:

- Chicken Vegetable Soup*
- Paleo-Correct Meat Loaf*
- Avocado and tomato slices
- Steamed broccoli
- Fresh peaches
- Glass of wine

Snack:† cucumber slices, cold beef slices

SATURDAY

Breakfast:

- Fresh or frozen strawberries
- Two-egg (cage-free) omelet stuffed with spinach, mushrooms, and onions sautéed in olive oil
- Water with lemon slice

Lunch:

- Kenny's Barbecued Spicy Chicken*
- Steamed vegetables
- Fresh fruit

Dinner:

- Marinated Mushrooms*
- Red Snapper in Snappy Sauce*
- Spicy Stuffed Squash*
- Baked Walnut-Cinnamon Apples*
- Glass of wine

Snack:† Basic Beef Jerky,* dried apple slices

WEEK 2 FOR LEVEL II

SUNDAY

Breakfast:
- Honeydew melon and fresh blueberries covered with walnuts
- Chilled steamed crab legs
- Cup of decaffeinated coffee

Lunch:
- Tossed green salad with Omega-3 Russian Salad Dressing*
- Broiled flounder with lemon juice and dill
- Glass of nonalcoholic wine

Dinner:
- Tomato and avocado wedges with garlic and cayenne powders
- Sicilian Skillet Veal Chops*
- Steamed cauliflower served with lemon juice
- Carrot sticks
- Strawberry-Blueberry Horizon*
- Iced herbal tea

Snack:[†] celery and carrot sticks dipped in Veggie Dip,* unsalted macadamia nuts

MONDAY

Breakfast:
- Kyle's Apple Breakfast*
- Cold sliced turkey breast
- Herbal tea

Lunch:
- Auroch Beef Cabbage Rolls*
- Fresh fruit
- Iced herbal tea

Dinner:
- Gazpacho*
- Mackerel steaks with dill and lemon juice
- Steamed asparagus with lemon juice
- Fresh fruit
- Glass of nonalcoholic wine

Snack:[†] Spicy Beef Jerky,* dried apricots without sulfur

TUESDAY

Breakfast:
- Fresh orange slices
- Scrambled Basil Eggs Topped with Salsa*
- Cup of decaffeinated coffee

Lunch:
- Carrot Salad*
- Salmon Steaks in Curry Sauce*
- Mineral water

Dinner:
- Baked Tomatoes*
- Rocky Mountain Elk Steaks*
- Walnut Broccoli with Carrots*
- Almost Frozen Mashed Bananas*
- Ice water

Snack:[†] Dried Salmon,* kiwifruit, celery sticks

*Please note: All meal suggestions with an * are recipes featured in Chapter 10.*

[†]*Snacks are permitted anytime.*

WEDNESDAY

Breakfast:
- Fresh papaya
- Pork Chops Stuffed with Chicken Livers*
- Ice water with lime slice

Lunch: Open

Dinner:
- Tossed green salad with olive oil and lemon juice
- Burgundy Beef Roast*
- Steamed orange peppers and onions
- Peach-Almond Delight*
- Iced tea

Snack:[†] cold trout with slices of Vidalia or Maui sweet onions, oranges

THURSDAY

Breakfast:
- Grapefruit
- Cold beef slices
- Cup of decaffeinated coffee

Lunch:
- Spinach salad with shrimp
- Apple slices with lemon juice
- Herbal tea

Dinner:
- Tossed green salad dressed with flaxseed oil and lemon juice
- Paleo Zucchini Soup*
- Broiled chicken breasts covered with Raspberry Barbecue Sauce*
- Fresh Cinnamon Applesauce*
- Iced tea

Snack:[†] walnuts, grapes, cherry tomatoes

FRIDAY

Breakfast:
- Cantaloupe
- Poached Eggs with Peach Salsa*
- Herbal tea

Lunch:
- Tossed green salad with Omega-3 Russian Salad Dressing*

- Lime and Dill Crab*
- Steamed carrots
- Water with lemon slice

Dinner: Open

Snack:† cold boiled shrimp, celery sticks, pecans

SATURDAY

Breakfast:
- Citrus bowl (grapefruit, orange, and tangerine sections)
- Cold Paleo-Correct Meat Loaf*
- Herbal tea

Lunch:
- Tomato, cucumber, and purple onion salad with olive oil
- Beef and Spinach Scramble*
- Mineral water

Dinner:
- Sliced cucumber and radish tray
- Chez Lorraine's Baked Salmon*
- Steamed asparagus
- Pecans, raisins, and blueberries
- Cup of decaffeinated coffee

Snack:† cold chicken breasts, sunflower seeds, dried pear slices

*Please note: All meal suggestions with an * are recipes featured in Chapter 10.

†Snacks are permitted anytime.

Level III: Maximal Weight Loss Level

At Level III, it's the 95-5 rule—one Open Meal a week, and the balance of meals made up of all the delicious modern Paleo meals I've discussed in this chapter. At this level, you should restrict or eliminate all the transitional foods, except during your Open Meals. As in Levels I and II, all snacks should be chosen from the list of Paleo Snacks. This is the highest level, designed for the true Paleo Diet aficionado who wants to maximize health and well-being, or for individuals suffering from obesity or high levels of chronic disease who need to maximize the therapeutic effects of the diet.

Sample 2-Week Meal Plan for Level III

WEEK 1 FOR LEVEL III

SUNDAY

Breakfast: Open

Lunch:
- Tossed green salad with lemon juice and olive oil dressing
- Savory Steamed Mussels*
- Mineral water

Dinner:
- Tomato and avocado slices
- Altamira Stuffed Chicken*
- Steamed Swiss chard and carrots
- Steamed artichoke
- Bowl of fresh blueberries, raisins, and almonds
- Mineral water

Snack:† Basic Beef Jerky,* carrot sticks

MONDAY

Breakfast:
- Bowl of diced apples, shredded carrots, and raisins with cinnamon
- Poached eggs
- Cup of decaffeinated coffee

Lunch:
- Brockway Tuna Salad*
- Handful of walnuts
- Mineral water

Dinner:
- Cold boiled shrimp
- Tossed green salad
- Chez Lorraine's Baked Salmon*
- Steamed asparagus with fresh-squeezed lemon
- Sliced kiwifruit and strawberries

Snack:† cold beef slices, celery sticks

TUESDAY

Breakfast:
- Honeydew melon and blackberries
- Broiled pork chops
- Herbal tea

Lunch:
- Waldorf Salad*
- Broiled halibut steak with lime juice
- Steamed cauliflower
- Apple
- Mineral water

Dinner:
- Tossed green salad with scallions and cucumbers
- Chicken Vegetable Soup*
- Stir-Fried Beef with Vegetables*
- Figs and walnuts
- Iced tea

Snack:† hard-boiled eggs, pecans, raisins

WEDNESDAY

Breakfast:
- Strawberries and apricots
- Zesty Shrimp-Avocado Omelet*
- Cup of decaffeinated coffee

Lunch:
- Cucumber and tomato slices with Veggie Dip*
- Steamed crab
- Dried apricots without sulfur
- Mineral water

Dinner:
- Oysters on the half shell
- Cucumber slices dipped in Guacamole Fiesta*
- Grilled chicken
- Ratatouille*
- Bowl of fresh boysenberries, raisins, and almonds
- Glass of nonalcoholic wine

Snack:† papaya, walnuts, Spicy Beef Jerky*

THURSDAY

Breakfast:
- Strawberries
- Small beefsteak with Peach Salsa*
- Herbal tea

Lunch:
- Tossed green salad with flaxseed oil and lemon juice
- Sand Harbor Baked Cod*
- Medjool dates and fresh nectarines
- Iced tea

Dinner:
- Marinated Mushrooms*
- Green salad with olive oil and lemon juice
- Broiled Tenderloin of Pork with Spicy Rub*
- Steamed cabbage with lemon juice and paprika
- Baked Walnut-Cinnamon Apples*

Ice water

Snack:† cold chicken breast, cantaloupe

*Please note: All meal suggestions with an * are recipes featured in Chapter 10.*

†*Snacks are permitted anytime.*

FRIDAY

Breakfast:
- Fresh or frozen blueberries and cantaloupe
- Cold steamed king crab legs
- Water with lemon slice

Lunch:
- Green salad with avocado, quartered tomatoes, and black olives (rinsed of salt) dressed with Anaheim Cilantro Salsa*
- Gingery Chicken and Veggies*
- Apple
- Mineral water

Dinner:
- Spinach salad with walnuts and flaxseed oil dressing
- Cold trout
- Baked Tomatoes*
- Chopped pecans, raspberries, and Medjool dates
- Mineral water

Snack:† hard-boiled egg, cold boiled shrimp

SATURDAY

Breakfast:
- Cold chicken breasts covered with Anaheim Cilantro Salsa*
- Watermelon
- Herbal tea

Lunch:
- Tahoe Shrimp Salad*
- Melon slices and strawberries

Dinner:
- Carrot, radish, cherry tomato, sliced cucumber tray
- Baked Haddock Italiano*
- Steamed asparagus
- Almonds, raisins, and peaches
- Mineral water

Snack:† Basic Beef Jerky,* oranges

WEEK 2 FOR LEVEL III

SUNDAY

Breakfast:
- Bowl of sliced banana, pears, and walnuts
- Soft-boiled eggs
- Cup of decaffeinated coffee

Lunch:
- Tossed green salad dressed with olive oil and lemon juice
- Red Snapper in Snappy Sauce*
- Apple slices with lemon juice
- Mineral water

Dinner:
- Ambrosia Salad*
- Broiled lobster tails with olive oil and fresh pepper
- Steamed artichoke with lemon juice
- Strawberry-Blueberry Horizon*
- Cup of decaffeinated coffee

Snack:† mango and kiwifruit, Dried Salmon*

MONDAY

Breakfast:
- Cantaloupe Stuffed with Blackberries and Pecans*
- Cold leftover lobster
- Herbal tea

Lunch:
- Tossed green salad with olive oil and lemon juice
- Kenny's Barbecued Spicy Chicken*
- Tangerine sections
- Glass of nonalcoholic wine

Dinner:
- Marinated Mushrooms*
- Chicken Vegetable Soup*
- London broil sprinkled with fresh ground pepper and garlic powder
- Spicy Stuffed Squash*
- Peach-Almond Delight*
- Iced tea

Snack:† Kyle's Apple Breakfast,* Spicy Beef Jerky*

TUESDAY

Breakfast:
- Grapefruit
- Cold leftover London broil
- Herbal tea

Lunch:
- Gazpacho*
- Broiled turkey burgers
- Sliced star fruit
- Mineral water

Dinner:
- Butter Leaf Avocado Salad*
- Cajun Catfish Bake*
- Steamed collard greens
- Fresh or frozen strawberries
- Mineral water

Snack:† cold boiled shrimp, cauliflower florets, pecans

*Please note: All meal suggestions with an * are recipes featured in Chapter 10.*

†*Snacks are permitted anytime.*

WEDNESDAY

Breakfast:
- Fresh mangos and papayas
- Breakfast beefsteak smothered with Peach Salsa*
- Herbal tea

Lunch:
- Celery and carrot sticks dipped in Guacamole Fiesta*
- Paleo Zucchini Soup*
- Sautéed Rocky Mountain Chicken Livers*
- Fresh blueberries
- Water with lemon slice

Dinner:
- Spinach Salad à la Cordani*
- Tender Buffalo Roast*
- Steamed asparagus and carrots with lemon juice and garlic powder
- Fresh Cinnamon Applesauce*
- Cup of decaffeinated coffee

Snack:† hard-boiled egg, walnuts, raisins

THURSDAY

Breakfast:
- Fresh plums
- Cold leftover Tender Buffalo Roast* slices covered with fresh Anaheim Cilantro Salsa*
- Water with lemon slice

Lunch:
- Spicy Tomato Soup*
- Shrimp-Stuffed Avocados*
- Watermelon

Dinner:
- Tomato, cucumber, and purple onion salad with olive oil
- Roast Pheasant with Fruit and Nut Stuffing*
- Carrot-Mushroom Stir-Fry*
- Waldorf Salad*
- Glass of wine or mineral water

Snack:† cold steak slices, tomato quarters

FRIDAY

Breakfast:
- Cantaloupe
- Eggs scrambled in olive oil and basil
- Herbal tea

Lunch:
- Almond Chicken Salad*
- Water with lemon slice

Dinner:
- Marinated Mushrooms*
- Isola Baked Pork Chops*
- Ratatouille*
- Baked Walnut-Cinnamon Apples*

Snack:[†] cold chicken breasts, sunflower seeds

SATURDAY

Breakfast:
- Fresh or frozen strawberries
- Poached eggs
- Cold boiled shrimp
- Herbal tea

Lunch: Open

Dinner:
- Tossed green salad with flaxseed oil and lemon juice
- Barbecued Venison Steaks with Herbs*
- Steamed summer squash with lemon juice
- Walnut Broccoli with Carrots*
- 2 or 3 Medjool dates
- Ice water

Snack:[†] carrot and celery sticks, raisins, walnuts

So there you have it—three delicious and healthful meal plans. Use these meal plans to familiarize yourself with Paleo Diet principles. Once you have become a seasoned Paleo Dieter, use your own creativity and ingenuity to develop your own scrumptious Paleo feasts!

Chapter 10

Paleo Recipes

With the Paleo Diet, you'll end up eating enormously diverse and bountiful meals that include all sorts of fruits, vegetables, meats, and seafood—many of which are rarely or never eaten on "normal" diets.

Throughout this book, I've been telling you how good this food is. In this chapter, I'm going to prove it. On the following pages you'll find a wide variety of breakfast, lunch, and dinner recipes, as well as recipes for making Stone Age snacks and desserts, salt- and sugar-free sauces, dressings, salsas, and condiments to help you launch the Paleo Diet in your own kitchen. Consider them a starting point for your own creativity and ingenuity. Starting the Paleo Diet doesn't mean you'll have to throw out your old cookbooks. It is easy to modify almost any basic recipe to conform to Stone Age dietary principles.

One cautionary note: In all your cooking, do your best to follow the spirit of the diet. If you eat certain Paleo foods or food combinations excessively, you can sabotage and defeat this lifetime nutrition plan and even gain weight. With modern food-processing techniques and creative recipes, a clever cook can assemble Stone Age ingredients in a manner that defies the basic logic of the diet. For instance, it is possible to make nut and root flours in food processors that can be combined with honey, olive oil, and eggs and later baked to resemble almost any modern processed food with very un-Paleo characteristics—high levels of carbohydrates, sugar, and fats. Those high-fat, high-sugar, high-carbohydrate Paleo food combinations may taste good, but they're not much better for your health and well-being than cookies, cakes, breads, and doughnuts. These foods are great treats to be eaten every once in a while and are better for you than the commercially available, processed versions. But if they become common fare—particularly if you're trying to lose weight—many of the potential benefits of the Paleo Diet will be lost.

When eaten in excessive quantities, even unprocessed or minimally processed foods that would have been available to our Paleolithic ancestors, such as dried fruits (raisins, dates, figs, and others), nuts, and honey, can throw the diet off balance and can be particularly troublesome if you're trying to lose weight. The best way to satisfy your craving for sweets is to eat fresh fruit. Instead of pie, think melons—or blueberries, blackberries, pears, peaches, strawberries, or any other favorite fresh fruit. If you still feel hungry after eating a Paleo meal, eat more lean protein—chicken or turkey breasts, fish, lean beef, shrimp, crab, or game meat if you can get it—or more crisp, succulent vegetables or juicy, sweet, fresh fruit.

When you carefully examine the Paleo Diet recipes, you'll notice that most of them contain only fresh meats, seafood, fruits, vegetables, nuts, and seeds, with added spices, certain oils, and condiments made from all of these ingredients. Stick to these foods. Depending on your level of the Paleo Diet (I, II, or III), you may occasionally want to include a few recipes that contain vinegar, wine, honey, or a dash of salt. There's nothing wrong with eating these foods *occasionally,* unless you have a health problem or an autoimmune disease, as discussed earlier in the book. Enjoy a glass of wine, a trace of salt in your food, a bit of honey in your dessert, or even an occasional bagel—but don't make them your norm.

Many thanks to Don Wiss, Patti Vincent, and all of the other cooks, Paleo chefs, gourmets, and gourmands at paleofood.com for inspiring me.

Basic Recipe Principles

When you make Paleo recipes with modern foods, make sure that all the ingredients are free of:

- Grains
- Legumes, including peanuts
- Dairy products
- Salt
- Processed sugars
- Potatoes
- Added fats (except for permitted oils in limited quantities)

Try to choose fresh meats and avoid processed, canned, salted, and pickled meats. Cook simply by baking, broiling, steaming, or sautéing in a little oil.

Stone Age Food Substitutions

Salt

Substitute powdered garlic, powdered onion, lemon juice, lime juice, lemon crystals, lemon pepper free of salt, cayenne pepper, chile powder, commercially available salt-free spice mixes, black pepper, cumin, turmeric, ground cloves, oregano, ground allspice, celery seeds, coriander seeds, and ground cardamom seeds. Actually, any spice or combination of spices can be used to replace salt. I do not recommend using any of the so-called lite salts or potassium chloride salts, because chloride, like sodium, is not good for your health.

Healthful Oils

Replace unhealthful fats and oils with olive oil, coconut oil, flaxseed oil, walnut oil, avocado oil, or macadamia nut oil. As I've discussed, olive oil has a wonderful flavor and is high in the health-promoting monounsaturated fats but generally has a poor omega-6 to omega-3 fat ratio. The same holds true for avocado oil. These two oils should frequently be complemented by, or blended with, other oils containing better omega-6 to omega-3 ratios, such as flaxseed or walnut oils. The only oils you should cook with are olive or coconut oils. Flaxseed and walnut oils are unstable during cooking and may produce toxic by-products.

Sugars

Concentrated sugars of any kind—even natural sugars (honey, maple sugar, and date sugar)—were not staple components for our Paleolithic ancestors. Sugars in the Paleo Diet should be obtained mainly from fruits and vegetables, not from concentrated sources. However, fruit purees flavored with lemon juice and spices (cinnamon, nutmeg, mint leaves, ginger, and vanilla, to name a few) can be used in recipes to add sweetness to sauces, condiments, and desserts.

Alcohol

Alcoholic beverages clearly were not a component of true Paleolithic diets, and yours should be limited to an occasional glass of wine, beer (preferably gluten-free brands), or spirits. Wine, as long as it does not contain salt (as most cooking wines do), can be used to marinate meats and add flavor to many cooked dishes. When wine is used in this context, the amount of added alcohol and sugar is negligible; also, wine contains a number of health-promoting phytochemicals and antioxidants. Note: If you suffer from an autoimmune disease, the alcohol and the yeast in wine or other alcoholic beverages can potentially cause problems, and you would be wise to avoid them altogether.

Nut Flours

Nut flours (almond, pecan, walnut, hazelnut) can be made in food processors or purchased at some health food or specialty stores, and they can be used to thicken sauces or to add flavor to condiments. Again, these products should be used sparingly. They have the potential to unbalance your diet and disrupt your health when they're used excessively or in combination with oils, honey, dried fruit, or fruit purees. The foundation of Paleo Diet carbohydrates is fresh fruits and vegetables—not nut flours, honey, fruit juices, or purees.

Now, bon appetit!

Fish and Seafood

Cajun Catfish Bake

2 lb catfish	1½ tsp black pepper
4 T olive oil	½ tsp cayenne pepper
1 clove garlic, minced	½ tsp turmeric
3 T freshly squeezed lemon juice	

Thoroughly wash the catfish and place in a 9 x 13-inch baking dish greased with a little olive oil. Heat the rest of the olive oil in a saucepan and sauté the garlic. Pour over the catfish. Sprinkle the lemon juice and remaining spices evenly over the fish. Bake at 350 degrees for 20 to 25 minutes. Serves three to four.

Sand Harbor Baked Cod

1 lb cod filets	2 T lemon juice
½ c white wine	1 T dried dill weed
¼ yellow onion, sliced	1 tsp turmeric

Wash the fish thoroughly in cool water, and lay it in a shallow baking dish. Pour in the white wine. Spread the onion slices evenly over the fish, and sprinkle with the lemon juice, dill, and turmeric. Cover with foil, and bake at 375 degrees for 20 minutes or until fish flakes easily with a fork. Serves two to three.

Lime and Dill Crab

2 large Dungeness crabs, cooked, cracked, shelled, and chilled

2 T lime juice

2 tsp paprika

2 tsp dried dill weed

2–3 limes, cut into wedges

3–4 sprigs parsley, finely chopped

Drizzle the crabmeat with lime juice and sprinkle with the paprika and dill. Serve with the lime wedges and garnish with the parsley. Serves two.

Baked Haddock Italiano

2 lb haddock

6 T olive oil

3 cloves garlic, minced

1 red onion, minced

1 green pepper, chopped

4 tomatoes, diced

6 T fresh chopped parsley

1 tsp dried basil

1 tsp dried dill weed

$\frac{1}{8}$ tsp black pepper

2 T lemon juice

Thoroughly wash the haddock in cool water and set it aside. Heat the oil in a heavy skillet, and sauté the garlic and onion until tender. Add the green pepper and continue to sauté on low heat until tender. Add the tomatoes, parsley, basil, dill, and black pepper. Remove from the heat and spread half the sauce in the bottom of a 9 x 13-inch baking dish. Place the fish on top, and pour the remaining sauce over the entire fish. Sprinkle with lemon juice. Cover with foil, and bake at 375 degrees for 15 to 20 minutes or until flaky. Serves four.

Savory Steamed Mussels

1 lb fresh mussels in shells   1 tsp dried dill weed

½ c water   1 T fresh lemon juice

1 clove garlic, minced   ½ c dry white wine

2 T olive oil

Steam the mussels in water until the shells open. While the mussels are steaming, sauté the garlic in olive oil. Add the dill, lemon juice, and wine. Simmer
for 3 minutes. When the mussels are open, put on a serving plate and pour the
mixture over each. Serves two.

Salmon Steaks in Curry Sauce

Two 8-ounce salmon steaks   ½ tsp cayenne pepper

2 tsp curry powder   1 c chicken stock (salt-free)

1 tsp turmeric   4 tsp white wine

Wash the salmon, and place it in a shallow baking dish. Mix the curry, turmeric, and pepper with the chicken stock, and pour it over the fish. Pour in the
white wine, and cover with foil. Bake at 350 degrees for 20 to 30 minutes. The
salmon should flake easily with a fork. Serves two.

Chez Lorraine's Baked Salmon

4 salmon steaks (about
1¾–2 lb)

4 T lemon juice

1 tsp dried dill weed

2 T finely chopped fresh
chives

Lime wedges

Place each salmon steak on a piece of aluminum foil large enough to wrap it. Pour lemon juice over each steak, sprinkle with the dill, and seal each steak in its aluminum pouch. Put the aluminum-sealed steaks in a baking dish and bake at 350 degrees for 30 minutes or until the fish flakes easily with a fork. Serve salmon with sprinkled chives and lime wedges. Serves four.

Shrimp-Stuffed Avocados

4 large avocados, peeled
and halved, seeds removed

1½ c small salad shrimp,
cooked and washed

1 T lemon juice

1 T onion powder

1 tsp black pepper

1 T paprika

Set the avocados on a serving plate with the cut side facing up. Combine the shrimp, lemon juice, onion powder, and pepper in a medium-size mixing bowl. Spoon the shrimp mixture onto each avocado, covering generously. Sprinkle the top of each stuffed avocado with paprika before serving. Serves four.

Barbecued Alaskan Shrimp

2½ lb shelled and steamed jumbo shrimp with tails left on

¼ c virgin olive oil

3 garlic cloves, minced

⅛ tsp paprika

Dash of cayenne pepper

2 T lemon juice

2 fresh limes, cut into wedges

3–4 sprigs fresh parsley

Place the cooked shrimp in a large bowl. Mix the olive oil, garlic, spices, and lemon juice in a separate bowl. Brush the shrimp with the spice mixture, and place on a hot grill or under a broiler for 1 to 2 minutes. Turn the shrimp and continue cooking for an additional 1 to 2 minutes. Garnish with the lime wedges and parsley. Serves three to four.

Tahoe Shrimp Salad

1 lb small salad shrimp, cooked

½ red onion, minced

1 T dried dill weed

1 T paprika

2 T fresh-squeezed lemon juice

3 c chopped lettuce

1 hard-boiled egg, sliced

Rinse and drain the shrimp, and set aside. In a small bowl, mix together the onion, dill, paprika, and lemon juice. Fold in the shrimp. Serve the shrimp salad on lettuce, and top with hard-boiled egg slices. Serves two.

Red Snapper in Snappy Sauce

¼ c olive oil	1 tsp black pepper
2 cloves garlic	2 tomatoes, diced
2 lb red snapper filets	4 scallions, sliced thin
½ c freshly squeezed lime juice	½ green bell pepper, seeded and chopped
2 T freshly squeezed lemon juice	½ red bell pepper, seeded and chopped
1 tsp cayenne pepper	Cilantro for garnish

Heat the oil in a skillet, and sauté the garlic until golden brown. Lay the fish in the oil, and sprinkle with the lime and lemon juice. Sprinkle the cayenne and black peppers over all, then add the tomatoes, scallions, and green and red bell peppers. Cover and simmer for 15 minutes or until the fish flakes easily with a fork. Garnish with cilantro. Serves four.

Brockway Tuna Salad

1 can albacore tuna, packed in water, low sodium	1 c shredded romaine lettuce
½ red onion, chopped	1 T flaxseed oil
½ c chopped celery	1 T lemon juice
1 small jar diced pimentos (no salt)	1 tsp paprika
½ c Omega-3 Mayonnaise (see recipe on page 182)	½ tsp freshly ground pepper

Drain the tuna, then place in a colander and rinse thoroughly to remove any remaining salt. In a mixing bowl, combine the tuna with the onion, celery, pimentos, and mayonnaise, mixing thoroughly. Toss the lettuce with flaxseed oil and lemon juice, and make a bed of lettuce in a medium-size serving bowl. Dollop the tuna mixture on the lettuce bed. Sprinkle with the paprika and pepper. Serves one.

Domestic Meat Entrées
(Beef, Chicken, Veal, Pork, Organ Meats, Game Meats)

BEEF

Stir-Fried Beef with Vegetables

12 oz boneless sirloin steak, thinly sliced into small, bite-size strips

2 T olive oil

1 clove garlic, minced

¼ c Burgundy wine

1 yellow onion, cut thinly into wedges

1 red bell pepper, seeded and cut into slender strips

2 celery stalks, chopped

4 oz thinly sliced carrots

4 oz sliced mushrooms

3 T lemon juice

Sauté the beef in half of the oil with garlic and half of the wine until the beef is browned. Remove from the skillet. Heat the remaining oil in the skillet. Sauté the onion, red pepper, celery, and carrots until the onion is tender—about 4 minutes. Add the remainder of the wine. Add the mushrooms and lemon juice. Stir-fry the mixture for approximately 3 more minutes. Combine the vegetables with the meat. Serves two.

Omega Meatballs

1 lb ground beef

1 T olive oil

1 medium carrot, grated

1 small scallion, finely diced

1 cage-free egg, beaten

¼ tsp powdered garlic

¼ tsp powdered onion

Combine all of the ingredients and make into small balls. Place the meatballs in a glass baking dish greased with olive oil. Bake covered at 350 degrees for 30 to 45 minutes or until done. Serves two to three.

Beef and Spinach Scramble

2 T olive oil

1 lb ground beef

3 scallions, chopped

2 cloves garlic, minced

1 tsp black pepper

1 tsp basil

1 c fresh spinach, washed and steamed

4 cage-free eggs, scrambled

In a large, heavy skillet, heat the olive oil. Add the beef, scallions, garlic, pepper, and basil. Cook on low heat until the meat is thoroughly browned. Turn the heat up to medium and add the spinach, stirring for 5 minutes. Add the eggs and continue stirring for about 1 minute or until the eggs are cooked. Serves four.

Auroch Beef Cabbage Rolls

1 head cabbage

1½ lb ground beef

1 medium red onion, chopped

2 cage free eggs

¼ tsp black pepper

1 tsp oregano

1 clove garlic, minced

6–8 medium tomatoes, peeled and pureed

Wash the cabbage and remove the core. Steam it for 5 minutes or until the leaves are loose and slightly limp. Pull off the leaves and set them aside. Mix together all of the remaining ingredients, reserving ⅓ c of the tomato puree for later. Fill each cabbage leaf with the meat mixture and roll. Place in a 9 x 13-inch glass baking dish. Spread the rolls with the remaining tomato puree, and cover with foil. Bake at 350 degrees for 1 hour. Serves four to six.

Paleo-Correct Meat Loaf

2 lb ground beef

2 red onions, finely chopped

4 cloves garlic, minced

½ red pepper, chopped

½ c fresh cilantro, chopped

½ c fresh parsley, chopped

2 tsp cumin

1 tsp pepper

3 cage-free eggs, beaten

2 T olive oil

Mix all of the ingredients in a large mixing bowl. Spread the mixture evenly in an 8 ½ x 11-inch baking dish. Bake at 400 degrees for 45 minutes or until cooked through. Serves eight.

Burgundy Beef Roast

1 beef roast (2–3 lb)

6 large tomatoes, diced

¼ tsp black pepper

2 cloves garlic, minced

1 c Burgundy wine

1 red onion, diced

2 T freshly squeezed lemon juice

3 T olive oil

1 T dry mustard

Place the meat in a deep roasting pan with a cover. Mix all the other ingredients, and pour over the meat. Cover and bake at 350 degrees for 1 to 1½ hours, and baste two or three times while baking. Serves six.

CHICKEN

Kenny's Barbecued Spicy Chicken

2 T fresh lemon juice

1 T fresh orange juice

2 scallions, finely chopped

1 tsp finely chopped fresh tarragon

1 tsp finely chopped fresh thyme

1 tsp finely chopped fresh sage

1 tsp fennel seeds, toasted and crushed

Freshly ground black pepper to taste

4 boneless chicken breast halves

In a large bowl, combine all ingredients except the chicken. Mix well to produce a marinade. Place the chicken in the bowl, coat thoroughly, and marinate for 1 to 2 hours. For grilling: Fire up the barbecue and grill the chicken on medium heat, turning constantly while basting with the marinade until the breasts are cooked. For broiling: Baste the chicken with the marinade and broil, turning and basting until the breasts are cooked. Serves four.

Altamira Stuffed Chicken

½ red onion, chopped

1 T olive oil

3–4 chopped chicken livers

½ c Pinot Noir red wine

¼ c raisins

½ c walnuts

¼ c celery

1 apple, cored, peeled, and diced

1 whole, large chicken

Sauté the onion in the oil until tender. Mix in the chopped chicken livers and brown. Pour in the wine, add the raisins, walnuts, celery, and apple, and simmer for 5 minutes. Stuff the chicken with the mixture and bake in a covered dish at 400 degrees for 1 hour or until done. Serves three to four.

Gingery Chicken and Veggies

½ c olive oil

2 cloves garlic, minced

½ red onion, sliced

1 tsp powdered ginger

2 c cooked diced chicken breast meat

1 c chicken broth (no salt)

½ c chopped celery

1 c thinly sliced carrots

½ bell pepper, sliced

Heat the oil in a heavy skillet, and sauté the garlic and onion. Add the remaining ingredients and simmer until the vegetables are tender. Serves four.

Chicken Cacciatore

2 whole chickens, cut up

1 tsp pepper

1 tsp oregano

1 red onion, sliced

1 c sliced mushrooms

4 celery stalks, cut into ½-inch pieces

½ c water

8 tomatoes, diced

1 tsp basil

1 tsp parsley

Place the chicken pieces in a large baking dish. Sprinkle with the pepper and oregano. Lay the onion, mushrooms, and celery on top of the chicken pieces. Pour in the water to cover the bottom of the dish. Spread the tomatoes over the chicken, and sprinkle with the basil and parsley. Bake at 325 degrees for 2 hours or until the chicken is done. Serves six.

VEAL

Slow-Cooked Veal with Salsa

2 lb veal, sliced ½ inch thick	2 c tomato salsa (see recipe below)

Place the veal slices in a slow cooker, cover with the salsa, and cook on low heat for 5 hours. Remove from the pot and pour the remaining salsa over the meat before serving. Serves four.

Salsa

6 large tomatoes, diced	½ c lime juice
1 yellow onion, minced	1 tsp cayenne pepper
3 cloves garlic, minced	⅓ c finely chopped fresh cilantro
1 tsp black pepper	

Combine all of the ingredients and mix well. Makes 2 cups.

Sicilian Skillet Veal Chops

8 veal chops	1 T chopped parsley
4 T olive oil	2 cloves garlic, minced
Pepper to taste	2 lb tomatoes, skinned, boiled, and mashed
1 T oregano	

In a large skillet, brown the chops in oil. Season with the pepper. Sprinkle with the oregano and parsley. Add the garlic and tomatoes. Cover and simmer until tender, 30 to 40 minutes. Serves eight.

PORK

Pork Chops Stuffed with Chicken Livers

6 double rib pork chops	4 T olive oil
6 chicken livers, chopped	Pepper to taste
½ lb mushrooms, chopped	1 T finely chopped parsley

Slit the chops to make pockets. Sauté the livers and mushrooms in 2 T of the olive oil. Season the chops with the pepper and parsley. Stuff the pork chips with the liver mixture and use toothpicks to hold the pockets closed. Heat the remaining oil in a heavy skillet, add the chops, and sear them over high heat on both sides. Place in a large casserole dish, and bake at 350 degrees for 25 minutes or until tender. Serves six.

Broiled Tenderloin of Pork with Spicy Rub

1 clove garlic, minced	2 T olive oil
1 T paprika	1 T red wine
1 T dry mustard	1 lb pork tenderloin, cut
1 T ground coriander	butterflied down the middle

Mix the garlic and dry spices in a mortar and pestle. Add in the oil and wine to make a paste. Rub the paste on the butterflied pork and refrigerate for 1 hour. Broil the pork 2 to 3 inches from a heat source for about 6 minutes per side or until it is cooked through. Serves four.

Isola Baked Pork Chops

4 tomatoes, quartered

1½ c peeled and diced eggplant

2 c sliced zucchini

½ lb mushrooms, halved

1 clove garlic, minced

1 bay leaf

¼ tsp thyme

¼ tsp basil

¼ tsp chopped parsley

½ tsp black pepper

1 T olive oil

4 pork chops

Combine all of the ingredients except the oil and pork chops. Grease a 9 x 13-inch baking dish with the oil. Layer the vegetable and spice mixture on the bottom, and place the pork chops on top. Cover and bake at 350 degrees for 1 hour or until the meat is tender. Remove bay leaf. Serves four.

ORGAN MEATS

Lorrie's Liver and Onions

¼ c olive oil

1 red onion, sliced thin

2 cloves garlic, minced

½ tsp basil

½ tsp rosemary

1 lb calf's liver

½ c Burgundy wine

Heat the oil in a heavy skillet. Sauté the onion, garlic, basil, and rosemary until the onions are tender. Add the liver, reduce the heat, and simmer for 10 minutes. Pour in the wine and continue to simmer for 15 minutes. Serves four.

Sautéed Rocky Mountain Chicken Livers

1 medium yellow onion, diced

2 garlic cloves, minced

1 green pepper, seeded and diced

2 T olive oil

¼ c Burgundy wine

1 lb chicken livers

Sauté the onion, garlic, and pepper in the oil with half of the wine. Add the livers and remaining wine. Sauté the livers until they are firm and brown. Serves four.

Buffalo Burgers

1 lb ground buffalo   1 T basil

½ red onion, finely chopped 1 T oregano

2 garlic cloves, minced   2 tsp black pepper

Mix all of the ingredients together in a large mixing bowl until well blended. Shape the meat into patties, and grill or broil on low heat, turning often. Serves four.

Tender Buffalo Roast

3–4 lb buffalo roast   ½ tsp black pepper

1 red onion, chopped   1 c red wine

1 small turnip, chopped   ⅓ c water

2 carrots, sliced thin   3 T chopped parsley

2 cloves garlic, minced

Place the meat in a large baking dish. Add all of the remaining ingredients. Cover and cook at 400 degrees for 90 minutes or until the meat is cooked through. Slice thinly and place on a serving plate. Pour the remaining juices over the meat before serving. Serves six.

Rocky Mountain Elk Steaks

4 medium elk steaks

½ c olive oil

2 garlic cloves, minced

½ red onion, sliced

1 tsp ground sage

1 tsp basil

1 tsp rosemary

1 c Burgundy wine

Wash the steaks thoroughly, and place them in a 9 x 13-inch baking dish. Heat the olive oil on low heat in a heavy skillet. Sauté the garlic, onion, and spices until tender. Stir in the wine, and remove from the heat. Pour over the elk steaks. Cover and refrigerate for 2 to 3 hours. Grill or broil slowly until cooked as desired. Serves four.

Roast Pheasant with Fruit and Nut Stuffing

1 pheasant (2–3 lb)

¼ c olive oil

1 T fresh ground pepper

1 T garlic powder

1½ c freshly squeezed orange juice

½ c raisins

3 cloves

½ tsp ginger

½ c dried and coarsely chopped apricots without sulfur

½ tsp grated orange peel

1 c chopped pecans

Preheat the oven to 350 degrees. Wash and dry the pheasant, and brush with the olive oil inside and out. Sprinkle inside and out with the pepper and garlic powder. In a saucepan, combine the orange juice, raisins, and cloves. Bring to a boil, reduce the heat, and simmer for 5 minutes. Strain the mixture, discarding the cloves and reserving the orange juice and raisins. In a mixing bowl, combine the orange juice and raisin mixture, ginger, apricots, orange peel, and pecans. Mix well and use to stuff the pheasant. Place the pheasant, breast up, on a rack in a roasting pan and roast until tender, about 30 minutes per pound; brush frequently with the remaining orange juice. Place the pheasant on a serving platter, and trickle the liquid from the roasting pan over the pheasant. Serves two.

Barbecued Venison Steaks with Herbs

2 T chopped rosemary

2 T chopped garlic

2 T chopped thyme

¼ c olive oil

4 venison steaks (4 oz each)

Fresh ground pepper to taste

Make a marinade by combining the herbs and olive oil in a mixing bowl. Marinate the venison for 4 hours in the refrigerator, covered. Remove the steaks from the marinade, and shake off the excess oil. For grilling: Place the steaks on the grill, season with pepper, and brush frequently with the marinade. Cook the steaks for 2 to 4 minutes per side until well cooked. For broiling: Place the steaks on the broiler in the oven for about 5 minutes per side or until cooked to your taste. Serves four.

Dried Salmon

**2 lb wild-caught salmon
filets, including skin, cut
into ½- to 1-inch-wide,
⅛-inch-thick strips**

Dry the salmon strips using the same method as with the beef jerky on page 161 or in the oven. Dry the meat until it is just a little chewy, but not hard.

Basic Beef Jerky

**2 lb beef, cut into 1-inch-
wide, ⅛-inch-thick strips
with the grain of the
muscle, when possible**

The easiest way to make jerky is to buy your own food dehydrator. Place beef strips on the racks of a home food dryer (available at any large discount store), and dry the meat until it is tough and chewy (usually overnight). Alternatively, dry meat in your oven on ungreased cookie sheets. Set the oven temperature between 140 and 150 degrees. Drying time varies among ovens but typically takes from 4 to 12 hours. The jerky is done when it is chewy and tough.

Spicy Beef Jerky

2 lb beef, cut into 1-inch-wide, ⅛-inch-thick strips* with the grain of the muscle, when possible

Chili powder

Cumin

Garlic powder

Onion powder

Dry mustard

Cayenne pepper

Lemon pepper

Turmeric

Coarse ground black pepper

Curry powder

White pepper

Mix any and all combinations of the spices listed above in a medium-size bowl to make a dry rub. Let your personal taste and imagination guide you, varying the amount of each ingredient according to preference. Our favorite is equal amounts of cumin, garlic powder, coarse ground black pepper, turmeric, and cayenne pepper. Dip each meat strip in the bowl of spices, then refrigerate overnight in a covered bowl in the refrigerator. Prepare the jerky using the method in the recipe above.

*Almost any meat can be dried; try lean pork, venison, buffalo, and even poultry and fish.

Egg Dishes

Zesty Shrimp-Avocado Omelet

2 cage-free eggs

1 T olive oil

1 T chopped scallions

1 T chopped tomatoes

¼ c small shrimp (fresh or thawed frozen)

1 tsp dried dill weed

½ tsp black pepper

Guacamole Fiesta (see page 184 for recipe)

Crack the eggs into a small bowl, and mix thoroughly with a fork or a wire whisk. Using a small, nonstick omelet skillet, heat the oil on medium heat. Pour in the eggs, and cook slowly until bubbles appear in the middle. Using a spatula, gently lift the edges of the omelet and allow uncooked egg to run off to the sides. Once the omelet is firm, sprinkle the scallions, tomatoes, and shrimp in the center of the omelet, and top with the dill and pepper. Fold the omelet in half, and cook for 30 seconds. Remove from the pan, and top with Guacamole Fiesta. Serves one.

Scrambled Basil Eggs Topped with Salsa

2 cage-free eggs

1 tsp dried basil

2 T Anaheim Cilantro Salsa (see page 184 for recipe)

Crack the eggs into a small bowl, add the basil, and mix thoroughly with a fork or a wire whisk. Scramble the eggs in a nonstick skillet. Remove the eggs with a spatula, and top with Anaheim Cilantro Salsa. Serves one.

Poached Eggs with Peach Salsa

Olive oil

2 cage-free eggs

2 T Peach Salsa (see page 185 for recipe)

Bring ½ inch of water to a boil in a saucepan. Rub a little olive oil in the egg wells of an egg poacher (available at most kitchen and cooking specialty stores). Crack the eggs into the egg wells and reduce the heat to a slow boil. Place the poacher in the saucepan and cover. Extra-large eggs take about 7 minutes for soft yolks; medium eggs, about 6 minutes. Remove the egg poacher from the pan with an oven mitt, and free the eggs with a flexible rubber spatula. Gently transfer the eggs to a plate, and smother with Peach Salsa. Serves one.

Soups

Chicken Vegetable Soup

6 c water

Meat of 1 whole chicken, diced

2 cloves garlic, minced

1 yellow onion, diced

1 bay leaf

1 tsp black pepper

6 fresh tomatoes, diced

2 small zucchini, sliced thin

3 carrots, diced

In a large pot, combine the water, chicken, garlic, onion, bay leaf, and pepper. Bring to a boil. Reduce the heat, cover, and simmer for about 2 hours or until the chicken is tender. Remove the bay leaf and discard. Add the remaining ingredients, and bring to a boil. Reduce the heat and cover. Simmer for about 20 minutes or until the vegetables are tender. Serves six.

Gazpacho

4 large tomatoes, chopped

1 small onion, coarsely chopped

1 clove garlic, peeled

1 c unsalted tomato juice

2 T lemon juice

Pepper to taste

Cayenne pepper to taste (optional)

1 sprig fresh parsley

4 ice cubes

1 medium cucumber, peeled and coarsely chopped

In a blender or food processor, combine all of the ingredients. Blend or process until the vegetables are small but not pureed. Serves two.

Source: Cooking Healthy with One Foot Out the Door by Polly Pritchford and Delia Quigley. Summertown, TN: The Book Publishing Company, 1995.

Paleo Zucchini Soup

2 T olive oil

1 red onion, chopped

5 cloves garlic, minced

2 qts water

2 c cooked, chopped beef, chicken, or pork

2 T dried basil

2 T dried parsley

2 T dried thyme

1 T black pepper

2 c chopped carrots

2 c chopped celery

2 c chopped zucchini

2 c fresh chopped tomatoes

½ c fresh chopped parsley

In a skillet, heat the olive oil, and sauté the onion and garlic. In a large pot, bring the water to a boil, and add the sautéed onion and garlic, meat, basil, parsley, thyme, and pepper. Lower the heat, and simmer for 1 hour. Add the carrots and celery, simmering for 30 minutes. Add the zucchini and simmer for an additional 30 minutes. Add the chopped tomatoes and fresh parsley, and simmer for 10 minutes. Serve immediately. Serves six.

Spicy Tomato Soup

8 fresh tomatoes, pureed

1 c water

¼ c diced green chiles

1 c chicken broth

1 red onion, finely minced

2 cloves garlic, minced

¼ c diced chives

1 bell pepper, seeded and diced

1 tsp cayenne pepper

1 tsp paprika

Combine all of the ingredients in a large soup pot, and cook on low heat for 1 hour. Serves six.

Vegetable Dishes

Carrot-Mushroom Stir-Fry

6 carrots, sliced thin

4 T olive oil

5 scallions, sliced into
1-inch pieces

10 medium mushrooms,
sliced thin

1 T lemon juice

½ tsp black pepper

Steam the carrots until they're tender. Heat the oil in a large skillet. Add the carrots, scallions, and mushrooms, and stir-fry until all are cooked. Add the lemon juice and pepper, and mix well. Serves four.

Baked Mushrooms Contra Costa

12 large white mushrooms

4 T lemon juice

2 T olive oil

2 T minced parsley

1 clove garlic, minced

2 T minced onion

1 tsp black pepper

2–4 T dry sherry

Wash the mushrooms, removing and reserving the stems. Sprinkle the lemon juice on each cap, and set in 9 x 13-inch baking dish. Mince the stems and sauté them in the olive oil. In a medium-size bowl, combine the sautéed mushroom stems with the remaining ingredients. Spoon stuffing generously into each mushroom cap. Cover and bake at 350 degrees for 15 minutes. Serves three to four.

Marinated Mushrooms

20 medium mushrooms

2 red onions, sliced

¼ c fresh chopped parsley

1 c olive oil

½ c dry white wine

¼ c lemon juice

1 clove garlic, minced

¼ tsp black pepper

1 tsp oregano

Wash the mushrooms, and slice them in half. Combine with the onions. In a blender, puree the remaining ingredients. Pour over the mushrooms and onions, mixing well. Refrigerate overnight or longer. Serves four.

Ratatouille

2 large onions, chopped

2 cloves garlic, minced

4 T olive oil

2 green peppers, seeded and cut into strips

1 lb sliced zucchini

1 lb diced eggplant

4 large tomatoes, skinned and diced

3 T fresh chopped parsley

½ tsp oregano

¼ tsp black pepper

Sauté the onions and garlic in the olive oil until tender. Add the remaining ingredients, and simmer. Reduce the heat, cover, and let simmer until the vegetables are tender (30 to 45 minutes). Serves six to eight.

Spicy Stuffed Squash

2 medium acorn squash	1 T olive oil
½ c water	½ tsp ground cinnamon
2 medium carrots, cooked and chopped	¼ tsp nutmeg
2 small turnips, cooked and chopped	1 c peeled, coarsely chopped apple

Cut the squash in half, and remove the seeds and strings. Place the squash, cut side down, in a 9 x 13-inch baking dish. Add the water, and cover with foil. Bake at 350 degrees for 30 minutes. Remove from the oven, and turn the squash so that the cut side is facing up. Cover with foil, and bake for 20 to 30 minutes more or until tender. Scoop the pulp out of each squash half, keeping the shells intact. Place the pulp in a blender, and add the carrots and turnips. Blend until smooth. Stir in the oil, cinnamon, and nutmeg, blending well. Fold in the apple, and spoon into the squash shells. Return to the baking dish, and bake for 15 to 20 minutes or until heated through. Serves four.

Baked Tomatoes

2 large tomatoes	1 scallion, chopped
½ c minced mushrooms	1 tsp finely chopped fresh basil
1 tsp chopped parsley	½ tsp thyme
1 clove garlic, minced	¼ c olive oil

Slice the tomatoes in half, scoop out most of the pulp, and set them in a medium-size baking dish. Combine the pulp with the remaining ingredients, and fill each tomato half. Bake at 375 degrees for 10 to 15 minutes. Serves four.

Walnut Broccoli with Carrots

½ c olive oil

1 medium onion, sliced into rings

2 large carrots, sliced diagonally ⅛ inch thick

2 large stalks broccoli, sliced ¼ inch thick

½ c raw, shelled walnuts

Heat the oil in a heavy skillet, and sauté the onion until tender. Add the carrots and broccoli, and stir-fry until tender yet crispy. Add the walnuts, and cook 3 to 5 minutes longer. Serves two.

Salads

Spinach Salad à la Cordani

½ lb pork tenderloin, sliced and chopped into small pieces

2 T olive oil

1 bunch fresh spinach, washed, drained, and torn into small pieces

1 can sliced water chestnuts (rinsed of salt)

1 lb fresh mushrooms, sliced thin

4 hard-boiled cage-free eggs, sliced

Sauté the pork tenderloin pieces in the olive oil until lightly browned. In a large serving bowl, toss together the spinach, water chestnuts, and mushrooms. Top the salad with egg slices and pork tenderloin pieces. Allow diners to add their own favorite dressings (see pages 185–186 for dressing recipes). Serves four.

Ambrosia Salad

6 carrots, shredded

2 c fresh pineapple chunks

¼ c walnuts

¼ c raisins

1 T lemon juice

In large bowl, combine all of the ingredients. Cover and chill before serving. Serves four.

Spinach Salad with Crabmeat

2 large bunches fresh
spinach leaves, washed and
dried

1 Walla Walla, Vidalia, or
Maui sweet onion, sliced
thin

2 large tomatoes, sliced
thin

½ lb cooked, shredded
crabmeat

2 hard-boiled cage-free or
omega-3–enriched eggs,
sliced thin

Tear the spinach leaves into small pieces, and mix with the onions, tomatoes, and crabmeat. Just before serving, toss with the Spinach Salad Dressing (see page 185) and top with egg slices. Serves four.

Carrot Salad

8 carrots

1 medium red onion, sliced
thin

1 green pepper, seeded and
sliced thin

4 medium tomatoes, peeled
and pureed

½ c flaxseed oil

¾ c lemon juice

4 T dry mustard

½ tsp black pepper

Steam the carrots until tender. Slice them thinly crosswise, and place them in a large bowl. In a separate bowl, combine the remaining ingredients until well mixed, and then add to the carrots, stirring until the carrots are well coated. Refrigerate overnight, and serve well chilled. Serves four.

Almond Chicken Salad

1 c cooked, diced chicken breast meat

1 c chopped romaine lettuce

1 c shredded butter leaf lettuce

¼ c chopped red cabbage

½ c sliced almonds

¼ c chopped Medjool dates

1–2 T flaxseed oil

1–2 T freshly squeezed orange juice

Combine the chicken, lettuces, cabbage, almonds, and dates in a large serving bowl. Toss with the flaxseed oil and freshly squeezed orange juice. Serves two.

Cauliflower Salad with Lemon Marinade

1 head cauliflower, cut into small florets

½ red onion, sliced

½ green bell pepper, seeded and chopped

⅔ c marinade (recipe follows)

In a medium-size salad bowl, combine the cauliflower, onion, and pepper. Pour the lemon marinade over the entire mixture, and refrigerate overnight. Serves four.

Lemon Marinade

1 tsp black pepper

1 tsp dry mustard

6 tsp lemon juice

3 tsp red wine

1 c flaxseed oil

1 T dried onion flakes

1 T finely chopped fresh parsley

Mix all of the dressing ingredients in a blender. Makes 1½ cups.

Butter Leaf Avocado Salad

2 c shredded butter leaf lettuce

1 c chopped iceberg lettuce

¼ c raisins

1 c quartered tomatoes

1 c avocado slices

Avocado oil

Lemon juice

Combine the lettuces, raisins, and tomatoes in a serving bowl, and layer the avocado slices around the top. Dress with avocado oil and lemon juice. Serves three.

Waldorf Salad

2 T lemon juice

2 T flaxseed oil

2 c diced, unpeeled red apples (cored)

1 c thinly sliced celery

½ c chopped walnuts

½ c raisins

2 c chopped iceberg lettuce leaves

Mix together the lemon juice and flaxseed oil. Toss together with the apples, celery, walnuts, and raisins. Serve on top of a bed of lettuce. Serves two.

Condiments, Dips, Salsas, Salad Dressings, and Marinades

Omega-3 Mayonnaise

1 cage-free egg

1 T lemon juice

¼ tsp dry mustard

½ c olive oil

½ c flaxseed oil

Put the egg, lemon juice, and mustard in a blender, and blend for 3 to 5 seconds. Continue blending, and slowly add the oils. Blend until the mayonnaise is thick. Scrape mayonnaise into a resealable plastic container and refrigerate. The mayonnaise should keep for 5 to 7 days. Makes 1 cup.

Veggie Dip

1 c Omega-3 Mayonnaise
(see recipe above)

1 tsp dried dill weed

½ tsp garlic powder

Pepper to taste

Mix all of the ingredients together. It is better if refrigerated for 1 hour before serving, but it is not necessary. Makes a great dip for raw veggies or to use as a salad dressing. Makes 1 cup.

Tartar Sauce

1 c Omega-3 Mayonnaise (see recipe opposite)

¼ c finely chopped red onion

½ T lemon juice

½ tsp dried dill weed

¼ tsp paprika

Pinch of garlic powder

Mix all of the ingredients together. Chill prior to serving. Makes 1¼ cups.

Ray's Catsup

3½ lb tomatoes, washed and sliced

2 medium onions, sliced

⅛ clove garlic

½ bay leaf

½ red pepper

¼ c unsweetened fruit juice (white grape, pear, or apple)

1 tsp whole allspice

1 tsp whole cloves

1 tsp whole mace

1 tsp celery seeds

1 tsp black peppercorns

½ inch cinnamon stick

½ c lemon juice

Pinch of cayenne pepper

Boil the tomatoes, onions, garlic, bay leaf, and pepper until soft. Add the fruit juice. In a small separate bowl, combine the allspice, cloves, mace, celery seeds, peppercorns, and cinnamon, and put into a small cloth spice bag. Add the spice bag to the mixture; bring to a boil and continue boiling, stirring frequently, until reduced by half. Remove the spice bag. Add the lemon juice and cayenne pepper. Continue boiling for 10 minutes more. Remove the bay leaf and bottle the catsup in clean jars, with ¾ inch of space at the top of the jar to allow for expansion. Seal and freeze immediately. Always refrigerate the container that is currently in use. Makes about 2 cups.

Source: Neanderthin: A Caveman's Guide to Nutrition, by Ray Audette. New York: St. Martin's Press, 1999.

Guacamole Fiesta

3 ripe avocados

1 tsp freshly squeezed
lemon juice

1 tsp coarsely ground black
pepper

1 tsp garlic powder

1 jalapeño pepper, finely
diced, stemmed, and
seeded*

Mash avocados together with a fork or potato masher until smooth, and then stir in all of the other ingredients until well mixed. Makes 1 ½ cups.

Wear plastic gloves when handling.

Anaheim Cilantro Salsa

2 cloves garlic

1 large yellow onion,
quartered

1 Anaheim pepper,
quartered and seeded

3 jalapeño peppers,
stemmed and seeded*

6 tomatoes, peeled, seeded,
and chopped

1 c fresh cilantro

1 tsp ground cumin

Freshly ground pepper to
taste

In a blender or food processor, combine the garlic, onions, and peppers. Blend or process until minced. Add the tomatoes and cilantro, and continue blending until the ingredients are mixed but still slightly chunky. Add the cumin and pepper. Refrigerate until ready to use. Makes 2 cups.

Wear plastic gloves when handling.

Peach Salsa

1 c fresh peaches, peeled and finely chopped

¼ c chopped red onions

¼ c seeded and chopped yellow or green bell peppers

1 T lime juice

2 tsp chopped fresh cilantro

Cayenne pepper to taste

In a medium-size bowl, stir all of the ingredients together. Cover and chill for up to 6 hours. Makes 2 cups.

Spinach Salad* Dressing

3 T dry mustard

1 clove garlic, minced

1 T black pepper

1 tsp cayenne pepper

1 tsp paprika

1 c Burgundy wine

1 c fresh tomatoes, pureed

2 c flaxseed oil

1 c lemon juice

Combine all of the ingredients in a blender and blend until pureed. Pour into a cruet or bottle, and shake well before each use. Makes 5 cups.

*Use with the recipe on page 179.

Omega-3 Russian Salad Dressing

1 c fresh tomatoes

½ c flaxseed oil

½ c lemon juice

3 T freshly squeezed orange juice

1 tsp paprika

1 small scallion or 1 tsp onion powder

1 tsp horseradish powder (optional)

1 clove garlic (optional)

Put all of the ingredients in a blender, and blend until smooth. Makes 1 cup.

Raspberry Barbecue Sauce

2 tsp olive oil

¼ c minced onion

1 T seeded and minced jalapeño pepper*

¼ c Ray's Catsup (see page 183 for recipe)

¼ tsp dry mustard

¼ tsp cayenne pepper

2 c fresh or frozen raspberries

Heat the oil in a heavy skillet, and sauté the onion and jalapeño for about 10 minutes. Add the catsup, mustard, and cayenne, and heat until simmering. Add the raspberries, and simmer for an additional 10 minutes. Remove from the heat and let cool. Pour into a blender, and blend until smooth. Makes about 1 ½ cups.

*Wear plastic gloves when handling.

Kona Local Marinade

½ c unsweetened fresh pineapple juice

¼ c olive oil

3 T lime juice

2 T finely grated fresh gingerroot

Combine all of the ingredients in a small bowl, and whisk until well blended. Use to marinate beef, chicken, pork, or fish when barbecuing. Makes about 1 cup.

Garlic and Herb Marinade

4 cloves garlic

4 T olive oil

⅓ c chopped fresh basil

⅓ c chopped fresh oregano

⅓ c chopped fresh parsley

6 T lemon juice

1 tsp black pepper

Mince the garlic, and place it in a blender. Add the remaining ingredients, and blend until well mixed. Use to brush on vegetables, chicken, or meat before and during grilling or broiling. Makes ½ cup.

Fruit Dishes and Desserts

Kyle's Apple Breakfast

1 large apple (any type),   Handful of raisins
chopped into bite-size
pieces   Cinnamon

1 medium carrot, grated

Combine the apple, carrot, and raisins in a bowl, and sprinkle cinnamon over the top. Serves one.

Almost Frozen Mashed Bananas

3–4 ripe bananas   1 tsp natural vanilla extract

Mash bananas with a fork or potato masher in a bowl, and thoroughly stir in vanilla. Put the mixture in the freezer for 20 to 30 minutes, until it is thick but not frozen solid. Serves three to four.

Fresh Cinnamon Applesauce

6 apples   1 tsp cinnamon
2–3 T fresh lemon juice

Core, peel, and slice the apples. Combine with the lemon juice in a blender until smooth. Sprinkle with the cinnamon and serve. Serves two.

Emerald Bay Fruit and Nut Mix

½ c walnuts   ½ c almonds
½ c pecans   ½ c chopped Medjool dates
½ c raisins   2 T lemon juice
½ c chopped fresh apples   1 tsp cinnamon

Combine all of the nuts and fruits in a large serving bowl. Mix in the lemon juice and cinnamon. Serves four.

Baked Walnut-Cinnamon Apples

4 apples

1 c raisins

¼ c chopped walnuts

¼ tsp cinnamon

½ tsp natural vanilla extract

½ c water

Preheat the oven to 375 degrees. Core and pierce the apples with a fork in several places around the center, to prevent them from bursting. Mix the raisins, walnuts, cinnamon, and vanilla in a small bowl. Fill the center of each apple with this mixture. Place in a glass baking dish, and pour water into the bottom of the baking dish. Cover with foil, and bake for about 30 minutes or until tender. Serves four.

Peach-Almond Delight

3 fresh peaches

4 oz slivered almonds

2 T diced Medjool dates

1 tsp natural vanilla extract

2 tsp cinnamon

Wash the peaches, and cut each one into eight sections. Mix with the almonds and dates, drizzle with the vanilla, and toss to evenly coat; sprinkle the cinnamon on top. Serves two.

Cantaloupe Stuffed with Blackberries and Pecans

1 cantaloupe

1 c blackberries

½ c chopped pecans

Mint or spearmint leaves
for garnish

Cut the cantaloupe in half, and scoop out the seeds. Fill each cavity with half of the blackberries and pecans. Garnish with mint or spearmint leaves. Serves two.

Strawberry-Blueberry Horizon

1 c fresh strawberries

1 c fresh blueberries

½ tangerine, sectioned

1 T freshly squeezed orange juice

1 tsp natural vanilla extract

Ground nutmeg

Fresh mint

Mix the strawberries, blueberries, and tangerine sections in a bowl. Drip with the orange juice and vanilla, toss to coat, and sprinkle with nutmeg. Chill for at least an hour and serve garnished with mint. Serves three.

Part 3

From the Paleo Perspective

Chapter 11

The Truth about Saturated Fat

If you are a Paleo Dieter or follow a low-carb diet, you know a storm has been brewing for some time about saturated fats. This question of saturated fats and disease has been hotly debated in recent years and has created a rift in both the Paleo and the scientific communities. My perspective on dietary saturated fat has changed substantially in the last decade as new data has arisen and as we gain a better understanding of atherosclerosis, the process that clogs arteries and promotes heart disease.

The correct answer to the saturated fat issue lies in the wisdom of our evolutionary past. By examining the dietary and lifestyle patterns of our hunter-gatherer ancestors, we can gain insight into this difficult problem. The evolutionary template allows us to peer into the future and provides us with the proper solution to complex dietary and health questions before any laboratory experiments are ever conducted. This powerful tool gives us a huge advantage. The Paleo evolutionary template allows us to connect the dots, piecing together and making sense of the scientific evidence so that we can truly understand how to eat for optimal health the way nature intended. To find an answer to the saturated fat problem, I examined the saturated fat intake of the world's 229 hunter-gather societies and published the results of my analysis in 2006; the outcome changed the way I now view saturated fats.

Wonderful Results with Paleo

Marilyn's Story

I started following this diet after it was recommended by an osteopath I was seeing. I am about to turn 65 and have been struggling with high blood pressure for about 4 years and elevated cholesterol for about 15 years. Until very recently, I was taking 25 mg of a diuretic and 40 mg of lisinopril (a blood pressure drug).

The first 2 weeks on the diet were not easy because I was especially weak until I adjusted my blood pressure medication, first cutting out my diuretic and then lowering the dosage of my lisinopril. I monitor my blood pressure daily, and with my doctor's supervision I am now keeping it within a normal range, usually about 110/75, with only 10 mg of lisinopril daily.

As to my lipids, the change is remarkable. Before I started the Paleo Diet, my total cholesterol was 263, HDL was 48, and LDL was 158, with a ratio of 5.4. My triglycerides were 284. My results today: Total cholesterol is 163 (in my entire life I have never been this low), with an HDL of 53, an LDL of 94, and a ratio of 3.1. My triglycerides are 76.

Prior to following this eating program, I was a fairly health-conscious person who exercised regularly yet was never able to control my weight or other health issues. I tried for 20 years to lose my last 10 pounds and was never successful. I have already lost at least 8 pounds and hope to drop 5 more. Most important, I am very excited to finally find a program that keeps me off medication.

Saturated Fat, Blood Cholesterol Levels, and Heart Disease

Let us critically evaluate both sides of the saturated fat argument. The traditional viewpoint is that dietary saturated fats raise blood cholesterol levels and increase our risk for heart disease. On the opposite side of the argument, a growing number of scientists, physicians, and writers now believe that dietary saturated fats have little or nothing to do with atherosclerosis and heart disease. Both factions strongly rely on epidemiological (population) studies to support their opposing viewpoints. Who's right and who's wrong? You may ask yourself how in the world could two seemingly well-informed and well-educated groups of scientists interpret similar studies in such different ways? And does it matter?

One of the reasons why epidemiological studies frequently yield conflicting results for identical topics is because of variables that cause confusion in the interpretation of the results. For example, although some studies have shown a link between animal protein consumption and symptoms of heart disease, it is entirely possible that this association was false because the measurement of animal protein was confounded by another variable also linked to heart disease symptoms: Meat is a major source of animal protein in the US diet, but it is also a major source of saturated fat. Because meat often comes as an inseparable package of protein plus saturated fat, animal protein is highly related to saturated fat, thereby making it difficult to separate the effects of saturated fat from those of animal protein.

Given the shortcomings of epidemiological studies, human experimental studies are more helpful because they can separate factors and determine which specific variable may be causing certain effects. So is it the protein or the saturated fat that elicits heart disease symptoms? To answer this question, an experiment was conducted by Dr. Andy Sinclair and coworkers at Deakin University in Australia in 1990. Ten adults were fed a low-fat, lean beef–based diet for 5 weeks. Caloric intake was kept constant during the entire experiment. Total blood cholesterol concentrations fell significantly within 1 week of beginning the high-protein diet but rose as beef fat drippings were added back into the diet during weeks 4 and 5. The authors concluded, "[I]t is the beef fat, not lean beef itself, that is associated with elevations in cholesterol concentrations."

More research conducted during the last 5 years has confirmed that increases in dietary protein have a beneficial effect on our blood cholesterol and blood lipid profiles.

Saturated Fats Defined

When most people align themselves with the saturated fat issue one way or another, they are frequently unaware that the term "saturated fat" is not a single item. Although most people know that saturated fats are concentrated in foods such as butter, eggs, lard, cheese, shortening, cream, fatty meats, and baked goods, few realize that not all saturated fats affect our blood cholesterol equally. There are four dietary saturated fats (actually, fatty acids) we need to concern ourselves with.

1. Lauric acid
2. Myristic acid
3. Palmitic acid
4. Stearic acid

Each of these dietary saturated fatty acids has slightly different effects on our blood.

Early studies supported the viewpoint that myristic acid and palmitic acid generally raised total blood cholesterol levels, whereas lauric acid did so slightly, and stearic acid didn't increase it at all. In those days, it was routine to carry out nutritional experiments under meticulous "metabolic ward" conditions—meaning that the subjects could eat only the food provided to them and nothing else. All meals were designed to precisely control the types of fats consumed. Subjects who didn't faithfully comply with the experimental diets were eliminated from the study.

The precision and accuracy of these early experiments are unquestionable, and the conclusion that saturated fats increase blood cholesterol is indisputable. As you will soon see, however, there are important limitations to these experiments that were unrecognized in their day. The most important shortcoming was that the endpoint variable that was measured—total blood cholesterol—was misleading and incomplete. We now realize that additional blood chemistry measurements are required to more accurately predict the risk of heart disease.

Total blood cholesterol levels are a crude marker for heart disease, as they don't reflect the dynamics of cholesterol entering or leaving the bloodstream. Some cholesterol is taken out of our bodies by HDL (good) particles, while other cholesterol is deposited in our arteries by LDL (bad) particles and forms part of the plaque that clogs our arteries. Because total cholesterol represents a summation of both good (HDL) and bad (LDL) cholesterol, by itself it is a poor measure of heart disease risk. The total cholesterol/HDL cholesterol ratio is a much better index for heart disease risk—and it is even more predictive if we know our general state of inflammation.

Putting It All Together

Lower values for the total cholesterol/HDL cholesterol ratio reduce our risk for heart disease, whereas higher values increase it. Let's go back and reevaluate Dr. Sinclair's experiment, in which he fed subjects a low-fat, beef-based diet for 5 weeks and then added beef fat back into the subjects' diets during weeks 4 and 5—all the while keeping the calories constant. Remember that total blood cholesterol increased during weeks 4 and 5 after the beef fat drippings were added back in, leading the authors of the study to conclude that saturated fats raise total blood cholesterol. Dr. Sinclair didn't report the total cholesterol/HDL cholesterol ratio in his experiment, but it is easy to calculate these numbers, as I have done in the table below. As you can see, the addition of high-saturated-fat beef drippings worsened total blood cholesterol values but actually improved the total cholesterol/HDL cholesterol ratio. If you were to look only at the total blood cholesterol values, it would appear as if saturated fats increased the risk for heart disease. And herein lies the problem with much of the human experimental studies conducted from the 1960s until the late 1980s—the single measurement of total cholesterol was an inappropriate and misleading endpoint.

Don't get too excited about my reanalysis of Dr. Sinclair's study. Remember, it is only a single experiment and, by itself, can't overturn the dogma of 30 or more years of studies examining only total blood cholesterol as the endpoint risk factor for heart disease. What we really need to look at are analyses combining all experiments that have examined how saturated fats affect the total cholesterol/HDL cholesterol ratio. Studies that combine the results from many experiments are called meta-analyses. In addition, we can check out what meta-analyses tell us about how the four different types of saturated fatty acids—lauric acid, myristic acid, palmitic acid, and stearic acid—affect the total cholesterol/HDL cholesterol ratio, as well as other blood markers that increase heart disease risk.

How Dietary Changes Affect Your Cholesterol

	Week 1	Week 2	Week 3	Week 4	Week 5
Calories	2,264	2,164	2,175	2,234	2,213
% Carbohydrate	43.8	62.6	62.5	53.3	43.6
% Fat	38.2	8.8	9.3	19.2	29.1
% Protein	16.1	25.6	26.9	25.4	25.4
Total Blood Cholesterol	5.84	4.69	4.84	4.94	5.39
HDL Cholesterol	1.71	1.41	1.60	1.64	1.76
Total Cholesterol/HDL	3.42	3.33	3.03	3.01	3.06

Amazingly, these types of comprehensive meta-analyses of human dietary interventions are few and far between. A recent meta-analysis involving saturated fats and blood chemistry was published in 2010 by Drs. Micha and Mozaffarian of the Harvard School of Public Health. Let's examine an important issue these authors have stirred up. If national nutritional policy dictates that dietary saturated fats should be slashed across the board for every man, woman, and child in the country, what should they be replaced with: carbohydrates, polyunsaturated fats, monounsaturated fats, or what? The default nutrient that the government decided on to replace saturated fats became carbohydrates—this official governmental dictate occurred with very little discussion or debate on the issue. Incredibly, this recommendation was never rigorously tested using human dietary interventions or meta-analyses. It simply became the unquestioned national policy that was spoon-fed to our entire medical and health-care system for decades. The simplistic thinking of the day was that if carbs contained no saturated fats, how could they possibly be dangerous?

Now let's take a look at the facts about saturated fats that should have been considered before national policy unilaterally rejected them. Drs. Micha and Mozaffarian's 2010 meta-analysis showed that when carbs were used to replace saturated fats, carbs *increased the risk for heart disease* by increasing blood triglycerides and lowering HDL cholesterol levels. More important, this comprehensive meta-analysis showed that the substitution of carbs for saturated fats neither raised nor lowered the total cholesterol/HDL cholesterol ratio. In effect, when compared to carbs, saturated fats were shown to be neutral and neither increased nor decreased the risk for heart disease. In addition, when individual saturated fatty acids were compared to carbs, it was demonstrated that lauric acid, myristic acid, and stearic acid actually lowered the total cholesterol/HDL cholesterol ratio. The authors concluded the most wide-ranging meta-analysis on saturated fats and heart disease ever with this statement: These meta-analyses suggest no overall effect of saturated fatty acid consumption on coronary heart disease events.

What a turn of events! The best science of 2010 with the most comprehensive database ever assembled flew in the face of more than 40 to 50 years of public and private recommendations that we should severely reduce dietary saturated fats to diminish our risk for heart disease. From the time I was 20 until very recently, I grew up with dietary recommendations that were flawed. Fortunately for me, during the last 20 years I have not followed the USDA MyPyramid Guidelines, which were in effect until mid-2011 but rather have followed humanity's original diet as my road map for optimal health and well-being.

So, should you go out and eat bacon, hot dogs, salami, and fatty processed meats until you can't eat any more? Absolutely not. Processed meats are synthetic mixtures of meat and fat combined artificially at the meatpacker's or the butcher's whim with no regard for the true fatty acid profile of the wild animal carcasses our hunter-gatherer ancestors ate. In addition to their unnatural fatty acid profiles—high in omega-6 fatty acids, low in omega-3 fatty acids, and high in saturated fatty acids—

processed fatty meats are chock-full of the preservatives nitrites and nitrates, which are converted into potent cancer-causing nitrosamines in our guts. To make a bad situation worse, these unnatural meats are typically laced with salt, high-fructose corn syrup, wheat, grains, and other additives that have multiple adverse health effects. In a 2010 meta-analysis, scientists from the Harvard School of Public Health reported that red meat consumption was not associated with either heart disease or type 2 diabetes, whereas eating processed meats resulted in a 42 percent greater risk for heart disease and a 19 percent greater risk for type 2 diabetes.

Blood Miracles

Sam's Story

Dr. Cordain spoke last semester at the USAF Academy. I listened to his lecture, bought and read *The Paleo Diet,* and decided to try the diet myself, due to concerns about coronary artery disease. I had my lipid profile checked the day before starting the diet and again after 2½ weeks—I had dropped my total cholesterol by 66 points, and my total cholesterol was lower than my LDL had been when I started. (Total cholesterol 141, down from 207; LDL 86, down from 145; HDL 42, down from 44; risk factor 3.4, down from 4.7.) Phenomenal!

Saturated Fats in Hunter-Gatherer Diets

In 2006, I published a chapter in a scientific book that essentially overturned my prior convictions about saturated fat and health. The correct science behind the saturated fat issue and heart disease did not happen overnight, and had I used the evolutionary template as my guide quite a bit earlier, I would have known that population-wide recommendations to reduce saturated fats were flawed. The US Dietary Guidelines and the World Health Organization both recommend consuming less than 10 percent of our calories as saturated fats. The American Heart Association's recommendations are lower still, advising us to get less than 7 percent of our daily calories as saturated fat. Let's take a look at the evolutionary evidence and see how it compares to these official recommendations.

In 2001, I published a paper in the *American Journal of Clinical Nutrition,* in which my colleagues and I examined the dietary macronutrient (protein, fat, and carbohydrate) content in 229 hunter-gatherer societies. We showed that animal fare almost always made up the greater part of hunter-gatherers' daily food intake. In fact, most (73 percent) of the world's hunter-gatherers obtained more than 50 percent of their subsistence from hunted and fished animal foods. In contrast, only 14 percent of worldwide hunter-gatherers obtained more than 50 percent of their daily subsistence from plant foods. You can see from these numbers that our ancestors ate a lot of meat. It is possible to look at any nutrient, including saturated fats, using the same mathematical model I developed for this study.

The results of this study are compiled in the following table. Notice that in my model I varied two factors: (1) the percentage of plant and animal foods in the diet and (2) the percentage of fat for the animal foods. These procedures allowed me to calculate the saturated fat in a wide range of hunter-gatherer diets. Finally, any combination of values that exceeded 35 percent protein was excluded, as protein is toxic above 35 percent of a person's daily calories.

Saturated Fat Intake for Different Levels of Dietary Meats and Plant Foods

Ratio of Plant to Animal Foods	% Animal Fat	% Protein	% Carb	% Fat	% Saturated Fat
35/65	20	21	22	58	17.6
35/65	15	28	22	50	16.3
35/65	10	35	22	43	14.1
45/55	20	20	28	52	15.8
45/55	15	26	28	46	14.5
45/55	10	32	28	40	12.3
50/50	20	20	31	49	15.1
50/50	15	25	31	44	13.8
50/50	10	31	31	38	11.6
55/45	20	19	34	47	14.5
55/45	15	24	34	42	13.1
55/45	10	29	34	37	11.0
65/35	20	19	40	41	13.1
65/35	15	22	40	37	11.8
65/35	10	26	40	34	9.6
65/35	5	32	40	28	6.1

A few key points can be determined from this table. First and foremost is the average dietary saturated fat intake, which comes in at 13.1 percent of the total calories. If we look at the typical hunter-gatherer diet, in which animal food consumption falls between 55 and 65 percent of the total calories, the dietary saturated fat intake is higher still at 15.1 percent. Even in plant-dominated hunter-gatherer diets, the dietary saturated fat (11.3 percent) is considerably higher than the American Heart Association's recommended healthful values of less than 7 percent.

You can see that the normal dietary intake of saturated fats for historically studied hunter-gatherers likely accounted for 10 to 15 percent of their total energy. Values lower than 10 percent or higher than 15 percent would have been the exception, rather than the rule.

I cannot lend my support to population-wide recommendations to lower dietary saturated fat below 10 percent to reduce our risk for heart disease. This advice has little or no support from an evolutionary basis. Just as the replacement of saturated fats with carbohydrates was a poor idea that had not been adequately tested, studies of sufficient duration examining how low-saturated-fat diets may affect our health and well-being have never been carried out. They certainly don't protect us from heart disease, and recommendations to reduce dietary saturated fats may potentially have adverse health consequences.

So my new advice for you is this: *If you are faithful to the basic principles of the Paleo Diet, consumption of saturated fats within the range of 10 to 15 percent of your daily calories will not increase your risk for heart disease.* In fact, the opposite may be true, as new information suggests that elevations in LDL cholesterol may actually reduce systemic inflammation, a potent risk factor for heart disease. Consumption of fatty meats and organs had survival value in an earlier time, because fat provided a lot of energy and organs were rich in nutrients including iron, vitamin A, and the B vitamins.

In Paleolithic times, humans didn't eat grains, legumes, dairy products, refined sugars, and salty processed foods, the modern foods that produce chronic low-level inflammation in our bodies. Some medical studies now attribute many diseases, including heart disease, to chronic inflammation. Perhaps inflammation will prove to be more of a risk factor than high total cholesterol was thought to be.

Good and Bad Saturated Fats

Saturated fats have always been part of the ancestral human diet, and you should not avoid them when they are found in "real," nonprocessed foods. The table on the following page shows the sources of most of the saturated fats in the typical American diet. Notice that two-thirds of all of the saturated fats that Americans consume come from processed foods and dairy products. These are the foods you want to eliminate or restrict when you adopt the Paleo Diet. Remarkably, computerized dietary analyses from our laboratory show that despite their high meat content, modern-day Paleo diets actually contain lower quantities of saturated fats than are found in the typical US diet.

Sources of Saturated Fats	% of Total Saturated Fats
NON-PALEO FOODS	
Milk, cheese, butter, and dairy	20.0
Processed foods with grains and beef (burritos, tacos, spaghetti)	9.8
Bread, cereals, rice, pasta, tortilla chips, potato chips	9.5
Desserts (ice cream, cakes)	8.6
Processed foods with grains and cheese (pizza, macaroni and cheese)	6.9
Beverages, miscellaneous	3.7
French fries, hash browns	3.3
Salad dressings	3.0
Margarine	1.2
Total	**66.0**
PALEO FOODS	
Beef	13.2
Pork	8.8
Poultry	6.0
Eggs	3.2
Seafood	1.8
Total	**33.0**

Stay away from saturated fats in processed foods. These artificial concoctions carry the baggage of refined grains, sugars, vegetable oils, trans fats, dairy, salt, preservatives, and additives that are definitely not good for our bodies. The saturated fats you consume from grass-fed beef, poultry, pork, eggs, fish, and seafood will not promote heart disease, cancer, or any chronic health problem. In fact, these foods can ensure your birthright—a long, healthy, and happy life.

Chapter 12

Just Say No to Milk, Grains, Beans, and Potatoes

My signature lecture, "Origins and Evolution of the Western Diet: Health Implications for the 21st Century," is based on a scientific paper I published in the *American Journal of Clinical Nutrition* in 2005. In this lecture, I trace the chronological introductions of all of the food groups and the foods that have become part of the contemporary US and Western diet. When I lecture, I like to engage the audience so that it becomes not just a one-way presentation by me but rather an interactive give-and-take conversation. When I get to the part about milk and dairy products, I pose a question: "How do we know that our hunter-gatherer ancestors never ate this food group?" In the ensuing pause before a few people raise their hands and give the correct answer, I flip to the next slide. Immediately appears an unruly herd of about 30 African Cape buffalo, snorting and pawing the earth with powerful hooves supporting their 1-ton bodies, crowned by enormous menacing horns.

Have you ever tried to approach a wild animal? How about milking one? This is an impossible task, to say the least. Until the dawn of agriculture 10,000 years ago and the subsequent domestication of dairy animals, milk, butter, cheese, and yogurt were never part of our ancestors' menu.

Although 10,000 years ago seems unimaginably distant compared to a single human life span, it is very recent on an evolutionary time scale. Only 333 human generations have come and gone since we first domesticated animals and began to consume their milk. As a species, we have had scant evolutionary experience to adapt to a food that now makes up about 10 percent of the calories in the American diet. Milk and dairy products have the enormous potential to disrupt our health and well-being through a variety of means that I barely touched on. If you had any prior doubts about whether you should eat dairy foods, the information contained in this chapter should help you make an informed decision in the best interests of your health.

Milk and dairy products became part of the current Western diet during the period known as the Neolithic or New Stone Age, which began about 10,000 years ago and ended 5,500 years ago. Unless you are lactose intolerant, have an allergy to milk and dairy products, or have been a devoted follower of the Paleo Diet, you probably don't give a second thought to whether you should consume a food group that seems to be found nearly everywhere in the Western diet. Your favorite dairy foods may include ice cream, chocolate milk, fruit-flavored yogurt, or fancy imported cheeses. You may think that you are doing your body a favor by eating these calcium-rich foods. But remember this: We are the only species on the planet to consume another animal's milk throughout our adult lives.

An increasing body of scientific evidence supports the evolutionary caution that this dietary practice is not necessarily harmless, as dairy products are put into almost all processed foods. Take some time to read labels. If you are a milk chocolate addict, you are eating dairy, and the same goes for latté lovers. Nonfat milk solids, a major ingredient in chocolate, are also put into candy, cereal, bread, salami, bologna, sausages, baked goods, salad dressings, chips, condiments, soft drinks, and many other foods that come in a can, a jar, a bottle, a bag, or a plastic wrapper.

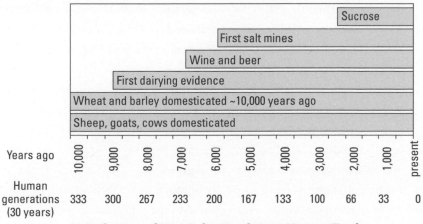

Introduction of Non-Paleo Foods into Human Foods

Even though these tiny residues of milk in processed foods seem to be trivial, don't fool yourself. Milk proteins and peptides (the building blocks of proteins) have a high potential to promote heart disease, cancer, allergies, and other health problems.

The Dairy Advertising Hype

Let's take a step back and look at the vast advertising campaign that the milk-processing industry has shoved down our throats for nearly 20 years. This glitzy promotional crusade with the "Got Milk?" slogan depicts movie stars, sports personalities, politicians, and other public figures with a wet, white film of what appears to be milk on their upper lips. Implied in magazine ads, TV and radio commercials, and social media is the notion that all public figures with "milk mustaches" endorse dairy products, presumably because these are healthy and nutritious foods. Let's stop for a minute and touch base with reality.

I haven't drunk a glass of milk in nearly 40 years, but if I were to, I certainly wouldn't spill it all over my upper lip. This issue really doesn't matter and is simply part of the industry's advertising strategy—if the movie stars and the sports heroes do it, so should you. My question: Why would a Wimbledon tennis champion, an Oscar-winning actress, and an Indy 500 race car driver blindly support a product they know virtually nothing about?

These public figures have spent their lifetimes honing talents, skills, and knowledge specific to their life callings. Yet when it comes to understanding milk's intricate influence on our metabolism, hormonal function, and long-term health, most of these people are novices operating completely outside their areas of expertise, without knowledge or understanding of the facts. Like the public, they have bought into the milk-processing industry's ad campaign, which portrays milk right along with motherhood, apple pie, and the American way.

This is exactly the message the milk-processing industry wants to convey to consumers because it sells more milk and dairy products, plain and simple. Is there a conspiracy by dairy industry middlemen, executives, and CEOs to sabotage our health and promote disease? Of course not. By and large, these people, just like the movie stars and the sports figures who endorse milk, are uninformed and blindly believe in their product. To them, the Got Milk? and Milk Mustache advertising campaigns simply represent a logical corporate tactic to increase sales and maximize profits of a supposedly nutritious and healthful product.

As was the case with saturated fats, whether people should consume dairy products is divisive within the scientific community because the human experimental and epidemiological evidence is not necessarily conclusive and still can be interpreted in a variety of ways. Does milk prevent disease or does milk promote disease—or is the answer somewhere in between?

In an ideal world, this question could be decisively answered by well-controlled human experimental studies conducted during entire lifetimes. Unfortunately, these hypothetical lifelong experiments in real people will never be carried out because they would be impossible to control, incredibly expensive, and unethical. In lieu of these studies, conventional nutrition researchers are left with four scientific procedures to unravel the milk-drinking dilemma: (1) epidemiological studies, (2) animal studies, (3) tissue studies, and (4) short-term human experiments.

Unfortunately, traditional nutrition researchers are unaware of or don't appreciate the most powerful research tool in all of biology. This concept could point them in the right direction when it comes to deciphering all of the conflicting information about dairy products and human health: the evolutionary template. Anybody who doesn't use it might just as well do calculations with a pencil and paper, rather than with a computer. When the evolutionary template is combined with the four procedures scientists use to establish causality between diet and disease, we can make sense of all of the contradictory data and be sure of arriving at the correct answer.

Healing Gastrointestinal Problems

Annie's Story

I have to share what an altering life change the Paleo Diet has been for me. As far back as I can remember, I have had GI [gastrointestinal] problems. I remember going to the hospital to receive barium treatments and always being mortified. I was constantly drinking castor oil, having Metamucil with my orange juice, and suppositories at 4 years old.

As I became an adult, I had terrible acid reflux, but I just assumed that the reflux was due to my pregnancies. At 20 years old, I started to have severe abdominal cramping—food would run through my body faster than it took to consume it. I was always exhausted and could gain 10 pounds at a time.

Finally, when my weight was up to 163 pounds, I was not able to hang onto anything I ate, and I was always so tired I felt drugged, I made an appointment with one of my state's top gastroenterologists. He immediately gave me a prescription for an antispasmodic because he believed that I had IBS [irritable bowel syndrome], and then scheduled a day to do an EDG [esophagogastroduodenoscopy]. I came back for my EDG, and the doctor found that I have GERD [gastrointestinal reflux disease] and a hiatal hernia; he suspects IBS. I still seemed to have a difficult time with eating anything baked or dairy, and I was still gaining weight and still "dumping" my food.

A month later, I went in to see my GI doctor. He told me not to drink any mixed drinks, white wines, or beer. I thought, Well, that is okay. I do not drink that often.

Two months went by. A coworker suggested the Paleo Diet. I immediately started it and eventually began hiking 4 miles every morning—I am now up to running, and I am not a runner!

My results: Since the middle of March, I have lost 44 pounds. I am now 119 pounds and a size 2! I have energy again and feel fabulous. Oh yes, I have a flat tummy again!

The food I was eating was slowly killing me. That sounds so dramatic, but it seriously was. My doctor said my body was in starvation mode and would hang onto anything it could. My belly was always distended, and I appeared to be 6 months pregnant.

I love the Paleo Diet and cannot say enough about it. I truly believe my tummy issues are genetic, and I have been dealing with celiac symptoms, lactose intolerance, GERD, and IBS all of my life. I have bought *The Paleo Diet* for everyone in my family.

Evolutionary Clues

George Santayana's famous quote has influenced my thinking about life, as well as diet, for decades: "Those who cannot remember the past are condemned to repeat it."

I am not the first scientist to recognize that milk and dairy consumption may have adverse effects on our health. One of the most vocal opponents to milk drinking was a physician, Dr. Frank Oski (1932–1996), who was the department chairman of pediatrics at Johns Hopkins University from 1985 until 1996. He was a member of the National Academy of Sciences and the author or coauthor of 300 academic papers and 20 books. A book he wrote in 1977, *Don't Drink Your Milk*, was decades ahead of its time. Here is an excerpt:

The fact is: the drinking of cow milk has been linked to iron-deficiency anemia in infants and children; it has been named as the cause of cramps and diarrhea in much of the world's population, and the cause of multiple forms of allergy as well; and the possibility has been raised that it may play a central role in the origins of atherosclerosis and heart attacks . . . . In no mammalian species, except for the human (and the domestic cat), is milk consumption continued after the weaning period [the period of breast-feeding]. Calves thrive on cow milk. Cow milk is for calves.

When you apply the evolutionary template to milk drinking, it becomes absolutely clear that cow's milk was never intended to nourish another species—us—throughout our entire adult lives. It was specifically designed by natural selection to encourage rapid growth, support immune function, and prevent disease in young suckling animals. Newborn calves, like most mammals, are nearly helpless for the first few hours after birth. They are unable to stand up, much less sprint away from potential predators. For the first few days and weeks after birth, they can't forage for food and are almost entirely dependent on their mothers' milk for nourishment.

Milk is designed to make young animals grow rapidly and to prime their immune systems and prevent disease by allowing hormones and other substances in their mothers' milk to enter their bloodstream. This is a brilliant evolutionary strategy to encourage survival for young suckling animals at the beginning of their lives, but it is a formula for disaster when adult humans consume a food intended only for the young of another species.

One of the telltale signs that there may be something wrong with milk drinking is that about 65 percent of all people on the planet can't do it without experiencing gas, bloating, and digestive distress. Maybe we should be listening to our bodies.

Milk is a mixture of carbohydrate, protein, and fats. Most of the carbohydrates in milk occur in the form of a sugar called lactose, which in turn is made up of two simple sugars: glucose and galactose. When we consume milk, ice cream, and other dairy products rich in lactose, it must first be broken down into these two simple sugars by an enzyme in our guts called lactase. About 65 percent of the world's people haven't inherited the genes to make lactase and are therefore lactose intolerant. The notable exceptions to this rule are people from Northern Europe and their descendants—because they maintain high gut lactase activity as adults, they can metabolize lactose into its two simple sugars and don't experience gastrointestinal upset after drinking milk. Most people on the planet can't drink milk without gastrointestinal upset because their genes haven't had enough time to adapt to this newcomer food. Milk is foreign fare that their bodies reject, as should we all, whether we can digest lactose or not. The lactose evidence is like a canary in a coal mine and hints at even greater health problems with milk and dairy consumption.

Dairy: A Nutritional Lightweight

Based on the dairy ad campaigns, cow's milk appears to be nothing less than an extraordinary food to perk up our health and avoid illness. This milky white liquid served cold is touted as "good for everybody" and high in nine nutrients, including calcium and vitamin D.

If the truth be known, milk is a lousy source of vitamin D, as well as of the top 13 nutrients most lacking in the US diet (zinc, calcium, magnesium, vitamin A, vitamin B_6, iron, vitamin C, folate, vitamin B_1, vitamin B_2, vitamin B_3, protein, vitamin B_{12}). Let's take a look at the facts.

In a paper published in the *American Journal of Clinical Nutrition*, my research group and I pointed out how dairy products were nutritional lightweights when compared to lean meats, seafood, fresh fruits, and vegetables. Based on the 13 vitamins and minerals most lacking in the US diet, our analysis showed that whole milk ended up near the bottom of the stack for all food groups.

The highest sources of these 13 nutrients are:

1. Fresh vegetables
2. Seafood
3. Lean meats
4. Fresh fruits
5. Whole milk
6. Whole grains
7. Nuts and seeds

To suggest that milk is a good source of vitamin D is a total stretch of the facts. In the last year, the official Institute of Medicine's recommended intake for vitamin D has increased from 400 IU to 600 IU per day for most people. Although this advice represents a substantial increase, it still falls far short of human experimental evidence showing that at least 2,000 IU per day is required to keep blood levels of vitamin D at the ideal concentration of 30 ng/ml.

An 8-ounce glass of raw milk (280 calories) straight from the cow, without fortification, gives you a paltry 3.6 IU of vitamin D. At this rate, you'd have to drink 167 of these 8-ounce glasses of milk just to achieve the 600 IU daily recommendation. Because most of the milk we drink is fortified with vitamin D, an 8-ounce glass typically yields 100 IU of this nutrient. Even with fortification, you would have to drink six 8-ounce glasses (1,680 calories or around 75 percent of your daily caloric intake) of milk to meet the daily requirement for vitamin D. If you wanted to reach the 2,000 IU level suggested by the world's best vitamin D researchers, you would have to drink twenty 8-ounce glasses of fortified milk, amounting to 5,600 calories. No one in his or her right mind would drink twenty glasses of milk a day, even if it were possible.

As you can see from these simple calculations, whether fortified or raw, milk is a very poor source of vitamin D. The best way to get your vitamin D is not by drinking milk, but rather by getting a little daily sun exposure, as nature intended.

Milk, Ulcers, and Heart Disease

One of the more remarkable tales in recent medical history involves peptic ulcers. This is a chronic condition in which the linings of the stomach or the small intestine are eroded away, causing painful internal wounds. Complications include bleeding and perforation of the gastrointestinal tract, which are potentially life threatening.

For the better half of my adult life, peptic ulcers were routinely attributed to excessive stomach acid production caused mainly by stress, spicy foods, or too much gum chewing. Even as recently as the mid 1980s, ulcer patients were advised to take antacids, make lifestyle changes to reduce stress, cut back on spicy foods, and stop chewing gum. Yet this advice didn't do much to alleviate symptoms or cure the problem.

One of the more unusual ideas that surfaced to treat peptic ulcers came from an early 20th-century doctor, Bertram Sippy. Dr. Sippy authored an influential paper that appeared in the *Journal of the American Medical Association* in 1915 suggesting that peptic ulcers could be effectively treated by feeding patients milk and cream on a regular basis throughout the day. The doctor's advice became known as the Sippy Diet and was employed widely across the United States to care for patients with ulcers, even as recently as 25 to 30 years ago.

One of the downsides to the Sippy Diet, first recognized by Dr. Hartroft in 1960, was that it noticeably increased fatal heart attacks in ulcer patients. In

Dr. Hartroft's study, three groups were examined at autopsy: (1) subjects with peptic ulcers who followed the Sippy Diet, (2) subjects with peptic ulcers who didn't follow the Sippy Diet, and (3) subjects without peptic ulcers. The fatal heart attack rate was similar between subjects without peptic ulcers and those with peptic ulcers who hadn't been on the Sippy Diet; however, the fatal heart attack rate in ulcer patients who had adhered to the Sippy Diet was a staggering 42 percent. *Close to half of all ulcer patients following the Sippy Diet had died of heart attacks!* Thank goodness for us all that the medical community no longer recommends the Sippy Diet.

The reason that physicians no longer recommend the Sippy Diet or any other dietary regime for the treatment of ulcers is one of the most unlikely tales in modern medicine. For almost 100 years, peptic ulcers were looked at as a disease of excessive stomach acid production caused by stress, spicy food—whatever. No one considered that this condition might be caused by an infectious organism until the publication of two revolutionary papers in 1983 and 1984 by two Australian scientists, Barry Marshall and Robin Warren, showing that 70 to 90 percent of peptic ulcers resulted from infection by the bacterium *Helicobacter pylori.* At first, these innovative publications were generally dismissed and discredited by the medical community. Yet it didn't take long for practicing physicians to realize that ulcers could be effectively cured simply by giving their patients a good dose of antibiotics.

Unfortunately, it took about a decade for these brilliant scientists' ideas to be accepted worldwide. Now, because of their groundbreaking insights, antibiotics are routinely used to successfully treat and cure almost all peptic ulcer cases. In 2005, Drs. Marshall and Warren were awarded the Nobel Prize in medicine for their discoveries.

The information about Sippy Diets and the risk of heart attacks has been buried in the scientific literature for nearly 50 years and is virtually lost to contemporary scientists. I would no longer necessarily hang my hat on 50-year-old studies than I would drink a cup of milk, but the knowledge, wisdom, and insight of our parents', grandparents', and great-grandparents' generations shouldn't be swept under the rug. Is it possible that they were on to something?

Dairy and Heart Disease: Contemporary Studies

The data from the early 1960s studies on milk and heart attacks bears further scrutiny. As we move forward from the past, numerous studies support the view that milk and dairy products may not be heart healthy and good for everybody. A 1993 epidemiological study involving 40 countries worldwide demonstrated that milk and its components—calcium, protein, and fat—had the highest relationship with cardiovascular death rates for any food or nutrient examined. Similar results implicating milk consumption as a cause for high mortality from heart disease were reported by Drs. Renaud and De Lorgeril in 1989, by Dr. Appleby in 1999, by Dr. Segall in 2002, and by Drs. Moss and Freed in 2003.

Milk isn't simply a creamy white liquid that is good for everybody but rather is a complex mixture of many substances suspected of causing heart disease, including its high calcium content, saturated fats, lactose, and certain proteins. Because milk contains so many compounds that could potentially promote heart disease, it is difficult or impossible for epidemiological studies to sort out all of the facts. Let's take a closer look at some specific elements in milk that may promote heart disease.

Most people know that milk and dairy products are two of our best sources of calcium. The dairy-manufacturing industry has pounded this message into our brains for decades—so much so, that many women fear they will develop osteoporosis if they don't consume dairy foods. Until recently, the prevailing knowledge was that if a little calcium was good for us, then more certainly must be even better. Not necessarily so.

In 2002, I wrote a scientific paper covering this topic, and my analysis showed that modern-day Paleo diets provide us with only about 70 percent of the daily recommended calcium intake, no matter what we eat. Given this evolutionary clue, it is not surprising to find that the supranormal intake of calcium that can be achieved by milk and dairy consumption may cause unexpected health problems.

A 2010 meta-analysis published in the *British Journal of Medicine* by Dr. Bolland from the University of Auckland confirmed the health hazards of too much calcium. His comprehensive analysis involving 26 separate studies and more than 20,000 participants revealed that calcium supplementation significantly increased the risk for heart attacks and sudden death. High blood levels of calcium from either supplementation or from excessive milk consumption are likely involved in atherosclerosis—the artery-clogging process—because too much calcium promotes the formation and fragility of the plaque that blocks our arteries.

High dietary calcium also tends to cause imbalances in magnesium, and this mineral is generally protective against heart disease for many reasons. In 1974,

Dr. Varo pointed out in one study that high dietary calcium-to-magnesium ratios were a better predictor of heart disease than was high calcium intake alone. The bottom line is that if you get too much calcium and not enough magnesium in your diet, it puts you at an increased risk for heart disease. Because milk's calcium-to-magnesium ratio is quite high (about 12:1), the inclusion of dairy products in our diets can easily raise the overall calcium-to-magnesium ratio to about 5:1, thereby reducing cellular magnesium stores and promoting heart disease. Our studies of hunter-gatherers confirm that the dietary calcium-to-magnesium ratio was much lower—close to 2:1.

Supplementation studies of magnesium show that it reduces heart disease risk via multiple mechanisms. It improves our blood lipid profiles, prevents heartbeat irregularities called arrhythmias, improves insulin metabolism, and lowers markers of inflammation. When you consume dairy products, you effectively negate each of these therapeutic effects of magnesium, either fully or in part.

Let's consider just a few other nutritional features in milk that further promote heart disease. In the 1950s and the early 1960s, when nutritional researchers were just beginning to understand how atherosclerosis and heart attacks developed, it was assumed to be a simple plumbing problem. Eat too much saturated fat and cholesterol, and your total blood cholesterol levels skyrocketed, clogging your arteries and thereby predisposing you to a heart attack or a stroke. Unfortunately, these simplistic views did not stand up well to the test of time, as hundreds of studies beginning in the 1990s showed that inflammation and immune reactions were just as important as or more important in the artery-clogging process than the consumption of either saturated fat or cholesterol.

What elements in the diet may be responsible for causing the chronic low-level inflammation that is now known to underlie not only heart disease, but also cancer and autoimmune diseases? The evolutionary template again brings us back to foods we never consumed in our ancestral past. Is there any possibility that these recent foods, such as milk and dairy, grains, and legumes, may cause chronic low-level inflammation and promote immune responses that lead to heart disease?

Milk is an amalgamation of nutrients, proteins, and hormones that have only recently been discovered and appreciated. It certainly is not the pure white liquid, high in calcium, vitamin D, and other vitamins and minerals, portrayed by milk manufacturers and their lobbyists. Milk is essentially nothing more than filtered cow's blood. It contains almost all of the hormones, immunological factors, and body-altering proteins that are found in bovine blood.

Let's not get too alarmed at this information; most of these compounds in milk have very short half-lives and are spontaneously degraded within minutes or hours after the manufacture of modern dairy foods, so they should not enter our bloodstream. Furthermore, a healthy human gut lining rarely allows intact large proteins such as those found in milk hormones to bypass its protective barrier.

So why should we worry? Are there proteins or hormones in cow's milk that bypass the gut barrier and eventually get into our bloodstream to wreak havoc with our immune systems and promote atherosclerosis?

Although no smoking gun has yet been found that implicates milk in the proinflammatory and immune processes that underlie atherosclerosis, a suspect substance is well known. One of the more important cow's milk proteins that may penetrate the gut barrier and get into our bloodstream is an enzyme in milk called xanthine oxidase. Numerous human studies show that our immune systems recognize this bovine enzyme as a foreign protein and produce antibodies to fight off this perceived foreign invader. Because we have a molecular duplicate of bovine xanthine oxidase located in the endothelial cells lining our arteries, it may also become a simultaneous target for the immune system's attack and may promote atherosclerosis. Even though we don't know for sure whether milk is involved in this process, there are no known health risks to not drinking milk, whereas the health benefits from abstaining might be enormous.

Milk, Insulin Resistance, and Metabolic Syndrome

The glycemic index gauges how much a food raises our blood glucose concentrations. Processed foods such as white bread, candies, breakfast cereals, cookies, and potatoes have high glycemic indices because they cause rapid and marked increases in our blood glucose levels. These foods tend to promote the metabolic syndrome, a condition that includes diseases of insulin resistance such as type 2 diabetes, hypertension, cardiovascular disease, obesity, gout, and detrimental blood chemistry profiles. Natural foods such as lean meats, fish, eggs, fresh fruits, and nonstarchy veggies typically have moderate to low glycemic indices and are not associated with the metabolic syndrome.

Normally, when our blood-sugar levels soar after we consume high-glycemic-index carbohydrates, our blood insulin concentrations also rise. Shortly after the glycemic index was developed in the early 1980s, it was discovered that milk, yogurt, and most dairy foods had low glycemic responses. Presumably, these foods should be healthy and should help prevent the metabolic syndrome. About 5 to 10 years ago, however, experiments from our laboratory and others unexpectedly revealed that low-glycemic dairy foods paradoxically caused huge rises in blood insulin levels. The table below shows that despite their low glycemic indices, dairy foods maintain high insulin responses similar to white bread.

Food	Glycemic Index	Insulin Index
White bread	70	100
Skim milk	32	90
Whole milk	27	90
Reduced-fat yogurt	27	115
Nonfat yogurt	24	115
Fermented milk (3% fat)	11	90

This information posed a challenge to nutritional scientists. It was unclear whether milk's insulin-stimulating effect but low glycemic response was healthful or harmful. To date, only one human study conducted by Dr. Hoppe in 2005 has addressed this question; it put twenty-four 8-year-old boys on either a high-milk or a high-meat diet for 7 days. The high-milk diet worsened the boys' insulin response almost 100 percent, and the entire group became insulin resistant in only a week's time. In contrast, the high–meat eating group's insulin levels did not change, and the boys' overall insulin metabolism remained healthy.

The results of this experiment are alarming, particularly if future studies also demonstrate this effect in teenagers and adults. As insulin resistance is the fundamental metabolic defect underlying the metabolic syndrome, it would not be surprising to discover that drinking milk may cause other diseases of insulin resistance.

Unsafe Milk Hormones

Of all of the milk hormones and the bioactive peptides, very few have been examined directly in human experiments. Nonetheless, evidence from animal, tissue, and epidemiological studies suggests that the consumption of milk and cow hormones at best may be unwise and at worst may be responsible for a number of life-threatening diseases. Let's take a look at the most problematic of these hormones.

Bovine Insulin

The regular, everyday milk you buy at the supermarket is loaded with bovine insulin. This cow hormone not only survives your gut's digestive enzymes, it also seems to frequently cross the gut barrier and make its way into the bloodstream, as revealed by telltale signs from our immune systems. Because the structure of bovine insulin varies from the human form, if it enters circulation, it is immediately recognized as a foreign particle and is flagged by the immune system. The large number of children who display immune system flags (antibodies) to bovine insulin means that it has indeed crossed the gut barrier intact and has caused an immune reaction. Although the mechanism is not entirely clear, the presence of bovine insulin antibodies in our bloodstream is associated with a greatly increased risk for type 1 diabetes.

Type 1 diabetes is an autoimmune disease in which the immune system destroys beta cells in the pancreas so that it can no longer make insulin. Type 1 diabetic patients must take insulin injections for the remainder of their lives. This devastating disease most frequently strikes children before their teen years. Epidemiological studies have time and again identified cow's milk as a major risk factor for the disease, particularly if children are exposed to milk or milk-containing formula before the age of 3. The bottom line: Milk is a potentially lethal toxin for infants and young children.

Insulin-like Growth Factor 1

Another hormone found in milk that may have disastrous effects on our health and well-being is insulin-like growth factor 1 (IGF-1). As implied by its name, this hormone encourages growth. Unfortunately, it promotes growth not only in healthy tissues and organs but also in cancerous growths. Like all milk hormones, IGF-1 is a large protein molecule that normally should not breach the gut barrier and get into our bloodstream. Nevertheless, recent meta-analyses of 15 epidemiological studies and eight human dietary interventions by Dr. Qin have shown without a doubt that milk drinking robustly elevates IGF-1 in our bloodstream. This effect may result directly from the additional ingested bovine IGF-1 that crosses our gut barriers or via indirect mechanisms. Milk drinking causes our blood insulin levels to rise sharply, and whenever blood insulin concentrations increase, a series of connected hormonal events simultaneously cause IGF-1 to increase. During a 24-hour period, blood insulin concentrations are a good marker for IGF-1 concentrations. When one increases, so does the other.

Whether IGF-1 in our blood is increased either directly from ingested bovine IGF-1 or indirectly from milk's insulin-raising effects doesn't really matter. The end result is the same—milk raises our total blood levels of IGF-1. This particular consequence of milk drinking is especially ominous because it encourages the growth of many types of cancer. Numerous worldwide meta-analyses during the last 40 years show that high blood levels of IGF-1 strongly increase the risk for prostate and breast cancer. If this outcome doesn't alarm you, additional meta-analyses will: These comprehensive studies show that milk drinking also increases the risk for ovarian cancer in women.

If you or any close relatives have a history of cancer, one of the best lifestyle changes you can make to reduce your risk of developing these life-threatening diseases is to wipe your upper lip clean of the milk mustache and get milk and dairy completely out of your life.

Estrogen

By now, you can see that milk isn't simply an innocuous high-calcium food that builds strong bones, but rather is a concoction of body-altering hormones, enzymes, and proactive peptides whose wide-ranging effects promote cardiovascular disease, insulin resistance, cancers, allergies, and autoimmune diseases. Another dangerous cancer-promoting hormone in milk is the female hormone estrogen. Cow's milk is chock-full of it. It is present in bovine milk in a variety of forms, including estrone, estradiol-17, estriol, estrone sulfate, and progesterone.

Modern dairy farmers maximize milk production from their cows. Dairy farmers are in the business to make money, and the more milk they can get from a single cow in a year, the more money they make. Female cows, like all mammals, produce milk only in the latter half of pregnancy and during the suckling period. The trick for modern dairy farmers is to get cows to make large amounts of milk during the early months of pregnancy, when milk is normally not produced. Dairy farmers achieve this goal by artificially inseminating cows within 3 months after they have just given birth. In effect, these unfortunate cows become pregnant once again while they are still nursing the young of their previous birth. This totally contrived interference by humans causes the mother cow to produce milk 305 days out of the year. From an economic perspective, this strategy makes perfect sense—more milk means more money. From a dietary and health perspective, this practice is disastrous for us because it strikingly increases the estrogen content in the milk we drink.

The main form of estrogen in cow's milk is estrone sulfate, which also happens to be the most frequently prescribed hormone replacement therapy for menopausal women. This pharmaceutical form of estrogen has high oral bioactivity—meaning that when you ingest it in pill form, it readily gets into your bloodstream. There is no reason to believe that estrone sulfate from cow's milk acts any differently. So, whether you are a man, a woman, or a child, if you drink milk and eat other dairy products, your blood concentration of female hormones will be higher than if you don't drink milk. This situation is not good.

For women, elevated blood estrogen and its metabolites increase your lifetime risk for developing breast and ovarian cancers. For men, milk's added estrogen may increase your risk for getting prostate and testicular cancers.

Asthma and Excessive Mucous Production

Too much milk consumption has long been associated with increased mucous production in the respiratory tract and the incidence of asthma. A few years back, I went to a high school cross-country meet and watched the young athletes cross the finish line. I noticed a few runners who were literally foaming at their mouths because they had so much mucus being produced from their respiratory systems. I wondered whether milk drinking had anything to do with it, but at the time, the science hadn't yet caught up with my observations and those of others. An intriguing 2010 hypothesis by Drs. Bartley and McGlashan from New Zealand may have found the answer.

Milk contains substances called casomorphins. These compounds are produced in our guts from the breakdown of the milk protein casein. One of these casomorphins, beta-casomorphin-7, directly stimulates mucous production from specific glands located in the gut. If the gut becomes leaky, which it invariably does on a typical Western diet, beta-casomorphin-7 can enter our bloodstream and travel to our chests, where it stimulates mucous production from MUC5AC glands located in our lungs and respiratory tracts. A final piece of this puzzle is that beta-casomorphin-7 is much more likely to trigger mucous production if the lungs and the respiratory tract are inflamed by asthma. Many people's exercise-induced asthma symptoms disappear on the Paleo Diet.

Treating Asthma

Shannon's Story

I'm a trainer, and I work with a very overweight woman, Jenny, who recently started my boot camp. She weighs 260 pounds at present. Until recently, she also suffered from exercise-induced asthma. For the first week of boot camp, she could not get through a class without her inhaler. Although I admired her dedication, it was painful and a bit scary to watch.

Then I put her on the Paleo Diet. This week, after doing this for a little less than 2 weeks, she no longer needs her inhaler. Miraculous!

Jenny's also doing great on the diet—she's not hungry at all, so I know the weight will be coming off soon as well.

Parkinson's Disease

Parkinson's disease is a nervous system disorder that primarily affects areas of the brain that control movement. Disease symptoms include tremors, stiffness, and difficulty moving, and its two most famous victims are Muhammad Ali and Michael J. Fox. Although the cause of Parkinson's disease isn't known, both genetic and environmental elements seem to be involved. Like autoimmune diseases, it appears that environmental factors may be the most important triggers of this debilitating illness.

When we talk about environmental origins of any chronic disease with an unknown cause, diet is at the top of our list. The first items that we should examine are the foods that were not part of our ancestral human diet. This leads us once again to milk and dairy products.

A comprehensive 2007 meta-analysis by researchers at the Harvard School of Public Health has identified a high intake of dairy foods as a prominent risk factor for Parkinson's disease. Men who consumed the highest quantities of dairy products had an 80 percent greater risk of developing the disease than did men who ate the lowest amounts. These results are consistent with a study of Japanese men showing that people who consumed more than 16 ounces of milk daily had a 130 percent greater risk of Parkinson's disease than non–milk drinkers. No one really knows how and why milk drinking increases the risk for this illness, but autoimmune mechanisms seem likely, particularly those directed at insulin. When you adopt the Paleo Diet, you will reduce your risk for developing

Parkinson's disease and other conditions with autoimmune components because this lifetime nutritional plan eliminates milk and all other foods that are suspected of causing autoimmune diseases.

Milk and Cataracts

Senile cataracts are cloudy opacities that form in the lenses of the eyes as people age, and they can ultimately cause blindness. The bad news is that if you live long enough, you will probably develop cataracts. The good news is that you can probably forestall their appearance until very late in life by following the Paleo Diet. For people between 52 and 62 years of age, 42 percent develop cataracts. This percentage increases to 60 percent between ages 65 and 75 and rises further to 91 percent for people between 75 and 85 years of age. In the United States and other Westernized countries, cataracts are treated by surgical removal, whereas left untreated they are the leading cause of blindness in older adults worldwide.

Milk drinking has a lot to do with cataract formation. Scientists routinely produce cataracts in rats, pigs, and guinea pigs even before they reach old age simply by feeding them high-milk and -lactose diets. As you recall, the main sugar in milk is lactose, which is broken down into its two constituent sugars, glucose and galactose, by the gut enzyme lactase. Numerous epidemiological studies show that lactose and galactose are involved in premature cataract formation. Due to the way cataracts form, we can probably never prevent them completely, but chances are good that if you adopt a dairy-free diet, you can live most of your life, even into old age, without developing cataracts.

Milk Impairs Iron and Zinc Absorption

As you saw earlier in the chapter in the list of the top 13 missing nutrients in our diets, zinc is number one: More than 73 percent of all people in the United States don't get enough of this essential mineral. Iron is number six, and about 40 percent of the population are deficient in this nutrient. Milk and dairy products are lousy sources of both iron and zinc, and the high concentration of calcium in cow's milk strongly interferes with the absorption of both iron and zinc. If you were to add a slice of melted cheese to your burger, it would severely reduce the amount of iron and zinc you could absorb from the burger.

Both zinc and iron are crucial minerals for our health and well-being. Low iron stores are the most frequent cause of anemia, and in children and teens, low iron can impair mental functioning. Pregnant women with iron deficiency are at greater risk for delivering preterm babies, and low iron may adversely affect athletic performance and work ability. The list of health problems associated with zinc deficiency includes low sperm counts, reduced libido, reduced immune function, increased susceptibility to upper respiratory infections, acne, white spots on fingernails, rough skin, lack of sexual development, stretch marks, macular degeneration, reduced collagen, and increased wrinkling. When you follow the Paleo Diet, you will be eating meat at almost every meal, and meat is a primary source of the most highly absorbable forms of both zinc and iron.

Milk, Dairy, and Bone Health

One of the biggest selling points the milk manufacturers would like us to believe is that by drinking lots of milk, we can reduce our risk of osteoporosis and future hip fractures. The foremost danger associated with osteoporosis is hip fracture in the elderly. Between 18 and 33 percent of all elderly people who suffer hip fractures die within a year after breaking their hips—not a pretty statistic. Although most people, including dairy lobbyists, believe that a low intake of calcium is a risk factor for hip and other bone fractures, the data say that's not the case.

A 2007 meta-analysis from the Harvard School of Public Health reported that high calcium intake had no therapeutic effect on hip fractures in 170,000 women and 68,000 men. In the same study, a pooled analysis of five human experimental trials showed no benefit of calcium supplementation on nonvertebrae fractures but, rather, showed that increased calcium intake actually increased the risk for hip fracture. A follow-up 2010 meta-analysis specifically examining milk consumption and hip fracture risk in 195,000 women and 75,000 men also showed that low milk intakes didn't increase fracture risk, nor did a high intake reduce it.

These studies show that we have been misled by the dairy manufacturers' overhyped advertising and marketing campaigns. It's clear that dairy doesn't prevent bone fractures, and it might contribute to heart disease and cancer. I cannot come up with one single reason to drink milk or eat dairy products.

Grains Are Antinutritious

In the United States, a number of governmental, institutional, and private organizations determine official national nutritional policy. The USDA's MyPyramid, recently renamed MyPlate, is probably the most visible governmental program that attempts to sway our perspective on what is and is not a healthy diet. The USDA guidelines tell us that we must consume foods from *all five* of their self-proclaimed food groups—grains, vegetables, fruits, dairy, and meat/beans. The USDA cautions us, *"For good health, eat a variety of foods from each food group every day."*

The USDA suggests that women between the ages of 19 and 30 should eat at least 6 ounces of grains daily, and half should come from whole grains. For men, this figure is increased to 8 ounces of daily grains. Implicit in these recommendations is the notion that cereal grains represent an essential component of human nutrition. In other words, healthy human diets are difficult or impossible to achieve without cereal grains because they are nutrient-rich foods that we all require.

As a scientist, I can tell you that we should never blindly trust recommendations from the USDA or anyone else without first examining the data. The data speaks without the overtones of either charismatic individuals or rigid governmental organizations.

Grains are not part of the Paleo Diet. I'm going to meticulously show you the science underlying why cereal grains are inferior foods and why they should be avoided. In the decade since the publication of my first book, startling new information has surfaced about wheat consumption and human health. So much so that the National Institutes of Health, the FDA, and the Centers for Disease Control and Prevention have now taken an active interest in this newly recognized public health threat.

The USDA guidelines encourage us to replace refined grains—white bread, white flour, white rice, and degermed corn meal—with whole grains because refined grains have been stripped of fiber, vitamins, and minerals. In the chart on the following page, you can see how the refining process reduces the nutrient content of whole wheat.

Percentage of Vitamins and Minerals in Whole-Wheat versus White Flour

	Whole-Wheat Flour	White Flour
Calcium	100%	50%
Chromium	100%	33%
Copper	100%	20%
Iron (enriched)	100%	20%
Magnesium	100%	18%
Manganese	100%	10%
Selenium	100%	75%
Zinc	100%	20%
Potassium	100%	22%
Biotin	100%	20%
Vitamin B_6	100%	17%
Vitamin E	100%	2%
Folic acid (enriched since 1998)	100%	25%
Vitamin B_3 (enriched)	100%	20%
Vitamin B_2 (enriched)	100%	33%
Vitamin B_1 (enriched)	100%	18%
Pantothenic acid	100%	50%
Vitamin K	100%	24%

At least on paper, compared to refined grains, it may appear that whole grains are indeed nutrient-rich foods packed with vitamins and minerals. Unfortunately, it just isn't so. What we need to do is to compare whole grains on a calorie-by-calorie basis to other foods such as fresh fruit, veggies, lean meats, and seafood, which are the staples of the Paleo Diet.

In a paper I published in 2005 in the *American Journal of Clinical Nutrition*, I examined the 13 nutrients most lacking in the US diet and then ranked seven food groups—whole grains, milk, fruits, veggies, seafood, lean meat, and nuts and seeds—for each of these 13 vitamins and minerals in 100-calorie samples. Food groups were ranked from 7 to 1—where 7 represented the highest-nutrient-density food group for a particular vitamin or mineral and 1 the lowest. We then summed up all of the rank scores to determine the most nutrient-dense food groups. Fresh veggies were far and away the most nutrient-rich foods, followed by seafood, lean meats, and fruits. When we ranked the scores of the most nutrient-rich foods, whole grains and milk are in fifth and sixth place, respectively. So much for the USDA's suggestion that whole grains are a nutrient-rich food essential for good human nutrition!

How about Fiber?

Almost everyone, including the USDA, assumes that whole grains are a good source of fiber. Traditional, dyed-in-the-wool nutritionists may ask, "If you eliminate whole grains from your diet, how in the world will you ever get enough fiber?" In the following graph, I depict the average fiber content in a 1,000-calorie serving of 3 refined cereals, 8 whole-grain cereals, 20 fresh fruits, and 20 nonstarchy vegetables. Although whole grains have four times more fiber than refined grains do, they are lightweights when compared to either fresh fruits or veggies. Furthermore, out of all the whole grains, only oats contain an insoluble fiber that mimics the blood cholesterol–lowering effects of the soluble fiber present in fresh fruits and vegetables.

Phytate: One Antinutrient in Grains

Another piece of the whole-grain story that the USDA's MyPyramid/MyPlate doesn't mention is nutrient availability. It may seem as if whole grains are great sources of calcium, magnesium, iron, and zinc. Not true. All whole grains contain an antinutrient called phytate or phytic acid, which binds these minerals

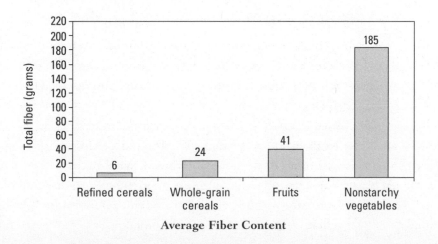

Average Fiber Content

and makes them unavailable for absorption in our gastrointestinal tracts. Phytate binds these nutrients in a dose-dependent manner, meaning that the more whole grains you eat, the more likely you will become deficient in these minerals.

Just such an effect was verified in rural Iranians who frequently consume about 50 percent of their daily calories from a whole wheat flat bread called tanok. A series of studies in the early 1970s by Dr. Reinhold demonstrated that excessive consumption of tanok caused zinc deficiency in young boys and teenagers, which resulted in a condition called hypogonadal dwarfism. This nutritional disease prevents normal growth and development, reduces stature, severely delays puberty, and adversely affects reproductive function.

By following the USDA guidelines, whole grains can easily make up a third or more of your caloric intake. A 25-year-old sedentary woman has an energy requirement of about 1,600 calories per day. If she consumes 6 ounces of grains, as recommended by the USDA, this amount of cereal translates into about 29 percent of her daily calories. If this woman considers herself "health conscious" and purchases only whole grain breads and cereals and has made a decision to reduce or completely eliminate meat, eggs, and other animal foods from her diet, whole grains can easily compose 50 percent or more of her diet. Like many Americans, she thinks she is following a healthy plant-based diet that will reduce her risk of developing many chronic diseases and nutritional deficiencies. In reality, she will most likely develop both iron deficiency anemia and zinc deficiency. Her whole grain–based diet, because of its high phytate and antinutrient content, will also promote calcium loss and osteoporosis.

Whole Grains and Bone Health

One of the best-kept secrets about excessive whole grain consumption is that it adversely affects skeletal health by impairing vitamin D and calcium metabolism. If you were to research the vitamin and mineral contents of various food groups, you would discover that the average amount of calcium in a 100-calorie serving of whole grains is a paltry 7.6 mg, whereas the same serving of fresh vegetables gives you 15 times more calcium (116.8 mg). More important, vegetable calcium is well assimilated, whereas calcium in whole grains is virtually unabsorbable because it is bound to phytate. The more whole grains you include in your diet, the less calcium will be available to build and maintain a healthy skeleton.

As if an extremely low calcium content that is poorly absorbed were not bad enough, whole grains also have other adverse nutrient characteristics that harm calcium metabolism and bone health. Whole grains have a calcium to phosphorus ratio that is quite low (0.08). Consumption of excess phosphorus when calcium intake is adequate or low leads to a condition called secondary hyperparathyroidism, which causes progressive bone loss. The recommended, ideal calcium to phosphorous ratio is 1.00, whereas it averages 0.64 for women and 0.62 for men in the United States. High-grain diets such as those recommended by the USDA (around 30 percent of your total calories) will further reduce the calcium to phosphorus ratio in your diet and increase your risk for developing osteoporosis.

Whole grains are bad news not only for adults' calcium metabolism but also for children's. In an experiment involving infants, Dr. Zoppi and coworkers showed that wheat bran given to infants for just 1 month caused their blood calcium to plummet. Most consumers believe that whole grains are vastly superior to refined grains in every respect. This assumption is simply untrue, particularly when it comes to calcium metabolism and bone mineral health. Animal experiments show that whole grain oats and wheat are worse for your health than their refined counterparts for a variety of reasons, including their adverse effect on vitamin D metabolism.

Whole Grains Impair Vitamin D Metabolism

One of the most disturbing effects of whole grains is their capacity to impair vitamin D metabolism. Besides calcium, vitamin D is one of the most important nutrients when it comes to our bone health. Within the last 10 years, scientists have determined that vitamin D deficiency spans the globe and has turned into a worldwide epidemic. Scores of studies indicate that anywhere from 40 to 100 percent of elderly men and women in the United States and Europe are vitamin D deficient. This epidemic is not limited only to the elderly. A study in Maine revealed that 48 percent of preteen girls had deficiencies in this important nutrient, while a study in Boston indicated that 52 percent of Hispanic and black teenagers were vitamin D depleted. Other studies have demonstrated that vitamin D deficiency is common in middle-aged adults, with as many as 60 to 90 percent of them maintaining inadequate blood concentrations of this crucial vitamin. Moreover, if you follow government guidelines and consume a third of your calories as grains and whole grains, you will make the potentially severe health problem of vitamin D deficiency even worse.

In 1919, Dr. Edward Mellanby of London University experimentally demonstrated that excessive whole grain consumption caused rickets in puppies. Rickets is a debilitating bone disease that afflicts puppies and human children by causing a softening of bones that leads to fractures and deformities that may persist throughout life. Since Dr. Mellanby's pioneering work, numerous experiments in other laboratory animals and even humans have shown without question that whole grains impair vitamin D metabolism.

There appear to be at least two elements in whole grains and whole wheat in particular that undermine vitamin D metabolism in our bodies. Most of us are either borderline or vitamin D deficient to start with, so any losses caused by whole-grain consumption exacerbate the problem. A study of vitamin D in human beings who consumed 60 grams of wheat bran daily for 30 days demonstrated an increased elimination of vitamin D from the intestines. It is not entirely clear how whole grains promote losses of vitamin D from our bodies, but they may interrupt the normal recycling process of vitamin D between the intestines and the liver.

Recent work from our research group suggests that one substance found in whole wheat may play an even more important role in disrupting normal vitamin D metabolism than previously suspected substances do. Wheat contains a lectin known as wheat germ agglutinin, or WGA, that has been shown to easily penetrate the gut barrier of rats and enter their bloodstream. Experiments from our laboratory, as well as those from Dr. Roberto Chignola and coworkers at the University of Verona, support the view that WGA from whole and refined wheat bypasses the gut barrier and enters human circulation as well. This is definitely not a good thing because WGA is a lectin that can bind to almost any cell in our bodies and disrupt normal cellular function.

Lectins are protein molecules found in plant and animal cells that firmly bind to carbohydrate and sugar molecules. They were originally discovered when researchers noticed lectins' ability to cause red blood cells to clump together in test tubes. In plants, their main function is to act as an antinutrient to discourage potential predators such as insects, birds, and small animals from eating their various leaves, seeds, and roots. Most plant lectins in our food supply are harmless because they can't bind to cells in our gastrointestinal tract and therefore can't get into our bloodstream. Two notable exceptions are cereal grain and legume lectins, which bind to cells in our intestines and enter circulation.

Once WGA finds its way into the bloodstream, it attaches itself to red blood cells and is carried to almost every cell in our bodies. At this point, WGA crosses cell membranes and binds to a structure on the cell nucleus called the nuclear pore. This action effectively blocks the entry of many hormones into the nucleus and prevents their intended cellular actions.

Vitamin D is actually not a vitamin at all. It is classified as a hormone because it affects so many of our body's cells and organs. In order for vitamin D to produce its beneficial effects in our bodies, it normally must enter the cell nucleus through the nuclear pore. Unfortunately, this process can't occur when WGA binds and blocks the nuclear pore. This series of events has been experimentally demonstrated in tissue studies in vitro but has yet to be confirmed in living human experiments in vivo. Yet the bottom line remains the same—excessive whole wheat and grain consumption disrupts vitamin D metabolism and disturbs normal bone health.

Whole Grains and Celiac Disease

One of the most shortsighted aspects of the USDA's population-wide recommendation for all of us to consume grains is its failure to recognize that wheat, rye, and barley are troublesome to a large percentage of the US population. In a landmark paper published in 2003, Dr. Alessio Fasano at the University of Maryland determined that 1 in 133 people in the United States has celiac disease, an autoimmune disease triggered by the consumption of gluten proteins found in all wheat, rye, and barley food products. Celiac disease arises when the immune system does not recognize the body's own intestinal tissues as part of itself and mounts an attack on them. In celiac patients, the range of symptoms runs the spectrum from intense inflammation, tissue destruction, diarrhea, and malabsorption of nutrients to virtually no symptoms at all. In infants and children, celiac disease can stunt normal growth and in adults it increases the risk of developing other autoimmune diseases and associated illnesses, with outcomes that range from inconsequential to lethal.

At least 2,316,000 Americans have celiac disease. Unfortunately, most are unaware that they have the disease, because about 80 percent of all celiac patients remain undiagnosed. If we do the math, you can see that at least 1,852,800 people in the United States don't have a clue that they have celiac disease and that they shouldn't be eating wheat, barley, and rye. Despite these compelling figures, the USDA has completely failed us with its recommendation for every man, woman, and child in the United States to eat grains on a daily basis.

At first, these numbers may seem trivial because they imply that most people have no trouble whatsoever when eating gluten-containing grains. Not true. Until very recently, the classical medical view of gluten was that it caused only one autoimmune illness (celiac disease) or possibly one other (dermatitis herpetiformis—an itchy skin rash). In the last 5 years, a few of the most well-recognized celiac researchers in the world, including Drs. Alessio Fasano and Marios Hadjivassiliou, have completely demolished this traditional perspective on gluten. These scientists have coined the term gluten sensitivity and have shown that celiac disease is just one of many illnesses and autoimmune diseases caused by gluten-containing grains. Intriguing evidence uncovered by these researchers and others shows that gluten sensitivity may underlie an extraordinary number of health problems and disorders, including those discussed below.

Diseases and Disorders Linked to Gluten Sensitivity

- Acid reflux
- Addison's disease (adrenal disease)
- Alopecia (hair loss)
- Anemia
- Aphthous ulceration (canker sores)
- Asthma
- Ataxias (a nervous system dysfunction causing grossly uncoordinated movements)
- Attention deficit disorder (ADD)
- Atopic diseases (flaky, itchy skin)
- Autism
- Autoimmune thyroid diseases
- Dementia
- Dental enamel defects
- Depression and anxiety
- Dermatitis herpetiformis (itchy skin disease)
- Eating disorders
- Epilepsy with cerebral calcifications
- Graves' disease

- Hashimoto's thyroiditis
- Hyperactivity
- Infertility
- IgA nephropathy (kidney inflammation)
- Irritable bowel syndrome
- Liver disease
- Chronic active hepatitis
- Primary biliary cirrhosis
- Primary sclerosing cholangitis
- Migraine headaches
- Peripheral neuropathies (nerve damage causing pain, muscle weakness, tingling, spasms, cramps)
- Psoriasis
- Rheumatoid arthritis
- Schizophrenia
- Selective IgA deficiency (immune system dysfunction)
- Sjögren's syndrome (dry eyes, mouth)
- Systemic lupus erythematosus (whole body autoimmune disease)
- Type I diabetes
- Uveitis (autoimmune eye disease)
- Vitiligo (skin depigmentation)

If even a small percentage of these diseases and disorders are directly caused by the consumption of gluten-containing grains, we really need to rethink governmental recommendations for all of us to eat cereals. In a recent interview, Dr. Fasano estimated that 20 million people nationwide are sensitive to gluten. These numbers are truly staggering and represent an epidemic—so much so that the Centers for Disease Control and Prevention now considers celiac disease and gluten sensitivity to be major public health threats.

One of the greatest improvements you can make in your physical and mental health will be to eliminate not only wheat from your diet, but the other seven major cereal grains, as well: rye, barley, oats, corn, rice, millet, and sorghum.

Pseudo Grains

All eight of the commonly consumed cereal grains are true cereals because they are the seeds of grasses that botanically belong to the *Poaceae* family of plants. By now, there should be little doubt in your mind that true cereal grains are inferior foods and should be avoided. Yet what about starchy seeds that are frequently used by celiac patients and others to replace gluten-containing grains? Technically, these seeds are not true grasses because they are not members of the *Poaceae* family. They include chia seeds, amaranth, quinoa, and buckwheat. Let's take a look at the nutritional pros and cons of these seeds.

Antinutrients in Seeds

As with all aspects of human nutrition, we first need to look at the evolutionary clues before we come to sweeping conclusions about which foods and food groups we should regularly include in, or omit from, our diets. From what we know about historically studied foragers, they hunted, gathered, and fished for foods in a manner that maximized their caloric intake versus the energy they expended to obtain these foods. This food-gathering strategy is referred to by anthropologists as the optimal foraging theory. Based on the optimal foraging theory, hunter-gatherers typically maintained the following order of food preferences:

1. Large animals
2. Medium-size animals
3. Small animals, birds, and fish
4. Roots and tubers
5. Fruit
6. Honey
7. Nuts and seeds
8. Grass seeds (cereals)

You can see from this list that hunter-gatherers always preferred large animals if they were available—simply because they got more food calories for their caloric expenditure. Notice that seeds and cereals were at the bottom of the list. There is no doubt that foragers were opportunists, and if something was edible, it was probably consumed, but only if preferred foods couldn't be acquired first.

So yes, the evolutionary evidence supports the notion that if pseudo grains or even cereal grains were available, they would have been occasionally consumed.

Nevertheless, seeds and grains would never have been eaten on a daily basis as staple foods that make up 25 to 50 percent of one's daily energy. In support of this conclusion is my 2000 analysis of 229 hunter-gatherer diets revealing that animal foods—not plant foods—were the preferred staples. Moreover, most wild plant foods, particularly seeds, are not available on a year-round basis but can be harvested and consumed seasonally for only a few weeks or months out of the year. Let's see how this evolutionary insight is an important nutritional concept that has relevance today.

Seeds of any mature plant represent their reproductive future. If they are entirely consumed by animals such as insects, birds, rodents, or mammals or are destroyed by fungi and microorganisms, the seeds can't make their way into the soil, germinate, and produce the next generation of plants. In other words, plants don't produce seeds simply to feed other animals or microorganisms—if they did, they would rapidly become extinct.

Natural selection has come up with a number of strategies to ensure that a plant's seeds are not completely eaten or destroyed by predators and microorganisms. First, the seed can be protected by a hard shell that makes it difficult or impossible for the predator to eat the inner seed. An example that comes to mind is a Brazil nut. Second, plants frequently evolve thorns, spikes, and other hazardous structures to keep animals away, such as what we find with cactus thorns. Another seed-saving strategy is the evolution of a very hard seed surrounded by sweet fruit. With this evolutionary solution, the predator is encouraged to eat the entire fruit, seed and all. The hard seed survives the predator's digestive system and exits fully intact in a nice pile of fertilizing dung. Strawberries and crab apples are a good example of this evolutionary approach.

One important strategy a plant can take to protect its seeds is the evolution of lethally toxic or moderately toxic compounds to discourage predation and damage by animals and microorganisms. These compounds are called antinutrients. Unfortunately, antinutrients not only adversely affect microorganisms, insects, birds, rodents, and animals, but they also cause varying degrees of harmful effects in our own bodies. The good news about antinutrients found in our food supply is that their toxicity is generally dose dependent, meaning that they become more and more poisonous as we eat more and more foods that contain antinutrients.

Not all food antinutrients affect us in exactly the same manner. Some have minimal or subtle effects, a few are lethally toxic, and others have long-term adverse health effects that we are only beginning to understand.

Pseudo grains such as chia seeds, amaranth, quinoa, and buckwheat are loaded with a variety of moderately toxic antinutrients that probably have minimal adverse health effects if we eat them occasionally, in limited quantities, or for only short periods. This dietary pattern mimics how hunter-gatherers would have consumed plant seeds. In the wild, plants produce seeds seasonally for only a few weeks or months out of the year. With the advent of agriculture and long-term storage technologies, we can now eat any plant seed that we like every single day of the year.

That's the problem. Repeated high exposure to seed antinutrients can undermine the nutrient quality of our diets but, more important, may impair intestinal function, promote chronic low-level inflammation, and increase our susceptibility to allergies and autoimmune and other inflammatory diseases.

Chia Seeds

Chia seeds are small and oval shaped, either black or white colored; they resemble sesame seeds. They are native to southern Mexico and northern Guatemala and were cultivated as a food crop for thousands of years in this region by the Aztecs and other native cultures. Chia seeds can be consumed in a variety of ways, which include roasting and grinding the seeds into a flour known as chianpinolli that can then be made into tortillas, tamales, and beverages. The roasted ground seeds are traditionally consumed as a gruel called pinole.

In the last 20 years, chia seeds have become an increasingly popular item in co-ops and health food stores, primarily because of their high content of the healthful omega-3 fatty acid alpha linolenic acid (ALA). Chia seeds have also been fed to domestic livestock and chickens to enrich their meat and eggs with omega-3 fats. I can endorse feeding chia seeds to animals but have serious reservations when it comes to humans eating these seeds as staple foods.

At least on paper, it would appear that chia seeds are a nutritious food that is not only high in ALA but is also a good source of protein, fiber, certain B vitamins, calcium, iron, manganese, and zinc.

Unfortunately, as is the case with many other plant seeds, chia seeds contain numerous antinutrients that reduce their nutritional value. Chia seeds contain high phosphorus levels and are concentrated sources of phytate, an antinutrient that binds to many minerals, such as calcium, iron, zinc, magnesium, and copper, making them unavailable for absorption. In our bodies, chia seeds actually become inferior sources of all of these minerals. Chia seeds are also good sources of vitamin B_6; unfortunately, in our bodies the utilization of this vitamin from plant foods such as chia seeds is quite low, whereas the bioavailability of B_6 from animal products is quite high—approaching 100 percent.

One unusual characteristic of chia seed pinole or food products comes from a clear mucilaginous gel that surrounds the seeds. This sticky gel forms a barrier that impairs digestion and fat absorption and causes a low protein digestibility. Animal and human studies indicate that it is likely that other antinutrients, together with this gel, may promote a leaky gut, chronic systemic inflammation, and food allergies.

Don't eat grains, which include wheat, rye, barley, oats, corn, rice, sorghum, and millet. Avoid pseudo grains such as buckwheat, chia seeds, amaranth, and quinoa.

Amaranth, Quinoa, and Buckwheat

Many celiac patients or people who want to avoid gluten-containing grains frequently eliminate wheat, rye, and barley foods and substitute products that contain one or more pseudo grains—amaranth, quinoa, and buckwheat—or their flours. The market for gluten-free food items has become enormous in the last decade, with estimated consumer demand totaling 60 million people in the United States alone. If you have purchased gluten-free foods or are considering doing so, make sure that you read labels carefully, as sometimes the seed flours that replace gluten flours have nearly as many nutritional shortcomings as the foods they replace. The health problems associated with the habitual consumption of amaranth, quinoa, and buckwheat have not been as well studied as those for gluten-containing cereal grains. Nevertheless, there are important red flags that should grab your attention.

As I mentioned, all pseudo grains are chock-full of antinutrients. These substances represent the plant's evolutionary defense mechanisms against predation by insects, birds, rodents, and other animals, as well as a means to discourage infection by microorganisms. When we examine the chemical composition of almost all seed antinutrients, whether they come from cereals, legumes, or pseudo grains, a familiar pattern of compounds emerges.

When you think about any poisonous or toxic substance, it has to follow a number of key steps in your body to do its poisoning and cause illness. First, it has to get into your body—this means that it has to survive digestive processes and resist gut enzymes that normally break down toxic food proteins into their harmless amino acid components. We know from human and animal studies that almost all plant seeds contain protease inhibitors. These compounds neutralize predator gut enzymes that normally would degrade seed proteins or toxins into nonhazardous substances. If a plant seed is to deliver a lethal or partially lethal protein to a potential predator, the toxic compound has to survive the predator's digestive enzymes. Protease inhibitors found in plant seeds do precisely this. They allow plant seeds to deliver additional poisons to the host's next line of defense—its gut barrier.

In addition to protease inhibitors that protect seed toxins from the host's digestive enzymes, plant seeds have evolved a number of compounds that allow their toxins to penetrate the gut barrier. The most common gut-breeching chemicals are called saponins. Other gut-penetrating seed proteins are lectins; gliadin proteins from wheat, rye, and barley; and another category of substances known as thaumatin-like proteins. Each of these compounds works in a slightly different manner to compromise intestinal permeability, resulting in a condition known as leaky gut.

Once the gut barrier has been damaged, plant seed antinutrients can find their way into the bloodstream to disturb normal bodily functions, causing illnesses and disease. Antinutrient damage to the intestinal barrier allows toxins from bacteria and viruses found in the gut contents to enter the bloodstream as well.

Amaranth

As with all pseudo grains, unless you consume them as staples to replace cereals in your diet, they probably will have few adverse effects on your long-term health and well-being. Nevertheless, amaranth seeds and flour contain at least three potentially harmful antinutrients. First, the saponin content (790 mg/kg) of amaranth seeds is higher than in a variety of common human foods that have been shown to impair intestinal function and cause leaky gut, which can lead to an increased risk for allergies, autoimmune diseases, and chronic low-level inflammation.

Amaranth seeds are also concentrated sources of oxalic acid and contain four to five times more of this antinutrient than either cereals or legumes. Dietary oxalic acid is problematic because the more of it you consume, the greater your risk is for developing kidney stones.

The most disturbing antinutrient found in amaranth is a lectin commonly known as ACA. Experiments by Dr. Jonathan Rhodes have revealed that ACA is a potent promoter of cancer cell growth in the intestines.

Quinoa

Quinoa is a pseudo grain with origins in South America. Like amaranth and chia seeds, it contains numerous antinutrients, including saponins, protease inhibitors, phytate, and tannins. A potential health-threatening component in quinoa is its high saponin content—up to 5,000 mg/kg. In both rat and tissue experiments, saponins from quinoa seeds increased intestinal permeability.

As I mentioned, a leaky gut may lead to many health problems and is thought to be one of the essential triggers for autoimmune diseases. If you currently have an autoimmune disease or if you have a family history of these illnesses, I would definitely recommend that you avoid quinoa and all other pseudo grains.

Buckwheat

This plant produces a starchy seed that is ground into flour that is frequently made into noodles widely consumed in Japan, China, and Korea. It can be made into porridges or even mixed with yeast to produce pancakes. Because buckwheat contains no gluten, the flour and its products are often used by celiac patients as substitutes for wheat, rye, and barley.

From a health and nutrition perspective, buckwheat has not been examined in nearly the same detail as true cereal grains or even other pseudo grains, so the jury is still out on how it may affect our long-term health and well-being. Nevertheless, allergists worldwide have taken a great interest in buckwheat because it is such a potent and fatal allergen. Buckwheat allergy seems to be common in Asian countries and frequently causes life-threatening allergic reactions called anaphylactic shock that do not lessen after childhood.

Like other pseudo grains, buckwheat is a concentrated source of protease inhibitors, which are suspected in causing buckwheat's powerful allergic responses. One unusual detrimental health effect of buckwheat consumption is a damaging skin reaction frequently shown in many animal experiments. This response is caused when sunlight reacts with dietary buckwheat compounds that make their way into the skin. How this adverse effect occurs is currently unknown.

As with other pseudo grains, I cannot recommend that you eat buckwheat, except on an infrequent basis. You will be much better off completely avoiding buckwheat and eating more fresh meats, seafood, fish, and fruits and veggies.

The Trouble with Beans

One question that comes up time and again is, "Why can't I eat beans?" I'll show you why legumes are inferior foods that should not be part of the Paleo Diet.

It may come as a surprise to you, but as recently as 15 years ago, imports of red kidney beans into South Africa were legally prohibited because of "their potential toxicity to humans." Many people think about kidney beans as nutritious, plant-based, high-protein foods, but indeed they are toxic. Unless adequately soaked and boiled, kidney beans and almost all legumes produce detrimental effects in our bodies. Starting in the early 1970s, a number of scientific papers reported that consumption of raw or undercooked red kidney beans caused nausea, vomiting, abdominal pain, severe diarrhea, muscle weakness, and inflammation of the heart. Similar symptoms were documented in horses and cattle. Furthermore, raw kidney beans were lethally toxic to rats when fed at more than 37 percent of their daily calories.

These clues should make us proceed cautiously as we consider the nutritional benefits and liabilities of beans and legumes.

The Questionable Nutrient Content of Beans and Legumes

As a child growing up in Southern California in the 1950s, I was always playing around swimming pools and open water. My mother enrolled me in a swim class by the time I was a toddler. Later in my childhood, one of my great disappointments on hot summer afternoons was that Mom made me wait an entire hour after lunch before I could get back into the water. As did almost everyone else of that era, Mom assumed that if she didn't take this precaution, I could potentially end up with paralyzing stomach cramps, which in turn would cause me to drown. A decade later, as I trained to become a beach lifeguard, this same belief was repeated in the lifesaving manual that was used to educate every lifeguard in the country. At the time, I never questioned this fundamental rule. I didn't even think about it. It simply was the way it was—yesterday, today, and presumably forever.

In nutrition we can frequently find these same dyed-in-the-wool beliefs, which, on careful scrutiny, make little sense. After the full story is presented to us in a logical and straightforward manner, we wonder why we ever believed in such silly ideas in the first place. If we examine the USDA's recommendations, governmental nutritionists have arbitrarily created five food groups: (1) grains, (2) vegetables, (3) fruits, (4) dairy, and (5) protein foods. I would agree that most common foods could logically be placed into one of these five categories, except for one glaring exception—protein foods.

The USDA has decided that protein foods should include: (1) meat, (2) poultry, (3) fish, (4) eggs, (5) nuts and seeds, and (6) dried beans and peas. I have little disagreement that meat, poultry, fish, and eggs are good sources of protein. The USDA, however, tells us that these six protein foods items are equivalent and can be used interchangeably with one another—that animal protein sources, including meats, poultry, fish, and eggs, are nutritionally comparable to plant protein sources: nuts, seeds, and dried beans and peas. I quote the USDA MyPyramid/MyPlate recommendations: "Beans and peas are the mature forms of legumes. They include kidney beans, pinto beans, black beans, lima beans, black-eyed peas, garbanzo beans (chickpeas), split peas and lentils. They are available in dry, canned, and frozen forms. These foods are excellent sources of plant protein, and also provide other nutrients such as iron and zinc. They are similar to meats, poultry, and fish in their contribution of these nutrients. Therefore, they are considered part of the Protein Foods Group. Many people consider beans and peas as vegetarian alternatives for meat."

Let's see how beans and peas stack up to meats, poultry, fish, and eggs in terms of protein, iron, and zinc, as alluded to by the USDA. In the graph on the following page you can see that on a calorie-by-calorie basis, legumes are utter lightweights when compared to the protein content of lean poultry, beef, pork, and seafood. Nuts and seeds fare even worse. Beans, peas, and other legumes contain 66 percent less protein than either lean chicken or turkey and 61 percent less protein than lean beef, pork, and seafood. What the USDA doesn't tell us is that our bodies don't process bean and legume proteins nearly as efficiently as they do animal proteins—meaning that the proteins found in beans, peas, and other legumes have poor digestibility.

The Food and Agricultural Organization and World Health Organization of the United Nations have devised a protein quality index known as the Protein Digestibility-Corrected Amino Acid Score (PDCAAS). This index reveals that beans and other legumes maintain second-rate PDCAAS ratings that average 20 to 25 percent lower than animal protein ratings. So legumes and beans not

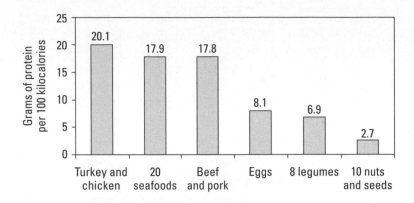

Protein in Various Foods

only contain about three times less protein than animal foods, but what little protein they do have is poorly digested. Their poor PDCAAS scores stem from a variety of antinutrients that impair protein absorption and from low levels of two essential amino acids, cysteine and methionine.

I have no idea how the USDA concluded that legumes are "excellent sources of plant protein . . . similar to meats, poultry, and fish in their contribution of these nutrients."

The same questionable conclusions are applied to the average iron and zinc content of eight commonly eaten legumes: green peas, lentils, kidney beans, lima beans, garbanzo beans (chickpeas), black-eyed peas, mung beans, and soybeans. When you look at straight data, the iron content of legumes appears to be similar to that of seafood and about twice as high as in lean meats and eggs. This data is misleading, though, because it doesn't tell us how legume iron is handled in our bodies. Experimental human studies from Dr. Cook in Switzerland and from Dr. Hallberg in Sweden have shown that only 20 to 25 percent of the iron in legumes is available for absorption because it is bound to phytate. In reality, the high iron content of legumes (2.2 mg/100 kcal) plummets by 75 to 80 percent when our bodies attempt to digest beans and peas, thereby making legumes a poor source of iron compared to animal foods. A similar situation occurs with zinc, as phytate and other antinutrients in legumes severely reduce its absorption in our bodies. Given that this information has been known for more than 30 years, it defies logic how the USDA could misinform the American public.

Healing Inflammation

Craig's Story

I had not been feeling well for several years. After I saw several rheumatologists and many doctors, they were not sure what was happening except that I was exhibiting symptoms of inflammation throughout my body (muscular and gut)—minimal joint pain but back and hip stiffness. My energy level was very low. I visited chiropractors and took Celebrex on an as-needed basis.

I searched and found an article dated April 18, 2000, in the WebMD archives that was written by Elizabeth Tracey on possible (lectin) grain, pea, and bean/gut changes/inflammation linkages to arthritis. Loren Cordain's name was mentioned. Beans and peas cause me great digestive and bowel issues.

I immediately stopped eating wheat, barley, peas, and beans and then began to feel great! People even notice a difference. It seems within a few days all of my symptoms have disappeared. My energy level and general feeling of well-being have increased dramatically! I am most relieved and hope I have finally found the answer.

The Purpose of Antinutrients

You can see how misleading it is to evaluate the nutritional and health effects of beans and other legumes simply by analyzing their nutrient content on paper, as the USDA has done. Before we can pass nutritional judgment on any food, it is essential to determine how it actually acts within our bodies. Beans are not good sources of either zinc or iron, and they have low protein digestibility because legumes are chock-full of antinutrients that impair our bodies' ability to absorb and assimilate potential nutrients found in these foods.

As was the case with the antinutrients found in whole grains, the primary purpose of most antinutrients in legumes is to discourage predation and prevent destruction of the plant's seeds, its reproductive materials, by microorganisms, insects, birds, rodents, and large mammals. We most frequently refer to legume seeds as beans. I've included peanuts here, which are not nuts at all; they are actually legumes. If you're unfamiliar with scientific names for plants, you may be surprised that many different versions of the beans we frequently eat are actually the exact same species—and contain comparable concentrations of toxic antinutrients. If you enjoy Mexican food, then you have probably tasted *Phaseolus vulgaris* as either refried beans or black beans, because these two beans are the same species, differing only by color. Great northern beans, green beans, kidney beans, navy beans, pinto beans, and white kidney beans are also members of the same species, *Phaseolus vulgaris*. All beans that are members of *Phaseolus vulgaris* contain some of the highest concentrations of antinutrients known.

The list of antinutrients found in legumes, beans, and soy includes lectins, saponins, phytate, polyphenols such as tannins and isoflavones, protease inhibitors, raffinose oligosaccharides, cyanogenic glycosides, and favism glycosides. This list looks formidable at first because of all of the scientific terms, but don't worry—the concepts underlying how these toxins may impair our health are easily understood. Let's go through this list so that you can clearly understand why you should avoid legumes.

Lectins

Earlier in the book, when I discussed cereals, I mentioned that almost all whole grains are concentrated sources of lectins. The same can be said for virtually all legumes. Lectins are potent antinutrients that plants have evolved as toxins to ward off predators. Raw or undercooked kidney beans have caused severe cases of food poisoning in humans and were shown to be lethally toxic in rats. Although several kidney bean antinutrients probably contributed to these poisonous effects, animal experiments indicate that a specific lectin found in kidney beans was the main culprit. Kidney beans and all other varieties of beans within the *Phaseolus vulgaris* species—black beans, kidney beans, pinto beans, string beans, navy beans, and so on—contain a lectin called phytohemagglutinin (PHA). The more PHA we ingest, the sicker we become. This is why raw beans are so toxic—they contain much higher concentrations of PHA than cooked beans do. Cooking doesn't completely eliminate PHA, however, and even small amounts of this lectin are known to produce adverse health effects, providing they can penetrate our gut barrier.

The trick with lectins is that they must bypass our intestinal walls and enter into our bloodstream if they are to wreak havoc within our bodies. So far, no human studies of PHA have been conducted. Yet in laboratory animals, PHA easily breeches the gut barrier and enters into the bloodstream, where it may travel to many organs and tissues and disrupt normal cell function, causing disease.

Human tissue experiments reveal that PHA and other food lectins can cause a leaky gut. A leaky gut represents one of the first steps implicated in many autoimmune diseases. Impaired intestinal integrity produced by dietary lectins may also cause low-level inflammation in our bloodstream—a necessary precursor in developing atherosclerosis and cancer.

Besides kidney beans and other bean varieties within *Phaseolus vulgaris* species, all other legumes contain lectins with varying degrees of toxicity, ranging from mild to lethal. Soybean lectin (SBA) is also known to impair intestinal permeability and cause a leaky gut. Peanut lectin (PNA) is the only legume lectin to have been tested in living humans by Dr. Rhodes's research group in London. Within less than an hour after ingestion by healthy normal subjects, PNA entered their bloodstreams—not a good thing because it then had the capacity to interact with virtually every cell in their bodies.

The lectins found in peas (PSA) and lentils (LCA) seem to be much less toxic than PHA, SBA, or PNA, but they are not completely without adverse effects in tissue and animal experiments. Although no long-term lectin experiments have yet been conducted in humans, from animal and tissue studies we know that these antinutrients damage the intestinal barrier, impair growth, alter normal immune function, and cause inflammation.

Saponins

The word "saponin" is derived from the Latin word for "soap." Saponins are antinutrients found in almost all legumes. They have soaplike properties that punch holes in the membranes lining the exterior of every cell. As was the case with lectins, this effect is dose dependent—the more saponins we ingest, the greater will be the damage to our bodies' cells. Our first line of defense against any antinutrient is our gut barrier. Human tissue and animal studies confirm that legume saponins can easily disrupt the cells that line our intestines and rapidly make their way into our bloodstream. Once in the bloodstream in sufficient quantities, saponins can cause ruptures in our red blood cells in a process known as hemolysis, which can temporarily impair our blood's oxygen-carrying capacity. The main threat to our health from legume saponins stems not from red blood cell damage but rather from saponins' ability to increase intestinal permeability. A leaky gut likely promotes low-level inflammation because it allows toxins and bacteria in our guts to interact with our immune systems. This process is known to be a necessary first step in developing autoimmune diseases and may promote the inflammation necessary for heart disease and cancer to develop and progress.

The other major problem with legume saponins is that cooking does not destroy them. In fact, even after extended boiling for 2 hours, 85 to 100 percent of the original saponins in most beans and legumes remain intact. And the concentration of saponins in soy protein isolates and textured vegetable protein is dangerously high. If you are an athlete or anyone else trying to increase your protein intake by supplementing with soy protein isolates, I suggest that you reconsider. A much healthier strategy would be to eat more lean meats and sea-food. These protein-packed foods taste a lot better than artificial soy isolates and are much better for your body. If we eat legumes only occasionally, saponin dam-age to our intestines will quickly repair itself; however, when legumes or soy products are consumed in high amounts as staples or daily supplements, the risk for developing a leaky gut and the diseases associated with it is greatly increased. On the other hand, by eating fermented soy products such as tofu, tempeh, or sprouted beans, you can lower your saponin intake.

Phytate

Because phytate prevents the full absorption of iron, zinc, calcium, and magne-sium in legumes and whole grains, reliance on these plant foods frequently causes multiple nutritional deficiencies in adults, children, and even nursing infants. Boiling and cooking don't seem to have much effect on the phytate con-tent of legumes, whereas sprouting and fermentation can moderately reduce phytate concentrations. Also, vitamin C counteracts phytate's inhibitory effects on mineral absorption. That said, the best tactic to reduce phytate in your diet is to adopt the Paleo Diet—humanity's original legume- and grain-free diet.

Polyphenols: Tannins and Isoflavones

Polyphenols are antioxidant compounds that protect plants from UV sunlight damage and from insects, pests, and other microorganisms. Just as sunscreens protect our skin from ultraviolet damage, polyphenols are one of the compounds that plants have evolved to prevent the harmful effects of ultraviolet (UV) radia-tion from the sun, along with damage caused by animal and microorganism predators. Polyphenols come in many different varieties and forms and are com-mon throughout the plant kingdom.

When we eat these compounds, they seem to have both healthful and detri-mental effects in our bodies. For instance, resveratrol is a polyphenol found in red grapes that may increase the life span of mice and slow or prevent many diseases. On the other hand, at least two types of polyphenols—tannins and isoflavones—in beans, soy, and other legumes may have adverse effects in our bodies.

Tannins are bitter-tasting polyphenols and give wine its astringent qualities. As with all antinutrients, the more tannin you ingest, the greater is the potential to disrupt your health. Tannins are similar to phytate, in that they reduce protein digestibility and bind iron and other minerals, preventing their normal absorption. Tannins damage our intestines, causing a leaky gut and allowing gut bacteria entry into our circulatory systems, thus encouraging low-level inflammation—a process intimately tied to heart disease, cancer, and autoimmune illnesses. By now you can see that legumes, beans, and soy represent a triple threat to our intestinal integrity because three separate antinutrients—lectins, saponins, and tannins—all work together to cause a leaky gut.

Isoflavones are some of nature's weirder plant compounds, in that they act like female hormones in our bodies. Certain isoflavones concentrated in soybeans and soy products are called phytoestrogens or plant estrogens. Isoflavones from soy products can cause goiters, an enlargement of the thyroid gland, particularly if your blood levels of iodine are low. Two phytoestrogens in soy, genistein and daidzein, produced goiters in experimental animals.

You don't have to develop full-blown goiters by consuming these soy isoflavones to impair your health. In a study of elderly subjects, Dr. Ishizuki and colleagues demonstrated that when subjects with an average age of 61 were given 30 grams of soy daily for 3 months, they developed symptoms of low thyroid function—malaise, lethargy, and constipation. Half of these people ended up with goiters.

For women, the regular intake of soy or soy isoflavones may disrupt certain hormones that regulate the normal menstrual cycle. In a meta-analysis of 47 studies, Dr. Hooper demonstrated that soy or soy isoflavone consumption caused two female hormones, follicle-stimulating hormone (FSH) and luteinizing hormone (LH), to fall by 20 percent.

Dr. Pirke at the University of Trier in Germany studied the effect of vegetarian diets on menstrual health and he found that seven of nine women who adhered to vegetarian diets for only 6 weeks stopped ovulating. One of the hormonal changes reported in this study, concurrent with the cessation of normal periods, was a significant decline in LH. Because Western vegetarian diets almost always contain lots of soy and soy isoflavones, it is entirely possible that soy isoflavones were directly responsible for the decline in LH and the disruption of normal menstrual periods documented in this study.

I have received e-mails from women all over the world whose menstrual and infertility problems subsided after they adopted the Paleo Diet. Their stories paint a credible picture that modern-day Paleo diets contain multiple nutritional elements that may improve or eliminate female reproductive and menstrual problems. Unfortunately, scientific validation of these women's experiences still lies in the future. But you don't have to wait—the potential benefits of the Paleo Diet are enormous, and the risks are minimal.

Perhaps the most worrisome effects of soy isoflavones may occur in developing fetuses with iodine-deficient mothers and in infants who receive soy formula. A 2007 paper by Dr. Gustavo Roman implicated soy isoflavones as risk factors for autism via their ability to impair normal iodine metabolism and thyroid function. Specifically, the soy isoflavone known as genistein may inhibit a key iodine-based enzyme required for normal brain development. Pregnant women with borderline iodine status can become iodine deficient if they have a diet that is high in soy. Their deficiency may then be conveyed to their developing fetuses, impairing growth in fetal brain cells known to be involved in autism. Infants born with iodine deficiencies are made worse if they are fed a soy formula.

Once again, the evolutionary lesson repeats itself. If a food or a nutrient generally was not a part of our ancestral diet, it has a high probability of disrupting our health and that of our children.

Protease Inhibitors

Very few people on the planet know about protease inhibitors. Yet I can tell you that when you eat beans, soy, or other legumes, you should be as aware of protease inhibitors as you are of a radar trap on the freeway.

When we eat any type of protein, enzymes in our intestines break the protein down into its component amino acids. These enzymes are called proteases and must be operating normally for our bodies to properly assimilate dietary proteins. Almost all legumes are concentrated sources of antinutrients called protease inhibitors, which prevent our gut enzymes from degrading protein into amino acids. Protease inhibitors found in beans, soy, peanuts, and other legumes are part of the reason why legume proteins have lower bioavailability than meat proteins. In experimental animals, ingestion of protease inhibitors in high amounts depresses normal growth and causes pancreatic enlargement.

Heating and cooking effectively destroy about 80 percent of the protease inhibitors found in most legumes, so the dietary concentrations of these antinutrients found in beans and soy are thought to have few harmful effects in our bodies. Yet at least one important adverse effect of protease inhibitors may have been overlooked.

When the gut's normal protein-degrading enzymes are inhibited by legume protease inhibitors, the pancreas works harder and compensates by secreting more protein-degrading enzymes. Consequently, the consumption of protease inhibitors causes levels of protein-degrading enzymes to rise within our intestines. One enzyme in particular, called trypsin, increases significantly. The rise in trypsin concentrations inside our gut is not without consequence, because elevated trypsin levels increase intestinal permeability, contributing to a leaky gut.

Raffinose Oligosaccharides

Here's another big scientific term for a little problem almost every one of us has had to deal with at one time or another after we ate beans: "Beans, beans, the musical fruit; the more you eat the more you . . . " Almost every schoolchild in the United States could complete this limerick. Plain and simple, beans cause gas or flatulence. Almost all legumes contain complex sugars called oligosaccharides. In particular, two complex sugars, raffinose and stachyose, are the culprits and are the elements in beans that give us gas. We lack the gut enzymes to break down these complex sugars into simpler sugars. Consequently, bacteria in our intestines metabolize these oligosaccharides into a variety of gases—hydrogen, carbon dioxide, and methane.

Beans don't affect everyone equally. Some people experience extreme digestive discomfort, with diarrhea, nausea, intestinal rumbling, and flatulence, whereas others are almost symptomless. These differences among people seem to be caused by varying types of gut flora.

Cyanogenic Glycosides

Some of us have food dislikes that have been with us since childhood. Perhaps the world's most well-known food dislike comes from the 41st president of the United States, George H. W. Bush: "I do not like broccoli and I haven't liked it since I was a little kid, and my mother made me eat it. And I'm president of the United States, and I'm not going to eat any more broccoli." My personal aversion is to coconuts. My father-in-law absolutely can't tolerate the thought of lima beans. His dislike is a good one that may involve heightened sensitivity to antinutrients in lima beans called cyanogenic glycosides. When digested, these compounds are turned into the lethal poison hydrogen cyanide in our intestines. Fortunately, cooking eliminates most of the hydrogen cyanide in lima beans. Nevertheless, a number of fatal poisonings have been reported in the medical literature from people eating raw or undercooked lima beans.

Although most of us would never consider eating raw lima beans, the problem doesn't end here. When cooked, most of the hydrogen cyanide in lima beans is converted into a compound called thiocyanate, which, along with soy isoflavones, is a dietary antinutrient that impairs iodine metabolism and causes goiter. Remember that in iodine-deficient children, these so-called goitrogens are suspect dietary agents underlying autism.

Favism Glycosides

Most of us in the United States have never tasted broad beans, also known as fava or faba beans. In Mediterranean, Middle Eastern, and North African countries, broad beans are more popular. Unfortunately for many people in these countries, particularly young children, the consumption of fava beans can be lethal. It has been intuitively known for centuries that fava bean consumption was fatal in certain people. Yet the biochemistry of the disease favism has been worked out only in the last 50 years or so.

Favism can only occur in people with a genetic defect called G6PD deficiency. This mutation is the most common human enzyme defect, which is present in more than 400 million people worldwide. It is thought to confer protection against malaria. People whose genetic background can be traced to Italy, Greece, the Middle East, or North Africa are at a much higher risk for carrying this mutation.

If you or your children don't know whether you have the genes that cause favism, a simple blood test available at most hospitals and medical clinics can diagnose this problem. Consumption of fava beans in genetically susceptible people causes a massive rupturing of red blood cells that is called hemolytic anemia. It may frequently be fatal in small children unless blood transfusions are given immediately. Not all people with G6PD deficiency experience favism symptoms after they eat broad beans, but if your family background is from the Mediterranean region, you may be particularly susceptible.

Although it is not completely known how broad bean consumption causes favism, three antinutrient glycosides (divicine, isouramil, and convicine) found in these legumes likely do the damage. These compounds enter our bloodstream, and in people with the G6PD mutations they interact with red blood cells in a manner that causes them to rupture.

Peanuts and Heart Disease

What's wrong with peanut oil and peanuts? Most nutritional experts would tell us that they are heart-healthy foods because they contain little saturated fat and most of their fat is made up of cholesterol-lowering monounsaturated and polyunsaturated fats. On the surface, you might think that peanut oil would probably be helpful in preventing the artery-clogging process that underlies heart disease. Your thoughts were not much different from those of nutritional scientists—until they actually tested peanuts and peanut oil in laboratory animals.

Beginning in the 1960s and continuing into the 1980s, scientists unexpectedly found peanut oil to be highly atherogenic, causing arterial plaques to form in rabbits, rats, and primates. Only a single study showed otherwise. Peanut oil was found to be so atherogenic that it continues to be routinely fed to rabbits to produce atherosclerosis to study the disease.

Initially, it was unclear how a seemingly healthful oil could be so toxic in such a wide variety of animals. Dr. David Kritchevsky was able to show with a series of experiments that peanut oil lectin (PNA) was most likely responsible for its artery-clogging properties. Lectins are large protein molecules; most scientists had presumed that digestive enzymes in our guts would degrade lectins into their component amino acids. It was assumed that the intact lectin molecule would not be able to get into the bloodstream to do its dirty work. But they were wrong—it turned out that lectins were highly resistant to the gut's protein-degrading enzymes.

An experiment conducted by Dr. Wang and colleagues and published in the prestigious medical journal *Lancet* revealed that PNA got into the bloodstream intact in as few as 1 to 4 hours after subjects ate a handful of roasted, salted peanuts. Even though the concentrations of PNA in the subjects' blood were quite low, they were still at concentrations known to cause atherosclerosis in experiments on animals. Lectins are a lot like superglue—it doesn't take much. These proteins can bind to a wide variety of cells in the body, including the cells lining the arteries. And indeed, it was found that PNA did its damage to the arteries by binding to a specific sugar receptor. The takeaway is to stay away from both peanuts and peanut oil. There are much better options!

As you adopt the Paleo Diet or any diet, listen to your body. If a food or a food type doesn't agree with you or makes you feel ill or unwell, don't eat it. I should have listened to my own advice 25 years ago when I was experimenting with vegetarian diets. Whenever I ate beans or legumes, I experienced digestive upset and gas and frequently had diarrhea. Since I've embraced the Paleo Diet almost 20 years ago, these symptoms have become a thing of the past.

Potatoes Should Stay below Ground

Should we be eating potatoes, sweet potatoes, yams, and other tubers, or not? There was a time in my life back in the late 1970s and early 1980s when I thought that if I eliminated red meat, eggs, and other animal products and ate a mainly plant-based diet, I would become healthier, decrease my risk for developing heart disease and cancer, and live a longer, fuller life. Part of this conceptual package meant that I should replace meat proteins with whole grains, legumes, potatoes, and other tubers. I faithfully followed the recommendations of such vegetarian gurus of that time as Frances Moore Lappe, Dick Gregory, and others.

Once I started to eat in this manner, I immediately noticed gastrointestinal tract problems—bloating, gas, intermittent diarrhea, joint aches, back problems, increased upper respiratory illnesses, and an inability to train and run at higher intensities. The vegetarian diet books of that era simply told us that it would take time for our bodies to adjust to beans, legumes, whole grains, and tubers. Well, after months and months, my body never did adapt—my symptoms got worse, not better. I should have listened to my body, but no—I simply assumed that the nutritional experts of this era knew better than I and that my symptoms must be some sort of anomaly.

Being a trusting soul, I continued with these nutritional experiments into my early and midthirties. Each and every time I went back to vegan or vegetarian dieting, everything about my health, well-being, and athletic performance declined. It took me a while to get it—diets based on whole grains, legumes, and tubers simply did not work in my body.

Even after all of these on-and-off-again experiments in my life, I tried plant-based diets one last time. Just before I got married and was approaching my fourth decade, I revisited vegetarian dieting. For breakfast, I would eat either brown rice, skim milk, and sliced bananas or a big bowl of boiled potatoes with salt and pepper. In those days, I typically got up and did a 3- to 5-mile run before 7:00 am and then ate breakfast. By 9:00 or 10:00 o'clock, I was famished and agitated, and it was all I could do to make it through until noon to put more high-starch, plant-based foods into my body. By 3:00 o'clock, I was in the same boat and couldn't wait to get home and eat more plant starch—brown rice, potatoes, chili with beans—anything.

I'll never forget how bad early morning breakfasts of potatoes made me feel. They left me drained of energy and feeling nervous, agitated, and depressed— only a few hours after my morning meal. I lived with it.

In the early 1980s, a brand new concept called the glycemic index, developed by Dr. David Jenkins at the University of Toronto, had just emerged. It showed us that certain foods—such as potatoes—caused our blood sugar levels to precipitously rise and then dramatically fall. It was this effect that made me feel so bad. Potatoes for breakfast caused my blood sugar levels to spike—only to fall drastically below their original levels shortly thereafter.

Once I figured out how potatoes affected my body, I began to finally question whether vegetarian diets were nourishing or actually caused harmful effects. I now fully understand how potatoes are one of the worst foods we can eat. As with all plant foods, sporadic consumption of potatoes will have little impact on your overall health, but if you eat them regularly as the majority of your daily calories, your health will suffer. Let me explain why.

In the United States, we eat a lot of potatoes. The per capita consumption of potato foods for every person in the United States in 2007 was 126 pounds. Out of that total, we ate:

Frozen potatoes: 53 percent

Fresh potatoes: 44 percent

Potato chips: 16 percent

Dehydrated potatoes: 13 percent

From this breakdown, you can see that most of the potatoes consumed in the United States are highly processed in the form of french fries, mashed potatoes, dehydrated potato products, and potato chips. Processed potato foods typically are made with multiple additives—salt, vegetable oils, trans fats, refined sugars, dairy products, cereal grains, and preservatives—that may adversely affect our health in a variety of ways.

Let's take a look at the glycemic indices of various potato foods (see the chart on the following page) and contrast them with those of refined sugars, and you can clearly see that almost all potato products have glycemic indices that are substantially higher than sucrose—table sugar—or high-fructose corn syrup. Eating potatoes is a lot like eating pure sugars, but it's even worse for you because of the harm these starchy tubers do to your blood sugar levels.

Comparison of Glycemic Indices among Refined Sugars and Potato Foods

Item	Glycemic Index
POTATO FOODS	
Russet Burbank potatoes, baked without fat	111
Potato, white, without skin, baked	98
Pontiac potato, peeled and baked	93
Red potatoes, boiled with skin	89
Sebago potato, peeled, boiled 35 minutes	87
Mashed potatoes	83
French fries, frozen, reheated in microwave	75
Potato chips	60
REFINED SUGARS	
Glucose (dextrose)	100
Sucrose	60–65
High-fructose corn syrup	60–65
Honey	48

It is obvious why those potato breakfasts I ate 25 years ago made me feel so awful. I may just as well have been consuming pure sugar or several candy bars for breakfast.

Because potatoes maintain one of the highest glycemic index values of any food, they cause our blood sugar levels to rise rapidly, which in turn immediately makes our blood insulin concentrations increase. When these two metabolic responses occur repeatedly for a week or two, we start to become insulin resistant—a condition that frequently precedes the development of a series of diseases known as metabolic syndrome.

During the course of months and years, insulin resistance leads to a multitude of devastating health effects. The list of metabolic syndrome diseases is long: obesity, type 2 diabetes, cardiovascular disease, high blood pressure, high blood cholesterol and other abnormal blood chemistries, systemic inflammation, gout, acne, skin tags, and breast, colon, and prostate cancers. A Paleo diet is your best medicine for metabolic syndrome because it eliminates not only high-glycemic potatoes from your diet, but also virtually every other food that spikes your blood sugar levels. When you trade in potatoes, grains, dairy, and processed foods for fresh fruits, veggies, meat, and seafood, diseases of insulin resistance and metabolic syndrome will no longer trouble you. A wonderful success story was sent to me by Dr. Lane Sebring, a general practitioner whose first prescription for his metabolic syndrome patients is *The Paleo Diet.*

Curing Metabolic Syndrome

Dr. Lane Sebring's Story

About half of the new patients to my clinic know I am a strong proponent of the Paleo Diet before they get here, and about one-third have either heard about the paleo diet. It truly is the best tool I have to help my patients. One day a 43-year-old, 5'8", 224-pound man—a pack-and-a-half-a-day smoker who had been on blood pressure meds for 3 years—was brought in by his wife, complaining of blurry vision. I noticed that he had lost 9 pounds since I last saw him, and his blood pressure was 170/100. I also noticed that his neck was smaller since I last saw him—more than you would expect with a 9-pound weight loss, something I've seen with new-onset diabetes. I asked him whether he had been getting up a lot in the middle of the night to go to the bathroom. He said, "Yes, how did you know?"

I checked his blood sugar, and it was 611. I increased his blood pressure medication and told him about diabetes. I started him on Avandia for diabetes and told him to read *The Paleo Diet.* Well, he didn't read it, but his wife did. She took away his lunch money and brought him lunch. At the 2-week follow-up visit, he had lost about 3 more pounds and was complaining about no salt and no potatoes, but his blood pressure was fine, and his blood glucose was 254. I gave him some more samples and a script and told him to come back in 8 weeks.

At follow-up, he had lost about 4 pounds, his blood glucose was 79, and his blood pressure was 112/72, so I praised him and his wife for their good work. The wife then said almost apologetically, "Dr. Sebring, I'm sorry, but we just couldn't afford the prescription you gave us. He hasn't taken any pills at all in 3 weeks."

He weighs 178 pounds now and is no longer diabetic or hypertensive, and you couldn't get him off the diet.

Dr. Sebring's success in curing metabolic syndrome diseases in his patients are not isolated examples, as I have had people from all over the world and from all walks of life contact me.

Root and Tuber Vegetables

Approximately 96 vegetable crops are grown worldwide that fit under the catch-all phrase "roots and tubers." Root and tuber vegetables are actually the underground food-storage organs of various plants. These edible below-ground organs are classified into one of five categories: roots, tubers, rhizomes, corms, and bulbs.

Some commonly consumed roots are carrots, parsnips, radishes, beets, rutabagas, sweet potatoes, cassava, and celeriac. Frequently eaten tubers include potatoes and yams. Examples of edible rhizomes are arrowroot, ginger, and turmeric. Corms include taro and Chinese water chestnuts; common edible bulbs include onions and garlic. Crops with an enlarged stem, such as leeks and kohlrabi, even when located underground, are generally not classified as roots and tubers.

My recommendation for overweight subjects or for people with diseases of insulin resistance—type 2 diabetes, hypertension, dyslipidemia (elevated triglycerides, low HDL, elevated small dense LDL), coronary heart disease, gout, and acne—is not to exceed a glycemic load of 10 for any given meal and to keep the day's glycemic load under 40. If you look at the table on the opposite page carefully, you can see that a 100-gram (around ¼-pound) serving of baked potato would provide you with half of your daily glycemic-load allotment. Not a good choice, for many reasons. A similar serving of sweet potato would be a better choice, with a glycemic load of 14.8; better choices still would be beets, rutabagas, or carrots, which under normal circumstances you can basically eat until you are full, as it would be quite difficult to consume enough of these foods to exceed a daily glycemic load of 40. Although the glycemic index and load values for celeriac have not yet been determined, the amount of carbohydrate per 100 grams (9.2 g) is similar to that for beets, rutabagas, and carrots. It is likely that celeriac has a similar low glycemic load and presents no problems. The same goes for turnips. Enjoy these healthful root and tuber vegetables.

Remember the 85-15 rule: If one is compliant with the diet 85 percent of the time, significant improvements in health could occur. I still adhere to this principle, and I believe that minor dietary indiscretions involving potatoes, sweet potatoes, or any other root or tuber on an occasional basis will have few unfavorable effects on your long-term health. In fact, for highly fit athletes or for healthy, normal-weight individuals who do a significant amount of exercise on a daily basis, sweet potatoes and yams represent a good source of carbohydrates, which

Comparison of Common Root Vegetables (in ¼-pound samples)

	Carbs	Glycemic Index	Glycemic Load
Cassava (manioc, tapioca)	38.1	70	26.6
Potato, baked	25.2	85	21.4
Taro	34.6	55	19.0
Parsnips	19.5	97	18.9
Sweet potato, baked	24.3	61	14.8
Yam	27.6	37	10.2
Beet	10.0	64	6.4
Rutabagas	8.7	72	6.3
Carrots	10.5	47	4.9
Jerusalem artichoke	17.4	na	na
Chicory	17.5	na	na
Burdock root	17.4	na	na
Celeriac	9.2	na	na
Turnip	62	na	na

are necessary to replenish your muscles' spent glycogen stores. All tubers are net base (alkaline) yielding vegetables; accordingly, they represent superior carbohydrate sources, compared to cereal grains, because they do not leach calcium from our bones or amino acids from our muscles, as do acid-yielding grains. Additionally, when fully cooked and peeled, these vegetables maintain low concentrations of antinutrients known to be harmful to our health. The two exceptions to this general rule are potatoes and cassava, both of which contain a number of antinutrients that, when present in high concentrations, can be toxic or even lethal.

We rarely consume cassava in the United States except as tapioca, and you can see from the table above that it has an exceptionally high glycemic load. This characteristic alone should make us shy away from eating this starchy root. Cassava, like lima beans, contains an antinutrient called cyanogenic glycoside, which, unless cooked sufficiently, can be converted into hydrogen cyanide, a deadly poison. Even when fully cooked, cassava root's cyanogenic glycosides are converted into thiocyanates, which may aggravate iodine deficiencies.

Potato Antinutrients

Cereal grains and legumes contain many antinutrients, which I discuss in the sections devoted to those foods; these compounds may have far-reaching effects on the quality of our diet and health. Unfortunately, most nutritionists have zero knowledge of antinutrients—much less how they may impair body function and promote disease. Even governmental and private agencies that determine and influence national nutritional policy have largely ignored these toxic dietary elements. As was the case with whole grains and legumes, potatoes are laden with antinutrients including saponins, lectins, and protease inhibitors.

Saponins

I can almost guarantee that if you ask your family physician about dietary saponins and your health, he or she will draw a complete blank. The same can be said for ADA-trained nutritionists at your local hospital or clinic. Even astute complementary health-care practitioners are usually in the dark when it comes to saponins in our daily food supply. Despite a mountain of scientific evidence showing that these compounds can be potent and even lethal toxins, they are rarely considered dietary threats to our health.

Saponins derive their name from their ability to form soaplike foams when mixed with water. Chemically, certain potato saponins are commonly referred to as glycoalkaloids. Their function is to protect the potato plant's root (tuber) from microbial and insect attack. When consumed by potential predators, glycoalkaloids protect the potato because they act as a toxin. These compounds exert their toxic effects by dissolving cell membranes. When rodents and larger animals, including humans, eat glycoalkaloid-containing tubers such as potatoes, these substances frequently create holes in the gut lining, thereby increasing intestinal permeability. If glycoalkaloids enter our bloodstream in sufficient concentrations, they destroy the cell membranes of our red blood cells.

Potatoes contain two glycoalkaloid saponins—Ð-chaconine and Ð-solanine—that may adversely affect intestinal permeability and aggravate inflammatory bowel diseases, including ulcerative colitis, Crohn's disease, and irritable bowel syndrome. Even in healthy normal adults, a meal of mashed potatoes results in the rapid appearance of both Ð-chaconine and Ð-solanine in the bloodstream. The toxicity of these two glycoalkaloids is dose dependent—meaning that the greater the concentration in the bloodstream, the greater is their toxic effect. At least 12 separate cases of human poisoning from potato consumption, involving nearly 2,000 people and 30 fatalities, have been recorded in the medical literature. Potato saponins can be lethally toxic once in the bloodstream in sufficient concentrations because these glycoalkaloids inhibit a key enzyme, acetyl cholinesterase, which is required for nerve impulse conduction.

The next logical question arises: Should we be eating a food that contains two known toxins that rapidly enter the bloodstream, increase intestinal permeability, and potentially impair the nervous and circulatory systems?

In the opinion of Dr. Patel, "If the potato were to be introduced today as a novel food, it is likely that its use would not be approved because of the presence of these toxic compounds."

In a comprehensive review of potato glycoalkaloids, Dr. Smith voiced similar sentiments:

> Available information suggests that the susceptibility of humans to glycoalkaloid poisoning is both high and very variable: oral doses in the range 1 to 5 mg/kg body weight are marginally to severely toxic to humans whereas 3 to 6 mg/kg body weight can be lethal. The narrow margin between toxicity and lethality is obviously of concern. Although serious glycoalkaloid poisoning of humans is rare, there is a widely held suspicion that mild poisoning is more prevalent than supposed.

The commonly accepted safe limit for total glycoalkaloids in potato foods is 200 mg/kg, a level proposed more than 70 years ago, whereas more recent evidence suggests this level should be lowered to 60–70 mg/kg. Many potato food products exceed this recommendation.

I believe that far more troubling than the toxicity of potato glycoalkaloids is their potential to increase intestinal permeability during the course of a lifetime, most particularly in people with diseases of chronic inflammation—cancer, autoimmune diseases, cardiovascular disease, and diseases of insulin resistance. Many scientists now believe that a leaky gut may represent a nearly universal trigger for autoimmune diseases.

When the gut becomes leaky, it is not a good thing, as the intestinal contents may have access to the immune system, which in turn becomes activated, thereby causing a chronic low-level systemic inflammation known as endotoxemia. In particular, a cell wall component of gut gram-negative bacteria called lipopolysaccharide (LPS) is highly inflammatory. Any LPS that gets past the gut barrier is immediately engulfed by two types of immune system cells. Once engulfed by these immune cells, LPS binds to a receptor on these cells, causing a cascade of effects that leads to increases in blood concentrations of proinflammatory hor-mones. Two recent human studies have shown that high-potato diets increase the blood inflammatory marker IL-6. Without chronic low-level systemic inflamma-tion, it is unlikely that few of the classic diseases of civilization—cancer, cardio-vascular disease, autoimmune diseases, and diseases of insulin resistance—would have an opportunity to take hold and inflict their fatal effects.

A final note on potatoes: This commonly consumed food is also a major source of dietary lectins. On average, potatoes contain 65 mg of potato lectins per kg. As is the case with most lectins, they have been poorly studied in humans, so we really don't have conclusive information on how potato lectins may affect human health. Yet preliminary tissue studies indicate that potato lectins resist degradation by gut enzymes, bypass the intestinal barrier, and can then bind to various tissues in our bodies. Potato lectins have been found to irritate the immune system and produce symptoms of food hypersensitivity in allergenic and nonallergenic patients.

Root and tuber vegetables such as sweet potatoes, yams, beets, carrots, tur-nips, and others are nutritious, tasty additions to the Paleo Diet. These foods complement the staples of modern-day Stone Age diets, and I encourage you to regularly include them in your diet.

Part 4

Maximum Living the Paleo Way

Chapter 13

Paleo Supplements
and Sunshine

*I promote the Paleo Diet every second I get. In my
private practice, it has cured more patients than any
other supplement or medication I have prescribed.*

—BROOKS RICE, MD

When you start eating Paleo, you simply won't require most vitamins and supplements. In fact, except for fish oil and vitamin D, if you take antioxidants or B vitamins, you will increase your risk of cancer, heart disease, and dying from all causes.

One of my first jobs after high school was with the US Forest Service on a wildfire crew in Markleville, California. During the summer of 1969, I bunked with eight other firefighters in a rustic shack where we shared a communal kitchen and bathroom. As an 18-year-old barely out of my parents' house, I had to buy groceries to last a week before my days off. I managed to purchase a box of Total cereal, thinking this was a sensible food to help me obtain 100 percent of my daily vitamins and minerals.

Forty years later, I realize that my naïve food choice reflected a global perspective on diet that has emerged since World War II. Instead of focusing on natural, healthy foods in my diet, I was suckered into focusing on micronutrients. Until only recently this perspective has dominated scientific, as well as lay, thought on nutritious diets. I quote a recent study by Drs. Lichtenstein and Russell from Tufts University that appeared in the prestigious *Journal of the American Medical Association*:

"The most promising data in the area of nutrition and positive health outcomes relate to dietary patterns, not nutrient supplements. These data suggest that other factors in food or the relative presence of some foods and the absence of other foods are more important than the level of individual nutrients consumed."

No amount of vitamins, minerals, or supplements added to breakfast cereals will ever make them a healthful food. Similarly, athletic drinks boasting vitamins, amino acids, and additives are nothing more than liquid candy. The food-processing industry "fortifies" highly processed foods such as breakfast cereals, soft drinks, designer yogurts, granola, mayonnaise, and orange juice with various nutrients and then recharacterizes them as "nutritious" or "heart healthy." These marketing ploys not only cause widespread adverse health effects, they also propagate the misleading idea that micronutrients (vitamins and minerals) are more important than foods.

As a lifelong skeptic, this is hard for me to believe. And now I'm telling my flabbergasted friends that I'm going for age 100. The only supplements I take are omega-3 and vitamin D.

We need to get back to healthy eating patterns characterized by a diet of traditional foods such as fresh fruits, vegetables, seafood, and grass-produced meats that have nourished and sustained our species from the very beginning. When we eat real, living foods, there is little or no need to supplement our diet with any single nutrient that is thought to be protective against disease.

The mentality that has dominated nutritional thought in the post–World War II era, since vitamins and supplements became widely available, was that if a little bit is good, more must be better. Let's take a look at the Dietary Reference Intake (DRI), which used to be called the Recommended Dietary Allowance (RDA), for the B vitamins in the table below.

Vitamin	DRI
Thiamine (vitamin B_1)	1.2 mg
Riboflavin (vitamin B_2)	1.3 mg
Niacin (vitamin B_3)	16 mg
Pantothenic acid (vitamin B_5)	5 mg
Pyrodoxine (vitamin B_6)	1.3 mg
Cyanocobalamin (vitamin B_{12})	2.4 mcg
Folate	400 mcg
Biotin	30 mcg

Notice that we actually need only tiny amounts of these essential nutrients. For instance, the daily DRI for vitamin B_1 is 1.2 milligrams. A milligram is just one-one-thousandth ($\frac{1}{1,000}$) of a gram, and a microgram (mcg) is just one-one-millionth of a gram ($\frac{1}{1,000,000}$). When I first started buying multivitamins back in the late 1960s and the early 1970s, about the only brand available was One-A-Day. Back then, these vitamins contained precisely the DRI—no more and no less.

These days, if you go down to your local pharmacy or health food store and decide to buy a mixed B-vitamin formula or a multivitamin, you are immediately met with a staggering number of choices. Do you want the 10-milligram (mg) version, the 50 mg form, or the 100 mg variety? You go with the 100 mg version because you're getting more vitamins for your buck. We all know that B vitamins are water soluble, so what you don't use will simply be excreted in your urine. Once again, let's allow the evolutionary template to give us guidance. Foraging human beings have always consumed vitamins, minerals, and phytochemicals in a range of concentrations that was available through diet alone. Processed foods were not on the menu, nor were vitamin supplements or fortified foods. Our ancestral vitamin, mineral, and nutrient intake always fell within a narrow range—not too low and not too high.

The relative levels of one B vitamin to another or any single nutrient to another fell within a range determined by the types of unprocessed plant and animal foods that were consumed. It would have been impossible for any hunter-gatherer ever to obtain 10 times the DRI for any B vitamin, much less 100 times this value. In addition, the natural ratio of one B vitamin to the next or any nutrient to another would never have been exactly one to one, as it is in most modern vitamin formulations.

Pain-Free Miracles
George's Story
I have been on a strict Paleo diet for 6 weeks, and I now believe in miracles. Five years ago, at the age of 64, I stopped playing golf because I had too many aches and pains in my muscles, joints, and bones, and my energy level was very low. At that time, I thought it was old age! Now, within 6 weeks I play golf, and I work or exercise 10 hours a day.

Paracelsus, one of the greatest Renaissance physicians of 16th-century Europe, is credited with the quote *"Dose makes the poison."* Indeed, this ancient wisdom is now coming back to haunt us in the 21st century as we indiscriminately lace our food supply with artificially produced vitamins and minerals that we perceive to enhance our health and prevent disease. When nutrient intake is low, it increases our risk for disease—this really isn't news to most of us. What may surprise you is that an excessive intake of many so-called safe vitamins and minerals has increasingly been shown to be harmful and to actually cause illness.

Our hunter-gatherer ancestors rarely or never would have ingested too few or too many nutrients that caused disease by landing on either the left- or the right-hand extremes of the curve. Prior to the agricultural revolution, it would have been difficult or nearly impossible for any forager to develop a vitamin or nutrient deficiency by falling on the left-hand side of the curve. Wild plant and animal foods are rich sources of all known nutrients required for optimal human health. When these foods or their modern counterparts are regularly consumed, nutrient deficiencies never develop. Only in the post-agricultural period could people have wound up on the left side of the curve.

Vitamin and mineral deficiencies became commonplace in early farmers as nutrient-poor cereal grains replaced wild meats, fish, fruits, and vegetables. With the Industrial Revolution and the introduction of refined grains, sugars, vegetable oils, canned foods, and eventually processed and junk food, the consumption of nutrient-depleted foods became the norm. It's high time that we return to the foods to which our species is genetically adapted. By doing so, you will never have to worry about landing on the left side of the curve.

Probably more alarming to you is not the left side of the curve but rather the right. I realize that you may be taking high doses of B and antioxidant vitamins because you think they provide protection from cancer and heart disease. Nothing could be further from the truth, and in fact this practice will increase your risk of dying from cancer, heart disease, and all causes combined. Except for fish oil and vitamin D, supplementation is a total waste of your time and money. It's high time to dismantle the myth of nutrient supplementation as our guiding light to health and well-being and replace it with the truth of nutrient-dense real foods.

Folic Acid Supplementation and Fortification

In 1947, scientists at Lederle Labs synthesized a compound called folic acid that had never previously existed on our planet. No human prior to 1947 had ever ingested this artificial substance. Fifty-one years later, in 1998, the FDA legis-lated that the entire US population would now be required to ingest this artifi-cial substance. We were never allowed to vote on this decision; it simply happened overnight. One day folic acid was not part of our food supply, and the next day every man, woman, and child in the United States was forced to ingest folic acid, whether they wanted to or not. This unilateral decision has turned into one of the worst health fiascos in the history of our country. In the years since its inception, this mandatory legislation has resulted in untold deaths, diseases, and disabilities.

If you are currently a Paleo Dieter, you probably don't have to worry about ingesting folic acid, provided that you are not taking any vitamin supplements that contain this compound. In 1998, the FDA mandated that all enriched wheat flour was to be fortified with folic acid. Because most commercial wheat prod-ucts—breakfast cereals, bread, cookies, cakes, crackers, doughnuts, pizza crust, hamburger and hot dog buns, wheat tortillas, and so on—are made with enriched wheat flour, essentially the entire US population began to consume folic acid in 1998. At the time, this national mandate seemed like a pretty good idea because convincing data existed to show that low folate status caused neural tube birth defects such as spina bifida. Folate is an entirely different compound than folic acid. In our bodies, folate and folic acid are metabolized in completely different ways. Folate is a natural vitamin found in leafy green vegetables, organ meats, and some nuts. Folic acid is a man-made substance that can be converted to folate in the liver. The problem is that folic acid is not efficiently converted to folate, thereby causing an excess pool of both folic acid and folate to build up in our bodies. It creates this pool even at doses as low as 200 mcg. And that's the problem.

I would be the first person to congratulate the FDA for mandating a national policy that could reduce or eliminate birth defects. Unfortunately, its shotgun approach to curing neural tube birth defects put the entire US population at risk for death and disability from other more serious diseases. In a 6-year period (1990–1996) before mandatory folic acid fortification, the average number of neural tube defects per year in the United States was 1,582. In the first year (1998–1999) following fortification, neural tube defects dropped to 1,337, so 245 cases of these diseases were prevented.

A much better strategy would be to selectively supplement pregnant women with folate—not with folic acid. Only fetuses, not the entire US population, are at risk for neural tube defects.

Folic Acid and Breast, Prostate, and Colorectal Cancers

In the last decade, an accumulating body of scientific evidence now makes it clear that the FDA's mandatory folic acid fortification program represents one of the worst blunders in the history of US public health. An alarming number of human clinical trials, animal experiments, and epidemiological studies convincingly show that excess folate via folic acid fortification has resulted in population-wide increases in the risk for breast, prostate, and colorectal cancers.

A 2010 meta-analysis at Bristol University demonstrated that high levels of blood folate were associated with an increased prostate cancer risk. Even more convincing evidence comes from a clinical trial by Dr. Figueiredo at the University of Southern California. In this experiment, 643 men were randomly assigned to either a folic acid supplementation group or a placebo group. After nearly 11 years, the percentage of men who developed prostate cancer in the folic acid treatment group was 9.7 percent, whereas only 3.3 percent of the men in the placebo group were diagnosed with prostate cancer.

Higher blood concentrations of folate from folic acid supplementation also cause a faster progression of this often fatal disease. Although scientists aren't completely sure how excess folate and folic acid promote cancer, animal experiments indicate that these compounds induce a cancer-causing reaction called hypermethylation in the DNA of cancer cells.

An alarming number of recent population studies have also suggested that high folate intake, largely from folic acid in supplements and fortified foods, may increase breast cancer risk. In a study of 70,656 postmenopausal women who were followed from 1992 until 2005, dietary folate intake from both folic acid and folate was positively associated with breast cancer risk.

I'd like to make it clear that folate and folic acid are not one and the same compound. Folate is the natural, healthful B vitamin that is found in leafy green veggies, organ meats, and some nuts. Folic acid is an artificial chemical that can be converted to folate in the liver. Because folic acid builds up and forms pools of this man-made chemical in our bodies at doses as low as 200 mcg (half the DRI), it is known to disrupt normal folate metabolism. Dietary folate from natural food sources does not produce harmful health effects, whereas folic acid does. A recent animal experiment by Dr. Ly at the University of Toronto demonstrated that folic acid supplementation led to an increased risk of mammary cancer in rats. It is notable that the equivalent (around 800 mcg) dietary levels of folic acid necessary to produce breast cancer in the rats could easily be achieved in humans by eating fortified foods and taking folic acid supplements.

The situation with colorectal cancers and folic acid supplementation or forti-fication is nearly identical to those for breast and prostate cancers. Animal, tis-sue, epidemiological, and human dietary trials all reveal that folic acid increases the risk for colorectal cancers. The most powerful type of research design in human supplementation experiments is called a double-blind, placebo-controlled, randomized trial. With these types of experiments, scientists can be relatively sure that a certain treatment causes a specific outcome. Such a study of 1,021 men and women was carried out during a 10-year period. I quote the authors of this study: "Folic acid was associated with higher risks of having three or more adenomas [cancers] and of noncolorectal cancers." A similar double-blind, placebo-controlled, randomized trial from Norway came up with similar conclu-sions: "Treatment with folic acid plus vitamin B_{12} was associated with increased cancer outcomes, and all-cause mortality in patients with ischemic heart disease in Norway, where there is no folic acid fortification of foods." Indeed, many Euro-pean nations, including the United Kingdom, have taken a more cautious approach and have decided not to fortify their food supplies with folic acid.

Folic Acid Fortification and Supplementation and Autism

A disturbing development involving folic acid fortification and supplementation has recently arisen. A number of scientists now believe that excessive folic acid may play an important role in the autism spectrum disorder (ASD), which includes autism, Asperger's syndrome, and other developmental problems. Recent epidemiological studies of autism show that the increasing prevalence of ASD in the United States coincides with the same time period that mandatory folic acid fortification began. It is known that excessive folic acid during the embryonic period may adversely affect normal brain development.

Unlike the folic acid/cancer story, the data for ASD is still preliminary. Large population studies will be required to determine whether the mandatory folic acid fortification program is responsible for the disturbing recent increase in ASD.

Antioxidant Supplements
Do More Harm Than Good

Of all of the supplements people take, antioxidants are one of the most popular, particularly with seniors and cancer patients. The most commonly supplemented antioxidants are beta-carotene, vitamin A, vitamin C, vitamin E, and selenium. About 11 percent of the US population supplement their diets with antioxidants on a daily basis; this number rises to almost 20 percent in adults 55 years of age and older. The perception with most antioxidant consumers is that these nutrients increase longevity and may prevent cancer, heart disease, and whatever else ails them. More is almost always thought to be better.

If people are deficient in nutrients, there is little doubt that health will suffer. On the other hand, more is definitely not better. Our bodies operate optimally when nutrients are supplied to them in the ranges for which they were designed. If you underinflate a tire, your car performs poorly—if you overinflate it, the tire ruptures. Just like tires, our bodies' natural defenses against disease, as well as the rate at which we age, is dependent on just the right amount of antioxidants from our diets—not too little, but also not too much.

The idea behind antioxidant supplements is that they capture and inactivate free radicals. These are highly reactive particles formed within our tissues as by-products of metabolism. Excessive free radicals may damage cells and tissues in many ways. In animal experiments, high free radical production can promote cancer, heart disease, and premature aging. Our bodies use dietary antioxidants to disarm free radicals and prevent damage to cells. We also manufacture antioxidants within our bodies that work together with dietary antioxidants to keep free radicals at bay.

An often-overlooked fact when it comes to free radicals is that they are necessary components of normal body function and a healthy immune system. Free radicals are used by the immune system to destroy cancer cells, kill invading microorganisms, and detoxify cells. If we overload our bodies with massive doses of antioxidants, these essential functions are impaired as normal free radical activity is suppressed. Alternatively, supranormal doses of antioxidant vitamins upset other delicate aspects of cellular machinery, which can actually turn antioxidants into pro-oxidants and ultimately increase free radical activity.

In 1994, one of the first realizations that high doses of antioxidants may be harmful arose with the ATBC study, a randomized, placebo-controlled experiment of 29,133 male smokers. The experiment wanted to determine whether beta-carotene or vitamin E supplementation could reduce lung cancer incidence in this group of heavy smokers. Following 5 to 8 years of supplementation, the researchers were shocked—treatment with beta-carotene actually increased lung cancer rates by 16 to 18 percent and overall death rates by 8 percent. Furthermore, the men who took vitamin E suffered more hemorrhagic strokes than did those taking placebo pills. A similar trial known as the CARET study had been ongoing concurrently with the ATBC study. In the CARET trial, smokers and former smokers received beta-carotene (20 mg) in combination with high doses of vitamin A (25,000 IU) for an average of 5 years. The men who received the antioxidants experienced a 28 percent greater incidence in lung cancer and a 17 percent higher death rate than those taking an inert placebo pill. The CARET trial was immediately stopped when the results of the ATBC trial were reported.

In the years since those studies, more convincing data has verified the harmful effects of antioxidant supplementation. A 2007 meta-analysis of 67 randomized, controlled trials studies involving 232,606 participants showed that supplementation with vitamin E, beta-carotene, or vitamin A increased overall death rates. In 2008, a large randomized controlled trial, the SELECT study of vitamin E and selenium supplementation in 35,533 men, was prematurely halted when it was discovered that these two antioxidants increased the risk for prostate cancer and type 2 diabetes. In addition, a large meta-analysis involving 20 randomized controlled trials and 211,818 subjects revealed that antioxidant supplementation (beta-carotene, vitamin A, vitamin C, vitamin E, and selenium) did not protect against gastrointestinal cancer and increased overall death rates.

A series of recent meta-analyses show that high vitamin E intake may be particularly dangerous. Dr. Miller at Johns Hopkins University analyzed 19 randomized trials that included more than 136,000 subjects and stated, "High-dosage (more than or equal to 400 IU a day) vitamin E supplements may increase all-cause mortality and should be avoided." In a meta-analysis of 118,765 people and nine randomized, controlled trials evaluating the effects of vitamin E on stroke, Dr. Schürks and coworkers at Harvard Medical School concluded, "In this meta-analysis, vitamin E increased the risk for hemorrhagic stroke by 22 percent . . . indiscriminate widespread use of vitamin E should be cautioned against."

Even the once-acclaimed vitamin C may have little therapeutic value for cancer or heart disease. In the Physicians' Health Study, a randomized, placebo-controlled trial of vitamins E and C in 14,641 male doctors, the authors summarized, "Neither vitamin E nor C supplementation reduced the risk of prostate or total cancer. These data provide no support for the use of these supplements for the prevention of cancer in middle-aged and older men."

The situation for cardiovascular disease and vitamin C and other antioxidants appears to be the same as for cancer—they are a waste of your money. Dr. Bleys demonstrated in a meta-analysis of 11 randomized, controlled trials: "Our meta-analysis showed no evidence of a protective effect of antioxidant vitamin-mineral or B vitamin supplementation on the progression of atherosclerosis. Our findings add to recent skepticism about the presumed beneficial effects of vitamin-mineral supplementation on clinical cardiovascular endpoints."

If you are an athlete, a series of recent human and animal experiments suggest that megadoses of vitamin C may have detrimental effects on your performance. Surprisingly, supplementation with vitamin C may decrease training efficiency, cancel the beneficial effects of exercise on insulin sensitivity, and delay healing after exercise. In addition, vitamin C supplementation did not decrease free radical damage to DNA that may occur following exercise.

These kinds of studies further cement the notion that fitness, vitality, and well-being can never be achieved by single isolated nutrients, supplements, or fortified foods. The available evidence conclusively shows that these compounds are harmful by causing nutritional imbalances within our bodies. The Paleo Diet has never been about supplements but rather about real, wholesome, living foods.

Depression, Anxiety, Fatigue Gone

Scott's Story

I'm 36 years old and 5 feet, 8½ inches tall. I started the Paleo Diet about 4 months ago. Since then, I've lost almost 25 pounds, bringing me down to my ideal weight of 150. My blood pressure went from 115/70 to 92/56. I decided to try the Paleo Diet because I read (on About.com) that it may help alleviate depression and anxiety. To my delight, it worked—my depression and anxiety have disappeared. My energy levels are much higher than before. I'm no longer tired throughout the day. My mind is clearer—I can focus much more easily, and my short-term memory has improved greatly. My skin is much smoother and less dry. Another improvement that I've found, which is kind of strange to me because I never expected it, is that my shinbones are no longer really sensitive. It used to be that if I barely bumped my shinbones against something, the pain was quite bad. Now they're hardly sensitive at all. Thanks much!

Sunshine

Starting in the summer of 1974, and for the next 20 consecutive summers, I worked as a lifeguard at Sand Harbor Beach on Lake Tahoe's pristine North Shore. Besides experiencing some of the greatest times of my life, I also took in a lot of sunshine—to say the least! Back in the 1970s, there were only two brands of "suntan lotions" (Coppertone and Sea & Ski) because "sunscreens" had yet to be invented. There were no sun-blocking agents in either lotion, and we used them mainly to moisturize our skin. No one on our lifeguarding crew worried about skin cancer, and if anybody got too much sun, he or she simply sat beneath an umbrella on the lifeguard tower. We wore short shorts and Vuarnet sunglasses. In the day, our goal was not to avoid the sun but rather to get the deepest, darkest tan possible.

Times and styles have changed considerably since then (thank God), but one big difference today that may produce adverse health effects is the universal application of sunscreen lotions.

I still spend my summers at Sand Harbor but no longer as a lifeguard. Very few beachgoers have deep tans the way they did back in the 1970s, and sunscreens are to be found in every beach bag because "everyone knows that sunscreens prevent skin cancer."

Just as the milk industry campaigned to convince us that milk drinking prevents osteoporosis, sunscreen manufacturers have promoted the myth that sunscreens prevent cancer. In a recent paper, Dr. Berwick from the University of New Mexico Cancer Center, summarized the most recent scientific findings on sunscreens: "Sunscreens protect against sunburn . . . . Thus far, no rigorous human evidence has shown that sunscreens prevent the major types of skin cancer: cutaneous melanoma and basal cell carcinoma." If the truth be known, melanoma risk is actually increased with the use of sunscreens because they allow you longer exposure to the sun without burning.

The part of sunlight that causes damage to our skin is ultraviolet (UV) radiation, a spectrum that is divided into two categories: UVA and UVB. Most of the sunlight that reddens our skin, causing sunburn, is UVB. Consequently, almost all sunscreens employ one or more ingredients in their formula to block UVB to various degrees. Until recently, few sunscreens blocked UVA. Although it hasn't been completely settled, a consensus in the scientific community now indicates that UVA sunlight is the chief cause of melanoma. If your sunscreen blocks only UVB and not UVA, it most likely increases the risk for melanoma.

You might think that the best sunscreen would be one that blocks both UVB and UVA equally, but this conclusion is erroneous and would actually end up increasing your risk of dying from numerous cancers. Sunlight exposure has a paradoxical effect that is both good and bad. Chronic, long-term exposure to the sun, such as what lifeguards and other outdoor workers experience, is protective from melanomas and many other cancers, whereas intermittent, infrequent intense burning, followed by little sun exposure, may promote this deadly form of skin cancer and many other cancers.

Blocking UVB sunlight turns out to be a very poor idea because this spectrum of light stimulates vitamin D production in our skin. Sunscreens that block UVB suppress the synthesis of vitamin D, one of the most powerful anticancer substances our bodies produce. In the last 20 years, compelling evidence reveals that low vitamin D blood status increases the risk for 16 cancers, many autoimmune diseases, cardiovascular disease, type 2 diabetes, hypertension, mental illness, osteoporosis, and susceptibility to infectious diseases. So what is the solution? How can you and your children enjoy a nice sunny summer day outdoors and not get sunburned but still benefit from the sun's healthy vitamin D–boosting effects?

If we look to the evolutionary template and use a little common sense and some modern technology, we can easily overcome this problem. The first thing you've got to do is change your mind-set—sunlight is not harmful but rather is incredibly healthy, providing that we get it in the same U-shaped dose that we get of other nutrients.

Lorrie and I have been taking our boys to the beach every summer of their lives. None has ever had a severe sunburn, and each of them gets a very dark tan by summer's end. Here's our strategy. At the beginning of summer, we apply lotion liberally for the first few days, preferably with sunscreens containing both UVA and UVB blockers and a moderate SPF value—8 to 15. As the boys gradually tan, we simultaneously reduce the sunscreen quantity and the SPF value.

After a week to 10 days, when they are tan, we pay little attention to sunscreens anymore, although we encourage them to sit under beach umbrellas or put on their shirts if they are hot or have had too much sun. A similar strategy will work for adults, depending on your skin color and initial tan. The key here is moderation and to gradually increase your exposure. The best protection from excessive sunlight is not a sunscreen, but rather shade, hats, and light clothing.

Regular sunlight exposure is one of the most healthy habits we can get into because it increases our blood levels of vitamin D, which in turn reduces our risk for developing most diseases and illnesses in the Western world. But how much sun do we need? This depends on your skin color. Very-dark-skinned people need almost twice the time in the sun as light-skinned people do to achieve similar blood concentrations of vitamin D.

Lifeguards and other outdoor workers can achieve blood concentrations that top out at about 60 ng/ml, but you don't need values this high. Most experts agree that values higher than 30 ng/ml will significantly reduce your risk for developing cancer and all of the other diseases associated with low vitamin D status. The good news is that daily sunlight exposure in the summertime for short periods of 15 to 30 minutes will rapidly boost your blood levels of vitamin D above 30 ng/ml. The bad news is that it is virtually impossible to do this with diet alone because almost all real foods that we commonly eat contain little or no vitamin D.

Vitamin D Supplementation

For most of us, regular sunlight exposure is a luxury that is difficult or impossible to come by on a year-round basis. Obviously, our hunter-gatherer ancestors did not have this problem. Consequently, you will need to supplement your diet with vitamin D_3 capsules. If we look at the official governmental recommendation for vitamin D intake—between 400 and 600 IU—it is woefully inadequate. This DRI, like the folic acid supplementation fiasco, represents a failure in public health policy. The most recent human experiments show that blood levels of 30 ng/ml could never be achieved with vitamin intakes between 400 and 600 IU. In fact, 400 IU does not raise insufficient blood concentrations of vitamin D at all.

The majority of Americans maintain blood levels of vitamin D that are either deficient or insufficient. One of the best strategies you can take with adopting the Paleo Diet is to supplement daily with vitamin D_3 if you are unable to get sunshine on a regular basis. Most vitamin D experts agree that daily supplementation of at least 2,000 IU of vitamin D_3 is necessary to achieve blood levels of 30 ng/ml or greater. People who have never supplemented with vitamin D or who have had little sunlight exposure for years may need 5,000 IU per day.

Fish Oil Supplementation

One of the absolutely essential elements of the Paleo Diet is to increase your consumption of foods containing the long-chain omega-3 fatty acids known as EPA and DHA. Your best sources of these vital nutrients come from fatty fish such as salmon, mackerel, sardines, and herring. A 4-ounce serving of salmon contains around 1,200 mg of EPA + DHA. If you're like most Americans, your normal daily diet provides only 100 to 200 mg of these healthy fatty acids.

Try to consume at least 500 to 1,800 mg of EPA + DHA per day, either by eating fish or taking fish oil supplements. If you have cardiovascular disease, you should include at least 1 gram of EPA + DHA in your diet. Patients with high blood triglycerides can lower their blood values by as much as 40 percent by taking 2 to 4 grams of EPA + DHA daily.

The problem with the typical American diet is that it contains insufficient EPA and DHA and excessive omega-6 fatty acids from vegetable oils. Today, vegetable oils used in cooking, salad oils, margarine, shortening, and processed foods supply 17.6 percent of the total daily calories in the US diet. This massive infusion of vegetable oils into our food supply, starting in the early 1900s, is to blame for elevating the ratio of dietary omega-6 to omega-3 to its current and damaging value of 10 to 1. In hunter-gatherer diets, the ratio of omega-6 to omega-3 was closer to 2 to 1.

Numerous diseases associated with this imbalance of omega-3 and omega-6 fatty acids include heart disease, cancer, autoimmune diseases, metabolic syndrome, and almost all inflammatory diseases that end with "-itis." If we use the evolutionary model exclusively, vegetable oils should make up a minimal part of contemporary Paleo diets. By using this strategy and regularly eating fatty fish or supplementing with fish oil, you will reduce your risk of developing almost all of the diseases of Western civilization.

To increase your intake of the long-chain omega-3 fatty acids:

- Eat fatty fish such as salmon, mackerel, sardines, or herring two or three times per week.

- Consume grass-fed fresh meats, rather than feedlot-produced meats.

- Eat cage-free or omega-3–enriched eggs.

- Enjoy shellfish, such as crab, lobster, oysters, and clams.

- Eat almost any fish, as even lean fish are moderate sources of EPA and DHA.

- Eat organ meats.

- Supplement with fish oil or fish oil capsules.

Chapter 14

Paleo Water

During my halcyon days of youth as a lifeguard, one of the brilliant ideas my fellow guards and I came up with was the notion that we should all be drinking pure water. As we sat in our lifeguard towers and sweltered all day long underneath the hot summer sun, the question arose—how should we replace the water we lost from our sweat? In those days, commercial bottled water in individual plastic containers didn't exist and was at least 10 years or more in the future. Even if such products were available, none of us, as underpaid young lifeguards, would have ever bought bottled water when we could have quenched our thirst for free from the tap.

A better idea surfaced. Why not drink Tahoe's crystal-clear, immaculate waters? In those days, contamination of Sierra Nevada mountain lakes and streams by bacterial pathogens such as Giardia was negligible, so we all bought into the idea. We all saw how Tahoe's waters close to the shoreline were clouded with pollen, insects, driftwood, crawdad carcasses, silt, and whatever, but moving out another hundred yards into deeper water was a completely different story. Tahoe's pristine waters at this depth were breathtakingly clear. From my lifeguard rescue board on the lake's surface, I remember staring down into incredibly clear images of granite boulders lying far below me, as if no water existed. I took a deep breath, fastened my goggles, and dove almost 20 feet down into Tahoe's exhilarating icy waters. When I reached bottom, I opened the nozzle of my water bottle and filled it.

This is how my fellow lifeguards and I regularly drank water during that magical summer of 1974. I drank deeply from Tahoe's clear, unpolluted waters, but at the time, I was unaware of what I was ingesting or what I wasn't ingesting.

All I knew was that this product of the High Sierra snowmelt tasted crisp and pure and better than any tap water I had ever drunk. I now know why. It was not contaminated with chlorine, fluoride, heavy metals, pesticides, solvents, fertilizers, sewer runoff, or other toxic elements. To me, Tahoe's pristine waters were a refreshing elixir that not only quenched my thirst but also cleansed my body as I swam in this unspoiled alpine lake.

Except for the air we breathe, perhaps the single most crucial element in maintaining our day-to-day health is water. Without a regular source of uncontaminated drinking water, we simply could not exist for more than a few days. Although our kidneys and immune systems are remarkably efficient at removing toxic compounds found in any polluted waters we may ingest, we are a lot better off drinking fresh, clear waters unadulterated by added chemicals, heavy metals, herbicides, toxic compounds, hormones, and pesticides.

The Problems with Tap Water

If I had to rate the most important achievements modern technology has made in public health, there is little doubt in my mind that uncontaminated drinking water and waste-water treatment would be at the top of my list. Prior to the advent of community-based water-treatment plants, infectious diseases such as cholera and typhoid fever caused death tolls as high as 1 per 1,000 in many major American cities. We can be thankful for the chlorination of our drinking waters, which first occurred in 1908 in Chicago and rapidly spread to the rest of the country and worldwide. Death from infectious diseases borne by contaminated water has been effectively eliminated since our water supply has been treated with chlorine.

Unfortunately, we unknowingly traded a huge problem—death by infectious disease—for a lesser predicament. It is now convincingly known that the chlorination process produces compounds that increase our risk for developing a variety of cancers. Although municipal water works regulate the maximal concentrations of these compounds that can be present in our drinking water, they cannot eliminate them.

In the 1970s, scientists discovered that when chlorine was added to our drinking water, it combined with naturally occurring organic matter such as vegetation and algae to produce toxic compounds called trihalomethanes. Since the discovery of these chemicals, epidemiological (population) studies have consistently demonstrated that trihalomethanes increase our risk for developing bladder and colorectal cancers. Additionally, trihalomethanes in our drinking water may impair normal menstrual function, increase the risk for miscarriage, and produce other undesirable reproductive effects in women.

When we think about the adverse health effects associated with tap water, most of us assume that they originate only from the water we drink from our faucets. Unfortunately, this is not the case. A 10-minute shower increases our blood chloroform (a chlorine by-product) levels almost 100 percent from the chlorine compounds we breathe in from the vaporized water. Hence, our chlorinated water supply hits us with a double whammy—we drink this noxious compound, and we also breathe it when we shower. Not all cities and municipalities employ chlorination to sanitize their water supplies, but alternative procedures such as ozone gas and ultraviolet light, which are used at a few hundred water treatment plants in the United States, are not without their own problems.

Given this scenario, how can we possibly find fresh, clean, unadulterated water to drink and shower with? Is plastic bottled water a viable solution for our daily drinking water? Our local municipal water-treatment plants have eliminated disease-causing microorganisms from our water supply, but unfortunately, most of these plants add chlorine and fluoride back into our water. They also frequently use outdated filtering technology that fails to remove known toxins and contaminants.

Feeling Great

Sam's Story

I am a lifelong sufferer of depression. I have long exercised 5 or 6 days a week, and I was still depressed. When I stumbled upon your Web site, I decided to start eating the Paleo way and have found that I have had no depressive episodes since. Even the mood swings are not evident. It feels great not to be battling depression every day. Thank you so much for the Paleo Diet.

The Problem with Plastic Bottled Water

As with the milk mustache, you should just say no to plastic bottled water. This product has been labeled one of the greatest cons of the 20th century, and I would totally agree. Compared to tap water, the cost of bottled water is staggering. A gallon of bottled water can run you from $1 to $10, whereas water from your tap costs less than a penny per gallon. The environmental impact of bottled water is worse still. It takes three times as much water to produce the plastic bottle as it does to fill it. An estimated 60 million plastic bottles are produced, filled, and bought daily in the United States, requiring 17 million barrels of oil, which represents enough energy to fuel 1 million cars for a year. Only one in five bottles is recycled—meaning that we dump 3 billion pounds of plastic into the environment each year.

The bottled-water middlemen with their slick advertising hype would have us think that we are getting higher-quality water when we buy their products. In reality, 40 percent of all bottled water is simply taken from municipal tap water. Almost 22 percent of bottled water brands contain chemical contaminants at higher concentrations than stipulated by governmental limits. Municipal water supplies are not allowed to have any fecal bacteria, whereas no such limitations are required for bottled water. Similarly, governmental regulations impose limits for bisphenol A (BPA) and phthalates in tap water, but no such rules exist for producers of bottled water.

The Problem with Plastics

As a Paleo Dieter, you realize that the closer we can mimic the beneficial aspects of our ancestral lifestyles, the better off we will be in the 21st century. We live in a world that is vastly different from that of our hunter-gatherer ancestors and is even very much different from the world of our grandparents and great-grandparents. One of the more important environmental pollutants that didn't exist 200 years ago is plastics. Plastics and plastic materials dominate our 21st-century world, whereas prior to World War II, most Americans rarely encountered these man-made compounds. It would be nearly impossible for any of us to get through a single day without touching, breathing, or ingesting plastic compounds. These materials are everywhere—from our cell phones to our computers, our cars, our food, and our clothing. We live in a "plastic, fantastic" world, to quote a lyric from one of my favorite sixties rock groups.

Only recently did we discover that tiny plastic particles pollute our world and may impair our health and well-being. Plastic chemicals are present in the dust we breathe in our homes and offices, and they contaminate our food, water supply, and medicines. In an earlier era, it was assumed that plastics were inert and had no harmful effects, but nothing could be further from the truth. We now know that at least two plastic compounds, bisphenol A (BPA) and phthalates, are injurious to our health and should be avoided whenever possible. Unfortunately, our contemporary world makes it difficult to escape these toxins.

As a modern-day hunter-gatherer, one of the best strategies you can take to reduce your BPA and phthalate load is to forgo any processed food item that comes in a can, a plastic container, or a plastic bottle—including water. Another unexpected source of BPA is from the thermally printed receipts you receive at many retail outlets. If you simply touch the printed label, BPA can permeate your skin. In the scientific community, BPA and phthalates are officially known as endocrine disruptors, meaning that these chemicals interfere with our bodies' normal hormonal functions, providing that they reach a high-enough concentration in our bloodstream.

It had always been assumed that we couldn't achieve harmful blood levels of BPA or phthalates while living, breathing, and eating in the normal Western environment. Regrettably, this assumption has turned out to be wrong. A 2008 study published by Dr. Lang and colleagues in the *Journal of the American Medical Association* demonstrated that even low blood levels of BPA increased the risk for cardiovascular disease, diabetes, and liver enzyme abnormalities in 1,455 adults. Although the mechanisms are not completely known, ingested BPA seems to act like one of the body's own female hormones and may bind hormonal receptors in various tissues, thereby producing its harmful effects.

Another reason why you should avoid processed foods packaged in plastics is the presence of phthalates. Like BPA, these chemicals can leach into our foods from their surrounding plastic containers and promote cancers, allergies, and infertility, among other health problems. Phthalates are found in adhesives, detergents, floorings, cosmetics, shampoos, fragrances, plastic bags, garden hoses, cleaning materials, toys, food packaging, and insecticides. As was the case with BPA, phthalates seem to initiate their harmful effects by mimicking the female hormone estrogen.

You can take a number of precautions to reduce your exposure to both BPA and phthalates. First, avoid foods sold in plastic containers and preferentially buy condiments, oils, or manufactured goods packaged in glass containers only. Canned goods are generally not part of the Paleo Diet—another good reason to avoid them is because some cans are lined with a plastic spray that contains BPA.

Another effective strategy to reduce your intake of these plastic compounds is to thoroughly rinse your fruits and produce before eating. Also, try to purchase cosmetics and deodorants that are free of these chemicals—read your labels carefully. Phthalates come in at least 10 different versions and are frequently abbreviated as MiBP, MnBP, DIBP, DNPB, MEP, and so on. Any time you see the word "phthalate" in the ingredients list, choose another product.

If you have the luxury, being outdoors is almost always better than being indoors, as we breathe in fewer plastic particles outside. We live in a plastic-polluted world, and there is no way that we can completely eliminate BPA, phthalates, and other plastics from our environments, but by adopting a modern-day Paleo diet filled with fresh fruits, veggies, fresh meats, seafood, and unprocessed foods, we can significantly lower our intake of these toxic chemicals.

Multiple Sclerosis (MS) in Remission
Elizabeth's Story

I was diagnosed in August 2003, 8 months and three severe MS episodes later. I was 16 at the time, 15 when symptoms first appeared. Postdiagnosis, I was told by the medical team to be aware of information claiming to aid MS, especially dietary. So I was a good, quiet patient and went onto Rebif, subcutaneously [Rebif is an interferon, to aid in reducing MS relapses]. I felt awful on these injections and was in the middle of school exams. I then decided it was time to research other therapies to aid MS. Several months later, after lots of research, I told my medical team I was coming off the Rebif. They were unsupportive and told me how shortsighted my decision was. I was committed to feeling better, however, not just staying clear of MS relapses. I haven't touched a medication—any—since 2004. The combination of these therapies (as well as a certain optimistic mind-set) has served me well. Despite a grim diagnosis and prognosis, here I am as an above-average 21-year-old. I'm studying for a tough university degree (in nutrition), I play college basketball, and I am virtually symptom free, though I have a slight balance and coordination problem, tracing back to my first MS attack. The power of nutrition in MS, autoimmune diseases, health, and longevity is so underrated.

Water for the Paleo Diet

I have spent a lot of time discussing the health problems associated with drinking tap or bottled water, but I haven't yet provided you with much of an alternative. Part of the problem is that it is difficult or impossible for municipal water-treatment plants to deliver to our doorsteps a chlorine-free product devoid of all major contaminants. And once treated water arrives at our homes, it can be further polluted by the lead, copper, and polyvinyl chloride (PVC) pipes within our own household plumbing systems.

Our water supply is not immune to political decisions about which we have little or no input. For instance, fluoride is routinely added to about 70 percent of America's municipal water supplies with the intent of reducing dental cavities. Yet this practice is controversial within the scientific community and may have a number of unexpected harmful health effects that we are only beginning to understand. The best protection against cavities is not fluoride but rather a Paleo diet devoid of refined sugars and processed foods, along with regular flossing and brushing.

The evolutionary template contraindicates chlorine, fluoride, heavy metals, pesticides, solvents, fertilizers, hormones, plastics, sewer runoff, and any other toxic element in our drinking water. Analyses of the few remaining pristine lakes and streams worldwide show these waterways to be generally free of bacterial contamination because their rain water or snow sources are naturally filtered through sand and gravel as they make their way to lower ground. Additionally, healthful minerals such as magnesium and calcium leached from earthen sources infiltrate free-flowing streams, rivers, and lakes, giving these waters the sweet taste I experienced when I drank of Tahoe's waters as a young man.

The evolutionary formula for our drinking water is obvious. What we should strive for with our contemporary water supply is the pristine quality our ancestors most frequently enjoyed. We need pure, clean water devoid of chlorine, fluoride, and all of the other toxic compounds detected in municipal water sources. To partially accomplish this, you will need to purchase a home filtration system that can elevate your tap water to the next level. A variety of commercial products are available. Most will improve the quality of your tap water but cannot guarantee absolute purity from all environmental contaminants. My recommendation is to make sure the filtration system you purchase removes chlorine, chloroform, trihalomethanes, fluoride, heavy metals (lead, copper, arsenic, rust), nitrates, volatile organic chemicals (industrial solvents, pesticides, herbicides, etc), sediments, and chlorine-resistant parasites (Giardia and Cryptosporidium).

When you purchase a home water filter, you will have two choices for its location: point of entry or point of use. Point-of-entry systems filter water as it comes into your house from the municipal water supply and consequently purify every tap in your entire house. Point-of-use devices filter water only at a single location—so if you want to filter one faucet for drinking water and another for showering, you obviously will have to buy a filter for each tap you want to treat. The highest-quality water is obtained from point-of-use filters because nothing stands between you and the purified water. The downside to point-of-entry (whole house) filters is that the filtered water must travel throughout your home plumbing system, where it may become contaminated from materials leaching in from the pipes in your house.

Most of us don't have a clue about the plumbing in our homes, much less the types of materials found in the pipes through which our home drinking water flows. Modern houses and apartments are most frequently plumbed with copper pipes, but plastic pipes made from PVC and chlorinated polyvinylchloride (CPVC) are becoming more popular. The most recent darling of the plastics industry for plumbing houses is cross-linked polyethylene, more commonly known as PEX. All of these materials are not ideal—they all may leak toxic compounds into our home water supplies that potentially affect our health and well-being.

Although copper pipes have served us for more than 100 years, a number of problems remain. If you live in an area where the water is soft or acidic, your in-house copper pipes can become corroded as they age. If excessive copper finds its way into your drinking water, numerous serious health problems can arise, including anemia, nausea, diarrhea, kidney and liver damage, and an increased risk for developing Alzheimer's disease.

If your house was built before 1987 and contains copper plumbing, your drinking water may also contain excessive lead. Prior to the passage of the Safe Drinking Water Act on June 19, 1986, lead was routinely used in plumbing fixtures, pipes, and the solder that joined pipes. Even such seemingly miniscule amounts of lead in copper pipe solder joints represent a powerful poison known to cause irreversible learning disabilities in young children and health problems in adults. If you live in an older home, another potential source of lead poisoning comes from the service line that connects your house to the water main in the street. Prior to the passage of the Safe Drinking Water Act, lead pipes were routinely used to bring water into your home from their municipal supply. These pipes are well-recognized sources of lead poisoning. Do yourself and your family a favor and examine the water pipe leading into your house. If it is light gray in color and can be easily scraped with a pen knife, it is probably made of lead. Contact officials at your city's water department and have them immediately replace this pipe.

In recent years, copper plumbing systems have been replaced with plastics. I cannot recommend either PVC or CPVC, as residual toxic chemicals from these pipes are known to leak into our in-house water supplies and increase our risk for developing numerous cancers. Both PVC and CPVC are sources of BPA. Initial reports suggest that PEX does not contain BPA, but it does harbor other compounds, such as ETBE, which make their way into our water and give it an unpleasant odor.

The Bottom Line for in-Home Water-Purification Systems

To date, the safest plumbing material for your house appears to be copper, unless you live in areas of the country where the water is acidic or soft. These types of waters cause copper in your plumbing to dissolve in your drinking water, and this situation is definitely not a good thing. By employing high-quality point-of-use filtration systems, you can minimize copper contamination, along with most other municipal water pollutants, for everyone in your home.

If money is not an issue, the best way to decontaminate your in-house water supply is to employ both point-of-entry and point-of-use filters. Point-of-entry filtration systems will entirely eliminate chlorine and chloroform compounds for everybody who showers or bathes at every location in your home. Point-of-use filters then become necessary only where drinking or cooking water is drawn. Typically, the kitchen faucet would be the most likely location for an additional point-of-use filter.

Drinking Water Storage

Glass bottles are always best for storing your filtered water; stainless steel bottles come in a close second. Both of these containers are virtually inert, and the water you put into them will remain pure and free of chemicals. Although polycarbonate plastic bottles are sometimes viewed as the next-best alternative to glass and stainless steel, the most recent experiments don't support this assumption. Experiments from Dr. Amiridou's laboratory at Aristotle University in Greece show that polycarbonate containers leaked the most BPA into bottled waters. Hence, I believe it is best that you entirely avoid plastic bottles and containers for water and food storage. One final thought: Be sure to refrigerate your stored filtered water, as it no longer contains chlorine and consequently can become contaminated with bacteria if opened and left at room temperature.

Chapter 15

Paleo Exercise

*Eating alone will not keep a man well; he must
also take exercise.*

—HIPPOCRATES

Regular physical activity is every bit as important as diet in achieving good health and permanent weight loss. Regular exercise can:

- Improve your insulin metabolism
- Increase HDL cholesterol and reduce blood triglycerides
- Lower your blood pressure
- Strengthen your heart and blood vessels
- Reduce your risk of developing heart disease and type 2 diabetes
- Alleviate stress, improve your mental outlook, and help you to sleep better
- Possibly increase bone mineral density in people under 30 and slow bone loss in older people

Here again, we need to follow the example set by our hunter-gatherer ancestors and use their activity levels as a guide for our own.

I must tell you that when asked to choose between doing long, hard, repetitive work and simply relaxing, or having fun, hunter-gatherers—just like their modern descendants—invariably would have opted for the latter two choices. In fact, the idea of exercise itself would have baffled these people. After all, no reasonable hunter-gatherers would have lifted heavy stones or run in circles for the mere sake of getting a "workout." Convincing them to continue these boring activities—or to develop a fitness plan—would have been impossible.

The huge difference between Paleolithic people and us is that they had no choice but to do hard manual labor on a regular basis. Their lives depended on it. Most of ours do not.

Exercise Plus Paleo Diet Equals Health

Joe's Story

Joe Friel is an internationally known expert on fitness who has coached Olympic triathletes and is the author of a number of bestselling books for triathletes and cyclists. Here are his experiences with Paleo diets.

I have known Dr. Cordain for many years, but I didn't become aware of his work until 1995. That year, we began to discuss nutrition for sports. As a longtime adherent to a very-high carbohydrate diet for athletes, I was skeptical of his claim that eating less starch would benefit performance. Nearly every successful endurance athlete I had known ate as I did, with a heavy emphasis on cereals, bread, rice, pasta, pancakes, and potatoes. In fact, I had done quite well on this diet, having been an All-American age-group duathlete (bike and run), finishing in the top 10 at World Championships. I had also coached many successful athletes, both professional and amateur, who ate the same way I did.

Our discussions eventually led to a challenge. Dr. Cordain suggested I try eating a diet more in line with what he recommended for 1 month. I took the challenge, determined to show him that eating as I had for years was the way to go. I started by simply cutting back significantly on starches and replacing those lost calories with fruits, vegetables, and very lean meats.

For the first 2 weeks I felt miserable. My recovery following workouts was slow, and my workouts were sluggish. I knew that I was well on my way to proving that he was wrong. But in week three, a curious thing happened. I began to notice that I was not only feeling better, but that my recovery was speeding up significantly. In the fourth week I experimented to see how many hours I could train.

Since my early forties (I was 51 at the time), I had not been able to train more than about 12 hours per week. Whenever I exceeded this weekly volume, upper-respiratory infections would soon set me back. In week four of the "experiment," I trained 16 hours without a sign of a cold, a sore throat, or an ear infection. I was amazed. I hadn't done that many hours in nearly 10 years. I decided to keep the experiment going.

That year I finished third at the US national championship, with an excellent race, and qualified for the US team for the World Championships. I had a stellar season, one of my best in years. This, of course, led to more questions of Dr. Cordain and my continued refining of the diet he recommended.

I was soon recommending it to the athletes I coached, including Ryan Bolton, who was on the US Olympic Triathlon team. Since 1995 I have written four books on training for endurance athletes and have described and recommended the Paleo Diet in each of them. Many athletes have told me a story similar to mine: They have tried eating this way, somewhat skeptically at first, and then discovered that they also recovered faster and trained better.

"Exercise": A Funny Idea to Hunter-Gatherers

In the late 1980s, the world community became increasingly alarmed at the shrinking tropical rain forest in the Amazon basin (due to clear-cut logging, mining, and industrialization). Politicians and environmentalists launched a host of programs to curb this deforestation and even brought native Amazon Indians to environmental conferences in New York City. At one such conference, a group of Indians came across joggers exercising in Central Park—and found this concept absolutely hilarious. That adults would run for no apparent reason was comically absurd to these practical hunters. In their tropical forest home, every movement had a function and a purpose. What could possibly be gained by running to no destination, with no predators or enemies to escape from, and with nothing to capture?

Physical Fitness:
Naturally, and with No Exercise Programs

The mind-set of these Amazonian Indians was undoubtedly very similar to that of any of the world's hunter-gatherers. They got plenty of exercise simply by carrying out the day's basic activities—finding food and water, building shelters, making tools, and gathering wood. These activities were more than enough to allow them to develop superb physical fitness. Strength, stamina, and good muscle tone were the natural by-products of their daily routine.

Our Stone Age ancestors worked hard or they didn't eat. Sustained labor wasn't necessary every day; periods of intense exertion generally alternated with days of rest and relaxation. But the work was always there, an inevitable fact of life. There were no retirement plans, no vacations, and definitely no labor-saving devices. Everybody, except for the very young or the very old, helped out. And their daily efforts were astonishing. The amount of physical activity performed by an average hunter-gatherer would have been about four times greater than that of a sedentary office worker—and about three times greater than anybody needs to get the health benefits of exercise. An office worker who jogged 3 miles a day for a whole week would use less than half the energy of an average hunter-gatherer, such as the !Kung people of Africa. !Kung men on average walk 9.3 miles per day; the women average 5.7 miles per day. As you may expect, all this walking and regular physical activity pays off with high levels of physical fitness for everyone. In fact, my research team has shown that the average aerobic capacity of the world's hunter-gatherers and less-Westernized peoples is similar to that of today's top athletes.

Exercise and Obesity

There are few physicians or health professionals who would argue that exercise shouldn't accompany dietary programs. Most of the scientific experiments that have monitored weight loss with and without exercise programs have shown that moderate exercise (20 to 60 minutes of walking or jogging five times a week) doesn't help you lose weight any faster—but it is very effective in helping you keep the extra pounds off over the long term.

Why Exercise by Itself Doesn't Promote Weight Loss

The idea of exercising the extra pounds away—if this is your only means of weight loss—is not terribly practical. Exercise combined with diet is no more effective than diet alone in causing weight loss. How can this be? The answer is a scientific equation: To lose a pound of fat, you need to achieve a caloric deficit of 3,500 calories.

Imagine that a mildly obese woman, weighing 154 pounds, would like to lose 30 pounds, or 105,000 calories, by walking or jogging for 3 miles (45 minutes) a day. On days when she walks or jogs, she expends 215 additional calories (compared to the 80 calories she expends for that same 45-minute period on other days). The 3-mile walk or jog causes a net deficit of 135 calories—not a lot, considering the amount of work she's doing. At this rate, it will take her 26 days to lose 1 pound and 780 days (more than 2 years) to lose 30 pounds. Most dieters simply don't have the patience to wait that long. (Frankly, most of us need the encouragement of seeing the scale change more rapidly to help us keep up the good work. Otherwise, it's easy to become discouraged and give up.)

Experiments by my colleague Dr. Joe Donnelly and coworkers at the University of Nebraska at Kearney, and by Dr. David Nieman at Appalachian State University in Boone, North Carolina, have demonstrated that *diet alone is just as effective as diet plus exercise in causing weight loss.*

The real benefit from exercise for weight loss comes not from the modest caloric deficit that it may create, but from its ability to *keep weight off* once it has been lost. Dr. Rena Wing of Brown University School of Medicine in Providence, Rhode Island, reviewed a large number of exercise trials in which participants either dieted only or dieted and exercised. Reporting on the participants a year later, Dr. Wing noted, "In all of the long-term randomized trials reviewed, weight losses at follow-up were greater in *diet plus exercise* than in *diet only.*"

Why Should You Exercise?

Regular exercise, though, is great for your body. One major benefit: It improves your insulin metabolism. As I've discussed earlier in this book, many overweight people are insensitive to insulin, a hormone secreted by the pancreas that aids the entry of glucose from the bloodstream into all cells of the body, including the muscle cells. When muscle cells become insensitive to insulin, the pancreas responds by secreting more insulin. This, in turn, raises the normal level of insulin in the bloodstream. The resulting elevation of blood insulin levels, called hyperinsulinemia, is the underlying cause of the metabolic syndrome diseases. Insulin is a master hormone that influences many other critical cellular functions. An elevated level of insulin in the bloodstream encourages fat deposition and the development of obesity.

Regular exercise has been shown in clinical studies to improve the muscles' sensitivity to insulin and to lower the level of insulin in the bloodstream. In other words, although exercise alone does not cause the large caloric deficits needed for weight loss, it sets the metabolic stage for weight loss to occur by improving your insulin metabolism—as long as you cut back on calories.

Improving your insulin sensitivity may also reduce your appetite by preventing the large swings in blood sugar levels that are a direct consequence of too much insulin secretion. When you eat a carbohydrate-heavy meal, digestive enzymes convert most of the carbohydrates to glucose, which then enters the bloodstream. Normally, the pancreas secretes just the right amount of insulin to help convert glucose into muscle and other cells of the body and to help keep the blood sugar level on an even keel. However, when your muscles are resistant to insulin's action and the pancreas must secrete extra insulin, this drives the blood glucose level even lower. This reduction in blood sugar, called hypoglycemia, makes you hungry—even if you've just eaten a large meal. Exercise can help break this vicious cycle by making the muscles more sensitive to insulin.

Exercise and Blood Lipids

Medical evidence suggests that exercise training alone has little or no effect on the LDL blood cholesterol level. However, it can improve the total cholesterol to HDL cholesterol ratio and reduce your risk of heart disease by significantly increasing the good HDL blood cholesterol level. Also, exercise has been shown to lower the triglyceride level, which may also be an independent risk factor for atherosclerosis and coronary heart disease.

The best way to improve your levels of total and HDL cholesterol is through a combination of exercise and diet. Do your heart a favor when you adopt the Paleo Diet, and start to exercise as well.

Exercise Prevents Heart Disease and High Blood Pressure

Exercise can also decrease your risk of dying from heart disease by triggering a variety of other healthful changes in your heart and circulatory system. Regular physical exertion has been shown to widen and increase the elasticity of the coronary arteries that carry blood to the heart. This widening is good: Even if there are plaques, or chunky deposits, in the coronary arteries of people who regularly exercise, their chances of having a heart attack are reduced because these arteries are wider—which makes it less likely that any blockage will completely cut off blood flow to the heart. With regular exercise, the heart gets bigger and stronger and may even develop new blood vessels to supply more blood and oxygen.

Also, exciting new evidence suggests that regular physical exertion may reduce the risk of a blood clot forming in a coronary artery—a key event leading to a heart attack. The net result of all these beneficial changes from physical activity is a significant reduction in your risk of dying from all forms of heart and blood vessel diseases. This has been demonstrated in a medical study of more than 40,000 women from Iowa.

The most pervasive of all chronic Western diseases is hypertension, or high blood pressure. It affects at least 50 million Americans, and by age 65 almost 60 percent of all Americans have blood pressure that is too high. Blood pressure is measured when the heart contracts (this is called systolic pressure) and when it relaxes (diastolic pressure). You are considered to have hypertension if your systolic blood pressure readings are 140 or greater and if your diastolic readings are 90 or greater. Many studies have demonstrated that regular exercise alone—without other lifestyle changes—is effective in lowering blood pressure. Because hypertension can accelerate the risk of stroke, exercise programs that lower blood pressure may also reduce the risk of stroke. Exercise, along with the foods you will be eating on the Paleo Diet, will put you on the right track for lowering your blood pressure and reducing your risk of developing diseases of the heart and the blood vessels.

Exercise, Type 2 Diabetes, and Other Health Benefits of Exercise

Type 2 diabetes affects an estimated 17 million Americans and normally arises from insulin resistance—the same dangerous condition that promotes obesity, hypertension, heart disease, and blood lipid abnormalities. Exercise can be of great help: A single round of exercise improves insulin sensitivity within 3 hours and keeps working all day long—even 24 hours after your exertion.

Exercise is one of nature's best cures for whatever ails you. Regular physical exertion can reduce stress and optimize your mental well-being, help you sleep better, improve your digestion and lung function, reduce bone mineral loss, and slow the physical changes associated with aging. It may decrease your risk of developing certain types of cancer. So go for it! Embrace the active lifestyle that is part of your ancestral heritage. Activity and movement are built into your genes. Your body absolutely requires it.

Modern Exercises for Your Paleolithic Body

Any activity is better than no activity. It doesn't have to be some ambitious plan devised by a personal trainer. Basically, whenever you can exert yourself physically—at work, at home, while traveling, or during leisure time—you should do it. On a typical day, most Americans walk about 30 feet from the house to the car, drive to work, walk 100 feet to the office, and sit virtually motionless in front of a computer for hours at a time. At the end of the day, they walk back to their cars, drive home, and then sit motionless in front of a TV screen until they go to sleep. Even in once highly active professions, such as construction, it is now possible to do almost as little physical activity as somebody performing a desk job. Operating an air-conditioned backhoe with fully hydraulic controls takes barely more effort than operating a personal computer.

Increasing Your Activity Level While at Home or at Work

In this highly mechanized, technological world, you can increase your physical exertion level while doing your daily tasks at home or at work, during your leisure activities, and by incorporating a regular exercise routine into your schedule. I encourage you to take full advantage of all three of these opportunities to get activity back into your life. At every occasion, when you have the chance to use your body, you should. Look upon activity not as something you have to do but rather as a fleeting opportunity to give your body a gift. Get it when you can! You'll feel better when you do.

Is it possible for you to sneak in some exercise on the way to or from work? Could you walk to work? Ride your bicycle? How about parking your car a half mile from work—or getting off at a bus or subway stop farther away and walking the rest of the way? How about taking the stairs or walking instead of driving to lunch? Better yet, go for a walk at lunchtime and brown-bag a Paleo lunch for afterward. You can even keep a portable stair-stepping device and a few small dumbbells in your office. Maybe you have access to a health club or a gym near work where you can take a quick swim, do some weight lifting, or get in a game of racquetball during your lunch hour. When you go to the restroom, take a roundabout route up and down a couple of flights of stairs. Because almost everybody notices an increase in daily energy levels (there is no mid-afternoon slump) within days of starting the Paleo Diet, you will have the energy and spirit for these extra activities. Look for physical activity—lifting, walking, climbing stairs, digging in the garden—whenever you can. Anything extra you can do is better than doing nothing, and all of these little increments add up.

At home, try not to use some of your labor-saving devices. For example, a snowblower gets the job done faster, but unless you're going to use the time saved for exercise later in the day, shoveling the snow would be much better for you. Important note: Beware the "weekend warrior" syndrome. If you have been sedentary, don't charge in with major aerobic exercise all at once. Talk to your doctor and figure out the safest, best way for you to get back in shape.

Increasing Your Activity Level During Leisure Time

During your leisure time, instead of watching a fishing show on TV, go fishing. Instead of watching a football game on TV, go out and throw the football around with your children. Instead of playing games on the computer, go for a walk or a hike or do some gardening. When you go to the beach, don't just sit there; try a bit of swimming, a walk, or maybe even jog in the sand. Leisure-time activities can be enjoyable and still involve exertion. When you go shopping, make sure you do as much walking as possible. Camping trips don't necessarily have to be junk-food feasts involving little or no physical activity. You can enjoy the great outdoors by doing something in it, such as hiking, chopping wood, or swimming. Be creative. Developing a more active life at home and at work will give you a great start in emulating the exercise patterns of our Paleolithic ancestors and will go a long way toward improving your health. Unless you do very strenuous work on the job or at home, however, you will probably need to complement your daily work and leisure activities with a structured exercise program as well.

Structured Exercise Programs

The physical activities of hunter-gatherers most closely resembled those of modern cross-training athletes, in that they were required to do both aerobic and strength activities periodically. Men commonly hunted from 1 to 4 days a week, with intervening days of rest. Hunting involved long walks and jogging (up to 10 to 15 miles) to find herd animals; dramatic sprints, jumps, and turns; occasionally violent struggles; and lengthy hikes home carrying the kill. Every 2 or 3 days, women routinely gathered; they spent many hours walking to sources of food, water, and wood. Foraging often involved strenuous digging, climbing, and then carrying heavy loads back to camp—usually with an infant or a young child on the woman's hip or back. Other common activities, some physically taxing, included taking care of children, making tools, building shelters, butchering animals, preparing food, and visiting. Dances were a major pastime and could take place several nights a week—often lasting for hours. The overall activity pattern of these people was cyclic: days of intense physical exertion (both aerobic and resistive) alternated with days of rest and light activity.

These activity patterns suggest that most of us are best adapted to exercise programs that alternate strength and aerobic activities, accompanied by intervening days of rest or low-level activities. As you develop an exercise program, you should keep these concepts in mind. Hard days should be followed by one or more easy days, and strength training (weight lifting) should accompany aerobic training. Although the bottom line is that any exercise is better than no exercise, you will be less susceptible to injury and will obtain superior overall fitness if you can follow these fundamental principles.

Aerobic Training Programs

You may already be fit and exercising regularly. Or you may do sporadic exercise. Or maybe you are overweight, and you hardly ever exercise. What you begin to do now—the amount and intensity of your exercise program—will necessarily depend on your starting point.

In order to gain the minimal health effects of exercise, you will need to accumulate at least *30 minutes of aerobic activity* (walking, jogging, swimming, cycling, aerobic dance, stair climbing, racquetball, basketball, etc.) of *moderate intensity* on most, and *preferably all, days of the week*. Additional health and functional benefits of physical activity can be achieved by devoting more time to the activity, by increasing the vigor of the activity, or by increasing the number of times per week you exercise.

If you're a beginner, you may not be able to walk for 30 minutes a day, every day, right away. Always listen to your body and increase or decrease your exercise accordingly. If you have a family history of heart disease, are very obese, or have other health problems, you should talk to your doctor or even have a checkup before you begin your exercise program. However, don't use this as an excuse to avoid exercising. *Not* exercising is more hazardous to your health than exercising is. If you feel sore or tired from a day's exercise, take the next day off, just as our hunter-gatherer ancestors would have done. Gradually, as you become more and more fit, you will be able to increase the frequency, intensity, and duration of your exercise program. Your fitness level will generally change more rapidly if you heighten the intensity of exercise, rather than increase the frequency or duration.

The key to any successful aerobic training program is to stick with it. You need to keep it interesting and stimulating. The best way to sabotage an aerobic training program is to walk in boring circles around a track or ride a stationary bicycle in your closet. Personally, I find jogging or walking on hiking trails or little-used dirt roads on the edge of town to be much more stimulating and peaceful than jogging on city streets. I can see birds and wildlife. The terrain and the view are constantly changing, and I don't have to fight traffic. It may take you a little longer to drive to a trailhead or a walking path, but you may find that it's worth it. If you live in a metropolitan area, a large city park may be ideal for walks and jogs. You may prefer swimming or bicycling, or you may be more sociable and prefer the company of others while doing aerobic dance, stair climbing, or stationary bicycling in a health club or a gymnasium. Vary your aerobic activities; take your dog with you; bring a pair of binoculars and look for birds;

travel to the park or hiking trails; swim at the ocean or the lake. Don't look at excrcise as a form of penance. Make it fun, and make it stimulating.

Strength Training Programs

Strength training should be performed at least twice a week, incorporating a minimum of 8 to 10 specific exercises that use the major muscle groups of the legs, trunk, arms, and shoulders. You should perform at least one or two sets of 8 to 12 repetitions in each set. To minimize the risk of muscle injury, it's a good idea to do plenty of stretching and light calisthenics as a warm-up—the same for aerobic exercise. If you do not have a weight machine or a set of free weights at home, visit your local health club or fitness center to get started. Most health clubs and fitness centers employ knowledgeable personnel who can help you get started and can show you how to lift properly and use the weight machines. Once you figure out the basics, you may want to purchase equipment for your home.

Cross-Train—Just Like Your Paleolithic Ancestors

I encourage you not just to walk or swim or lift weights. Try to incorporate both strength and aerobic activities into your fitness program. This is the way our Paleolithic ancestors did it, and this is the method that will increase your fitness levels most rapidly, while simultaneously preventing injuries. If your legs are sore or tired from walking, then take the next day off or do some weight lifting that emphasizes the muscles of your upper body. Swimming is a wonderful exercise that temporarily neutralizes the force of gravity and allows free movement of the joints and the muscles. Even if walking or jogging is your main aerobic activity, try to swim a few times a month. It will give your body a needed break from jogging's incessant pounding and will allow you to stretch your muscles and joints fully. Using a cross-training machine, bicycling, and stationary bicycling, like swimming, can also work wonders in relieving the stress from too much walking or jogging. When you alternate strength activities with various aerobic activities, you will not only speed up the development of fitness, but you will also lessen your chances of injury.

Think of exercise as a luxury—a wonderful, opulent pursuit that is not available to all. It is a miraculous elixir that will brighten your spirits, improve your well-being, and make you feel so much better! Exercise will help you complete and maintain your wonderful new Paleo way of life.

Chapter 16

The Paleo Diet for Women

The Paleo Diet is a lifetime way of eating that has been adopted by hundreds of thousands, perhaps millions, of people worldwide. Men, women, and children of all ages and from all walks of life have decided to replicate the diets of their hunter-gatherer ancestors, but with foods commonly available at their local supermarkets. There are many ways to approach the Paleo Diet—many different Paleo diets, so to speak. People can fine-tune this nutritional plan to their individual needs, and I have always felt that this is the correct approach.

We should use the Paleo Diet as a starting point for optimal nutrition, but we should always listen to our own bodies, as we adjust our diets to our specific nutritional and lifestyle requirements. For instance, I view freshly steamed crab legs with pleasure and consider it a favorite food, whereas others may have allergies to shellfish that would obviously exclude this nutritious food. Some people seem to do better on higher-fat versions of the Paleo Diet, whereas others prefer less meat and more fruits and veggies.

Protein and Pregnancy

It is becoming increasingly clear that one size doesn't necessarily fit all. Following a modern-day Paleo diet may be one of the best strategies for you and your partner to become pregnant. Once women have a successful conception, however, it is important for them to reduce their protein intake during pregnancy.

There is no doubt that contemporary Paleo diets will give you with considerably more protein than the amount consumed in the typical US diet. The average protein intake in the US diet is 98.6 grams per day (15.5 percent of total calories) for men and 67.5 grams per day (15.1 percent of total calories) for women. Animal products provide approximately 75 percent of the protein in the US food supply, followed by dairy, cereals, eggs, legumes, fruits, and vegetables. Because dairy, cereals, and legumes are not part of the Paleo Diet, you will be obtaining nearly all of your protein from animal foods. Diets that contain 20 percent or more protein have been labeled high-protein diets, and those that contain 30 percent or more protein have been dubbed very-high-protein diets. Accordingly, a high-protein diet (20 to 30 percent protein) for the average US man would contain between 125 and 186 grams of protein per day and for the average woman from 89 to 133 grams of protein per day. Most contemporary Paleo Dieters follow high-protein diets, because their protein intake falls between 20 and 30 percent of their daily calories.

I need to point out that there is a physiological limit to the amount of protein you can ingest before it becomes toxic. A by-product of dietary protein metabolism is nitrogen, which in turn is converted into urea by your liver and then excreted by the kidneys into your urine. The upper limit of protein ingestion is determined by your liver's ability to synthesize urea. When nitrogen intake from dietary protein exceeds the ability of the liver to synthesize urea, excessive nitrogen (as ammonia) and amino acids spill into the bloodstream, causing toxicity. For most people, the dietary protein ceiling occurs when protein exceeds 35 to 40 percent of their normal daily caloric intake. Consequently, very-high-protein diets for the average US man could range from 187 to 270 grams per day and for women, from 134 to 246 grams per day.

Our hunter-gatherer ancestors knew that they could get too much of a good thing and avoided eating very lean, fat-depleted animals. Anthropologists, including my colleague John Speth at the University of Michigan, have documented that hunter-gatherer women have a lower tolerance for protein when they become pregnant. The medical literature has recently substantiated the anthropological observations, and it is now known that during pregnancy, women have a reduced ability to metabolize dietary protein. High maternal protein intake increases the risk for low-birthweight babies and overall fetal mortality. During pregnancy, the estimated safe upper limit for dietary protein is about 25 percent of daily calories. Here's a breakdown of protein content in the average American diet.

- Average protein intake in the United States: 15 percent of caloric intake
- Diets considered to be high-protein: 20 to 30 percent of average caloric intake
- Diets considered very-high-protein: 30 to 40 percent of average caloric intake

Most modern-day Paleo Dieters eat high-protein diets that contain between 20 and 30 percent protein. If you are pregnant, a 25 percent protein limit would amount to no more than 110 grams of protein per day. This goal can easily be achieved by eating fattier cuts of meat; fatty fish such as salmon, mackerel, and herring; and more nuts, avocados, and eggs, along with using more olive oil in your salads and cooking. Besides including more fat in your diet, you should also displace lean proteins with more carbohydrates. Yams, sweet potatoes, bananas, and other fresh fruits are a great starting point.

Eating Paleo is perhaps the best strategy you can take in becoming pregnant, and by slightly lowering your protein intake during pregnancy, you can help assure yourself of an easy delivery and a healthy baby.

Paleo Diets and Gestational Diabetes Mellitus

One of the greatest risks for pregnant women and their fetuses is the development of diabetes during pregnancy. This condition is known as gestational diabetes mellitus (GDM) and is present in 4 to 7 percent of all pregnancies in the United States. GDM heightens the risk for premature births, birth defects, and stillbirths. For the mother-to-be, GDM increases her chances of developing pre-eclampsia, a blood pressure condition that can be life threatening to the mother and the child. The chief metabolic problem with GDM is that maternal blood sugar levels remain elevated during pregnancy; this condition is largely responsible for the health risks in both mother and fetus.

GDM is definitely bad news, but the good news is that low-glycemic-index and low-glycemic-load diets are known to improve pregnancy outcomes if they are followed starting with the first trimester. My colleague Dr. Jennie Brand-Miller from the University of Sydney demonstrated that low-glycemic-index diets effectively halved the number of women who required medication to control their high blood sugar levels during pregnancy. And a recent study from David Ludwig's group at Harvard Medical School showed that a low-glycemic-load diet resulted in longer pregnancy duration, greater infant head circumferences, and improved maternal cardiovascular risk factors.

Because the Paleo Diet is a low-glycemic-index nutritional plan, it represents one of the best steps pregnant women can adopt to prevent GDM and improve their own health and that of their children.

The Paleo Diet, Omega-3 Fatty Acids, and Pregnancy

One of the most therapeutic aspects of the Paleo Diet for virtually all chronic Western diseases is its high omega-3 fatty acid content, particularly EPA and DHA. So it should not surprise you that these essential nutrients will also help ensure a successful pregnancy and a healthy baby. Adequate maternal intake of EPA and DHA during pregnancy can improve your infant's cognitive and visual performance because these fatty acids represent the building blocks of fetal brain and retinal tissues. Omega-3 fatty acids play a key role in determining the length of gestation and may reduce the incidence of preterm birth. Some studies also suggest that sufficient consumption of fish (high sources of EPA and DHA) during pregnancy may be effective in preventing postpartum depression. Unfortunately, many pregnant women avoid fish because of concerns about adverse effects of mercury and other contaminants.

The Paleo Diet is an extraordinarily rich source of omega-3 fatty acids, particularly if you consume fatty fish such as salmon, mackerel, herring, or sardines a few times a week. Shellfish and leaner fish are good sources of EPA and DHA; grass-fed meats and omega-3–enriched eggs contain moderate amounts of these health-promoting fatty acids. Pregnant women should strive for a minimum of 200 milligrams (mg) of DHA per day. Note that a 100-gram serving, around 4 ounces, of Atlantic salmon gives you 300 mg of EPA and 900 mg of DHA. If you don't like to eat fish or seafood or have worries about mercury and other toxins in fish, I recommend that you supplement with fish oil, either capsules or liquid, during your pregnancy.

The Paleo Diet and Polycystic Ovary Syndrome

Polycystic ovary syndrome (PCOS) is the most common hormonal disease in females, afflicting between 5 and 10 percent of all women of childbearing age; it is a major cause of infertility. Common symptoms include menstrual irregu-

larities, ovarian cysts, and high levels of male hormones, producing acne, excessive body hair, and hair loss. The majority of women with PCOS have insulin
resistance and frequently are obese. They maintain a ten times greater incidence
of type 2 diabetes than healthy normal women and are at a much greater risk of
dying from premature cardiovascular disease.

The good news is that diet is known to be a major player underlying this
syndrome. Weight-loss programs seem to reduce disease symptoms, but more
important, so may low-glycemic-index diets. A new study by Dr. Jennie Brand-
Miller has shown that a low-glycemic-index diet could improve PCOS symptoms by preventing menstrual irregularities. Two other new studies have
demonstrated that supplementation with omega-3 fatty acids may also be therapeutic in PCOS patients. The Paleo Diet is just what the doctor ordered if you
have PCOS. Because our ancestral diet is a high-protein, low-glycemic nutritional plan, rich in omega-3 fats, it will help you to lose weight, normalize your
hormones, and reduce your risk for developing diabetes and cardiovascular
disease.

Relieving Menstrual Problems

Phyllis's Story

I have not read of any other women talking about relief from period pain on a Paleo diet, but if only I'd known about it years earlier!

I have always had extremely severe cramps in the first few hours of my period. I spoke to many women but have met only a few who seemed to experience the same degree of pain as me. If I didn't take medication in time, I always repeatedly vomited, even after my stomach was empty. I had diarrhea and terrible cramps. I just could not believe how painful they were. My hair was usually wet within minutes, due to my sweating from the pain, and I could see the sweat bead down my arms, too. I could not even sit upright; mostly, I just curled into a ball. I lived in terror of being caught away from home, without medication, when my cramps started.

Although being on the pill solved the problem for a couple of years in my twenties, I did not want to be on the pill long term. No other solution worked, and even
referrals to gynecologists did not help. Yet for the 2 years I lived in Japan in my mid-
twenties, I was free of all pain. I put this down to a diet high in seaweed, tofu, and fish
and was frustrated that I never managed to replicate the benefits at home in Australia, despite trying hard to achieve a similar diet.

It seems odd now that I didn't realize that the solution lay in what I was not eating in Japan: I was eating very little dairy and wheat. A doctor who specialized in

nutritional medicine made this clear to me. After 1 week on a Paleo diet, I had my first period in 11 years that did not require medication. I was astonished and jubilant.

I have experienced most of the other benefits that people have talked so much about, such as weight loss, increased energy, and no colds. My premenstrual tension is almost entirely gone after months of getting progressively worse. My favorite thing is not having an afternoon slump during my workday.

The Paleo Diet and Breast and Other Cancers

Although many women fear breast cancer—and rightly so—the greatest risk to health for both men and women comes not from cancer but rather from cardiovascular disease. Cancer is second. In both men and women, cardiovascular disease plus cancer are responsible for a little more than 60 percent of all deaths from all causes combined. The Paleo Diet contains many nutritional elements that can greatly reduce your risk of contracting both of these diseases.

There is no doubt that breast cancer is a serious illness that in many cases can be life threatening. The graphs on the opposite page show the top 10 causes of cancer deaths in the United States in 2007. Note that for both men and women, lung cancer is responsible for nearly twice as many fatalities as the next leading cancer deaths—breast for women and prostate for men. Almost all lung cancer is caused by smoking and consequently is preventable by eliminating this nasty habit.

Breast cancer was rare or nonexistent in historically studied hunter-gatherers and other less-Westernized peoples. Similar observations have been consistently noted for almost all of the other common modern cancers: prostate, colorectal, pancreatic, leukemia, and ovarian. Some of the most convincing evidence demonstrating that cancer is a disease of modern civilization comes from studies of the Inuit (Eskimo) people as they made the transition from their Stone Age way of life to the Space Age in less than two generations.

Here is a quote from an article on Eskimo health that appeared in the *Canadian Medical Association Journal* in 1936: "In the Western Arctic Dr. Urquhart has as yet not met with a single case of cancer in the 7 years of his practice. Cancer must be extremely rare in the Eastern Arctic also." Similar observations come from yet another frontier physician, Dr. Samuel Hutton, who treated non-Westernized Inuit people in Labrador from 1902 to 1913:

"Some diseases common in Europe have not come under my notice during a prolonged and careful survey of the health of the Eskimos. Of these diseases the most striking is cancer. I have not seen or heard of a case of malignant new growth in an Eskimo." As the Inuit people became more and more Westernized and began to replace their traditional foods with processed foods, their relative immunity to cancer diminished. In a paper published in 1984,

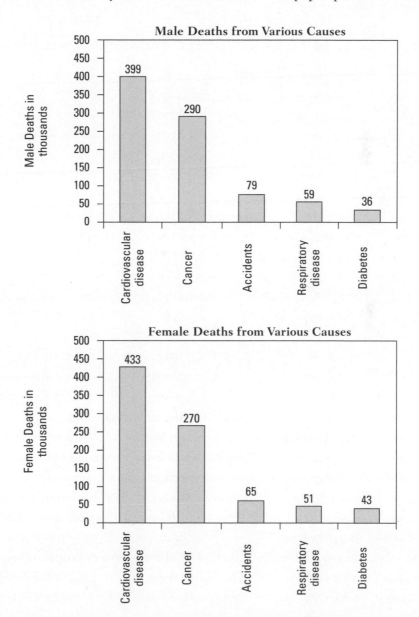

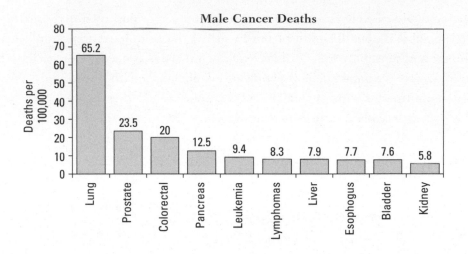

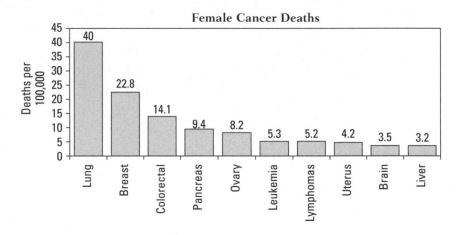

Drs. Hildes and Schaefer examined cancer rates in the Inuit from 1950 to 1980 and noted, "The most frequent tumours in the most recent period studied were lung, cervical and colorectal cancers. Breast cancer was absent before 1966 and was found in only 2 of 107 Canadian Inuit women stricken with cancer from 1967 to 1980, whereas the most recent rates in the longer-acculturated Inuit of Alaska and Greenland have approached those prevailing in modern Western women."

The virtual absence of breast cancer and other common Western cancers is not entirely restricted to the Inuit. The Nobel prize–winning physician Dr. Albert Schweitzer commented, "On my arrival in Gabon, in 1913, I was astonished to encounter no case of cancer. . . . I cannot, of course, say positively that there was no cancer at all, but, like other frontier doctors, I can only say that if any cases existed they must have been quite rare. This absence of cancer seemed to me due to the difference in nutrition of the natives as compared with the Europeans. . . . In the course of the years, we have seen cases of cancer in growing numbers in our region. My observations incline me to attribute this to the fact that the natives were living more and more after the manner of the whites." Dr. Schweitzer got it right. The virtual absence of breast, prostate, colorectal, and other common Western cancers in the hunter-gatherers of Gabon had everything to do with their diet.

The Paleo Diet maintains multiple nutritional characteristics that will help protect you against breast and other common Western cancers. The Paleo Diet is a low-glycemic-index, low-glycemic-load diet. A recent meta-analysis involving 10 studies and more than 575,000 subjects by Drs. Dong and Qin clearly shows that high-glycemic-index diets increase the risk for developing breast cancer. Similar results were observed in an even larger meta-analysis by Dr. Barclay and colleagues from the University of Sydney.

It is not only the Paleo Diet's low glycemic index and load that will protect you from breast cancer but also its rich omega-3 fatty acid content and low levels of high omega-6 vegetable oils. In tissue and animal models of breast cancer, omega-6 fatty acids from vegetable oils stimulate cancer growth, whereas omega-3 fatty acids inhibit it. A large meta-analysis by Dr. Saadatian-Elahi showed a significant protective effect of omega-3 fatty acids on breast cancer risk.

The Paleo Diet is a milk- and dairy-free diet. As discussed earlier, milk drinking boosts your blood concentrations of female hormones, whether you are a man or a woman. If you are a woman, elevated blood estrogen and its metabolites increase your lifetime risk for breast and ovarian cancers. For men, milk's added estrogen may heighten your risk for prostate and testicular cancer.

The Paleo Diet is also exceedingly rich in fresh fruits and veggies. These foods are Mother Nature's best medicine; meta-analyses of population studies confirm that fresh fruits and vegetables protect women from breast and many other cancers.

However you look at it, the Paleo Diet is a good natural way to prevent cancer.

Surviving Breast Cancer

Debbie's Story

I am a breast cancer survivor. I was first diagnosed with breast cancer on May 25, 2001: T1, Node Negative, HER2-positive, and nuclear grade 3. I had a lumpectomy, aggressive chemotherapy, and radiation. On March 26, 2004, my breast cancer returned to my L-1 disk in my spine. I had 6 months of weekly chemotherapy and radiation. By December 15, 2004, I was declared in remission.

Herceptin was part of the chemo protocol that I had received in 2004, and I have been receiving it every 3 weeks since the beginning of January 2005. Tumor marker tests are also conducted every other month. Unfortunately, my tumor markers started rising, and by the end-of-May tests, the upward trend was disturbing.

On May 28, I shared this news with my pharmacist, who is also a certified nutritionist. He recommended that I immediately eliminate sugar and grains from my diet. I found the Paleo Diet and started to eliminate sugar, grains, and dairy from my diet that day.

The results have been astonishing, to say the least. On May 24, 2005, my CA 27 29 marker was 43 and as of October 24, 2005, was 24. My CA 15 3 marker was 28.6 on May 24, 2005 and lowered to 22.9. I am 100 percent convinced that it is a result of my being a very compliant follower of the Paleo Diet. Cancer likes sugar. Sugar is not my friend and is an enemy to my health.

I am very thankful to an astute pharmacist/certified nutritionist who is on top of the current diets and their effects on one's health. We are what we eat. I do not miss any of the sweets that I craved so, and I love the fact that I have finally lost the 25 pounds of chemo/radiation weight that I could not lose, no matter how much exercise or dieting I did since 2002. Fresh fruits, fresh vegetables, and lean meats and fish are the mainstays of my current good health.

I will continue to spread the message to my support group and other women I meet who have breast cancer. Mind, body, and soul—keeping each healthy is essential to survive this terrible disease. The diet recommended to me on May 28, 2005, empowered me to continue to do everything possible to win this battle.

The Paleo Diet and Osteoporosis

One of the greatest fears many women have when they first adopt the Paleo Diet is how—without drinking milk or eating dairy products—they will get enough calcium to build strong bones to prevent osteoporosis. As I mentioned, large meta-analyses (combined population studies) clearly show that neither calcium supplementation nor increased milk drinking reduces the risk for osteoporotic fractures. The current obsession with calcium *intake* as the single and most important factor involved with bone health is misguided. What the dairy lobbyists don't tell us is that bone mineral content is determined not only by calcium *intake* but rather by *calcium balance*.

The calcium stores in your bones are like your checkbook. If you spend more money than you earn, your checking account will have a negative balance. Similarly, if we lose more calcium in our urine than we ingest, we will be in negative calcium balance. This phenomenon helps explain why US women maintain one of the worst rates of osteoporosis in the world, despite having one of the highest calcium intakes.

When we talk about calcium balance, calcium loss in the urine is just as important as the calcium we ingest from our diets. Urinary calcium losses are primarily dependent on dietary acid/base balance. After digestion, all foods ultimately report to the kidneys as either acid or base. If our diet is net acid producing, the acid must be buffered by the alkaline stores of base in our bones. Acid-producing foods are hard cheeses, cereal grains, salted foods, and almost all processed foods, meats, fish, and eggs. The only alkaline base–producing foods are fruits and vegetables. Because the average American diet is overloaded with grains, cheeses, and salty processed foods at the expense of fruits and vegetables, virtually everyone in the United States has an acid-yielding diet that leaches calcium from his or her bones.

Because Paleo Dieters consume anywhere from a third to half of their daily calories as fresh fruits and veggies, their diets are net alkaline yielding—reducing urinary calcium losses and restoring a positive calcium balance. High-protein diets such as the Paleo Diet are also bone healthy because protein increases calcium absorption and stimulates production of a hormone (IGF-1) that promotes new bone formation. Besides yielding a net alkaline load to the kidneys, most fresh veggies are rich sources of calcium, particularly leafy green vegetables—think broccoli, kale, cabbage, Brussels sprouts, cauliflower, kohlrabi, and mustard greens.

Vitamin C from fresh fruits and veggies, like protein from meats and fish, increases calcium absorption, further promoting a net positive calcium balance. Vitamin D is also one of our best allies in ensuring strong, fracture-resistant bones so be sure to implement dietary and lifestyle strategies to ensure adequate blood levels of vitamin D.

Rest assured, evolution via natural selection has engineered successful biological systems that build strong, fracture-resistant bones for every species of mammal on the planet—including us. Without drinking cow's milk.

Feeling Better

Liz's Story

I am a 61-year-old woman. I started the Paleo Diet in November 2005 and have been on it ever since. I do indulge in some of the forbidden foods such as coffee with half-and-half, a habit seemingly impossible for me to break. It gives me the energy to do the things I want to do, and unless you can give me a formula for getting more energy otherwise, I may be in trouble on that one. Also, after experimenting without or with drastically less salt, I have added back my habitual amounts of salt again. But it is a lot, lot less than in the typical American diet, I assure you. Other than that, I stick to meat, vegetables, and fruit. No dairy, no grains, no legumes, no potatoes. I don't miss any of it.

I found an organic farmer in Marin County near where I live and got a hog, a quarter steer, and chickens from him. The meat is lean and outstanding. I get fresh-caught fish and vegetables from the farmer's market, as well as organic eggs. My trips to the supermarket are now limited to bananas, half-and-half, and a few other things occasionally.

I feel good. Some friends say I am the picture of health. At the start of the diet, I weighed 145 pounds; now I weigh 130 pounds and have stayed there for months.

I never suffer from indigestion now. My husband, who is also on this diet, eats toast and butter and jam for breakfast, a gourmet lunch with his colleagues, and what I cook for dinner. Even so, he has gone from having a hiatal hernia, with daily doses of Mylanta and Prilosec, to no problems at all. And he has lost at least 30 pounds. I would like to see him eat better, and maybe he'll come around.

For a while I did experience daily leg cramps, then I read one of Dr. Cordain's papers on potassium and what contained the most potassium. I try to eat those vegetables, and I throw mushrooms into everything when I have them.

Since I have been on the diet, I have been virtually free of almost weekly, random, very debilitating headaches. I feel so free and at this point take it for granted. There used to be days when I just would have to stay in bed because the headaches were so bad, and the doctor always said they were tension headaches.

Bottom line—I like eating the way I do, and I will never change.

Chapter 17

Living the Paleo Diet

I have given you the key to the door, but I cannot open it for you. For the first time in your life, you should realize that by eating the diet nature devised for us, you can achieve permanent weight loss and significantly improve your health. All of this can occur without your experiencing continual feelings of hunger.

Humanity's original diet is not prescribed to you by a diet doctor or by governmental recommendations, but rather by more than 2 million years of evolutionary wisdom. This is the diet that every single person on the planet ate a mere 333 generations ago. Paleolithic people had no choice but to follow the Paleo Diet. Refined grains, sugars, salt, dairy products, fatty meats, and processed food simply didn't exist. Unfortunately, from a health and weight perspective, you have a choice. Burgers, fries, and a Coke are just down the block—but so are healthful fruits, vegetables, and lean meats. The choice is yours.

How can you empower yourself? How can you make the correct choice happen every time? Here are a few simple guidelines that will help.

The Right Reasons to Eat

Let's once more follow the course given to us by our hunter-gatherer ancestors. Eat when you are hungry, and stop eating when you are full. Many of us eat for all the wrong reasons.

Food is love. Remember that birthday cake you ate on your special day as a child? It brought you warmth and security—it may have represented your parents' love. Many of us still associate sugary, rich desserts with love and fond childhood memories. That's okay; in fact, food should still be associated with love. But why not try to love yourself, your family, or your friends with some of nature's original loving food, so that by eating, you are also loving your body and making yourself healthy? How about a few rich lobster tails or fresh crab legs, some creamy avocado slices, or a bowl of fresh blackberries topped with almond slices? These foods taste great and make you feel great. Those childhood love foods (cookies, cakes, candy, ice cream, chocolates—you know the rest) are a temporary fix that all too soon will make you feel tired, drowsy, and bloated. How many times do you need to "love yourself" with these foods to know that they always let you down in the long run?

Food is a reward. Remember going out to dinner after high school graduation, your wedding, or getting that new job? You rewarded yourself by eating a great meal—and rightly so. You deserved it, and you still do. However, many of us seek that reward or gratification from our food almost daily. Reward yourself with food, and do it daily, but do it with the delicious bounty of real foods: fruits, vegetables, and meats. You will be rewarding not only your psyche but your body, as well.

Food relieves boredom. Have you ever sat around on a Friday evening with nothing to do, knowing there is a half gallon of ice cream in the refrigerator? How about an afternoon home alone with some chocolate chip cookies fresh out of the oven? When you adopt the Paleo Diet, these situations will no longer be a problem. You will have a ton of food at home, but it will be fruits, veggies, meats, and seafood. Go ahead—get bored all you want, and please eat all you want, because your appetite will tell you when to stop. You could probably eat the entire half gallon of ice cream and the whole plate of cookies, but you will always stop eating when you've had your fill of chicken breasts, succulent tiger shrimp, or fresh tangerines. Use these foods to relieve your boredom, and you will find yourself losing weight and taking a new path toward terrific health.

One Day at a Time

If you are like almost everyone on this planet, you probably have never made it through a single day of your life without eating grains, dairy products, legumes, salt, refined sugars, fatty meats, or processed foods and drinks.

Go ahead, try it—just once!

I challenge you to eat nothing but fresh fruits, veggies, fish, seafood and fresh meats for a single day. You will not be hungry. Eat as much and as many of these foods as you want—eat until you are full. I can assure you that you will not develop vitamin or mineral deficiencies; on the contrary, you will be luxuriously nourished.

See for yourself—see how you feel when you wake up the next morning.

Follow the Paleo Diet principles all day long for a second day. You can do it. If you get hungry or are tempted, treat yourself to a big bowl of fruit or some cold chicken breasts or any of the wonderful Paleo snacks listed in Chapter 9. Monitor your energy level. Do you like waking up feeling positive and energized, looking forward to a bright new day? Do you like the way it feels *not* to have that midmorning or midafternoon slump? Well, this is just the beginning. Most people report these healthful benefits within days of adopting the Paleo Diet.

But the best is yet to come. Your weight will drop rapidly within the first few days, and then you will continue to lose weight until you reach your optimal weight. For some people, this may take a month or two; for those with severe weight problems, 6 months or more. But the bottom line is that you will continue to lose weight as long as you follow the Paleo Diet principles. If weight loss is your primary goal, then focus on how you would like to look in a month or two. Your confidence will soar as you begin to shed the pounds. Your clothes will begin to fit a bit looser. Good—you are well on your way! People will notice your new svelteness. Use these markers as your personal triumphs. Know that these little victories may take weeks or months but that the battle is won on a daily basis. Try to remember how good each morning feels when you stick with the diet. This is where it counts—day to day. The days become weeks, and the weeks become months, and you will eventually break through and reach your weight-loss goal—whatever it may be.

You may also notice that many health problems you had lived with or ignored for years begin to improve. Your joints are no longer as stiff in the morning, and your sinuses are now beginning to clear. Your skin and hair are becoming softer and less dry. Your heartburn and indigestion have become a thing of the past. And for the first time in years, your constipation or irritable bowel syndrome is gone. For those with more serious health problems, such as high blood pressure and elevated cholesterol or type 2 diabetes, symptoms may begin to improve within weeks of adopting the Paleo Diet.

You have the key to unlock the door of good health with humanity's original diet. What better reason to permanently adopt the Paleo Diet than to prevent heart disease, type 2 diabetes, hypertension, or other symptoms of metabolic syndrome? Play it smart. Remove the known or suspected causes of metabolic syndrome from your diet. When you do, you will also lower your risk of developing many types of cancer, as well.

The choice is yours. The risks are nil, the benefits are many. Eat your fill to health and the right weight. And don't forget to enjoy!

Resources

RECOMMENDED WEB SITES

Loren Cordain's Paleo Diet Web site
thepaleodiet.com

Loren Cordain's Dietary Cure for Acne Web site
thepaleodiet.com/dietary-cure-for-acne

Robb Wolf's Web site
robbwolf.com

Don Wiss's comprehensive Paleo Web site
donwiss.com

RECOMMENDED BOOKS

Cordain, Loren. *The Dietary Cure for Acne.* Fort Collins, CO: Paleo Diet Enterprises LLC, 2006, http://thepaleodiet.com/dietary-cure-for-acne/.

Cordain, Loren, and Joe Friel. *The Paleo Diet for Athletes: A Nutritional Formula for Peak Athletic Performance.* Emmaus, PA: Rodale Inc., 2005.

Cordain, Loren, Nell Stephenson, and Lorrie Cordain. *The Paleo Diet Cookbook: More Than 150 Recipes for Paleo Breakfasts, Lunches, Dinners, Snacks, and Beverages.* Hoboken, NJ: John Wiley & Sons, 2011.

SUPPLIERS OF GAME MEATS

Broken Arrow Ranch
3296 Junction Highway
Ingram, TX 78025
(800) 962-4263
brokenarrowranch.com

Exotic Meat Market
130 Walnut Avenue, #5
Perris, CA 92571
(877) 398-0141
exoticmeatmarkets.com

Exotic Meats USA
1330 Capital Blvd.
Reno, NV 89502
(800) 444-5687
exoticmeatsandmore.com
gamesalesintl.com

Grande Natural Meat
PO Box 10
Del Norte, Colorado 81132
(888) 338-4581
elkusa.com

Hills Foods Ltd.
Unit 1-130 Glacier Street
Coquitlam, British Columbia
Canada V3K 5Z6
(877) 368-7569
hillsfoods.com

Mount Royal Game Meat
3902 N. Main
Houston, TX 77009
(800) 730-3337
mountroyal.com

Polarica
105 Quint Street
San Francisco, CA 94124
(800) 426-3872
polarica.com

SUPPLIERS OF PASTURE- AND GRASS-PRODUCED MEATS, EGGS, AND DAIRY

Jo Robinson's comprehensive listing of pasture and grass-fed meats, eggs, and dairy in the United States and Canada.
eatwild.com

George Bass's free-range eggs
The Country Hen
16 Williamsville Road
Hubbardston, MA 01452
(978) 928-5333
countryhen.com

References

Abegaz EG, Bursey RG. Formaldehyde, aspartame, migraines: a possible connection. *Dermatitis* 2009 May-Jun;20(3):176–177; author reply 177–179.

Abrams HL. A dischronic perview of wheat in hominid nutrition. *J Appl Nutr* 1978;30:41–43.

———. The relevance of Paleolithic diet in determining contemporary nutritional needs. *J Applied Nutr* 1979;31:43–59.

Abrams SA, Griffin IJ. Microminerals and Bone Health. In Holick MF, Dawson-Hughes B, *Nutrition and Bone Health*. Totowa, NJ: Humana Press, 2004: 377–387.

Adachi J, Hasegawa M. Improved dating of the human/chimpanzee separation in the mitochondrial DNA tree: heterogeneity among amino acid sites. *J Mol Evol* 1995;40:622–628.

Adams M, Lucock M, Stuart J, Fardell S, Baker K, Ng X. Preliminary evidence for involvement of the folate gene polymorphism 19bp deletion-DHFR in occurrence of autism. *Neurosci Lett* 2007 Jul 5;422(1):24–29.

Adams PB, Lawson S, Sanigorski A, Sinclair AJ. Arachidonic acid to eicosapentaenoic acid ratio in blood correlates positively with clinical symptoms of depression. *Lipids* 1996;31:S157–S161.

Adebamowo CA, Spiegelman D, Berkey CS, Danby FW, Rockett HH, Colditz GA, Willett WC, Holmes MD. Milk consumption and acne in teenaged boys. *J Am Acad Dermatol* 2008;58(5):787–793.

———. Milk consumption and acne in adolescent girls. *Dermatol Online J* 2006;12(4):1.

Adebamowo CA, Spiegelman D, Danby FW, Frazier AL, Willett WC, Holmes MD. High school dietary dairy intake and teenage acne. *J Am Acad Dermatol* 2005;52(2):207–214.

Adly L, Hill D, Sherman ME, Sturgeon SR, Fears T, Mies C, Ziegler RG, Hoover RN, Schairer C. Serum concentrations of estrogens, sex hormone-binding globulin, and androgens and risk of breast cancer in postmenopausal women. *Int J Cancer* 2006 Nov 15;119(10):2402–2407.

Agren MS. Studies on zinc in wound healing. *Acta Derm Venereol Suppl (Stockh)* 1990;154:1–36.

Agren MS, Ostenfeld U, Kallchave F, Gong Y, Raffn K, Crawford ME, Kiss K, Friis-Møller A, Gluud C, Jorgensen LN. A randomized, double-blind, placebo-controlled multicenter trial evaluating topical zinc oxide for acute open wounds following pilonidal disease excision. *Wound Repair Regen* 2006 Sep–Oct;14(5):526–535.

Aiello LC, Wheeler P. The expensive tissue hypothesis. *Curr Anthropol* 1995;36: 199–222

Ainsleigh HG. Beneficial effects of sun exposure on cancer mortality. *Prev Med* 1993;22:132–140.

315

Aizawa H, Niimura M. Elevated serum insulin-like growth factor-1 (IGF-1) levels in women with postadolescent acne. *J Dermatol* 1995;22:249–252.

———. Mild insulin resistance during oral glucose tolerance test (OGTT) in women with acne. *J Dermatol* 1996;23:526–529.

Albanes D, Jones DV, Schatzkin A, Micozzi MS, Taylor PR. Adult stature and risk of cancer. *Can Res* 1988;48:1658–1662.

Albert CM, Hennekens CH, O'Donnell CJ, Ajani UA, Carey VJ, Willett WC, Ruskin JN, Manson JE. Fish consumption and risk of sudden cardiac death. *JAMA* 1998;279:23–28.

Albert LJ, Inman RD. Molecular mimicry and autoimmunity. *N Engl J Med* 1999;341:2068–2074.

Alcock N, Macintyre I. Inter-relation of calcium and magnesium absorption. *Clin Sci* 1962 Apr;22:185–193.

Alexander D, Ball MJ, Mann J. Nutrient intake and haematological status of vegetarians and age-sex matched omnivores. *Eur J Clin Nutr* 1994 Aug;48(8):538–546.

Alexiou P, Chatzopoulou M, Pegklidou K, Demopoulos VJ. RAGE: a multi-ligand receptor unveiling novel insights in health and disease. *Curr Med Chem* 2010;17(21):2232–2252.

Alvarez JR, Torres-Pinedo R. Interactions of soybean lectin, soyasaponins, and glycinin with rabbit jejunal mucosa in vitro. *Pediatr Res* 1982 Sep;16(9):728–731.

American Heart Association. *2000 Heart and Stroke Statistical Update.* Dallas, TX: American Heart Association, 1999.

American Heart Association, 2010 Heart & Stroke Statistical Update americanheart.org /presenter.jhtml?identifier=3000090.

American Society for Clinical Nutrition and American Institute of Nutrition/AIN Task Force on Trans Fatty Acids. Position paper on trans fatty acids. *Am J Clin Nutr* 1996 May;63(5):663–670.

Amiridou D, Voutsa D. Alkylphenols and phthalates in bottled waters. *J Hazard Mater* 2011 Jan 15;185(1):281–286.

ams.usda.gov/nop/NationalList/TAPReviews/morpholine.pdf.

ams.usda.gov/nop/NationalList/TAPReviews/shellac.pdf.

Anderson GH. Dietary patterns vs. dietary recommendations: identifying the gaps for complex carbohydrate. *Crit Rev Food Sci Nutr* 1994;5&6:435–440.

Ansaldi N, Palmas T, Corrias A, Barbato M, D'Altiglia MR, Campanozzi A, Baldassarre M, Rea F, Pluvio R, Bonamico M, Lazzari R, Corrao G. Autoimmune thyroid disease and celiac disease in children. *J Pediatr Gastroenterol Nutr* 2003 Jul;37(1):63–66.

Antonios TT, MacGregor GA. Deleterious effects of salt intake other than effects on blood pressure. *Clin Exp Pharmacol Physiol* 1995;22:180–184.

Appel LJ, Moore TJ, Obarzanek E, Vollmer WM, Svetkey LP, Sacks FM, Bray GA, Vogt TM, Cutler JA, Windhauser MM, Lin PH, Karanja N. A clinical trial of the effects of dietary patterns on blood pressure. *N Engl J Med* 1997;336: 1117–1124.

Appel LJ, Sacks FM, Carey VJ, Obarzanek E, Swain JF, Miller ER 3rd, Conlin PR, Erlinger TP, Rosner BA, Laranjo NM, Charleston J, McCarron P, Bishop LM, OmniHeart Collaborative Research Group. Effects of protein, monounsaturated fat, and carbohydrate intake on blood pressure and serum lipids: results of the OmniHeart randomized trial. *JAMA* 2005 Nov 16;294(19):2455–2464.

Appleby P, Roddam A, Allen N, Key T. Comparative fracture risk in vegetarians and nonvegetarians in EPIC-Oxford. *Eur J Clin Nutr* 2007 Dec;61(12):1400–1406.

Appleby PN, Thorogood M, Mann JI, Key TJ. The Oxford Vegetarian Study: an overview. *Am J Clin Nutr* 1999 Sep;70(3 Suppl):525S–531S.

Appleton KM, Rogers PJ, Ness AR. Updated systematic review and meta-analysis of the effects of n-3 long-chain polyunsaturated fatty acids on depressed mood. *Am J Clin Nutr* 2010 Mar;91(3):757–770.

Armelagos GJ. Human evolution and the evolution of disease. *Ethn Dis* 1991;1: 21–25.

Arrar L, Hanachi N, Rouba K, Charef N, Khennouf S, Baghiani A. Anti-xanthine oxidase antibodies in sera and synovial fluid of patients with rheumatoid arthritis and other joint inflammations. *Saudi Med J* 2008 Jun;29(6):803–807.

Arrieta MC, Bistritz L, Meddings JB.Alterations in intestinal permeability. *Gut* 2006 Oct;55(10):1512–1520.

Artaud-Wild S et al. Differences in coronary mortality can be explained by differences in cholesterol and saturated fat intake in 40 countries but not in France and Finland. *Circulation* 1993;88: 2771–2779.

Astrup A, Dyerberg J, Elwood P, Hermansen K, Hu FB, Jakobsen MU, Kok FJ, Krauss RM, Lecerf JM, Legrand P, Nestel P, Risérus U, Sanders T, Sinclair A, Stender S, Tholstrup T, Willett W. The role of reducing intakes of saturated fat in the prevention of cardiovascular disease: where does the evidence stand in 2010? *Am J Clin Nutr* 2011 Apr; 93(4):684–88.

ATBC Cancer Prevention Study Group. The effect of vitamin E and beta carotene on the incidence of lung cancer and other cancers in male smokers. The Alpha-Tocopherol, Beta Carotene Cancer Prevention Study Group. *N Engl J Med* 1994 Apr 14;330(15):1029–1035.

Attia N, Tamborlane WV, Heptulla R, Maggs D, Grozman A, Sherwin RS, Caprio S. The metabolic syndrome and insulin-like growth factor I regulation in adolescent obesity. *J Clin Endocrinol Metab* 1998;83:1467–1471.

Aude YW, Agatston AS, Lopez-Jimenez F, Lieberman EH, Almon M, Hansen M, Rojas G, Lamas GA, Hennekens CH. The national cholesterol education program diet vs a diet lower in carbohydrates and higher in protein and monounsaturated fat: a randomized trial. *Arch Intern Med* 2004 Oct 25;164(19):2141–2146.

Autier P. Sunscreen abuse for intentional sun exposure. *Br J Dermatol* 2009 Nov;161 Suppl 3:40–45.

Autier P, Boniol M, Doré JF. Sunscreen use and increased duration of intentional sun exposure: still a burning issue. *Int J Cancer* 2007 Jul 1;121(1):1–5.

Autier P, Doré JF, Eggermont AM, Coebergh JW. Epidemiological evidence that UVA radiation is involved in the genesis of cutaneous melanoma. *Curr Opin Oncol* 2011 Mar;23(2):189–196.

Autism and Developmental Disabilities Monitoring Network Surveillance Year 2006 Principal Investigators; Centers for Disease Control and Prevention (CDC). Prevalence of autism spectrum disorders—Autism and Developmental Disabilities Monitoring Network, United States, 2006. *MMWR Surveill Summ* 2009 Dec 18;58(10):1–20.

Baaregaard A. Dental conditions and nutrition among natives in Greenland. *Oral Surg, Oral Med, Oral Pathol* 1949;2:995–1007.

Baba NH, Sawaya S, Torbay N, Habbal Z, Azar S, Hashim SA. High protein vs. high carbohydrate hypoenergetic diet for the treatment of obese hyper-insulinemic subjects. *Int J Obes Relat Metab Disord* 1999;23:1202–1206.

Bai J, Hagenmaier RD, Baldwin EA. Volatile response of four apple varieties with different coatings during marketing at room temperature. *J Agric Food Chem* 2002 Dec 18;50(26):7660–7668.

Baines M, Kredan MB, Davison A, Higgins G, West C, Fraser WD, Ranganath LR. The association between cystcine, bone turnover, and low bone mass. *Calcif Tissue Int* 2007 Dec;81(6):450–454.

Baines S, Powers J, Brown WJ. How does the health and well-being of young Australian vegetarian and semi-vegetarian women compare with non-vegetarians? *Public Health Nutr* 2007 May;10(5):436–442.

Baker BP, Benbrook CM, Groth E 3rd, Lutz Benbrook K. Pesticide residues in conventional, integrated pest management (IPM)-grown and organic foods: insights from three US data sets. *Food Addit Contam* 2002 May;19(5):427–446.

Balam G, Gurri F. A physiological adaptation to undernutrition. *Ann Hum Biol* 1994;21: 483–489.

Baldwin EA. Edible coatings for fresh fruits and vegetables: past, present, and future. In *Edible Coatings and Films to Improve Food Quality*, Krochta, JM, Baldwin, EA, Nisperos-Carriedo, MO (eds). Lancaster, PA: Technomic Publishing Co., 1994: 25–64.

Bandyopadhyay A, Ghoshal S, Mukherjee A. Genotoxicity testing of low-calorie sweeteners: aspartame, acesulfame-K, and saccharin. *Drug Chem Toxicol* 2008;31(4):447–457.

Bang O, Dyerberg J. Lipid metabolism and ischemic heart disease in Greenland Eskimos. *Adv Nutr Res* 1980;3:1–22.

Banwell JG, Howard R, Kabir I, Costerton JW. Bacterial overgrowth by indigenous microflora in the phytohemagglutinin-fed rat. *Canadian Journal of Microbiology* 1988; 34:1009–1013.

Barbier O, Arreola-Mendoza L, Del Razo LM. Molecular mechanisms of fluoride toxicity. *Chem Biol Interact* 2010 Nov 5;188(2):319–333.

Barclay AW, Petocz P, McMillan-Price J, Flood VM, Prvan T, Mitchell P, Brand-Miller JC. Glycemic index, glycemic load, and chronic disease risk—a meta-analysis of observational studies. *Am J Clin Nutr* 2008 Mar;87(3):627–637.

Barkeling B, Rossner S, Bjorvell H. Effects of a high-protein meal (meat) and a high-carbohydrate meal (vegetarian) on satiety measured by automated computerized monitoring of subsequent food intake, motivation to eat and food preferences. *Int J Obes* 1990;14:743–751.

Barlovic DP, Thomas MC, Jandeleit-Dahm K. Cardiovascular disease: what's all the AGE/RAGE about? *Cardiovasc Hematol Disord Drug Targets* 2010 Mar;10(1):7–15.

Barratt SM, Leeds JS, Robinson K, Shah PJ, Lobo AJ, McAlindon ME, Sanders DS. Reflux and irritable bowel syndrome are negative predictors of quality of life in coeliac disease and inflammatory bowel disease. *J Gastroenterol Hepatol* 2011 Feb;23(2):159–165.

Barre A, Peumans WJ, Menu-Bouaouiche L, Van Damme EJ, May GD, Herrera AF, Van Leuven F, Rougé P. Purification and structural analysis of an abundant thaumatin-like protein from ripe banana fruit. *Planta* 2000 Nov;211(6):791–799.

Barsony J, Pike JW, DeLuca HF, Marx SJ. Immunocytology with microwave-fixed fibroblasts shows 1 alpha,25-dihydroxyvitamin D3-dependent rapid and estrogen-dependent slow reorganization of vitamin D receptors. *J Cell Biol* 1990 Dec;111(6 Pt 1):2385–2395.

Bartley J, McGlashan SR. Does milk increase mucus production? *Med Hypotheses* 2010 Apr;74(4):732–734.

Barzel US. The skeleton as an ion exchange system: implications for the role of acid-base imbalance in the genesis of osteoporosis. *J Bone Min Res* 1995;10:1431–1436.

Basford JR, Oh JK, Allison TG, Sheffield CG, Manahan BG, Hodge DO, Tajik AJ, Rodeheffer RJ, Tei C. Safety, acceptance, and physiologic effects of sauna bathing in people with chronic heart failure: a pilot report. *Arch Phys Med Rehabil* 2009 Jan;90(1):173–177.

Bastian SE, Dunbar AJ, Priebe IK, Owens PC, Goddard C. Measurement of betacellulin levels in bovine serum, colostrum and milk. *J Endocrinol* 2001 Jan;168(1):203–212.

Batchelor AJ, Watson G, Compston JE. Reduced plasma half-life of radio-labelled 25-hydroxyvitamin D3 in subjects receiving a high fiber diet. *Brit J Nutr* 1983;49:213–216.

Baumann E, Stoya G, Völkner A, Richter W, Lemke C, Linss W. Hemolysis of human erythrocytes with saponin affects the membrane structure. *Acta Histochem* 2000 Feb;102(1):21–35.

Beard CM, Panser LA, Katusic SK. Is excess folic acid supplementation a risk factor for autism? *Med Hypotheses* 2011 Jul;77(1):15–17.

Beaudet AL, Goin-Kochel RP. Some, but not complete, reassurance on the safety of folic acid fortification. *Am J Clin Nutr* 2010 Dec;92(6):1287–1288.

Belpoggi F, Soffritti M, Padovani M, Degli Esposti D, Lauriola M, Minardi F. Results of long-term carcinogenicity bioassay on Sprague-Dawley rats exposed to aspartame administered in feed. *Ann N Y Acad Sci* 2006 Sep;1076:559–577.

Belvedere P, Gabai G, Dalla VL, et al. Occurrence of steroidogenic enzymes in the bovine mammary gland at different functional stages. *J Steroid Biochem Mol Biol* 1996;59:339–347.

Bengmark S. Advanced glycation and lipoxidation end products—amplifiers of inflammation: the role of food. *JPEN J Parenter Enteral Nutr* 2007 Sep–Oct;31(5):430–440.

Benko S, Magyarics Z, Szabó A, Rajnavölgyi E. Dendritic cell subtypes as primary targets of vaccines: the emerging role and cross-talk of pattern recognition receptors. *Biol Chem* 2008 May;389(5):469–485.

Bennett M. Vitamin B12 deficiency, infertility and recurrent fetal loss. *J Reprod Med* 2001 Mar;46(3):209–212.

Berker B, Kaya C, Aytac R, Satiroglu H. Homocysteine concentrations in follicular fluid are associated with poor oocyte and embryo qualities in polycystic ovary syndrome patients undergoing assisted reproduction. *Hum Reprod* 2009 Sep;24(9):2293–2302.

Berkey CS, Rockett HR, Gillman MW, Field AE, Colditz GA. Longitudinal study of skipping breakfast and weight change in adolescents. *Int J Obes Relat Metab Disord* 2003 Oct;27(10):1258–1266.

Berlyne GM, Ben Ari J, Nord E, Shainkin R. Bedouin osteomalacia due to calcium deprivation caused by high phytic acid content of unleavened bread. *Am J Clin Nutr* 1973;26:910–911.

Bershad S, Poulin YP, Berson DS, Sabean J, Brodell RT, Shalita AR, Kakita L, Tanghetti E, Leyden J, Webster GF, Miller BH. Topical retinoids in the treatment of acne vulgaris. *Cutis* 1999;64(suppl 2):8–20.

Berwick M. The good, the bad, and the ugly of sunscreens. *Clin Pharmacol Ther* 2011 Jan;89(1):31–33.

Bhushan S, Pandey RC, Singh SP, Pandey DN, Seth P. Some observations on human semen analysis. *Indian J Physiol Pharmacol* 1978 Oct-Dec;22(4):393–396.

Bicchieri MG (ed.). *Hunters and Gatherers Today*. New York: Holt, Rinehart and Winston, 1972.

Biedermann S, Tschudin P, Grob K. Transfer of bisphenol A from thermal printer paper to the skin. *Anal Bioanal Chem* 2010 Sep;398(1):571–576.

Bies C, Lehr CM, Woodley JF. Lectin-mediated drug targeting: history and applications. *Adv Drug Deliv Rev* 2004 Mar 3;56(4):425–35.

Bigal ME, Krymchantowski AV. Migraine triggered by sucralose—a case report. *Headache* 2006 Mar;46(3):515–517.

Bigard AX, Boussif M, Chalabi H, Guezennec CY. Alterations in muscular performance and orthostatic tolerance during Ramadan. *Aviat Space Environ Med* 1998 Apr;69(4):341–346.

Billhult A, Lindholm C, Gunnarsson R, Stener-Victorin E. The effect of massage on immune function and stress in women with breast cancer—a randomized controlled trial. *Auton Neurosci* 2009 Oct 5;150(1–2):111–115.

Binkley N, Novotny R, Krueger D, Kawahara T, Daida YG, Lensmeyer G, Hollis BW, Drezner MK. Low vitamin D status despite abundant sun exposure. *J Clin Endocrinol Metab* 2007 Jun;92(6):2130–2135.

Binoux M, Gourmelen M. Statural development parallels IGF I levels in subjects of constitutionally variant stature. *Acta Endocrinol* 1987;114:524–530.

Bischoff-Ferrari HA. Optimal serum 25-hydroxyvitamin D levels for multiple health outcomes. *Adv Exp Med Biol* 2008;624:55–71.

Bischoff-Ferrari HA, Dawson-Hughes B, Baron JA, et al. Calcium intake and hip fracture risk in men and women: a meta-analysis of prospective cohort studies and randomized controlled trials. *Am J Clin Nutr* 2007;86:1780–1790.

Bischoff-Ferrari HA, Dawson-Hughes B, Baron JA, Kanis JA, Orav EJ, Staehelin HB, Kiel DP, Burckhardt P, Henschkowski J, Spiegelman D, Li R, Wong JB, Feskanich D, Willett WC. Milk intake and risk of hip fracture in men and women: a meta-analysis of prospective cohort studies. *J Bone Miner Res* 2011 Apr;26(4):833–39.

Bischoff-Ferrari HA, Shao A, Dawson-Hughes B, Hathcock J, Giovannucci E, Willett WC. Benefit-risk assessment of vitamin D supplementation. *Osteoporos Int* 2010 Jul;21(7):1121–1132.

Bissoli L, Di Francesco V, Ballarin A, Mandragona R, Trespidi R, Brocco G, Caruso B, Bosello O, Zamboni M. Effect of vegetarian diet on homocysteine levels. *Ann Nutr Metab* 2002;46(2):73–79.

Bitzer M, Feldkaemper M, Schaeffel F. Visually induced changes in components of the retinoic acid system in fundal layers of the chick. *Exp EyeRes* 2000;70:97–106.

Bjelakovic G, Gluud C. Surviving antioxidant supplements. *J Natl Cancer Inst* 2007 May 16;99(10):742–743.

Bjelakovic G, Nikolova D, Gluud LL, Simonetti RG, Gluud C. Antioxidant supplements for prevention of mortality in healthy participants and patients with various diseases. *Cochrane Database Syst Rev* 2008 Apr 16;(2):CD007176.

———. Mortality in randomized trials of antioxidant supplements for primary and secondary prevention: systematic review and meta-analysis. *JAMA* 2007 Feb 28;297(8):842–857. Review. Erratum in: *JAMA* 2008 Feb 20;299(7):765–766.

Bjelakovic G, Nikolova D, Simonetti RG, Gluud C. Systematic review: primary and secondary prevention of gastrointestinal cancers with antioxidant supplements. *Aliment Pharmacol Ther* 2008 Sep 15;28(6):689–703.

Black HS, Thornby JI, Gerguis J, Lenger W. Influence of dietary omega-6, -3 fatty acid sources on the initiation and promotion stages of photocarcinogenesis. *Photochem Photobiol* 1992;56:195–199.

Blair R, Misir R. Biotin bioavailability from protein supplements and cereal grains for growing broiler chickens. *Int J Vit Nutr Res* 1989;59:55–58.

Blank M, Barzilai O, Shoenfeld Y. Molecular mimicry and auto-immunity. *Clin Rev Allergy Immunol* 2007;32:111–118.

Bleys J, Miller ER 3rd, Pastor-Barriuso R, Appel LJ, Guallar E. Vitamin-mineral supplementation and the progression of atherosclerosis: a meta-analysis of randomized controlled trials. *Am J Clin Nutr* 2006 Oct;84(4):880–887.

Block G, Patterson B, Subar A. Fruit, vegetables, and cancer prevention: a review of the epidemiological evidence. *Nutr Cancer* 1992;18:1–29.

Blum WF, Albertsson-Wikland K, Rosberg S, Ranke MB. Serum levels of insulin-like growth factor I (IGF-I) and IGF binding protein 3 reflect spontaneous growth hormone secretion. *J Clin Endocrinol Metab* 1993;76:1610–1616.

Blumenschine RJ. Carcass consumption sequences and the archaeological distinction of scavenging and hunting. *J Hum Evol* 1986;15:639–659.

Blumenschine RJ, Cavallo JA. Scavenging and human evolution. *Sci Am* 1992;267:90–96.

Blumenschine RJ, Madrigal TC. Variability in long bone marrow yields of East African ungulates and its ooarchaeological implications. *J Archaeo Sci* 1993;20:555–587.

Boaz NT. *Evolving Health: The Origins of Illness and How the Modern World Is Making Us Sick.* New York: John Wiley & Sons, Inc., 2002.

Bocherens H, Drucker DG, Billiou D, Patou-Mathis M, Vandermeersch B. Isotopic evidence for diet and subsistence pattern of the Saint-Cesaire I Neanderthal: review and use of a multi-source mixing model. *J Hum Evol* 2005 Jul;49(1):71–87.

Boeda E, Geneste JM, Griggo C, Mercier N, Muhesen S, Reyss JL, Taha A, Valladas H. A Levallois point embedded in the vertebra of a wild ass (*Equus africanus*): hafting, projectiles and Mousterian hunting weapons. *Antiquity* 1999;73:394–402.

Bohn T, Davidsson L, Walczyk T, Hurrell RF. Phytic acid added to white-wheat bread inhibits fractional apparent magnesium absorption in humans. *Am J Clin Nutr* 2004 Mar;79(3):418–423.

Boivin J, Bunting L, Collins JA, Nygren KG. International estimates of infertility prevalence and treatment-seeking: potential need and demand for infertility medical care. *Hum Reprod* 2007 Jun;22(6):1506–1512.

Bolland MJ, Avenell A, Baron JA, Grey A, MacLennan GS, Gamble GD, Reid IR. Effect of calcium supplements on risk of myocardial infarction and cardiovascular events: meta-analysis. *BMJ* 2010 Jul 29;341:c3691.

Bomford R, Stapleton M, Winsor S, Beesley JE, Jessup EA, Price KR, Fenwick R. Adjuvanticity and ISCOM formation by structurally diverse saponins. *Vaccine* 1992;10(9):572–577.

Borer KT. Physical activity in the prevention and amelioration of osteoporosis in women: interaction of mechanical, hormonal and dietary factors. *Sports Med* 2005;35(9):779–830.

Bosland PW. Chiles: history, cultivation, and uses. In *Spices, Herbs and Edible Fungi (Herbs)*, Charalambous G (ed). Amsterdam: Elsevier Science Publishers, 1994: 347–366.

Boufassa C, Lafont J, Rouanet JM, Besancon P. Thermal inactivation of lectins (PHA) isolated from *Phaseolus vulgaris*. *Food Chem* 1986;20:295–304.

Boulet SL, Gambrell D, Shin M, et al. Racial/ethnic differences in the birth prevalence of spina bifida-United States, 1995–2005. *MMWR* 2009;57:1409–1413.

Bourne D, Prescott J. A comparison of the nutritional value, sensory qualities, and food safety of organically and conventionally produced foods. *Crit Rev Food Sci Nutr* 2002;42:1–34.

Boutton TW, Lynott MJ, Bumsted MP. Stable carbon isotopes and the study of prehistoric diet. *Crit Rev Food Sci Nutr* 1991;30:373–385.

Boxmeer JC, Brouns RM, Lindemans J, Steegers EA, Martini E, Macklon NS, Steegers-Theunissen RP. Preconception folic acid treatment affects the microenvironment of the maturing oocyte in humans. *Fertil Steril* 2008 Jun;89(6):1766–1770.

Boxmeer JC, Smit M, Utomo E, Romijn JC, Eijkemans MJ, Lindemans J, Laven JS, Macklon NS, Steegers EA, Steegers-Theunissen RP. Low folate in seminal plasma is associated with increased sperm DNA damage. *Fertil Steril* 2009 Aug;92(2):548–556.

Boxmeer JC, Smit M, Weber RF, Lindemans J, Romijn JC, Eijkemans MJ, Macklon NS, Steegers-Theunissen RP. Seminal plasma cobalamin significantly correlates with sperm concentration in men undergoing IVF or ICSI procedures. *J Androl* 2007 Jul–Aug;28(4):521–527.

Brand-Miller JC, Holt SHA. Australian aboriginal plant foods: a consideration of their nutritional composition and health implications. *Nut Res Rev* 1998;11:5–23.

Brenna JT, Salem N Jr, Sinclair AJ, Cunnane SC. Alpha-Linolenic acid supplementation and conversion to n-3 long-chain polyunsaturated fatty acids in humans. *Prostaglandins Leukot Essent Fatty Acids* 2009 Feb–Mar;80(2–3):85–91.

Breslow RA, Hallfrisch J, Guy DG, Crawley B, Goldberg AP. The importance of dietary protein in healing pressure ulcers. *J Am Geriatr Soc* 1993;41:357–362.

Brewer GJ. The risks of copper toxicity contributing to cognitive decline in the aging population and to Alzheimer's disease. *J Am Coll Nutr* 2009 Jun;28(3):238–342.

Briani C, Samaroo D, Alaedini A. Celiac disease: from gluten to autoimmunity. *Autoimmun Rev* 2008 Sep;7(8):644–650.

Briggs RD, Rubenberg ML, O'Neal RM, Thomas WA, Hartroft WS. Myocardial infarction in patients treated with Sippy and other high-milk diets: an autopsy study of fifteen hospitals in the U.S.A. and Great Britain. *Circulation* 1960 Apr;21:538–542.

Brismar K, Fernqvist-Forbes E, Wahren J, Hall K. Effect of insulin on the hepatic production of insulin-like growth factor-binding protein-1 (IGFBP-1), IGFBP-3, and IGF-1 in insulin dependent diabetes. *J Clin Endocrinol Metab* 1994;79:872–878.

Brooke OG, Brown IRF, Cleeve HJW. Observations of the vitamin D state of pregnant Asian women in London. *Brit J Obstet Gynaecol* 1981;88:18–26.

Brouwer IA, Katan MB, Zock PL. Dietary alpha-linolenic acid is associated with reduced risk of fatal coronary heart disease, but increased prostate cancer risk: a meta-analysis. *J Nutr* 2004;134(4):919–922.

Brown KH, Peerson JM, Baker SK, Hess SY. Preventive zinc supplementation among infants, preschoolers, and older prepubertal children. *Food Nutr Bull* 2009 Mar;30 (1 Suppl):S12–40.

Brown RJ, de Banate MA, Rother KI. Artificial sweeteners: a systematic review of metabolic effects in youth. *Int J Pediatr Obes* 2010 Aug;5(4):305–312.

Brown RJ, Walter M, Rother KI. Ingestion of diet soda before a glucose load augments glucagon-like peptide-1 secretion. *Diabetes Care* 2009 Dec;32(12):2184–2186.

Bruder G, Jarasch ED, Heid HW. High concentrations of antibodies to xanthine oxidase in human and animal sera. *J Clin Invest* 1984;74:783–794.

Bruning PF, Bonfrer JM, van Noord PA, Hart AA, de Jong-Bakker M, Nooijen WJ. Insulin resistance and breast cancer risk. *Int J Cancer* 1992;52:511–516.

Bucciarelli P, Martini G, Martinelli I, Ceccarelli E, Gennari L, Bader R, Valenti R, Franci B, Nuti R, Mannucci PM. The relationship between plasma homocysteine levels and bone mineral density in post-menopausal women. *Eur J Intern Med* 2010 Aug;21(4):301–305.

Buera MP, Pilosof AMR, Bartholomai GB. 1984 Kinetics of trypsin inhibitory activity loss in heated flour from bean *Phaseolus vulgaris*. *J Food Sci* 1984;49:124–126.

Bulkley JL. Cancer among primitive tribes. *Cancer* 1927;4:289–295.

Bunn, HT, Kroll EM. Systematic butchery by Plio-Pleistocene hominids at Olduvai Gorge, Tanzania. *Curr Anthropol* 1986;20:365–398.

Burch ES, Ellanna LJ (eds.). *Key Issues in Hunter-Gatherer Research*. Oxford, UK: Berg Publishers, 1994.

Bürk K, Farecki ML, Lamprecht G, Roth G, Decker P, Weller M, Rammensee HG, Oertel W. Neurological symptoms in patients with biopsy proven celiac disease. *Mov Disord* 2009 Dec 15;24(16):2358–2362.

Burnett ME, Wang SQ. Current sunscreen controversies: a critical review. *Photodermatol Photoimmunol Photomed* 2011 Apr;27(2):58–67.

Cahill, JP. Ethnobotany of chia, *Salvia hispanica L. (Lamiaceae). Economic Botany* 2003;57(4):604–618.

Calder PC, Yaqoob P. Omega-3 (n-3) fatty acids, cardiovascular disease and stability of atherosclerotic plaques. *Cell Mol Biol (Noisy-le-grand)* 2010 Feb 25;56(1):28–37.

Calloway DH, Carol A, Hickey CA, Murphy EL. Reduction of intestinal gas-forming properties of legumes by traditional and experimental processing methods. *J Food Sci* 1971;36:251–255.

Camacho-Hubner C, Woods KA, Miraki-Moud F, Hindmarsh PC, Clark AJ, Hansson Y, Johnston A, Baxter RC, Savage MO. Effects of recombinant human insulin-like growth factor I (IGF-I) therapy on the growth hormone-IGF system of a patient with a partial IGF-I gene deletion. *J Clin Endocrinol Metab* 1999;84:1611–1616.

Cameron A, Jones J, Elliott B, Gorman L. *The L.L. Bean Game and Fish Cookbook*. New York: Random House, 1983.

Campbell TC, Junshi C. Diet and chronic degenerative diseases: perspectives from China. *Am J Clin Nutr* 1994 May;59(5 Suppl):1153S–1161S.

Campbell TC, Parpia B, Chen J. Diet, lifestyle, and the etiology of coronary artery disease: the Cornell China study. *Am J Cardiol* 1998 Nov 26;82(10B):18T–21T.

Campbell-Brown M, Ward RJ, Haines AP, North WR, Abraham R, McFadyen IR, Turnlund JR, King JC. Zinc and copper in Asian pregnancies—is there evidence for a nutritional deficiency? *Br J Obstet Gynaecol* 1985 Sep;92(9):875–885.

Cani PD, Amar J, Iglesias MA, Poggi M, Knauf C, Bastelica D et al. Metabolic endotoxemia initiates obesity and insulin resistance. *Diabetes* 2007 Jul;56(7):1761–1772.

Canned tuna. *Consumer Reports* 1992(February);103–114.

Cao XL, Corriveau J, Popovic S. Sources of low concentrations of bisphenol A in canned beverage products. *J Food Prot* 2010 Aug;73(8):1548–1551.

Capaso LL. Antiquity of cancer. *Int J Cancer* 2005;113:2–13.

Cappellini MD, Fiorelli G. Glucose-6-phosphate dehydrogenase deficiency. *Lancet* 2008;371(9606):64–74.

Cappuccio FP, Bell R, Perry IJ, Gilg J, Ueland PM, Refsum H, Sagnella GA, Jeffery S, Cook DG. Homocysteine levels in men and women of different ethnic and cultural background living in England. *Atherosclerosis* 2002 Sep;164(1):95–102.

Caprio S. Differences between African American and white girls in the insulin-like growth factor-I and the binding proteins: importance of insulin resistance and hyperinsulinemia. *J Pediatr* 1999;135:270–271.

Carayol M, Grosclaude P, Delpierre C. Prospective studies of dietary alphalinolenic acid intake and prostate cancer risk: a meta-analysis. *Cancer Causes Control* 2010;21(3):347–355.

Carmalt J, Rosel K, Burns T, Janzen E. Suspected white kidney bean (*Phaseolus vulgaris*) toxicity in horses and cattle. *Aust Vet J* 2003 Nov;81(11):674–676.

Caron M, Steve, AP. *Lectins and Pathology.* London: Taylor & Francis, 2000.

Carreno-Gómez B, Woodley JF, Florence AT. Studies on the uptake of tomato lectin nanoparticles in everted gut sacs. *Int J Pharm* 1999 Jun 10;183(1):7–11.

Cary OJ, Locke C, Cookson JB. Effect of alterations of dietary sodium on the severity of asthma in men. *Thorax* 1993;48:714–718.

Cascella NG, Kryszak D, Bhatti B, Gregory P, Kelly DL, McEvoy JP, Fasano A, Eaton WW. Prevalence of celiac disease and gluten sensitivity in the United States clinical antipsychotic trials of intervention effectiveness study population. *Schizophr Bull* 2011 Jan;37(1):94–100.

Castillo-Duran C, Solomons NW. Studies on the bioavailability of zinc in humans. IX. Interaction of beef-zinc with iron, calcium and lactose. *Nutr Res* 1991;11:429–438.

Catlin, G. *Letters and Notes on the Manners, Customs, and Conditions of North American Indians.* New York: Dover Publications, 1973.

Ch'ng CL, Jones MK, Kingham JG. Celiac disease and autoimmune thyroid disease. *Clin Med Res* 2007 Oct;5(3):184–192.

Chaitow L. *Stone Age Diet.* London: Macdonald & Co. (Publishers) Ltd., 1987.

Chambers JC, Obeid OA, Refsum H, Ueland P, Hackett D, Hooper J, Turner RM, Thompson SG, Kooner JS. Plasma homocysteine concentrations and risk of coronary heart disease in UK Indian Asian and European men. *Lancet* 2000;355:523–527.

Chan JM. Nutrition and acid-base metabolism. *Fed Proc* 1981;40:2423–2428.

Chandrajith R, Dissanayake CB, Ariyarathna T, Herath HM, Padmasiri JP. Dose-dependent Na and Ca in fluoride-rich drinking water—another major cause of chronic renal failure in tropical arid regions. *Sci Total Environ* 2011 Jan 15;409(4):671–675.

Chanmugam P, Boudreau M, Hwang DH. Differences in the omega-3 fatty acid contents in pond-reared and wild fish and shellfish. *J Food Sci* 1986;51:1556–1557.

Chen H, O'Reilly E, McCullough ML, Rodriguez C, Schwarzschild MA, Calle EE, Thun MJ, Ascherio A. Consumption of dairy products and risk of Parkinson's disease. *Am J Epidemiol* 2007 May 1;165(9):998–1006.

Chen Y, Quick WW, Yang W, Zhang Y, Baldwin A, Moran J, Moore V, Sahai N, Dall TM. Cost of gestational diabetes mellitus in the United States in 2007. *Popul Health Manag* 2009 Jun;12(3):165–174.

Chew SJ, Balakrishnan V. Myopia produced in young chicks by intermittent minimal form visual deprivation—can spectacles cause myopia? *Singapore Med J* 1992;33:489–492.

Chiaffarino F, Ascone GB, Bortolus R, Mastroia-Covo P, Ricci E, Cipriani S, Parazzini F.

Effects of folic acid supplementation on pregnancy outcomes: a review of randomized clinical trials. *Minerva Ginecol* 2010 Aug;62(4):293–301.

Chiang EC, Shen S, Kengeri SS, Xu H, Combs GF, Morris JS, Bostwick DG, Waters DJ. Defining the optimal selenium dose for prostate cancer risk reduction: insights from the U-shaped relationship between selenium status, DNA damage, and apoptosis. *Dose Response* 2009 Dec 21;8(3):285–300.

Childers NF. *Arthritis—Childer's Diet to Stop It. Nightshades, Aging and Ill Health*, 4th ed. Gainesville, FL: Horticultural Publications, 1993.

Chinoy NJ, Rao MV, Narayana MV, Neelakanta E. Microdose vasal injection of sodium fluoride in the rat. *Reprod Toxicol* 1991;5(6):505–512.

Cho E, Hunter DJ, Spiegelman D, Albanes D, Beeson WL, van den Brandt PA, Colditz GA, et al. Intakes of vitamins A, C, and E and folate and multivitamins and lung cancer: a pooled analysis of 8 prospective studies. *Int J Cancer* 2006 Feb 15;118(4):970–978.

Chrispeels MJ, Raikel NV. Lectins, lectin genes, and their role in plant defense. *Plant Cell* 1991;3:1–9.

Clark LC, Combs GF Jr, Turnbull BW, Slate EH, Chalker DK, Chow J, Davis LS, Glover RA, Graham GF, Gross EG, Krongrad A, Lesher JL Jr, Park HK, Sanders BB Jr, Smith CL, Taylor JR. Effects of selenium supplementation for cancer prevention in patients with carcinoma of the skin. A randomized controlled trial. Nutritional Prevention of Cancer Study Group. *JAMA* 1996;276:1957–1963.

Clarke R. B-vitamins and prevention of dementia. *Proc Nutr Soc* 2008 Feb;67(1):75–81.

Clarke R, Birks J, Nexo E, Ueland PM, Schneede J, Scott J, Molloy A, Evans JG. Low vitamin B-12 status and risk of cognitive decline in older adults. *Am J Clin Nutr* 2007 Nov;86(5):1384–1391.

Clarke R, Frost C, Collins R, Appleby P, Peto R. Dietary lipids and blood cholesterol: quantitative meta-analysis of metabolic ward studies. *BMJ* 1997 Jan 11;314(7074):112–117.

Clarke R, Halsey J, Lewington S, Lonn E, Armitage J, Manson JE, et al. Effects of lowering homocysteine levels with B vitamins on cardiovascular disease, cancer, and cause-specific mortality: meta-analysis of 8 randomized trials involving 37 485 individuals. *Arch Intern Med* 2010 Oct 11;170(18):1622–1631.

Clarke R, Sherliker P, Hin H, Nexo E, Hvas AM, Schneede J, Birks J, Ueland PM, Emmens K, Scott JM, Molloy AM, Evans JG. Detection of vitamin B12 deficiency in older people by measuring vitamin B12 or the active fraction of vitamin B12, holotranscobalamin. *Clin Chem* 2007 May;53(5):963–970.

Clastres P. The Guayaki. In *Hunters and Gatherers Today*, Bicchieri MG (ed). New York: Holt, Rinehart and Winston, Inc., 1972, 151.

Cleave TL. *The Saccharine Disease*. Bristol: John Wright & Sons, 1974.

Clements MR, Johnson L, Fraser DR. A new mechanism for induced vitamin D deficiency in calcium deprivation. *Nature* 1987;325:62–65.

Clifton P. High protein diets and weight control. *Nutr Metab Cardiovasc Dis* 2009 Jul;19(6):379–382.

Close GL, Ashton T, Cable T, Doran D, Holloway C, McArdle F et al. (2006). Ascorbic acid supplementation does not attenuate post-exercise muscle soreness following muscle-damaging exercise but may delay the recovery process. *Brit J Nutr* 2006;95:976–981.

Clyne PS, Kulczycki A. Human breast milk contains bovine IgG. Relationship to Infant Colic? *Pediatrics* 1992;87:439–444.

Cockayne S, Adamson J, Lanham-New S, Shearer MJ, Gilbody S, Torgerson DJ. Vitamin K and the prevention of fractures: systematic review and meta-analysis of randomized controlled trials. *Arch Intern Med* 2006 Jun 26;166(12):1256–1261.

Cockburn A. Where did our infectious diseases come from? The evolution of infectious disease. *Ciba Found Symp* 1977;49:103–112.

Cogswell ME, Looker AC, Pfeiffer CM, Cook JD, Lacher DA, Beard JL, Lynch SR, Grummer-Strawn LM. Assessment of iron deficiency in US preschool children and nonpregnant females of childbearing age: National Health and Nutrition Examination Survey 2003–2006. *Am J Clin Nutr* 2009 May;89(5):1334–1342.

Cohen MN, Armelagos GJ. *Paleopathology at the Origins of Agriculture.* New York: Academic Press, 1984.

———. The significance of long-term changes in human diet and food economy. In Harris M, Ross EB (eds.), *Food and Evolution. Toward a Theory of Human Food Habits,* Philadelphia: Temple University Press, 1987, 261–283.

Cole BF, Baron JA, Sandler RS, Haile RW et al. Folic acid for the prevention of colorectal adenomas: a randomized clinical trial. *JAMA* 2007 Jun 6;297(21):2351–2359.

Coletta JM, Bell SJ, Roman AS. Omega-3 fatty acids and pregnancy. *Rev Obstet Gynecol* 2010 Fall;3(4):163–171.

Collin SM, Metcalfe C, Refsum H, Lewis SJ, et al. Circulating folate, vitamin B12, homocysteine, vitamin B12 transport proteins, and risk of prostate cancer: a case-control study, systematic review, and meta-analysis. *Cancer Epidemiol Biomarkers Prev* 2010 Jun;19(6):1632–1642.

Collin SM, Metcalfe C, Refsum H, Lewis SJ, Smith GD et al. Associations of folate, vitamin B12, homocysteine, and folate-pathway polymorphisms with prostate-specific antigen velocity in men with localized prostate cancer. *Cancer Epidemiol Biomarkers Prev* 2010 Nov;19(11):2833–2838.

Collins JL, Beaty BF. Heat inactivation of trypsin inhibitor in fresh green soybeans and physiological responses of rats fed the beans. *J Food Sci* 1980;45:542–546.

Cordain L. Atherogenic potential of peanut oil–based monounsaturated fatty acids diets. *Lipids* 1998;33:229–230.

———. Cereal grains: humanity's double-edged sword. *World Rev Nutr Diet* 1999;84:19–73.

———. Dietary implications for the development of acne: a shifting paradigm. In *U.S. Dermatology Review II 2006,* Bedlow J (ed). London: Touch Briefings Publications, 2006.

———. Implications for the role of diet in acne. *Semin Cutan Med Surg* 2005;24(2):84–91.

———. Paleodiet and Paleolithic Nutrition: The Cordain Files. beyondveg.com/cat/paleodiet/index.shtml.

———. Saturated fat consumption in ancestral human diets: implications for contemporary intakes. In *Phytochemicals, Nutrient-Gene Interactions,* Meskin MS, Bidlack WR, Randolph RK (eds.), CRC Press (Taylor & Francis Group), 2006, 115–126.

———. The nutritional characteristics of a contemporary diet based upon Paleolithic food groups. *J Am Nutraceut Assoc* 2002;5:15–24.

———. *The Paleo Diet.* John Wiley & Sons, New York, 2010.

Cordain L, Brand-Miller J, Eaton SB, Mann N. Reply to SC Cunnane. *Am J Clin Nutr* 2000;72:1585–1586.

———. Macronutrient estimations in hunter-gatherer diets. *Am J Clin Nutr* 2000; 72:1589–1590.

Cordain L, Brand-Miller J, Eaton SB, Mann N, Holt SH, Speth JD. Plant-animal subsistence ratios and macronutrient energy estimations in worldwide hunter-gatherer diets. *Am J Clin Nutr* 2000;71:682–692.

Cordain L, Bryan ED, Melby CL, Smith MJ. Influence of moderate daily wine consumption upon body weight regulation and metabolism in healthy, free living males. *J Am Coll Nutr* 1997;16:134–139.

Cordain L, Campbell TC. The protein debate. *Catalyst Athletics,* March 19, 2008 cathletics.com/articles/article.php?articleID=50.

Cordain L, Eades MR, Eades MD. Hyperinsulinemic diseases of civilization: more than just Syndrome X. *Comp Biochem Physiol A Mol Integr Physiol* 2003;136(1):95–112.

Cordain L, Eaton SB, Brand-Miller J, Lindeberg S, Jensen C. An evolutionary analysis of the aetiology and pathogenesis of juvenile-onset myopia. *Acta Ophthalmol Scand* 2002;80(2):125–135.

Cordain L, Eaton SB, Brand-Miller J, Mann N, Hill K. The paradoxical nature of hunter-gatherer diets: Meat based, yet non-atherogenic. *Eur J Clin Nutr* 2002 Mar;56 sup 1:S42–52.

Cordain L, Eaton SB, Sebastian A, Mann N, Lindeberg S, Watkins BA, O'Keefe JH, Brand-Miller J. Origins and evolution of the Western diet: health implications for the 21st century. *Am J Clin Nutr* 2005;81(2):341–354.

Cordain L, Friel J. *The Paleo Diet for Athletes.* Emmaus, PA: Rodale Inc., 2006.

Cordain L, Gotshall RW. Compiled ethnographic observations of the aerobic fitness, strength, and body composition of unacculturated humans. *Med Sci Sports Exerc* 1999;31:S213.

Cordain L, Gotshall RW, Eaton SB. Evolutionary aspects of exercise. *World Rev Nutr Diet* 1997;81:49–60.

Cordain L, Gotshall RW, Eaton SB, Eaton SB 3rd. Physical activity, energy expenditure, and fitness: an evolutionary perspective. *Int J Sports Med* 1998 Jul;19(5):328–335.

Cordain L, Lindeberg S, Hurtado M, Hill K, Eaton SB, Brand-Miller J. Acne vulgaris: a disease of Western civilization. *Arch Dermatol* 2002;138(12):1584–1590.

Cordain L, Martin C, Florant G, Watkins BA. The fatty acid composition of muscle, brain, marrow, and adipose tissue in elk: evolutionary implications for human dietary lipid requirements. *World Rev Nutr Diet* 1998;83:225.

Cordain L, Melby CL, Hamamoto AE, O'Neill S, Cornier MA, Barakat HA, Israel RG, Hill JO. Influence of moderate chronic wine consumption on insulin sensitivity and other correlates of syndrome X in moderately obese women. *Metabolism* 2000;49:1473–1478.

Cordain L, Miller JB, Eaton SB, Mann N, Holt SH, Speth JD. Plant-animal subsistence ratios and macronutrient energy estimations in worldwide hunter-gatherer diets. *Am J Clin Nutr* 2000 Mar;71(3):682–692.

Cordain L, Miller J, Mann N. Scant evidence of periodic starvation among hunter-gatherers. *Diabetologia* 1999;42:383–384.

Cordain L, Stephenson N, Cordain L. *The Paleo Diet Cookbook.* John Wiley & Sons, New York, 2010.

Cordain L, Toohey L, Smith MJ, Hickey MS. Modulation of immune function by dietary lectins in rheumatoid arthritis. *Br J Nutr* 2000 Mar;83(3):207–217.

Cordain L, Watkins BA, Florant G, Kehler M, Rogers L. A detailed fatty acid analysis of selected tissues in elk, mule deer, and antelope. *FASEB J* 1999:13:A887.

Cordain L, Watkins BA, Florant GL, Kehler M, Rogers L, Li Y. Fatty acid analysis of wild ruminant tissues: evolutionary implications for reducing diet-related chronic disease. *Eur J Clin Nutr* 2001;56:1–11.

Cordain L, Watkins BA, Mann NJ. Fatty acid composition and energy density of foods available to African hominids: evolutionary implications for human brain development. *World Rev Nutr Diet* 2001;90:144–161.

Correia M, Barroso Â, Barroso MF, Soares DB, Oliveira MBPP, and Delerue-Matos C. Contribution of different vegetable types to exogenous nitrate and nitrite exposure. *Food Chem* 2010;120:960–968.

Cotterman ML, Darby LA, Skelly WA. Comparison of muscle force production using the Smith machine and free weights for bench press and squat exercises. *J Strength Cond Res* 2005;19:169–176.

Couet C, Jan P, Debry G. Lactose and cataract in humans: a review. *J Am Coll Nutr* 1991;10:79–86.

Couzy F, Mansourian R, Labate A, Guinchard S, Montagne DH, Dirren H. Effect of dietary phytic acid on zinc absorption in the healthy elderly, as assessed by serum concentration curve tests. *Br J Nutr* 1998 Aug;80(2):177–182.

Craig WJ, Mangels AR; American Dietetic Association. Position of the American Dietetic Association: vegetarian diets. *J Am Diet Assoc.* 2009 Jul;109(7):1266–1282.

Crawford MA, Bloom M, Broadhurst CL, Schmidt WF, Cunnane SC, Galli C, Gehbremeskel K, Linseisen F, Lloyd-Smith J, Parkington J. Evidence for the unique function of docosahexaenoic acid during the evolution of the modern hominid brain. *Lipids* 1999;34:s39–s47.

Crawford MA, Gale MM, Woodford MH, Casped NM. Comparative studies on fatty acid composition of wild and domestic meat. *Int J Biochem* 1970;1:295–305.

Crawford MA, Sinclair AJ. The long chain metabolites of linoleic and linolenic acids in liver and brains of herbivores and carnivores. *Comp Biochem Physiol* 1976;54B:395–401.

Crinnion WJ. Toxic effects of the easily avoidable phthalates and parabens. *Altern Med Rev* 2010 Sep;15(3):190–196.

Crovetti R, Porrini M, Santangelo A, Testolin G. The influence of thermic effect of food on satiety. *Eur J Clin Nutr* 1998;52:482–488.

Crowe FL, Steur M, Allen NE, Appleby PN, Travis RC, Key TJ. Plasma concentrations of 25-hydroxyvitamin D in meat eaters, fish eaters, vegetarians, and vegans: results from the EPIC-Oxford study. *Public Health Nutr* 2011 Feb;14(2):340–346.

Cunliffe WJ, Cotteril JA. The acnes: clinical features, pathogenesis and treatment. In Rook A (ed.), *Major Problems in Dermatology.* Philadelphia: WB Saunders, 1975, vol. 6, 13–14.

Cusin I, Rohner-Jeanrenaud F, Terrettaz J, Jeanrenaud B. Hyperinsulinemia and its impact on obesity and insulin resistance. *Int J Obes Relat Metab Disord* 1992;16(suppl 4):S1–S11.

Cussons AJ, Watts GF, Mori TA, Stuckey BG. Omega-3 fatty acid supplementation decreases liver fat content in polycystic ovary syndrome: a randomized controlled trial employing proton magnetic resonance spectroscopy. *J Clin Endocrinol Metab* 2009 Oct;94(10):3842–3848.

Dagnelie PC, van Dusseldorp M, van Staveren WA, Hautvast JG. Effects of macrobiotic diets on linear growth in infants and children until 10 years of age. *Eur J Clin Nutr* 1994;48(supp 1):S103–S112.

Dalla Pellegrina C, Perbellini O, Scupoli MT, Tomelleri C, Zanetti C, Zoccatelli G, Fusi M, Peruffo A, Rizzi C, Chignola R. Effects of wheat germ agglutinin on human gastrointestinal epithelium: insights from an experimental model of immune/epithelial cell interaction. *Toxicol Appl Pharmacol* 2009 Jun 1;237(2):146–153.

Danielson C, Lyon JL, Egger M, Goodenough GK. Hip fractures and fluoridation in Utah's elderly population. *JAMA* 1992 Aug 12;268(6):746–748.

Dasarathy J, Gruca LL, Bennett C, Parimi PS, Duenas C, Marczewski S, Fierro JL, Kalhan SC. Methionine metabolism in human pregnancy. *Am J Clin Nutr* 2010 Feb;91(2):357–365.

Dauncey MJ, Bingham SA. Dependence of 24 h energy expenditure in man on the composition of the nutrient intake. *Br J Nutr* 1983;50:1–13.

Davey GK, Spencer EA, Appleby PN, Allen NE, Knox KH, Key TJ. EPIC-Oxford: lifestyle characteristics and nutrient intakes in a cohort of 33 883 meat-eaters and 31 546 non meat-eaters in the UK. *Public Health Nutr* 2003 May;6(3):259–269.

David AR, Zimmerman MR. Cancer: an old disease, a new disease, or something in between? *Nat Rev Cancer* 2010 Oct;10(10):728–733.

Davidson PW, Myers GJ, Cox C, Axtell C, Shamlaye C, Sloane-Reeves J, Cernichiari E, Needham L, Choi A, Wang Y, Berlin M, Clarkson TW. Effects of prenatal and postnatal methylmercury exposure from fish consumption on neurodevelopment: outcomes at 66 months of age in the Seychelles Child Development Study. *JAMA* 1998;280:701–707.

Davies DE, Chamberlin SG. Targeting the epidermal growth factor receptor for therapy of carcinomas. *Biochem Pharmacol* 1996 May 3;51(9):1101–1110.

Davies DF, Davies JR, Richards MA. Antibodies to reconstituted dried cow's milk protein in coronary heart disease. *J Atherocler Res* 1969;9:103–107.

Daviglus ML, Stamler J, Orencia AJ, Dyer AR, Liu K, Greenland P, Walsh MK, Morris D, Shekelle RB. Fish consumption and the 30-year risk of fatal myocardial infarction. *N Engl J Med* 1997;336:1046–1053.

Dawson-Hughes B. Protein intake and calcium absorption—Potential role of the calcium sensor receptor. In Burckhardt P, Heaney R, Dawson-Hughes B. *Proceedings of the International Symposium on Nutritional Aspects of Osteoporosis, 4–6 May 2006, Lausanne, Switzerland.* Elsevier, 2007:217–227.

De Bortoli MC, Cozzolino SM. Zinc and selenium nutritional status in vegetarians. *Biol Trace Elem Res* 2009 Mar;127(3):228–233.

De Heinzelin J, Clark JD, White T, Hart W, Renne P, WoldeGabriel G, Beyene Y, Vrba E. Environment and behavior of 2.5-million-year-old Bouri hominids. *Science* 1999 Apr 23;284(5414):625–629.

De Lorgeril M, Salen P, Martin JL, Monjaud I, Delaye J, Mamelle N. Mediterranean diet, traditional risk factors, and the rate of cardiovascular complications after myocardial infarction: final report of the Lyon Diet Heart Study. *Circulation* 1999;99:779–785.

De Rougemont A, Normand S, Nazare JA, Skilton MR, Sothier M, Vinoy S, Laville M. Beneficial effects of a 5-week low-glycaemic index regimen on weight control and cardiovascular risk factors in overweight non-diabetic subjects. *Br J Nutr* 2007 Dec;98(6):1288–1298.

De Swert LF, Cadot P, Ceuppens JL. Diagnosis and natural course of allergy to cooked potatoes in children. *Allergy* 2007 Jul;62(7):750–757.

Deeth HC. Homogenized milk and atherosclerotic disease: a review. *J. Dairy Sci* 1983;66:1419–1435.

DeFronzo RA, Cooke CR, Andres R, Faloona GR, Davis PJ. The effect of insulin on renal handling of sodium, potassium, calcium, and phosphate in man. *J Clin Invest* 1975; 55:845–855.

Denton D. *The Hunger for Salt.* New York: Springer-Verlag, 1984.

Department of Health and Human Services. Centers for Disease Control and Prevention. United States Cancer Statistics http://apps.nccd.cdc.gov/uscs/.

Deplewski D, Rosenfield RL. Growth hormone and insulin-like growth factors have different effects on sebaceous cell growth and differentiation. *Endocrinology* 1999;140:4089–4094.

Devine A, Criddle RA, Dick IM, Kerr DA, Prince RL. A longitudinal study of the effect of sodium and calcium intakes on regional bone density in postmenopausal women. *Am J Clin Nutr* 1995;62:740–745.

DeVoe D, Israel RG, Lipsey T, Voyles W. A long-duration (118-day) backpacking trip (2669 km) normalizes lipids without medication: a case study. *Wilderness & Environmental Medicine* 2009, 20(4):347–352.

DeVries A. *Primitive Man and His Food.* Chicago: Chandler Book Company, 1952.

Dhiman TR, Anand GR, Satter LD, Pariza MW. Conjugated linoleic acid content of milk from cows fed different diets. *J Dairy Sci* 1999;82:2146–2156.

Dhonukshe-Rutten RA, van Dusseldorp M, Schneede J, de Groot LC, van Staveren WA. Low bone mineral density and bone mineral content are associated with low cobalamin status in adolescents. *Eur J Nutr* 2005 Sep;44(6):341–347.

Diamond J. The worst mistake in the history of the human race. *Discover* 1987(May):64–66.

Dietary Reference Intakes for Calcium and Vitamin D. Institute of Medicine of the National Academies, 2010 iom.edu/Reports/2010/Dietary-Reference-Intakes-for-Calcium-and-Vitamin-D.aspx.

Dietary supplementation with n-3 polyunsaturated fatty acids and vitamin E after myocardial infarction: results of the GISSI-Prevenzione trial. Gruppo Italiano per lo Studio della Sopravvivenza nell'Infarto miocardico. *Lancet* 1999;354:447–455.

Dirlewanger M, Schneiter P, Jequier E, Tappy L. Effects of fructose on hepatic glucose metabolism in humans. *Am J Physiol Endocrinol Metab* 2000;279:E907–E911.

Do LG, Spencer AJ. Risk-benefit balance in the use of fluoride among young children. *J Dent Res* 2007 Aug;86(8):723–728.

Dobnig H, Pilz S, Scharnagl H, Renner W, Seelhorst U, Wellnitz B, Kinkeldei J, Boehm BO, Weihrauch G, Maerz W. Independent association of low serum 25-hydroxyvitamin d and 1,25-dihydroxyvitamin d levels with all-cause and cardiovascular mortality. *Arch Intern Med* 2008 Jun 23;168(12):1340–1349.

Dobzhansky T. *Am Biol Teacher* 1973 March;35:125–129.

Dohan FC. Genetic hypothesis of idiopathic schizophrenia: its exorphin connection. *Schizophr Bull* 1988;14(4):489–494.

————. Hypothesis: genes and neuroactive peptides from food as cause of schizophrenia. *Adv Biochem Psychopharmacol* 1980;22:535–548.

Dohan FC, Grasberger JC. Relapsed schizophrenics: early discharge from the hospital after cereal-free, milk-free diet. *Am J Psychiatry* 1973;130: 685–688.

Dohan FC, Harper EH, Clark MH, Rodrigue RB, Zigas V. Is schizophrenia rare if grain is rare? *Biol Psychiatry* 1984 Mar;19(3):385–399.

Dong JY, Qin LQ. Dietary glycemic index, glycemic load, and risk of breast cancer: meta-analysis of prospective cohort studies. *Breast Cancer Res Treat* 2011 Apr;126(2):287–294.

Donnelly J, Pronk NP, Jacobsen DJ, Pronk SJ, Jakicic JM. Effects of a very low-calorie diet and physical-training regimens on body composition and resting metabolic rate in obese females. *Am J Clin Nutr* 1991;54:56–61.

Douglas JWB, Ross JM, Simpson HR. The ability and attainment of shortsighted pupils. *J R Stat Soc Series A (Gen)* 1967;130:479–504.

Dreon DM, Fernstrom HA, Miller B, Krauss RM. Low-density lipoprotein subclass patterns and lipoprotein response to a reduced-fat diet in men. *FASEB J* 1994;8:121–126.

Dreon DM, Fernstrom HA, Williams PT, Krauss RM. A very low-fat diet is not associated with improved lipoprotein profiles in men with a predominance of large, low-density lipoproteins. *Am J Clin Nutr* 1999;69:411–418.

————. Reduced LDL particle size in children consuming a very-low-fat diet is related to parental LDL-subclass patterns. *Am J Clin Nutr* 2000;71:1611–1616.

Dror DK, Allen LH. Effect of vitamin B12 deficiency on neurodevelopment in infants: current knowledge and possible mechanisms. *Nutr Rev* 2008 May;66(5):250–255.

Duckett SK, Wagner DG, Yates LD, Dolezal HG, May SG. Effects of time on feed on beef nutrient composition. *J Anim Sci* 1993;71:2079–2088.

Dunbar AJ, Priebe IK, Belford DA, Goddard C. Identification of betacellulin as a major peptide growth factor in milk: purification, characterization and molecular cloning of bovine betacellulin. *Biochem J* 1999 Dec 15;344 Pt 3:713–721.

Durand ML, Dietrich AM. Contributions of silane cross-linked PEX pipe to chemical/solvent odours in drinking water. *Water Sci Technol* 2007;55(5):153–160.

Dwyer J, Foulkes E, Evans M, Ausman L. Acid/alkaline ash diets: time for assessment and change. *J Am Diet Assoc* 1985;85:841–845.

Eaton SB et al. Women's reproductive cancers in evolutionary context. *Quart Rev Biol* 1994;69:353–367.

Eaton SB, Cordain L, Lindeberg S. Evolutionary health promotion: a consideration of common counterarguments. *Prev Med* 2002;34(2):119–123.

Eaton SB, Eaton SB 3rd, Sinclair AJ, Cordain L, Mann NJ. Dietary intake of long-chain polyunsaturated fatty acids during the Paleolithic. *World Rev Nutr Diet* 1998;83:12–23.

Eaton SB, Konner M. Paleolithic nutrition. A consideration of its nature and current implications. *N Engl J Med* 1985;312:283–289.

Eaton SB, Konner M, Shostak M. Stone Agers in the fast lane: chronic degenerative diseases in evolutionary perspective. *Am J Med* 1988;84:739–749.

Eaton SB, Shostak M, Konner M. The first fitness formula. In *The Paleolithic Prescription*. New York: Harper & Row, 1988, 168–199.

———. *The Paleolithic Prescription*. New York: Harper & Row, 1988.

Eaton SB, Strassman BI, Nesse RM, Neel JV, Ewald PW, Williams GC, Weder AB, Eaton SB 3rd, Lindeberg S, Konner MJ, Mysterud I, Cordain L. Evolutionary health promotion. *Prev Med* 2002;34(2):109–118.

Ebbing M, Bønaa KH, Nygård O, Arnesen E, Ueland PM, et al. Cancer incidence and mortality after treatment with folic acid and vitamin B12. *JAMA* 2009 Nov 18;302(19):2119–2126.

Ebisch IM, Peters WH, Thomas CM, Wetzels AM, Peer PG, Steegers-Theunissen RP. Homocysteine, glutathione, and related thiols affect fertility parameters in the (sub)fertile couple. *Hum Reprod* 2006 Jul;21(7):1725–1733.

Ebisch IM, Pierik FH, DE Jong FH, Thomas CM, Steegers-Theunissen RP. Does folic acid and zinc sulphate intervention affect endocrine parameters and sperm characteristics in men? *Int J Androl* 2006 Apr;29(2):339–345.

Eigenmann PA. Mechanisms of food allergy. *Pediatr Allergy Immuol* 2009;20:5–11.

Elfström P, Montgomery SM, Kämpe O, Ekbom A, Ludvigsson JF. Risk of thyroid disease in individuals with celiac disease. *J Clin Endocrinol Metab* 2008 Oct;93(10):3915–3921.

Elli M, Cattivelli D, Soldi S, Bonatti M, Morelli L. Evaluation of prebiotic potential of refined psyllium (*Plantago ovata*) fiber in healthy women. *J Clin Gastroenterol* 2008 Sep;42 Suppl 3 Pt 2:S174–S176.

Elmadfa I, Singer I. Vitamin B-12 and homocysteine status among vegetarians: a global perspective. *Am J Clin Nutr* 2009 May;89(5):1693S–1698S.

El-Tawil AM. Prevalence of inflammatory bowel diseases in the Western nations: high consumption of potatoes may be contributing. *Int J Colorectal Dis* 2008 Oct;23(10):1017–1018.

Ercan N, Gannon MC, Nuttall FQ. Effect of added fat on the plasma glucose and insulin response to ingested potato given in various combinations as two meals in normal individuals. *Diabetes Care* 1994;17(12):1453–1459.

Estrada A, Li B, Laarveld B. Adjuvant action of *Chenopodium quinoa* saponins on the induction of antibody responses to intragastric and intranasal administered antigens in mice. *Comp Immunol Microbiol Infect Dis* 1998 Jul;21(3):225–236.

Etling K. The wild diet. *Outdoor Life.* 1992(August):52–64.

Evans GH et al. Association of magnesium deficiency with the blood pressure lowering effects of calcium. *J Hypertension* 1990;8:327–337.

Evans TRJ, Kaye SB. Retinoids: present role and future potential. *Br J Cancer* 1999;80:1–8.

Evershed RP, Payne S, Sherratt AG, Copley MS, Coolidge J, Urem-Kotsu D, et al. Earliest date for milk use in the Near East and southeastern Europe linked to cattle herding. *Nature* 2008 Sep 25;455(7212):528–531.

Ewer TK. Rachitogenicity of green oats. *Nature* 1950;166:732–733.

Ezzo JA, Larsen CS, Burton JH. Elemental signatures of human diets from the Georgia Bight. *Am J Phys Anthropol* 1995;98:471–481.

Fairweather D, Frisancho-Kiss S, Rose NR. Viruses as adjuvants for autoimmunity: evidence from Coxsackievirus-induced myocarditis. *Rev Med Virol* 2005 Jan–Feb;15(1):17–27.

Fairweather D, Kaya Z, Shellam GR, Lawson CM, Rose NR. From infection to autoimmunity. *J Autoimmun* 2001 May;16(3):175–186.

Fairweather D, Rose NR. Women and autoimmune disease. *Emerg Infect Dis* 2004;10:2005–2011.

Falkingham M, Abdelhamid A, Curtis P, Fairweather-Tait S, Dye L, Hooper L. The effects of oral iron supplementation on cognition in older children and adults: a systematic review and meta-analysis. *Nutr J* 2010 Jan 25;9:4.

Falsetti L, Eleftheriou GI. Hyperinsulinemia in the polycystic ovary syndrome: a clinical endocrine and echographic study in 240 patients. *Gynecol Endocrinol* 1996;10:319–326.

FAO/WHO Expert Consultation. Protein Quality Evaluation. Food and Agricultural Organization of the United Nations, FAO Food and Nutrition Paper 51, Rome.

Farlow DW, Xu X, Veenstra TD. Quantitative measurement of endogenous estrogen metabolites, risk-factors for development of breast cancer, in commercial milk products by LC-MS/MS. *J Chromatogr B Analyt Technol Biomed Life Sci* 2009;877(13):1327–1334.

Farnsworth E, Luscombe ND, Noakes M, Wittert G, Argyiou E, Clifton PM. Effect of a high-protein, energy-restricted diet on body composition, glycemic control, and lipid concentrations in overweight and obese hyperinsulinemic men and women. *Am J Clin Nutr* 2003 Jul;78(1):31–39.

Fasano A. Physiological, pathological, and therapeutic implications of zonulin-mediated intestinal barrier modulation: living life on the edge of the wall. *Am J Pathol* 2008 Nov;173(5):1243–1252.

———. Surprises from celiac disease. *Sci Am* 2009 Aug;301(2):54–61.

Fasano A, Berti I, Gerarduzzi T, Not T, Colletti RB, Drago S, Elitsur Y, Green PH, Guandalini S, Hill ID, Pietzak M, Ventura A, Thorpe M, Kryszak D, Fornaroli F, Wasserman SS, Murray JA, Horvath K. Prevalence of celiac disease in at-risk and not-at-risk groups in the United States: a large multicenter study. *Arch Intern Med* 2003 Feb 10;163(3):286–292.

Fedail SS, Murphy D, Salih SY, Bolton CH, Harvey RF. Changes in certain blood constituents during Ramadan. *Am J Clin Nutr* 1982 Aug;36(2):350–353.

Feldkaemper MP, Neacsu I, Schaeffel F. Insulin acts as a powerful stimulator of axial myopia in chicks. *Invest Ophthalmol Vis Sci* 2009;50(1):13–23.

Fernandes G, Velangi A, Wolever TM. Glycemic index of potatoes commonly consumed in North America. *J Am Diet Assoc* 2005 Apr;105(4):557–562.

Fernandez, S, Vidueiros M, Ayerza R, Coates W, Pallaro A. Impact of chia (*Salvia hispanica L*) on the immune system: preliminary study. *Proceedings of the Nutrition Society*, 2008 May;67(Issue OCE), E12.

Ferry RJ, Cerri RW, Cohen P. Insulin-like growth factor binding proteins: new proteins, new functions. *Horm Res* 1999;51:53–67.

Feskens EJ, Bowles CH, Kromhout D. Inverse association between fish intake and risk of glucose intolerance in normoglycemic elderly men and women. *Diabetes Care* 1991;14:935–941.

Field S, Newton-Bishop JA. Melanoma and vitamin D. *Mol Oncol* Apr;5(2):197-214.

Fields C, Dourson M, Borak J. Iodine-deficient vegetarians: a hypothetical perchlorate-susceptible population? *Regul Toxicol Pharmacol* 2005 Jun;42(1):37–46.

Fields M, Lewis CG, Lure MD. Copper deficiency in rats: the effect of type of dietary protein. *J Am Coll Nutr* 1993;12:303–306.

Figueiredo JC, Grau MV, Haile RW, Sandler RS, Summers RW, Bresalier RS, Burke CA, McKeown-Eyssen GE, Baron JA. Folic acid and risk of prostate cancer: results from a randomized clinical trial. *J Natl Cancer Inst* 2009 Mar 18;101(6):432–435.

Finlay DR, Newmeyer DD, Price TM, Forbes DJ. Inhibition of in vitro nuclear transport by a lectin that binds to nuclear pores. *J Cell Biol* 1987 Feb;104(2):189–200.

Firestein GS, Alvaro-Gracia JM, Maki R. Quantitative analysis of cytokine gene expression in rheumatoid arthritis. *Journal of Immunology* 1990;144: 33347–33353.

Fischer Walker CL, Ezzati M, Black RE. Global and regional child mortality and burden of disease attributable to zinc deficiency. *Eur J Clin Nutr* 2009 May;63(5):591–597.

Flegal KM. Evaluating epidemiologic evidence of the effects of food and nutrient exposures. *Am J Clin Nutr* 1999 Jun;69(6):1339S–1344S.

Flegal KM, Carroll MD, Ogden CL, Curtin LR. Prevalence and trends in obesity among US adults, 1999–2008. *JAMA* 2010;303(3):235–241.

Fogh K, Kragballe K. New vitamin D analogs in psoriasis. *Curr Drug Targets Inflamm Allergy* 2004 Jun;3(2):199–204.

Fontana L, Meyer TE, Klein S, Holloszy JO. Long-term calorie restriction is highly effective in reducing the risk for atherosclerosis in humans. *Proc Natl Acad Sci USA.* 2004 Apr 27;101(17):6659–6663.

Food habits of a nation. In *The Hindu*, August 14, 2006 hinduonnet.com/2006/08/14/stories/2006081403771200.htm.

Ford JA, Colhoun EM, McIntosh WB, Dunnigan MG. Biochemical response of late rickets and osteomalacia to a chupatty-free diet. *Brit Med J* 1972;2:446–447.

Ford JA, McIntosh WB, Dunnigan MG. A possible relationship between high-extraction cereal and rickets and osteomalacia. *Adv Exp Med Biol* 1977;81:353–362.

Ford RP. The gluten syndrome: a neurological disease. *Med Hypotheses* 2009 Sep;73(3): 438–440.

Forouhi NG, Luan J, Cooper A, Boucher BJ, Wareham NJ. Baseline serum 25-hydroxy vitamin D is predictive of future glycaemic status and insulin resistance: The MRC Ely prospective study 1990–2000. *Diabetes* 2008 Oct;57(10):2619–2125.

Fort P, Moses N, Fasano M, Goldberg T, Lifshitz F. Breast and soy-formula feedings in early infancy and the prevalence of autoimmune thyroid disease in children. *J Am Coll Nutr* 1990 Apr;9(2):164–167.

Foster-Powell K, Brand-Miller J. International tables of glycemic index. *Am J Clin Nutr* 1995;62:871s–893s.

Foster-Powell K, Holt SH, Brand-Miller JC. International table of glycemic index and glycemic load values: 2002. *Am J Clin Nutr* 2002 Jul;76(1):5–56.

Franceschi S, Favero A. The role of energy and fat in cancers of the breast and colon-rectum in a southern European population. *Ann Oncol* 1999;10(suppl 6):61–63.

Francis G, Kerem Z, Makkar HP, Becker K. The biological action of saponins in animal systems: a review. *Br J Nutr* 2002 Dec;88(6):587–605.

Fraser GE. A search for truth in dietary epidemiology. *Am J Clin Nutr* 2003 Sep;78(3 Suppl):521S–525S.

Frassetto L. Diet, evolution, and aging—the pathophysiologic effects of the post-agricultural inversion of the potassium-to-sodium and base-to-chloride ratios in the human diet. *Eur J Nutr* 2001 Oct;40(5):200–213.

Frassetto LA, Morris Jr RC, Sebastian A. A practical approach to the balance between acid production and renal acid excretion in humans. *J Nephrol* 2006 Mar–Apr;19 Suppl 9:S33–40.

———. Dietary sodium chloride intake independently predicts the degree of hyperchloremic metabolic acidosis in healthy humans consuming a net acid-producing diet. *Am J Physiol Renal Physiol* 2007 Aug;293(2):F521–525.

Frassetto LA, Morris RC, Sebastian A. Potassium bicarbonate reduces urinary nitrogen excretion in postmenopausal women. *J Clin Endocrinol Metab* 1997; 82:254–259.

Frassetto LA, Schloetter M, Mietus-Synder M, Morris RC Jr., Sebastian A. Metabolic and physiologic improvements from consuming a Paleolithic, hunter-gatherer type diet. *Eur J Clin Nutr* 2009 Aug;63(8):947-955.

Frassetto LA, Todd KM, Morris RC, Sebastian A. Estimation of net endogenous noncarbonic acid production in humans from diet potassium and protein contents. *Am J Clin Nutr* 1998;68:576–583.

Freeland-Graves JH, Bodzy PW, Eppright MA. Zinc status of vegetarians. *J Am Diet Assoc* 1980 Dec;77(6):655–661.

Freeland-Graves JH, Ebangit ML, Hendrikson PJ. Alterations in zinc absorption and salivary sediment zinc after a lacto-ovo-vegetarian diet. *Am J Clin Nutr* 1980 Aug;33(8):1757–1766.

Freni SC. Exposure to high fluoride concentrations in drinking water is associated with decreased birth rates. *J Toxicol Environ Health* 1994 May;42(1):109–121.

Freudenheim JL. Study design and hypothesis testing: issues in the evaluation of evidence from research in nutritional epidemiology. *Am J Clin Nutr* 1999 Jun; 69(6):1315S–1321S.

Freyre EA, Rebaza RM, Sami DA, Lozada CP. The prevalence of facial acne in Peruvian adolescents and its relation to their ethnicity. *J Adolesc Health* 1998;22:480–484.

Friborg JT, Melbye M. Cancer patterns in Inuit populations. *Lancet Oncol* 2008 Sep;9(9):892–900.

Friedman M. Potato glycoalkaloids and metabolites: roles in the plant and in the diet. *J Agric Food Chem* 2006 Nov 15;54(23):8655–8681.

Friedman M, Levin CE. Alpha tomatine content in tomato and tomato products determined by HPLC with pulsed amperometric detection. *J Agric Food Chem* 1995;43:1507–1511.

Fujimori S, Tatsuguchi A, Gudis K, Kishida T, Mitsui K, Ehara A, Kobayashi T, Sekita Y, Seo T, Sakamoto CJ. High dose probiotic and prebiotic cotherapy for remission induction of active Crohn's disease. *Gastroenterol Hepatol* 2007 Aug;22(8):1199–1204.

Gabor F, Bogner E, Weissenboeck A, Wirth M. The lectin-cell interaction and its implications to intestinal lectin-mediated drug delivery. *Adv Drug Deliv Rev* 2004 Mar 3;56(4):459–480.

Gabor F, Stangl M, Wirth M. Lectin-mediated bioadhesion: binding characteristics of plant lectins on the enterocyte-like cell lines Caco-2, HT-29 and HCT-8. *J Control Release* 1998 Nov 13;55(2–3):131–142.

Gabunia L, Vekua A, Lordkipanidze D, Swisher CC III, Ferring R, Justus A, Nioradze M, Tvalchrelidze M, Anton SC, Bosinski G, Joris O, Lumley MA, Majsuradze G, Mouskhelishvili A. Earliest Pleistocene hominid cranial remains from Dmanisi, Republic of Georgia: taxonomy, geological setting, and age. *Science* 2000;288:1019–1025.

Gandini S, Merzenich H, Robertson C, Boyle P. Meta-analysis of studies on breast cancer risk and diet: the role of fruit and vegetable consumption and the intake of associated micronutrients. *Eur J Cancer* 2000 Mar;36(5):636–646.

Ganmaa D, Sato A. The possible role of female sex hormones in milk from pregnant cows in the development of breast, ovarian, and corpus uteri cancers. *Med Hypotheses* 2005;65(6):1028–1037.

Ganmaa D, Tezuka H, Enkhmaa D, Hoshi K, Sato A. Commercial cows' milk has uterotrophic activity on the uteri of young ovariectomized rats and immature rats. *Int J Cancer* 2006 May 1;118(9):2363–2365.

Ganmaa D, Wang PY, Qin LQ, Hoshi K, Sato A. Is milk responsible for male reproductive disorders? *Med Hypotheses* 2001 Oct;57(4):510–514.

Gannon MC, Nuttall FQ, Krezowski PA, Billington CJ, Parker S. The serum insulin and plasma glucose responses to milk and fruit products in type 2 (non-insulin-dependent) diabetic patients. *Diabetologia* 1986 Nov;29(11):784–791.

Gannon MC, Nuttall FQ, Westphal SA, Fang S, Ercan-Fang N. Acute metabolic response to high-carbohydrate, high-starch meals compared with moderate-carbohydrate, low-starch meals in subjects with type 2 diabetes. *Diabetes Care* 1998;21:1619–1626.

Gao X, LaValley MP, Tucker KL. Prospective studies of dairy product and calcium intakes and prostate cancer risk: a meta-analysis. *J Natl Cancer Inst* 2005 Dec 7;97(23):1768–1777.

Garcia-Menaya JM, Gonzalo-Garijo MA, Moneo I, Fernandez B, Garcia- Gonzalez F, Moreno F. A 17-kDa allergen detected in pine nuts. *Allergy* 2000;55: 291–293.

Gardiner PA. Dietary treatment of myopia in children. *Lancet* 1958;1;1152–1155.

Gardner CD, Fortmann SP, Krauss RM. Association of small low-density lipoprotein particles with the incidence of coronary artery disease in men and women. *JAMA* 1996;276:875–881.

Gardner CD, Kraemer HC. Monounsaturated versus polyunsaturated dietary fat and serum lipids. A meta-analysis. *Arterioscler Thromb Vasc Biol* 1995;15:1917–1927.

Garland CF, Garland FC, Gorham ED. Calcium and vitamin D. Their potential roles in colon and breast cancer prevention. *Ann NY Acad Sci* 1999;889:107–119.

———. Epidemiologic evidence for different roles of ultraviolet A and B radiation in melanoma mortality rates. *Ann Epidemiol* 2003 Jul;13(6):395–404.

———. Rising trends in melanoma. An hypothesis concerning sunscreen effectiveness. *Ann Epidemiol* 1993;3:103–110.

Garland FC, Garland CF, Gorham ED, Young JF. Geographic variation in breast cancer mortality in the United States: a hypothesis involving exposure to solar radiation. *Prev Med* 1990;19:614–622.

Gaziano JM, Glynn RJ, Christen WG, Kurth T, Belanger C, MacFadyen J, Bubes V, Manson JE, Sesso HD, Buring JE. Vitamins E and C in the prevention of prostate and total cancer in men: the Physicians' Health Study II randomized controlled trial. *JAMA* 2009 Jan 7;301(1):52–62. Epub 2008 Dec 9.

Gazzano E, Bergandi L, Riganti C, Aldieri E, Doublier S, Costamagna C, Bosia A, Ghigo D. Fluoride effects: the two faces of janus. *Curr Med Chem* 2010;17(22):2431–2441.

Gee JM, Johnson IT. Interactions between hemolytic saponins, bile salts, and small intestinal mucosa in the rat. *J Nutr* 1988 Nov;118(11):1391–1397.

Gee JM, Price KR, Ridout CL, Wortley GM, Hurrell RF, Johnson IT. Saponin of quinoa (Chenopodium quinoa): effects of processing on their abundance in quinoa products and their biological effects on intestinal mucosal tissue. *J Sci Food Agric* 1993;63:201–209.

Gee JM, Wal JM, Miller K, Atkinson H, Grigoriadou F, Wijnands MV, Penninks AH, Wortley G, Johnson IT. Effect of saponin on the transmucosal passage of beta-lactoglobulin across the proximal small intestine of normal and beta-lactoglobulin-sensitised rats. *Toxicology* 1997 Feb 28;117(2–3):219–228.

Gee JM, Wortley GM, Johnson IT, Price KR, Rutten AA, Houben GF, Penninks, AJ. Effects of saponins and glycoalkaloids on the permeability and viability of mammalian intestinal cells and on the integrity of tissue preparations. *Toxicol in Vitro* 1996;10:117–128.

Gélinas B, Seguin P. Oxalate in grain amaranth. *J Agric Food Chem* 2007 Jun 13;55(12): 4789–4794.

Genkinger JM, Hunter DJ, Spiegelman D, et al. Dairy products and ovarian cancer: a pooled analysis of 12 cohort studies. *Cancer Epidemiol Biomarkers Prev* 2006 Feb;15(2):364–372.

George R, Bhopal R. Fat composition of free living and farmed sea species: implications for human diet and sea-farming techniques. *Br Food J* 1995;97:19–22.

German JB, Dillard CJ. Saturated fats: what dietary intake? *Am J Clin Nutr* 2004;80:550.

Gerrior S, Bente I. Nutrient Content of the U.S. Food Supply, 1909–99: A Summary Report. USDA, Center for Nutrition Policy and Promotion. *Home Economics Research Report No. 55*, 2002.

Ghafoorunissa. Requirements of dietary fats to meet nutritional needs & prevent the risk of atherosclerosis—an Indian perspective. *Indian J Med Res* 1998;108:191–202.

Gibson RS, Bailey KB, Gibbs M, Ferguson EL. A review of phytate, iron, zinc, and calcium concentrations in plant-based complementary foods used in low-income countries and implications for bioavailability. *Food Nutr Bull* 2010 Jun;31(2 Suppl):S134–S146.

Gibson RS, Bindra GS, Nizan P, Draper HH. The vitamin D status of East Indian Punjabi immigrants to Canada. *Brit J Nutr* 1987;58:23–29.

Gielkens HA, Verkijk M, Lam WF, Lamers CB, Masclee AA. Effects of hyperglycemia and hyperinsulinemia on satiety in humans. *Metabolism* 1998;47:321–324.

Gilani GS, Cockell KA, Sepehr E. Effects of antinutritional factors on protein digestibility and amino acid availability in foods. *J AOAC Int* 2005 May–Jun;88(3):967–987.

Gill ZP, Perks CM, Newcomb PV, Holly JM. Insulin-like growth factor–binding protein (IGFBP-3) predisposes breast cancer cells to programmed cell death in a non-IGF-dependent manner. *J Biol Chem* 1997;272:25602–25607.

Gilsing AM, Crowe FL, Lloyd-Wright Z, Sanders TA, Appleby PN, Allen NE, Key TJ. Serum concentrations of vitamin B12 and folate in British male omnivores, vegetarians, and vegans: results from a cross-sectional analysis of the EPIC-Oxford cohort study. *Eur J Clin Nutr* 2010 Sep;64(9):933–939.

Giovannucci E. Insulin-like growth factor-I and binding protein-3 and risk of cancer. *Horm Res* 1999;51(suppl S3):34–41.

———. Tomatoes, tomato-based products, lycopene, and cancer: review of the epidemiologic literature. *J Natl Cancer Inst* 1999;91:317–331.

Giovannucci E, Stampfer MJ, Colditz GA, Rimm EB, Trichopoulos D, Rosner BA, Speizer FE, Willett WC. Folate, methionine, and alcohol intake and risk of colorectal adenoma. *J Natl Cancer Inst* 1993;85:875–883.

Gomez-Cabrera M-C, Domenech E, Romagnoli M, Arduini A, Borras C, Pallardo FV et al. Oral administration of vitamin C decreases muscle mitochondrial biogenesis and hampers training-induced adaptations in endurance performance. *Am J Clin Nutr* 2008;87(1):142–149.

Gore F, Fawell J, Bartram J. Too much or too little? A review of the conundrum of selenium. J *Water Health* 2010 Sep;8(3):405–416.

Gorham ED, Mohr SB, Garland CF, Chaplin G, Garland FC. Do sunscreens increase risk of melanoma in populations residing at higher latitudes? *Ann Epidemiol* 2007 Dec;17(12): 956–963.

Gotshall RW, Mickelborough TD, Cordain L. Dietary salt restriction improves pulmonary function in exercise-induced asthma. *Med Sci Sports Exerc* 2000;32:1815–1819.

Gourmelen M, Le Bouc Y, Girard F, Binoux M. Serum levels of insulin-like growth factor (IGF) and IGF binding proteins in constitutionally tall children and adolescents. *J Clin Endocrinol Metab* 1984;59:1197–1203.

Govindarajan VS, Sathyanarayana MN. Capsicum—production, technology, chemistry, and quality. Part V. Impact on physiology, pharmacology, nutrition, and metabolism; structure, pungency, pain, and desensitization sequences. *Crit Rev Food Sci Nutr* 1991;29(6):435–474.

Grammer JC, McGinnis J, Pubols MH. 1983. The rachitogenic effects of fractions of rye and certain polysaccharides. *Poultry Science* 62:103–109.

Grant G. Anti-nutritional effects of soyabean: a review. *Prog Food Nutr Sci* 1989;13(3–4): 317–348.

Grant G, More LJ, McKenzie NH, Pusztai A. The effect of heating on the haemaggluti-nating activity and nutritional properties of bean (*Phaseolus vulgaris*) seeds. *J Sci Food Agric* 1982;33:1324–1326.

Grant G, More LJ, McKenzie NH, Stewart JC, Pusztai A. A survey of the nutritional and haemagglutination properties of legume seeds generally available in the UK. *Br J Nutr* 1983 Sep;50(2):207–214.

Gravis G, Bladou F, Salem N, Gonçalves A, Esterni B, Walz J, Bagattini S, Marcy M, Brunelle S, Viens P. Results from a monocentric phase II trial of erlotinib in patients with metastatic prostate cancer. *Ann Oncol.* 2008 Sep;19(9):1624–1628.

Gray JP. A corrected ethnographic atlas. *World Cultures J* 1999;10:24–85.

Gray R. *Eat Like a Wild Man: 110 Years of Great Sports Afield Recipes.* Minocqua, WI: Willow Creek Press, 1997.

Greenfield HJ. The origins of milk and wool production in the old world. *Curr Anthropol* 1988;29:573–594.

Greenough A, Shaheen SO, Shennan A, Seed PT, Poston L. Respiratory outcomes in early childhood following antenatal vitamin C and E supplementation. *Thorax* 2010 Nov;65(11): 998–1003.

Greer F, Pusztai A. (1985). Toxicity of kidney bean (*Phaseolus vulgaris*) in rats: changes in intestinal permeability. *Digestion* 1985 32:42–46.

Griffin BA. Lipoprotein atherogenicity: an overview of current mechanisms. *Proc Nutr Soc* 1999;58:163–169.

Guart A, Bono-Blay F, Borrell A, Lacorte S. Migration of plasticizersphthalates, bisphenol A and alkylphenols from plastic containers and evaluation of risk. *Food Addit Contam Part A Chem Anal Control Expo Risk Assess* 2011 Mar 11:1–10.

Gueux E, Azais-Braesco V, Bussiere L, Grolier P, Mazur A, Rayssiguier Y. Effect of magnesium deficiency on triacylglycerol-rich lipoprotein and tissue susceptibility to peroxidation in relation to vitamin E content. *Br J Nutr* 1995;74:849–856.

Gueux E, Cubizolles C, Bussière L, Mazur A, Rayssiguier Y et al. Oxidative modification of triglyceride rich lipoprotein in hypertriglyceridemic rats following magnesium deficiency. *Lipids* 1993;28:573–575.

Guinez C, Morelle W, Michalski JC, Lefebvre T. O-GlcNAc glycosylation: a signal for the nuclear transport of cytosolic proteins? *Int J Biochem Cell Biol* 2005 Apr;37(4):765–774.

Gupta YP. Anti-nutritional and toxic factors in food legumes: a review. *Plant Foods Hum Nutr* 1987;37:201–228.

Guthrie JF, Morton JF. Food sources of added sweeteners in the diets of Americans. *J Am Diet Assoc* 2000;100:43–51.

Gutowska I, Baranowska-Bosiacka I, Baskiewicz M, Milo B, Siennicka A, Marchlewicz M, Wiszniewska B, Machalinski B, Stachowska E. Fluoride as a pro-inflammatory factor and inhibitor of ATP bioavailability in differentiated human THP1 monocytic cells. *Toxicol Lett* 2010 Jul 1;196(2):74–79.

Hadjivassiliou M, Gibson A, Davies-Jones GA, Lobo AJ, Stephenson TJ, Milford-Ward A. Does cryptic gluten sensitivity play a part in neurological illness? *Lancet* 1996;347:369–371.

Hadjivassiliou M, Sanders DS, Grünewald RA, Woodroofe N, Boscolo S, Aeschlimann D. Gluten sensitivity: from gut to brain. *Lancet Neurol* 2010 Mar;9(3):318–330.

Hallberg L, Hulthén L. Prediction of dietary iron absorption: an algorithm for calculating absorption and bioavailability of dietary iron. *Am J Clin Nutr* 2000 May;71(5):1147–1160.

Hallberg L, Rossander-Hulten L, Brune M, Gleerup A. Calcium and iron absorption: mechanism of action and nutritional importance. *Eur J Clin Nutr* 1992 May;46(5):317–327.

Halldorsson TI, Strøm M, Petersen SB, Olsen SF. Intake of artificially sweetened soft drinks and risk of preterm delivery: a prospective cohort study in 59,334 Danish pregnant women. *Am J Clin Nutr* 2010 Sep;92(3):626–633.

Halperin EC. Pale-oncology the role of ancient remains in the study of cancer. *Perspect Biol Med* 2004;47:1–14.

Halsted JA, Ronaghy HA, Abadi P, Haghshenass M, Amirhakemi GH, Barakat RM, Reinhold JG. Zinc deficiency in man, the Shiraz experiment. *Am J Med* 1972;53:277–284.

Hammond AC, Rumsey TS, Haaland GL. Prediction of empty body components in steers by urea dilution. *J Anim Sci* 1988;66:354–360.

Han J, Isoda H, Maekawa T. Analysis of the mechanism of the tight-junctional permeability increase by capsaicin treatment on the intestinal Caco-2 cells. *Cytotechnology* 2002 Nov;40(1–3):93–98.

Han JK, Akutsu M, Talorete TP, Maekawa T, Tanaka T, Isoda H. Capsaicin-enhanced Ribosomal Protein P2 Expression in Human Intestinal Caco-2 Cells. *Cytotechnology* 2005 Jan;47(1–3):89–96.

Hanchette CL, Schwartz GC. Geographic patterns of prostate cancer mortality. Evidence for a protective effect of ultraviolet radiation. *Cancer* 1992;70:2861–2869.

Hankinson SE, Eliassen AH. Endogenous estrogen, testosterone, and progesterone levels in relation to breast cancer risk. *J Steroid Biochem Mol Biol* 2007 Aug-Sep;106(1–5):24–30.

Hansen CM, Leklem JE, Miller LT. Vitamin B-6 status indicators decrease in women consuming a diet high in pyridoxine glucoside. *J Nutr* 1996 Oct;126(10):2512–2518.

Hansen D, Dendale P, van Loon LJ, Meeusen R. The impact of training modalities on the clinical benefits of exercise intervention in patients with cardiovascular disease risk or type 2 diabetes mellitus. *Sports Med* 2010 Nov 1;40(11):921–940.

Harlan JR. The plants and animals that nourish man. *Sci Am* 1976;235:89–97.

Harris WS, Kris-Etherton PM, Harris KA. Intakes of long-chain omega-3 fatty acid associated with reduced risk for death from coronary heart disease in healthy adults. *Curr Atheroscler Rep* 2008 Dec;10(6):503–509.

Harrison DC, Mellanby E. Phytic acid and the rickets-producing action of cereals. *Biochem J* 1939 Oct;33(10):1660–1680.

Harrison R. Milk xanthine oxidase: hazard or benefit. *J Nutr Environ Med* 2002;12:231–238.

Härtig W, Reichenbach A, Voigt C, Boltze J, Bulavina L, Schuhmann MU, Seeger J, Schusser GF, Freytag C, Grosche J. Triple fluorescence labelling of neuronal, glial, and vascular markers revealing pathological alterations in various animal models. *J Chem Neuroanat* 2009 Mar;37(2):128–138.

Hartmann S, Lacorn M, Steinhart H. Natural occurrence of steroid hormones in food. *Food Chem* 1998;6:7–20.

Hartroft WS. The incidence of coronary artery disease in patients treated with Sippy diet. *Am J Clin Nutr* 1964 Oct;15:205–210.

Harvey R, Hannan SA, Badia L, Scadding G. Nasal saline irrigations for the symptoms of chronic rhinosinusitis. *Cochrane Database Syst Rev* 2007 Jul 18;(3):CD006394.

Haskell WL. The influence of exercise on the concentrations of triglyceride and cholesterol in human plasma. *Exerc Sport Sci Rev* 1984;12:205–244.

Hawkes K, Hill K, O'Connell JF. Why hunters gather: optimal foraging and the ache of eastern Paraguay. *Am Ethnologist* 1982;9:379–398.

Heal KG, Sheikh NA, Hollingdale MR, Morrow WJ, Taylor-Robinson AW. Potentiation by a novel alkaloid glycoside adjuvant of a protective cytotoxic T cell immune response specific for a preerythrocytic malaria vaccine candidate antigen. *Vaccine* 2001;19(30):4153–4161.

Hearsey H. The rarity of cancer among the aborigines of British Central Africa. *Brit Med J* 1906 Dec 1:1562–1563.

Hedlund LR, Gallagher JC. Increased incidence of hip fracture in osteoporotic women treated with sodium fluoride. *J Bone Miner Res* 1989 Apr;4(2):223–225.

Hegsted DM, Ausman LM, Johnson JA, Dallal GE. Dietary fat and serum lipids: an evaluation of the experimental data. *Am J Clin Nutr* 1993 Jun;57(6):875–883.

Hegsted DM, McGandy RB, Myers ML, Stare FJ. Quantitative effects of dietary fat on serum cholesterol in man. *Am J Clin Nutr* 1965;17:281–295.

Heilbronn LK, Ravussin E. Calorie restriction and aging: review of the literature and implications for studies in humans. *Am J Clin Nutr* 2003 Sep;78(3):361–369.

Heiser CB. *Nightshades, the Paradoxical Plants.* San Francisco: W.H. Freeman and Company, 1969.

Hellenäs KE, Nyman A, Slanina P, Lööf L, Gabrielsson J. Determination of potato glycoalkaloids and their aglycone in blood serum by high-performance liquid chromatography. Application to pharmacokinetic studies in humans. *J Chromatogr* 1992 Jan 3;573(1):69–78.

Hennekens CH, Buring JE. *Epidemiology in Medicine.* Boston: Little, Brown, 1987.

Henry CJ, Lightowler HJ, Strik CM, Storey M. Glycaemic index values for commercially available potatoes in Great Britain. *Br J Nutr* 2005 Dec;94(6):917–921.

Henson ES, Gibson SB. Surviving cell death through epidermal growth factor (EGF) signal transduction pathways: Implications for cancer therapy. *Cell Signal* 2006 Dec;18(12): 2089–2097.

Henson, WW. Cancer in Kafirs: suggested cause. *Guy's Hospital Gazette* 1904 Mar 26:131–133.

Herbert K, Fletcher S, Chauhan D, Ladapo A, Nirwan J, Munson S et al. (2006). Dietary supplementation with different vitamin C doses: no effect on oxidative DNA damage in healthy people. *Eur J Nutr* 2006;45(2):97–104.

Herbert V. Staging vitamin B-12 (cobalamin) status in vegetarians. *Am J Clin Nutr* 1994 May;59(5 Suppl):1213S–1222S.

Herrick K, Phillips DIW, Haselden S, Shiell AW, Campbell-Brown M, Godfrey KM. Maternal consumption of a high-meat, low-carbohydrate diet in late pregnancy: relation to adult cortisol concentrations in the offspring. *J Clin Endocrinol Metab* 2003;88(8): 3554–3560.

Herrmann M, Peter Schmidt J, Umanskaya N, Wagner A, Taban-Shomal O, Widmann T, Colaianni G, Wildemann B, Herrmann W. The role of hyperhomocysteinemia as well as folate, vitamin B(6) and B(12) deficiencies in osteoporosis: a systematic review. *Clin Chem Lab Med* 2007;45(12):1621–1632.

Herrmann M, Widmann T, Colaianni G, Colucci S, Zallone A, Herrmann W. Increased osteoclast activity in the presence of increased homocysteine concentrations. *Clin Chem* 2005 Dec;51(12):2348–2353.

Herrmann W, Obeid R, Schorr H, Geisel J. Functional vitamin B12 deficiency and determination of holotranscobalamin in populations at risk. *Clin Chem Lab Med* 2003 Nov;41(11):1478–1488.

Herrmann W, Obeid R, Schorr H, Hübner U, Geisel J, Sand-Hill M, Ali N, Herrmann M. Enhanced bone metabolism in vegetarians—the role of vitamin B12 deficiency. *Clin Chem Lab Med* 2009;47(11):1381–1387.

Herrmann W, Schorr H, Obeid R, Geisel J. Vitamin B-12 status, particularly holotrans-cobalamin II and methylmalonic acid concentrations, and hyperhomocysteinemia in vegetarians. *Am J Clin Nutr* 2003 Jul;78(1):131–136.

Heyland DK, Jones N, Cvijanovich NZ, Wong H. Zinc supplementation in critically ill patients: a key pharmaconutrient? *JPEN J Parenter Enteral Nutr* 2008 Sep–Oct;32(5):509–519.

Hibbeln JR. Fish consumption and major depression. *Lancet* 1998;351:1213.

Hibbeln JR, Salem N. Dietary polyunsaturated fatty acids and depression: when cholesterol does not satisfy. *Am J Clin Nutr* 1995;62:1–9.

Hidiroglou M, Ivan M, Proulx JG, Lessard JR. Effect of a single intramuscular dose of vitamin D on concentrations of liposoluble vitamins in the plasma of heifers winter-fed oat silage, grass silage or hay. *Can J Anim Sci* 1980;60:311–318.

Higami Y, Yamaza H, Shimokawa I. Laboratory findings of caloric restriction in rodents and primates. *Adv Clin Chem* 2005;39:211–237.

Higashihara M, Ozaki Y, Ohashi T, Kume S. Interaction of Solanum tuberosum agglutinin with human platelets. *Biochem Biophys Res Commun* 1984 May 31;121(1):27–33.

Hildes JA, Schaefer O. The changing picture of neoplastic disease in the western and central Canadian Arctic (1950–1980). *Can Med Assoc J* 1984;130:25–32.

Hinton PS, Sinclair LM. Iron supplementation maintains ventilatory threshold and improves energetic efficiency in iron-deficient nonanemic athletes. *Eur J Clin Nutr* 2007 Jan;61(1):30–39.

Hintz HF, Hogue DE, Krook L. Toxicity of red kidney beans (*Phaseolus vulgaris*) in the rat. *J Nutr* 1967 Sep;93(1):77–86.

Hirwe R, Jathar VS, Desai S, Satoskar RS. Vitamin B12 and potential fertility in male lactovegetarians. *J Biosoc Sci* 1976 Jul;8(3):221–227.

Ho-Pham LT, Nguyen ND, Nguyen TT, Nguyen DH, Bui PK, Nguyen VN, Nguyen TV. Association between vitamin D insufficiency and tuberculosis in a Vietnamese population. *BMC Infect Dis* 2010 Oct 25;10:306.

Ho-Pham LT, Nguyen ND, Nguyen TV. Effect of vegetarian diets on bone mineral density: a Bayesian meta-analysis. *Am J Clin Nutr* 2009 Oct;90(4):943–950.

Hobbs CJ, Plymate SR, Rosen CJ, Adler RAI. Testosterone administration increases insulin-like growth factor-I levels in normal men. *J Clin Endocrinol Metab* 1993;77:776–779.

Hobbes T. *The Leviathan*. Amherst, NY: Prometheus Books, 1988.

Hochman LG, Scher RK, Meyerson MS. Brittle nails: response to daily biotin supplementation. *Cutis* 1993;51:303–305.

Hokanson JE, Austin MA. Plasma triglyceride level is a risk factor for cardiovascular disease independent of high-density lipoprotein cholesterol level: a meta-analysis of population-based prospective studies. *J Cardiovasc Risk* 1996;3:213–219.

Holick MF. Optimal vitamin d status for the prevention and treatment of osteoporosis. *Drugs Aging* 2007;24(12):1017–1029.

———. Vitamin D and sunlight: strategies for cancer prevention and other health benefits. *Clin J Am Soc Nephrol* 2008;3:1548–1554.

———. Vitamin D deficiency. *N Engl J Med* 2007;357:266–281.

Holick MF, Chen TC. Vitamin D deficiency: a worldwide problem with health consequences. *Am J Clin Nutr* 2008 Apr;87(4):1080S–1086S.

Hollis BW. Circulating 25-hydroxyvitamin D levels indicative of vitamin D sufficiency: implications for establishing a new effective dietary intake recommendation for vitamin D. *J Nutr* 2005 Feb;135(2):317–322.

Holly JMP. The physiological role of IGFBP-1. *Acta Endocrinol* 1991;124: 55–62.

Holmes MD, Stampfer MJ, Colditz GA, Rosner B, Hunter DJ, Willett WC. Dietary factors and the survival of women with breast carcinoma. *Cancer* 1999;86:826–835.

Holt SH et al. An insulin index of foods: the insulin demand generated by 1000-kJ portions of common foods. *Am J Clin Nutr* 1997 Nov;66(5):1264–1276.

Holt SH, Miller JB. Increased insulin responses to ingested foods are associated with lessened satiety. *Appetite* 1995;24:43–54.

Honein MA, Paulozzi LJ, Mathews TJ, Erickson JD, Wong LY. Impact of folic acid fortification of the US food supply on the occurrence of neural tube defects. *JAMA* 2001 Jun 20;285(23):2981–2986.

Hooper L, Ryder JJ, Kurzer MS, Lampe JW, Messina MJ, Phipps WR, Cassidy A. Effects of soy protein and isoflavones on circulating hormone concentrations in pre- and post-menopausal women: a systematic review and meta-analysis. *Hum Reprod Update* 2009 Jul–Aug;15(4):423–440.

Hoorfar J, Buschard K, Dagnaes-Hansen F. Prophylactic nutritional modification of the incidence of diabetes in autoimmune non-obese diabetic (NOD) mice. *Br J Nutr* 1993 Mar;69(2):597–607.

Hoppe C, Mølgaard C, Vaag A, Barkholt V, Michaelsen KF. High intakes of milk, but not meat increase s-insulin and insulin resistance in 8-year-old boys. *Eur J Clin Nutr* 2005 Mar;59(3):393–398.

Hormi K, Lehy T. Developmental expression of transforming growth factor-alpha and epidermal growth factor receptor proteins in the human pancreas and digestive tract. *Cell Tissue Res* 1994 Dec;278(3):439–450.

Horner SM et al. Efficacy of intravenous magnesium in acute myocardial infarction in reducing arrhythmias and mortality. Meta-analysis of magnesium in acute myocardial infarction. *Circulation* 1992;86:774–779.

Høst A. Frequency of cow's milk allergy in childhood. *Ann Allergy Asthma Immunol* 2002 Dec;89(6 Suppl 1):33–37.

Hotz C. Dietary indicators for assessing the adequacy of population zinc intakes. *Food Nutr Bull* 2007 Sep;28(3 Suppl):S430–453.

Howell JM. Early farming in northwestern Europe. *Sci Am* 1987;257:118–126.

Howell WH, McNamara DJ, Tosca MA, Smith BT, Gaines JA. Plasma lipid and lipoprotein responses to dietary fat and cholesterol: a meta-analysis. *Am J Clin Nutr* 1997 Jun;65(6):1747–1764.

Hoyt G, Hickey MS, Cordain L. Dissociation of the glycaemic and insulinaemic responses to whole and skimmed milk. *Br J Nutr* 2005;93(2):175–177.

Hu FB, Stampfer MJ, Manson JE, Rimm E, Colditz GA, Speizer FE, Hennekens CH, Willett WC. Dietary protein and risk of ischemic heart disease in women. *Am J Clin Nutr* 1999 Aug;70(2):221–227.

Hu FB, Stampfer MJ, Rimm EB, Manson JE, Ascherio A, Colditz GA, Rosner BA, Spiegelman D, Speizer FE, Sacks FM, Hennekens CH, Willett WC. A prospective study of egg consumption and risk of cardiovascular disease in men and women. *JAMA* 1999;281:1387–1394.

Hua G, Reckhow DA. Comparison of disinfection byproduct formation from chlorine and alternative disinfectants. *Water Res* 2007 Apr;41(8):1667–1678.

Huang YC, Chang SJ, Chiu YT, Chang HH, Cheng CH.The status of plasma homocysteine and related B-vitamins in healthy young vegetarians and nonvegetarians. *Eur J Nutr* 2003 Apr;42(2):84–90.

Hughes JS, Acevedo E, Bressani R, Swanson BG. Effects of dietary fiber and tannins on protein utilization in dry beans (*Phaseolus vulgaris*). *Food Res Int* 1996;29:331–338.

Humbert P, Bidet A, Treffel P, Drobacheff C, Agache P. Intestinal permeability in patients with psoriasis. *J Dermatol Sci* 1991;2:324–326.

Humphrey LL, Fu R, Rogers K, Freeman M, Helfand M. Homocysteine level and coronary heart disease incidence: a systematic review and meta-analysis. *Mayo Clin Proc* 2008 Nov;83(11):1203–1212.

Hung S, Umemura T, Yamashiro S, Slinger SJ. The effects of original and randomized rapeseed oils containing high or very low levels of erucic acid on cardiac lipids and myocardial lesions in rats. *Lipids* 1977;12(2):215–221.

Hunt JR, Matthys LA, Johnson LK. Zinc absorption, mineral balance, and blood lipids in women consuming controlled lactoovovegetarian and omnivorous diets for 8 wk. *Am J Clin Nutr* 1998 Mar;67(3):421–430.

Hunt JR, Roughead ZK. Nonheme-iron absorption, fecal ferritin excretion, and blood indexes of iron status in women consuming controlled lactoovovegetarian diets for 8 wk. *Am J Clin Nutr* 1999 May;69(5):944–952.

Hunt SP, O'Riordan JLH, Windo J, Truswell AS. Vitamin D status in different subgroups of British Asians. *Br Med J* 1976;2:1351–54.

Hunter DJ, Willett WC. Diet, body size, and breast cancer. *Epidemiol Rev* 1993;15:110–132.

Hurrell RF, Juillerat MA, Reddy MB, Lynch SR, Dassenko SA, Cook JD. Soy protein, phytate, and iron absorption in humans. *Am J Clin Nutr* 1992 Sep;56(3):573–578.

Husain R, Duncan MT, Cheah SH, Ch'ng SL. Effects of fasting in Ramadan on tropical Asiatic Moslems. *Br J Nutr* 1987 Jul;58(1):41–48.

Hvas AM, Morkbak AL, Nexo E. Plasma holotranscobalamin compared with plasma cobalamins for assessment of vitamin B12 absorption; optimisation of a non-radioactive vitamin B12 absorption test (CobaSorb). *Clin Chim Acta* 2007 Feb;376(1–2):150–154.

Hwalla Baba N, Sawaya S, Torbay N, Habbal Z, Azar S, Hashim SA. High protein vs. high carbohydrate hypoenergetic diet for the treatment of obese hyperinsulinemic subjects. *Int J Obes* 1999;23:1202–1206.

Hyppönen E, Läärä E, Reunanen A, Järvelin MR, Virtanen SM. Intake of vitamin D and risk of type 1 diabetes: a birth-cohort study. *Lancet* 2001 Nov 3;358(9292):1500–1503.

Iablokov V, Sydora BC, Foshaug R, Meddings J, Driedger D, Churchill T, Fedorak RN. Naturally occurring glycoalkaloids in potatoes aggravate intestinal inflammation in two mouse models of inflammatory bowel disease. *Dig Dis Sci* 2010 Nov;55(11):3078–3085.

Ikeda K. Buckwheat: composition, chemistry, and processing. *Adv Food Nutr Res* 2002;44:395–434.

Ingram CJ, Mulcare CA, Itan Y, Thomas MG, Swallow DM. Lactose digestion and the evolutionary genetics of lactase persistence. *Hum Genet* 2009 Jan;124(6):579–591.

Inkielewicz-Stepniak I, Czarnowski W. Oxidative stress parameters in rats exposed to fluoride and caffeine. *Food Chem Toxicol* 2010 Jun;48(6):1607–1611.

Ip C, Scimeca JA, Thompson HJ. Conjugated linoleic acid. A powerful anticarcinogen from animal fat sources. *Cancer* 1994;74(suppl 3):1050–1054.

Is our fish fit to eat? *Consumer Reports* 1992(February);103–114.

Ishizuki Y, Hirooka Y, Murata Y, Togashi K. The effects on the thyroid gland of soybeans administered experimentally in healthy subjects. *Nippon Naibunpi Gakkai Zasshi* 1991 May 20;67(5):622–629.

Isoda H, Han J, Tominaga M, Maekawa T. Effects of capsaicin on human intestinal cell line Caco-2. *Cytotechnology* 2001 Jul;36(1–3):155–161.

Itami S, Kurata S, Takayasu S. Androgen induction of follicular epithelial cell growth is mediated via insulin-like growth factor-I from dermal papilla cells. *Biochem Biophys Res Commun* 1995;212:988–994.

Iuorio R, Mercuri V, Barbarulo F, D'Amico T, Mecca N, Bassotti G, Pietrobono D, Gargiulo P, Picarelli A. Prevalence of celiac disease in patients with autoimmune thyroiditis. *Minerva Endocrinol* 2007 Dec;32(4):239–243.

Ivarsson A, Persson LA, Juto P, Peltonen M, Suhr O, Hernell O. High prevalence of undiagnosed coeliac disease in adults: a Swedish population-based study. *J Intern Med* 1999 Jan;245(1):63–68.

Ivy JL. Role of exercise training in the prevention and treatment of insulin resistance and on insulin-dependent diabetes mellitus. *Sports Med* 1997;24:321–336.

Ixtainaa VY, Nolascoa SM, Tomás MC. Physical properties of chia (*Salvia hispanica L.*) seeds. *Industrial Crops and Products* 2008;28:286–293.

Jacob SE, Stechschulte S. Formaldehyde, aspartame, and migraines: a possible connection. *Dermatitis* 2008 May–Jun;19(3):E10–1.

Jacobson MS. Cholesterol oxides in Indian ghee: possible cause of unexplained high risk of atherosclerosis in Indian immigrant populations. *Lancet* 1987;2:656–658.

Jakobsson I, Lindberg T. Cow's milk proteins cause infantile colic in breast-fed infants: a double-blind crossover study. *Pediatrics* 1983 Feb;71(2):268–271.

Jathar VS, Hirwe R, Desai S, Satoskar RS. Dietetic habits and quality of semen in Indian subjects. *Andrologia* 1976;8(4):355–358.

Jenkins DJ, Kendall CW, Connelly PW, Jackson CJ, Parker T, Faulkner D, Vidgen E. Effects of high- and low-isoflavone (phytoestrogen) soy foods on inflammatory biomarkers and proinflammatory cytokines in middle-aged men and women. *Metabolism* 2002 Jul;51(7):919–924.

Jensen-Jarolim E, Gajdzik L, Haberl I, Kraft D, Scheiner O, Graf J. Hot spices influence permeability of human intestinal epithelial monolayers. *J Nutr* 1998;128:577–581.

Johnson FO, Gilbreath ET, Ogden L, Graham TC, Gorham S. Reproductive and developmental toxicities of zinc supplemented rats. *Reprod Toxicol* 2011 Feb;31(2):134–143.

Johnson IT, Gee JM, Price K, Curl C, Fenwick GR. Influence of saponins on gut permeability and active nutrient transport in vitro. *J Nutr* 1986 Nov;116(11):2270–2277.

Jönsson T, Ahren B, Pacini G, Sundler F, Wierup N, Steen S, Sjoberg T, Ugander M, Frostegard J, Göransson L, Lindeberg S. A Paleolithic diet confers higher insulin sensitivity, lower C-reactive protein and lower blood pressure than a cereal-based diet in domestic pigs. *Nutr Metab* (Lond) 2006;3:39.

Jönsson T, Granfeldt Y, Ahrén B, Branell UC, Pålsson G, Hansson A, Söderström M, Lindeberg S. Beneficial effects of a Paleolithic diet on cardiovascular risk factors in type 2 diabetes: a randomized cross-over pilot study. *Cardiovasc Diabetol* 2009;8:35.

Jönsson T, Granfeldt Y, Erlanson-Albertsson C, Ahren B, Lindeberg S. A Paleolithic diet is more satiating per calorie than a Mediterranean-like diet in individuals with ischemic heart disease. *Nutr Metab* (Lond) 2010 Nov 30;7(1):85.

Joyce SJ, Cook A, Newnham J, Brenters M, Ferguson C, Weinstein P. Water disinfection by-products and pre-labor rupture of membranes. *Am J Epidemiol* 2008 Sep 1;168(5):514–521. Epub 2008 Jul 16.

Jungers, WL. Biomechanics: barefoot running strikes back. *Nature* 2010;463(7280):433–434.

Juul A, Scheike T, Nielsen CT, Krabbe S, Muller J, Skakkebaek NE. Serum insulin-like growth factor I (IGF-1) and IGF-binding protein 3 levels are increased in central precocious puberty: effects of two different treatment regimens with gonadotropin-relating hormone agonists, without or in combination with an antiandrogen (cyproterone acetate). *J Clin Endocrinol Metab* 1995;80:3059–3067.

Kagnoff MF. Celiac disease: pathogenesis of a model immunogenetic disease. *J Clin Invest* 2007 Jan;117(1):41–49.

Kalhan S. Protein metabolism in pregnancy. *Am J Clin Nutr* 2000;71 (suppl):1249S–1255S.

Kallio P, Kolehmainen M, Laaksonen DE, Pulkkinen L, Atalay M, Mykkänen H, Uusitupa M, Poutanen K, Niskanen L. Inflammation markers are modulated by responses to diets differing in postprandial insulin responses in individuals with the metabolic syndrome. *Am J Clin Nutr* 2008 May;87(5):1497–1503.

Kane J. *Savages.* New York: Random House, 1995.

Kanis JA, Johansson H, Oden A, De Laet C, Johnell O, Eisman JA, Mc Closkey E, Mellstrom D, Pols H, Reeve J, Silman A, Tenenhouse A. A meta-analysis of milk intake and fracture risk: low utility for case finding. *Osteoporos Int* 2005 Jul;16(7):799–804.

Karabudak E, Kiziltan G, Cigerim N. A comparison of some of the cardiovascular risk factors in vegetarian and omnivorous Turkish females. *J Hum Nutr Diet* 2008 Feb;21(1):13–22.

Karas-Kuzelicki N, Pfeifer V, Lukac-Bajalo J. Synergistic effect of high lactase activity genotype and galactose-1-phosphate uridyl transferase (GALT) mutations on idiopathic presenile cataract formation. *Clin Biochem* 2008 Jul;41(10–11):869–874.

Katre P, Bhat D, Lubree H, Otiv S, Joshi S, Joglekar C, Rush E, Yajnik C. Vitamin B12 and folic acid supplementation and plasma total homocysteine concentrations in pregnant Indian women with low B12 and high folate status. *Asia Pac J Clin Nutr* 2010;19(3):335–343.

Katz KD, Hollander D. Intestinal mucosal permeability and rheumatological diseases. *Baillières Clinical Rheumatology* 1989;3:271–284.

Kavanaghi R, Workman E, Nash P, Smith M, Hazleman BL, Hunter JO. The effects of elemental diet and subsequent food reintroduction on rheumatoid arthritis. *British Journal of Rheumatology* 1995;34:70–273.

Keim NL, Van Loan MD, Horn WF, Barbieri TF, Mayclin PL.Weight loss is greater with consumption of large morning meals and fat-free mass is preserved with large evening meals in women on a controlled weight reduction regimen. *J Nutr* 1997 Jan;127(1):75–82.

Kelly J, Lanier A, Santos M, Healey S, Louchini R, Friborg J, Young K, Ng C. Cancer among the circumpolar Inuit, 1989–2003. I. Background and methods. *Int J Circumpolar Health* 2008 Dec;67(5):396–407.

Kelly RL. *The Foraging Spectrum. Diversity in Hunter-Gatherer Lifeways.* Washington, DC: Smithsonian Institution Press, 1995.

Kerstetter JE, Gaffney ED, O' Brien O et al. Dietary Protein increases intestinal calcium absorption and improves bone balance: an hypothesis. In Burckhardt P, Heaney R, Dawson-Hughes B. *Proceedings of the International Symposium on Nutritional Aspects of Osteoporosis, 4–6 May 2006, Lausanne, Switzerland.* Elsevier, 2007:204–216.

Keski-Rahkonen A, Kaprio J, Rissanen A, Virkkunen M, Rose RJ. Breakfast skipping and health-compromising behaviors in adolescents and adults. *Eur J Clin Nutr* 2003 Jul;57(7):842–853.

Keukens EA, de Vrije T, Jansen LA, de Boer H, Janssen M, de Kroon AI, Jongen WM, de Kruijff B. Glycoalkaloids selectively permeabilize cholesterol containing biomembranes. *Biochim Biophys Acta* 1996 Mar 13;1279(2):243–250.

Keukens EA, de Vrije T, van den Boom C, de Waard P, Plasman HH, Thiel F, Chupin V, Jongen WM, de Kruijff B. Molecular basis of glycoalkaloid induced membrane disruption. *Biochim Biophys Acta* 1995 Dec 13;1240(2):216–228.

Key TJ, Appleby PN, Rosell MS. Health effects of vegetarian and vegan diets. *Proc Nutr Soc* 2006 Feb;65(1):35–41.

Key TJ, Appleby PN, Spencer EA, Travis RC, Roddam AW, Allen NE. Cancer incidence in vegetarians: results from the European Prospective Investigation into Cancer and Nutrition (EPIC-Oxford). *Am J Clin Nutr* 2009 May;89(5):1620S–1626S.

———. Mortality in British vegetarians: results from the European Prospective Investigation into Cancer and Nutrition (EPIC-Oxford). *Am J Clin Nutr* 2009 May;89(5):1613S–1619S.

Key TJ, Fraser GE, Thorogood M, Appleby PN, Beral V, Reeves G, Burr ML, Chang-Claude J, Frentzel-Beyme R, Kuzma JW, Mann J, McPherson K. Mortality in vegetarians and nonvegetarians: detailed findings from a collaborative analysis of 5 prospective studies. *Am J Clin Nutr* 1999;70:516S–524S.

Keys A, Anderson IT, Grande F. Prediction of serum-cholesterol responses of man to changes in fats in the diet. *Lancet* 1957;2:959–966.

Khan AT, Graham TC, Ogden L, Ali S, Salwa, Thompson SJ, Shireen KF, Mahboob M. A two-generational reproductive toxicity study of zinc in rats. *J Environ Sci Health B* 2007 May;42(4):403–415.

Khedr E, Hamed SA, Elbeih E, El-Shereef H, Ahmad Y, Ahmed S. Iron states and cognitive abilities in young adults: neuropsychological and neurophysiological assessment. *Eur Arch Psychiatry Clin Neurosci* 2008 Dec;258(8):489–496. Epub 2008 Jun 20.

Kihara T, Biro S, Imamura M, Yoshifuku S, Takasaki K, Ikeda Y, Otuji Y, Minagoe S, Toyama Y, Tei C. Repeated sauna treatment improves vascular endothelial and cardiac function in patients with chronic heart failure. *J Am Coll Cardiol* 2002 Mar 6;39(5):754–759.

Kilpatrick DC, Pusztai A, Grant G, Graham C, Ewen SW. Tomato lectin resists digestion in the mammalian alimentary canal and binds to intestinal villi without deleterious effects. *FEBS Lett* 1985;185:299–305.

Kimber I, Dearman RJ. An assessment of the ability of phthalates to influence immune and allergic responses. *Toxicology* 2010 May 27;271(3):73–82.

King CR. A novel embryological theory of autism causation involving endogenous biochemicals capable of initiating cellular gene transcription: a possible link between twelve autism risk factors and the autism 'epidemic.' *Med Hypotheses* 2011 Mar 7. Epub ahead of print.

Kinjo Y, Beral V, Akiba S, Key T, Mizuno S, Appleby P, Yamaguchi N, Watanabe S, Doll R. Possible protective effect of milk, meat and fish for cerebrovascular disease mortality in Japan. *J Epidemiol* 1999 Aug;9(4):268–274.

Kirkwood TB, Shanley DP. Food restriction, evolution, and ageing. *Mech Ageing Dev* 2005 Sep;126(9):1011–1016.

Kitazawa M, Cheng D, Laferla FM. Chronic copper exposure exacerbates both amyloid and tau pathology and selectively dysregulates cdk5 in a mouse model of AD. *J Neurochem* 2009 Mar;108(6):1550–1560.

Klag MJ, Whelton PK. The decline in stroke mortality: an epidemiologic perspective. *Ann Epidemiol* 1993;3:571–575.

Klinger B, Anin S, Silbergeld A, Eshet R, Laron Z. Development of hyperandrogenism during treatment with insulin-like growth factor-I (IGF-I) in female patients with Laron syndrome. *Clin Endocrinol* 1998;48:81–87.

Knekt P, Jarvinen R, Dich J, Hakulinen T. Risk of colorectal and other gastro-intestinal cancers after exposure to nitrate, nitrite, and N-nitroso compounds: a follow-up study. *Int J Cancer* 1999 Mar 15;80(6):852–856.

Knopp RH, Walden CE, Retzlaff BM, McCann BS, Dowdy AA, Albers JJ, Gey GO, Cooper MN. Long-term cholesterol lowering effects of 4 fat restricted diets in hypercholesterolemic and combined hyperlipidemic men: The Dietary Alternatives Study. *JAMA* 1997;278:1509–1515.

Knovich MA, Storey JA, Coffman LG, Torti SV, Torti FM. Ferritin for the clinician. *Blood Rev* 2009 May;23(3):95–104.

Knudsen D, Jutfelt F, Sundh H, Sundell K, Koppe W, Frøkiaer H. Dietary soya saponins increase gut permeability and play a key role in the onset of soyabean-induced enteritis in Atlantic salmon (Salmo salar L.). *Br J Nutr* 2008 Jul;100(1):120–129.

Kobayashi M, Sasaki S, Hamada GS, Tsugane S. Serum n-3 fatty acids, fish consumption, and cancer mortality in six Japanese populations in Japan and Brazil. *Jpn J Cancer Res* 1999;90(9):914–921.

Koebnick C, Hoffmann I, Dagnelie PC, Heins UA, Wickramasinghe SN, Ratnayaka ID, Gruendel S, Lindemans J, Leitzmann C. Long-term ovo-lacto vegetarian diet impairs vitamin B-12 status in pregnant women. *J Nutr* 2004 Dec;134(12):3319–3326.

Kokkinos PF, Narayan P, Colleran JA, Pittaras A, Notargiacomo A, Reda D, Papademetriou V. Effects of regular exercise on blood pressure and left ventricular hypertrophy in African-American men with severe hypertension. *N Engl J Med* 1995;333:1462–1467.

Koldovský O. Hormones in milk. In *Vitamins and Hormones 50*, Litwack G (ed). New York: Academic Press, 1995, 77–149.

————.The potential physiological significance of milk-borne hormonally active substances for the neonate. *J Mammary Gland Biol Neoplasia* 1996;1:317–323.

Komori Y, Aiba T, Nakai C, Sugiyama R, Kawasaki H, Kurosaki Y. Capsaicin-induced increase of intestinal cefazolin absorption in rats. *Drug Metab Pharmacokinet* 2007 Dec;22(6):445–449.

Kopinski JS, Leibholz J, Bryden WL. Biotin studies in pigs. Biotin availability in feedstuffs for pigs and chickens. *Br J Nutr* 1989;62:773–780.

Kornsteiner M, Singer I, Elmadfa I. Very low n-3 long-chain polyunsaturated fatty acid status in Austrian vegetarians and vegans. *Ann Nutr Metab* 2008;52(1):37–47.

Kostraba JN, Cruickshanks KJ, Lawler-Heavner J, Jobim LF, Rewers MJ, Gay EC, Chase HP, Klingensmith G, Hamman RF. Early exposure to cow's milk and solid foods in infancy, genetic predisposition, and risk of IDDM. *Diabetes* 1993 Feb;42(2):288–295.

Kozio MJ. Chemical composition and nutritional evaluation of quinoa (*Chenopodium quinoa Willd.*) *J Food Comp Anal* 1992;5:35–68.

Kozukue N, Han JS, Kozukue E, Lee SJ, Kim JA, Lee KR, Levin CE, Friedman M. Analysis of eight capsaicinoids in peppers and pepper-containing foods by high-performance liquid chromatography and liquid chromatography-mass spectrometry. *J Agric Food Chem* 2005 Nov 16;53(23):9172–9181.

Krajcovicová-Kudláčková M, Bucková K, Klimes I, Seboková E. Iodine deficiency in vegetarians and vegans. *Ann Nutr Metab* 2003;47(5):183–185.

Krasner SW, Weinberg HS, Richardson SD, Pastor SJ, Chinn R, Sclimenti MJ, Onstad GD, Thruston AD Jr. Occurrence of a new generation of disinfection byproducts. *Environ Sci Technol* 2006 Dec 1;40(23):7175–7185.

————. The formation and control of emerging disinfection by-products of health concern. *Philos Transact A Math Phys Eng Sci* 2009 Oct 13;367(1904):4077–4095.

Kris-Etherton PM, Taylor DS, Yu-Poth S, Huth P, Moriarty K, Fishell V, Hargrove RL, Zhao G, Etherton TD. Polyunsaturated fatty acids in the food chain in the United States. *Am J Clin Nutr* 2000;71(suppl 1):179S–188S.

Kristiana I, Gallard H, Joll C, Croué JP. The formation of halogen-specific TOX from chlorination and chloramination of natural organic matter isolates. *Water Res* 2009 Sep;43(17):4177–4186.

Kritchevsky D et al. Influence of native and randomized peanut oil on lipid metabolism and aortic sudanophilia in the vervet monkey. *Atherosclerosis* 1982;42:53–58.

Kritchevsky D, Tepper SA, Klurfeld DM. Lectin may contribute to the atherogenicity of peanut oil. *Lipids* 1998 Aug;33(8):821–823.

Krivosíková Z, Krajcovicová-Kudláčková M, Spustová V, Stefíková K, Valachovicová M, Blazícek P, Ne˘mcová T. The association between high plasma homocysteine levels and lower bone mineral density in Slovak women: the impact of vegetarian diet. *Eur J Nutr* 2010 Apr;49(3):147–153.

Krober T. *Ishi in Two Worlds. A Biography of the Last Wild Indian in North America.* Los Angeles: University of California Press, 1961.

Kubow S. Lipid oxidation products in food and atherogenesis. *Nutr Rev* 1993;51:33–40.

Kukkonen-Harjula K, Kauppinen K. Health effects and risks of sauna bathing. *Int J Circumpolar Health* 2006 Jun;65(3):195–205.

Kull I, Bergström A, Melén E, Lilja G, van Hage M, Pershagen G, Wickman M. Early-life supplementation of vitamins A and D, in water-soluble form or in peanut oil, and allergic diseases during childhood. *J Allergy Clin Immunol* 2006 Dec;118(6):1299–1304.

Kumar J, Garg G, Sundaramoorthy E, Prasad PV, Karthikeyan G, Ramakrishnan L, Ghosh S, Sengupta S. Vitamin B12 deficiency is associated with coronary artery disease in an Indian population. *Clin Chem Lab Med* 2009;47(3):334–338.

Kumar J, Muntner P, Kaskel FJ, Hailpern SM, Melamed ML. Prevalence and associations of 25-hydroxyvitamin D deficiency in US children: NHANES 2001–2004. *Pediatrics* 2009 Sep;124(3):e362–370.

Kumar V, Rajadhyaksha M, Wortsman J. Celiac disease-associated autoimmune endocrinopathies. *Clin Diagn Lab Immunol* 2001 Jul;8(4):678–685.

Künzel W, Fischer T, Lorenz R, Brühmann S. Decline of caries prevalence after the cessation of water fluoridation in the former East Germany. *Community Dent Oral Epidemiol* 2000 Oct;28(5):382–389.

Kurahashi N, Inoue M, Iwasaki M, et al. Dairy product, saturated fatty acid, and calcium intake and prostate cancer in a prospective cohort of Japanese men. *Cancer Epidemiol Biomarkers Prev* 2008 Apr;17(4):930–937.

Kurtz TW, Al-Bander HA, Morris RC. "Salt-sensitive" essential hypertension in men. Is the sodium ion alone important? *N Engl J Med* 1987;317:1043–1048.

Kushi LH, Fee RM, Folsom AR, Mink PJ, Anderson KE, Sellers TA. Physical activity and mortality in postmenopausal women. *JAMA* 1997;277:1287–1292.

Kuzma JN, Cordain L. Ingestion of wheat germ in healthy subjects does not acutely elevate plasma wheat germ agglutinin concentrations. *FASEB J* 2010, 24:723.10.

Labrique-Walusis F, Keister KJ, Russell AC. Massage therapy for stress management: implications for nursing practice. *Orthop Nurs* 2010 Jul–Aug;29(4):254–257.

Laidlaw SA, Grosvenor M, Kopple JD. The taurine content of common foodstuffs. *JPEN J Parenter Enteral Nutr* 1990 Mar–Apr;14(2):183–188.

Laidlaw SA, Shultz TD, Cecchino JT, Kopple JD. Plasma and urine taurine levels in vegans. *Am J Clin Nutr* 1988 Apr;47(4):660–663.

Lang IA, Galloway TS, Scarlett A, Henley WE, Depledge M, Wallace RB, Melzer D. Association of urinary bisphenol A concentration with medical disorders and laboratory abnormalities in adults. *JAMA* 2008 Sep 17;300(11):1303–1310.

Lanier AP, Bender TR, Blot WJ, Fraumeni JF Jr. Cancer in Alaskan Natives: 1974–78. *Natl Cancer Inst Monogr* 1982;62:79–81.

Lansdown AB, Mirastschijski U, Stubbs N, Scanlon E, Agren MS. Zinc in wound healing: theoretical, experimental, and clinical aspects. *Wound Repair Regen* 2007 Jan–Feb;15(1): 2–16.

Larsen CS. Reading the bones of La Florida. *Sci Am* 2000;282:80–85.

Larsen CS, Schoeninger MJ, van der Merwe NJ, Moore KM, Lee-Thorp JA. Carbon and nitrogen stable isotopic signatures of human dietary change in the Georgia Bight. *Am J Phys Anthropol* 1992;89:197–214.

Larsen TM, Dalskov SM, van Baak M, Jebb SA, Papadaki A, Pfeiffer AF, Martinez JA, Handjieva-Darlenska T, Kunešová M, Pihlsgård M, Stender S, Holst C, Saris WH, Astrup A. Diet, Obesity, and Genes (Diogenes) Project. Diets with high or low protein content and glycemic index for weight-loss maintenance. *N Engl J Med* 2010 Nov 25;363(22):2102–2113.

Larsson SC, Orsini N, Wolk A. Milk, milk products, and lactose intake and ovarian cancer risk: a meta-analysis of epidemiological studies. *Int J Cancer* 2006 Jan 15;118(2):431–441.

Laugesen M, Elliott R. Ischaemic heart disease, Type 1 diabetes, and cow milk A1 beta-casein. *N Z Med J* 2003 Jan 24;116(1168):U295.

Layman DK, Boileau RA, Erickson DJ, Painter JE, Shiue H, Sather C, Christou DD. A reduced ratio of dietary carbohydrate to protein improves body composition and blood lipid profiles during weight loss in adult women. *J Nutr* 2003 Feb;133(2):411–417.

Leboff MS, Narweker R, LaCroix A, Wu L, Jackson R, Lee J, Bauer DC, Cauley J, Kooperberg C, Lewis C, Thomas AM, Cummings S. Homocysteine levels and risk of hip fracture in postmenopausal women. *J Clin Endocrinol Metab* 2009 Apr;94(4):1207–1213.

Ledesma MC, Jung-Hynes B, Schmit TL, Kumar R, Mukhtar H, Ahmad N. Selenium and vitamin E for prostate cancer: post-SELECT (Selenium and Vitamin E Cancer Prevention Trial) status. *Mol Med* 2011 Jan-Feb;17(1–2):134–143.

Lee RB. The !Kung Bushmen of Botswana. In *Hunters and Gatherers Today*, Bicchieri MG. (ed). New York: Holt, Rinehart and Winston, Inc., 1972, 151.

Lee RB, Daly RH (eds.). *The Cambridge Encyclopedia of Hunters and Gatherers*. Cambridge, UK: Cambridge University Press, 1999.

Lee S, Levin MC. Molecular mimicry in neurological disease: what is the evidence? *Cell Mol Life Sci* 2008 Apr;65(7–8):1161–1175.

Lee-Thorp J, Thackeray JF, van der Merwe N. The hunters and the hunted revisited. *J Hum Evol* 2000;39:565–576.

Lee-Thorp J, van der Merwe NJ, Brain CK. Diet of *Australopithecus robustus* at Swartkrans from stable isotopic analysis. *J Hum Evol* 1994;27:361–372.

Leeman M, Ostman E, Björck I. Glycaemic and satiating properties of potato products. *Eur J Clin Nutr* 2008 Jan;62(1):87–95.

Leeming RJ, Lucock M. Autism: Is there a folate connection? *J Inherit Metab Dis* 2009 Jun;32(3):400–402.

Legge AJ, Rowley-Conway PA. Gazelle killing in stone age Syria. *Sci Am* 1988;257:88–95.

Legro RS. Polycystic ovary syndrome: current and future treatment paradigms. *Am J Obstet Gynecol* 1998;179(6 Pt 2):S101–S108.

Leitzmann MF, Stampfer MJ, Michaud DS, Augustsson K, Colditz GC, Willett WC, Giovannucci EL. Dietary intake of n-3 and n-6 fatty acids and the risk of prostate cancer. *Am J Clin Nutr* 2004;80(1):204–216.

Lemann J, Lennon EJ. Role of diet, gastrointestinal tract and bone in acid-base homeostasis. *Kidney Int* 1972;1:275–279.

Leonard WR, Robertson ML. Evolutionary perspectives on human nutrition: the influence of brain and body size on diet and metabolism. *Am J Hum Biol* 1994;6:77–88.

Levine AJ, Figueiredo JC, Lee W, Conti DV, Kennedy K, Duggan DJ, Poynter JN, Campbell PT, Newcomb P, Martinez ME, Hopper JL, Le Marchand L, Baron JA, Limburg PJ, Ulrich CM, Haile RW. A candidate gene study of folate-associated one carbon metabolism genes and colorectal cancer risk. *Cancer Epidemiol Biomarkers Prev* 2010 Jul;19(7):1812–1821.

Lewin R. A revolution of ideas in agricultural origins. *Science* 1988;240:984–986.

Liao F, Folsom AR, Brancati FL. Is low magnesium concentration a risk factor for coronary heart disease? The Atherosclerosis Risk in Communities (ARIC) Study. *Am Heart J* 1998;136:480–490.

Lichtenstein AH, Russell RM. Essential nutrients: food or supplements? Where should the emphasis be? *JAMA* 2005 Jul 20;294(3):351–358.

Lidén M, Kristjánsson G, Valtýsdóttir S, Hällgren R. Gluten sensitivity in patients with primary Sjögren's syndrome. *Scand J Gastroenterol* 2007 Aug;42(8):962–967.

Lieb CW. The effects on human beings of a twelve months' exclusive meat diet. *JAMA* 1929;93:20–22.

Lieberman DE, Venkadesan M, Werbel WA, Daoud AI, D'Andrea S, Davis IS et al. Foot strike patterns and collision forces in habitually barefoot versus shod runners. *Nature* 2010;463(7280):531–535.

Liener IE. Implications of antinutritional components in soybean foods. *Crit Rev Food Sci Nutr* 1994;34:31–67.

———. Nutritional significance of lectins in the diet. In *The Lectins: Properties, Functions, and Applications in Biology and Medicine*, Liener IE, Sharon N, Goldstein IJ (eds). Orlando: Academic Press, 1986: 527–552.

Liljeberg Elmstahl H, Bjorck I. Milk as a supplement to mixed meals may elevate postprandial insulinaemia. *Eur J Clin Nutr* 2001;55:994–999.

Lin J, Lee IM, Cook NR, Selhub J, Manson JE, Buring JE, Zhang SM. Plasma folate, vitamin B-6, vitamin B-12, and risk of breast cancer in women. *Am J Clin Nutr* 2008 Mar;87(3): 734–743.

Lin PY, Huang SY, Su KP. A meta-analytic review of polyunsaturated fatty acid compositions in patients with depression. *Biol Psychiatry* 2010 Jul 15;68(2):140–147.

Lin X, Gingrich JR, Bao W, Li J, Haroon ZA, Demark-Wahnefried W. Effect of flaxseed supplementation on prostatic carcinoma in transgenic mice. *Urology* 2002;60(5):919–924.

Lindeberg S, Berntorp E, Carlsson R, Eliasson M, Marckmann P. Haemostatic variables in Pacific Islanders apparently free from stroke and ischaemic heart disease—the Kitava Study. *Thromb Haemost* 1997 Jan;77(1):94–98.

Lindeberg S, Eliasson M, Lindahl B, Ahrén B. Low serum insulin in traditional Pacific Islanders— the Kitava Study. *Metabolism* 1999;48(10):1216–1219.

Lindeberg S, Jonsson T, Granfeldt Y, Borgstrand E, Soffman J, Sjostrom K, Ahren B. A Palaeolithic diet improves glucose tolerance more than a Mediterranean-like diet in individuals with ischaemic heart disease. *Diabetologia* 2007;50(9):1795–1807.

Lindeberg S, Lundh B. Apparent absence of stroke and ischaemic heart disease in a traditional Melanesian island: a clinical study in Kitava. *J Intern Med* 1993;233(3):269–275.

Lindeberg S, Nilsson-Ehle P, Terént A, Vessby B, Scherstén B.Cardiovascular risk factors in a Melanesian population apparently free from stroke and ischaemic heart disease: the Kitava study. *J Intern Med* 1994 Sep;236(3):331–340.

Lindgren BF, Segovia B, Lassarre C, Binoux M, Gourmelen M. Growth retardation in constitutionally short children is related both to low serum levels of insulin-like growth factor-I and to its reduced bioavailability. *Growth Regul* 1996;6:158–164.

Lindseth G, Lindseth PD. The relationship of diet to airsickness. *Aviat Space Environ Med* 1995;66:537–541.

Lindzon GM, Medline A, Sohn KJ, Depeint F, Croxford R, Kim YI. Effect of folic acid supplementation on the progression of colorectal aberrant crypt foci. *Carcinogenesis* 2009 Sep;30(9):1536–1543.

Lipkin M, Newmark HL. Vitamin D, calcium, and prevention of breast cancer: a review. *J Am Coll Nutr* 1999;18(suppl 5):392S–397S.

Lipton RB, Newman LC, Cohen JS, Solomon S. Aspartame as a dietary trigger of headache. *Headache* 1989 Feb;29(2):90–92.

Lissowska J, Gaudet MM, Brinton LA, Peplonska B, Sherman M, Szeszenia-Dabrowska N, Zatonski W, Garcia-Closas M. Intake of fruits, and vegetables in relation to breast cancer risk by hormone receptor status. *Breast Cancer Res Treat* 2008;107:113–117.

Liu B, Lee HY, Weinzimer SA, Powell DR, Clifford JL, Kurie JM, Cohen P. Direct functional interaction between insulin-like growth factor–binding protein-3 and retionoid X receptor-alpha regulate transcriptional signaling and apoptosis. *J Biol Chem* 2000;275:33607–33613.

Liu S, Willett WC, Stampfer MJ, Hu FB, Franz M, Sampson L, Hennekens CH, Manson JE. A prospective study of dietary glycemic load, carbohydrate intake, and risk of coronary heart disease in US women. *Am J Clin Nutr* 2000;71:1455–1461.

Lochner N, Pittner F, Wirth M, Gabor F. Wheat germ agglutinin binds to the epidermal growth factor receptor of artificial Caco-2 membranes as detected by silver nanoparticle enhanced fluorescence. *Pharm Res* 2003 May;20(5):833–839.

Loganathan SN, Kannan K. Occurrence of bisphenol A in indoor dust from two locations in the Eastern United States and implications for human exposures. *Arch Environ Contam Toxicol* 2011 Jan 8;61(1):68–73.

Løland KH, Bleie O, Blix AJ, Strand E, Ueland PM, Refsum H, Ebbing M, Nordrehaug JE, Nygård O. Effect of homocysteine-lowering B vitamin treatment on angiographic progression of coronary artery disease: a Western Norway B Vitamin Intervention Trial (WENBIT) substudy. *Am J Cardiol* 2010 Jun 1;105(11):1577–1584.

Long C, Alterman T. Meet the real free-range eggs. *Mother Earth News*, 2007, motherearthnews.com/Real-Food/ 2007-10-01/Tests-Reveal-Healthier-Eggs.aspx.

Lopez-Bote CJ. Effect of free-range feeding on omega-3 fatty acids and alphatocopherol content and oxidative stability of eggs. *Anim Feed Sci Technol* 1998;72:33–40.

Lorenz K. Cereals and schizophrenia. *Adv Cereal Sci Technol* 1990;10:435–469.

Losso JN. The biochemical and functional food properties of the Bowman-Birk inhibitor. *Crit Rev Food Sci Nutr* 2008 Jan;48(1):94–118.

Lothe L, Lindberg T. Cow's milk whey protein elicits symptoms of infantile colic in colicky formula-fed infants: a double-blind crossover study. *Pediatrics* 1989 Feb;83(2):262–266.

Louie JC, Brand-Miller JC, Markovic TP, Ross GP, Moses RG. Glycemic index and pregnancy: a systematic literature review. *J Nutr Metab* 2010;2010:282464.

Ludwig DS. Dietary glycemic index and obesity. *J Nutr* 2000;130:280S–283S.

Ludwig DS, Majzoub JA, Al-Zahrani A, Dallal GE, Blanco I, Roberts SB. High glycemic index foods, overeating, and obesity. *Pediatrics* 1999; 103:E26.

Luo Z, Rouvinen J, Mäenpää PH. A peptide C-terminal to the second Zn finger of human vitamin D receptor is able to specify nuclear localization. *Eur J Biochem* 1994;223:381–387.

Luopajärvi K, Savilahti E, Virtanen SM, Ilonen J, Knip M, Akerblom HK, Vaarala O. Enhanced levels of cow's milk antibodies in infancy in children who develop type 1 diabetes later in childhood. *Pediatr Diabetes* 2008 Oct;9(5):434–441.

Luscombe-Marsh ND, Noakes M, Wittert GA, Keogh JB, Foster P, Clifton PM. Carbohydrate-restricted diets high in either monounsaturated fat or protein are equally effective at promoting fat loss and improving blood lipids. *Am J Clin Nutr* 2005 Apr;81(4):762–772.

Lynch SM, Strain JJ. Effects of copper deficiency on hepatic and cardiac antioxidant enzyme activities in lactose and sucrose fed rats. *Brit J Nutr* 1989;61:345–354.

Lyons TS, McLester JR, Arnett SW, Thoma MJ. Specificity of training modalities on upper-body one repetition maximum performance: free weights vs. hammer strength equipment. *J Strength Cond Res* 2010 Nov;24(11):2984–2988.

MacAuliffe T, Pietraszek A, McGinnis J. Variable rachitogenic effects of grain and alleviation by extraction or supplementation with vitamin D, fat, and antibiotics. *Poultry Sci* 1976;55:2142–2147.

MacDonald ML, Rogers QR. Nutrition of the domestic cat, a mammalian carnivore. *Ann Rev Nur* 1984;4:521–562.

Maclaurin BP, Matthews N, Kilpatrick JA. Coeliac disease associated with auto-immune thyroiditis, Sjogren's syndrome, and a lymphocytotoxic serum factor. *Aust N Z J Med* 1972 Nov;2(4):405–411.

Magkos F, Arvaniti F, Zampelas A. Organic food: nutritious food or food for thought? A review of the evidence. *Int J Food Sci Nutr* 2003;54:357–371.

Main PA, Angley MT, Thomas P, O'Doherty CE, Fenech M. Folate and methionine metabolism in autism: a systematic review. *Am J Clin Nutr* 2010 Jun;91(6):1598–1620.

Malaisse WJ, Vanonderbergen A, Louchami K, Jijakli H, Malaisse-Lagae F. Effects of artificial sweeteners on insulin release and cationic fluxes in rat pancreatic islets. *Cell Signal* 1998 Nov;10(10):727–733.

Mancilha-Carvalho JJ, Crews DE. Lipid profiles of Yanomamo Indians of Brazil. *Prev Med* 1990;19:66–75.

Mann N, Pirotta Y, O'Connell S, Li D, Kelly F, Sinclair A. Fatty acid composition of habitual omnivore and vegetarian diets. *Lipids* 2006 Jul;41(7):637–646.

Mann NJ, Li D, Sinclair AJ, Dudman NP, Guo XW, Elsworth GR, Wilson AK, Kelly FD. The effect of diet on plasma homocysteine concentrations in healthy male subjects. *Eur J Clin Nutr* 1999;53:895–899.

Manning PJ, Sutherland WH, McGrath MM, de Jong SA, Walker RJ, Williams MJ. Postprandial cytokine concentrations and meal composition in obese and lean women. *Obesity (Silver Spring)* 2008 Jun 26.

Marean CW, Assefa Z. Zooarchaeological evidence for the faunal exploitation behavior of neanderthals and early modern humans. *Evol Anthropol* 1999;8:22–37.

Mariani A, Chalies S, Jeziorski E, Ludwig C, Lalande M, Rodière M. Consequences of exclusive breast-feeding in vegan mother newborn—case report. *Arch Pediatr* 2009 Nov;16(11):1461–1463.

Marks BL, Rippe JM. The importance of fat free mass maintenance in weight loss programmes. *Sports Med* 1996;22:273–281.

Marmer WN, Maxwell RJ, Williams JE. Effects of dietary regimen and tissue site on bovine fatty acid profiles. *J Anim Sci* 1984;59:109–121.

Marsh KA, Steinbeck KS, Atkinson FS, Petocz P, Brand-Miller JC. Effect of a low glycemic index compared with a conventional healthy diet on polycystic ovary syndrome. *Am J Clin Nutr* 2010 Jul;92(1):83–92.

Marshall BJ. Unidentified curved bacillus on gastric epithelium in active chronic gastritis. *Lancet* 1 1983;(8336):1273–1275.

Marshall BJ, Warren JR. Unidentified curved bacilli in the stomach patients with gastritis and peptic ulceration. *Lancet* 1 1984;(8390):1311–1315.

Martin-Moreno JM, Willett WC, Gorgojo L, Banegas JR, Rodriguez-Artalejo F, Fernandez-Rodriguez JC, Maisonneuve P, Boyle P. Dietary fat, olive oil intake, and breast cancer risk. *Int J Cancer* 1994;58:774–780.

Mason SLR et al. Preliminary investigation of the plant macro-remains from Dolni Vestonice II, and its implications for the role of plant foods in Palaeolithic and Mesolithic Europe. *Antiquity* 1994;68:48–57.

Masoro EJ. Overview of caloric restriction and ageing. *Mech Ageing Dev* 2005 Sep;126(9):913–922.

Massey LK. Dietary influences on urinary oxalate and risk of kidney stones. *Front Biosci* 2003 May 1;8:s584–s594.

Mathews-Roth MM, Krinsky NI. Effect of dietary fat level on UV-B induced skin tumors, and anti-tumor action of b-carotene. *Photochem Photobiol* 1984;40:671–673.

Mattison JA, Lane MA, Roth GS, Ingram DK. Calorie restriction in rhesus monkeys. *Exp Gerontol* 2003 Jan–Feb;38(1–2):35–46.

Mattson MP. The need for controlled studies of the effects of meal frequency on health. *Lancet* 2005;365:1978–1980.

Mattson MP, Wan R. Beneficial effects of intermittent fasting and caloric restriction on the cardiovascular and cerebrovascular systems. *J Nutr Biochem* 2005 Mar;16(3):129–137.

McAuley KA, Hopkins CM, Smith KJ, McLay RT, Williams SM, Taylor RW, Mann JI. Comparison of high-fat and high-protein diets with a high-carbohydrate diet in insulin-resistant obese women. *Diabetologia* 2005 Jan;48(1):8–16.

McCance DR, Holmes VA, Maresh MJ, Patterson CC, Walker JD, Pearson DW, Young IS. Diabetes and Pre-eclampsia Intervention Trial (DAPIT) Study Group. Vitamins C and E for prevention of pre-eclampsia in women with type 1 diabetes (DAPIT): a randomised placebo-controlled trial. *Lancet* 2010 Jul 24;376(9737):259–266.

McCann JC, Ames BN. An overview of evidence for a causal relation between iron deficiency during development and deficits in cognitive or behavioral function. *Am J Clin Nutr* 2007 Apr;85(4):931–945.

McCarty MF. Sub-optimal taurine status may promote platelet hyperaggregability in vegetarians. *Med Hypotheses* 2004;63(3):426–433.

McClung JP, Karl JP, Cable SJ, Williams KW, Nindl BC, Young AJ, Lieberman HR. Randomized, double-blind, placebo-controlled trial of iron supplementation in female soldiers during military training: effects on iron status, physical performance, and mood. *Am J Clin Nutr* 2009 Jul;90(1):124–131.

McDermott CM, Beitz DC, Littledike ET, Horst RL. Effects of dietary vitamin D3 on concentrations of vitamin D and its metabolites in blood plasma and milk of dairy cows. *J Dairy Sci* 1985;68:1959–1967.

McDonald TA, Komulainen H. Carcinogenicity of the chlorination disinfection by-product MX. *J Environ Sci Health C Environ Carcinog Ecotoxicol Rev* 2005;23(2):163–214.

McDowell M, Briefel R, Alaimo K et al. Energy and macronutrient intakes of persons ages 2 months and over in the United States. *Third National Health and Nutrition Examination Survey, Phase 1, 1988–91*. Washington, DC: US Government Printing Office, Vital and Health Statistics, 1994. CDC publication No. 255.

McGough N, Cummings JH. Coeliac disease: a diverse clinical syndrome caused by intolerance of wheat, barley, and rye. *Proc Nutr Soc* 2005 Nov;64(4):434–450.

Meat and Livestock Association of Australia (mla.com.au/).

Medeiros LC, Belden RP, Williams ES. Selenium content of bison, elk and mule deer. *J Food Sci* 1993;4:731–733.

Melamed ML, Kumar J. Low levels of 25-hydroxyvitamin D in the pediatric populations: prevalence and clinical outcomes. *Ped Health* 2010 Feb;4(1):89–97.

Mellanby E. An experimental investigation of rickets. *Lancet* 1919;1:407–412.

Meloni G, Ogana A, Mannazzu MC, Meloni T, Carta F, Carta A. High prevalence of lactose absorbers in patients with presenile cataract from northern Sardinia. *Br J Ophthalmol* 1995 Jul;79(7):709.

Meneely GR, Battarbee HD. High sodium–low potassium environment and hypertension. *Am J Cardiol* 1976;38:768–785.

Mensinga TT, Sips AJ, Rompelberg CJ, van Twillert K, Meulenbelt J, van den Top HJ, van Egmond HP. Potato glycoalkaloids and adverse effects in humans: an ascending dose study. *Regul Toxicol Pharmacol* 2005 Feb;41(1):66–72.

Mensinga TT, Speijers GJ, Meulenbelt J. Health implications of exposure to environmental nitrogenous compounds. *Toxicol Rev* 2003;22(1):41–51.

Mensink RP, Zock PL, Kester AD, Katan MB. Effects of dietary fatty acids and carbohydrates on the ratio of serum total to HDL cholesterol and on serum lipids and apolipoproteins: a meta-analysis of 60 controlled trials. *Am J Clin Nutr* 2003 May;77(5):1146–1155.

Mertz JR, Wallman J. Choroidal retinoic acid synthesis: a possible mediator between refractive error and compensatory eye growth. *Exp Eye Res* 2000;70:519–527.

Messina M, Redmond G. Effects of soy protein and soybean isoflavones on thyroid function in healthy adults and hypothyroid patients: a review of the relevant literature. *Thyroid* 2006 Mar;16(3):249–258.

Metlapally R, Ki CS, Li YJ, Tran-Viet KN, Abbott D, Malecaze F, Calvas P, Mackey DA, Rosenberg T, Paget S, Guggenheim JA, Young TL. Genetic association of insulin-like growth factor-1 polymorphisms with highgrade myopia in an international family cohort. *Invest Ophthalmol Vis Sci* 2010 Sep;51(9):4476-9.

Meyer C, Mueller MF, Duncker GI, Meyer HJ. Experimental animal myopia models are applicable to human juvenile-onset myopia. *Surv Ophthalmol* 1999;44 (suppl 1):S93–S102.

Mezzano D, Kosiel K, Martínez C, Cuevas A, Panes O, Aranda E, Strobel P, Pérez DD, Pereira J, Rozowski J, Leighton F. Cardiovascular risk factors in vegetarians. Normalization of hyperhomocysteinemia with vitamin B(12) and reduction of platelet aggregation with n-3 fatty acids. *Thromb Res* 2000 Nov 1;100(3):153–160.

Mezzano D, Munoz X, Martinez C, Cuevas A, Panes O, Aranda E, Guasch V, Strobel P, Munoz B, Rodriguez S, Pereira J, Leighton F. Vegetarians and cardiovascular risk factors: hemostasis, inflammatory markers, and plasma homocysteine. *Thromb Haemost* 1999;81:913–917.

Micha R, Mozaffarian D. Saturated fat and cardiometabolic risk factors, coronary heart disease, stroke, and diabetes: a fresh look at the evidence. *Lipids* 2010 Oct;45(10):893–905. Epub 2010 Mar 31.

Micha R, Wallace SK, Mozaffarian D. Red and processed meat consumption and risk of incident coronary heart disease, stroke, and diabetes mellitus: a systematic review and meta-analysis. *Circulation* 2010 Jun 1;121(21):2271–2283.

Michaelsson G, Ahs S, Hammarstrom I, Lundin IP, Hagforsen E. Gluten-free diet in psoriasis patients with antibodies to gliadin results in decreased expression of tissue transglutaminase and fewer Ki67+ cells in the dermis. *Acta Derm Venereol* 2003;83(6):425–429.

Michaëlsson G, Gerdén B, Hagforsen E, Nilsson B, Pihl-Lundin I, Kraaz W, Hjelmquist G, Lööf L. Psoriasis patients with antibodies to gliadin can be improved by a gluten-free diet. *Br J Dermatol* 2000 Jan;142(1):44–51.

Michaëlsson G, Gerdén B, Ottosson M, Parra A, Sjöberg O, Hjelmquist G, Lööf L. Patients with psoriasis often have increased serum levels of IgA antibodies to gliadin. *Br J Dermatol* 1993 Dec;129(6):667–673.

Michie CA, Chambers J, Abramsky L, Kooner JS. Folate deficiency, neural tube defects, and cardiac disease in UK Indians and Pakistanis. *Lancet* 1998 Apr 11;351(9109):1105.

Mickleborough TD, Gotshall RW, Rhodes J, Tucker A, Cordain L. Elevating dietary salt exacerbates hypernea-induced airway obstruction in guinea pigs. *J Appl Physiol* (1985). 2001 Sep;91(3):1061-6.

Mielants H. Reflections on the link between intestinal permeability and inflammatory joint disease. *Clinical and Experimental Rheumatology* 1990;8:523–524.

Mikkelsen PB, Toubro S, Astrup A. Effect of fat-reduced diets on 24-hr energy expenditure: comparisons between animal protein, vegetable protein, and carbohydrate. *Am J Clin Nutr* 2000;72:1135–1141.

Millen AE, Dodd KW, Subar AF. Use of vitamin, mineral, nonvitamin, and nonmineral supplements in the United States: the 1987, 1992, and 2000 National Health Interview Survey results. *J Am Diet Assoc* 2004;104:942–950.

Miller ER 3rd, Pastor-Barriuso R, Dalal D, Riemersma RA, Appel LJ, Guallar E. Meta-analysis: high-dosage vitamin E supplementation may increase all-cause mortality. *Ann Intern Med* 2005 Jan 4;142(1):37–46.

Miller GJ, Field RA, Riley ML. Lipids in wild ruminant animals and steers. *J Food Qual* 1986;9:331–343.

Miller MM. Low sodium chloride intake in the treatment of insomnia and tension states. *JAMA* 1945;129:262–266.

Miller WC, Koceja DM, Hamilton EJ. A meta-analysis of the past 25 years of weight loss research using diet, exercise, or diet plus exercise intervention. *Int J Obes Relat Metab Disord* 1997;21:941–947.

Milner JD, Stein DM, McCarter R, Moon RY. Early infant multivitamin supplementation is associated with increased risk for food allergy and asthma. *Pediatrics* 2004 Jul;114(1):27–32.

Milton K. Primate diets and gut morphology: implications for hominid evolution. In Harris M, Ross EB (eds.), *Food and Evolution*, Philadelphia: Temple University Press, 1987, 93–108.

————. Diet and primate evolution. *Sci Am* 1993;269:86–93.

Misra A, Vikram NK, Pandey RM, Dwivedi M, Ahmad FU, Luthra K, Jain K, Khanna N, Devi JR, Sharma R, Guleria R. Hyperhomocysteinemia, and low intakes of folic acid and vitamin B12 in urban North India. *Eur J Nutr* 2002 Apr;41(2):68–77.

Mizushima T. HSP-dependent protection against gastrointestinal diseases. *Curr Pharm Des* 2010;16(10):1190–1196.

Moan J, Dahlback A, Setlow RB. Epidemiological support for an hypothesis for melanoma induction indicating a role for UVA radiation. *Photochem Photobiol* 1999;70:243–247.

Mohr SB, Garland CF, Gorham ED, Grant WB, Garland FC. Relationship between low ultraviolet B irradiance and higher breast cancer risk in 107 countries. *Breast J* 2008 May–Jun;14(3):255–260.

Mokdad AH, Serdula MK, Dietz WH, Bowman BA, Marks JS, Koplan JP. The spread of the obesity epidemic in the United States, 1991–1998. *JAMA* 1999;282:1519–1522.

Molloy AM, Kirke PN, Brody LC, Scott JM, Mills JL. Effects of folate and vitamin B12 deficiencies during pregnancy on fetal, infant, and child development. *Food Nutr Bull* 2008 Jun;29(2 Suppl):S101–S111.

Molloy AM, Kirke PN, Troendle JF, Burke H, Sutton M, Brody LC, Scott JM, Mills JL. Maternal vitamin B12 status and risk of neural tube defects in a population with high neural tube defect prevalence and no folic acid fortification. *Pediatrics* 2009 Mar;123(3):917–923.

Monroy-Torres R, Mancilla-Escobar ML, Gallaga-Solorzano JC, Medina-Godoy S, Santiago-Garcia EJ. Protein digestibility of chia seed *Salvia hispanica L. Revista Salud Publica y Nutricion* 2008 Enero–Marzo;9(1). Monterey, Mexico.

Moore WJ, Corbett ME. Distribution of dental caries in ancient British populations. I. Anglo-Saxon period. *Caries Res* 1975;9:163–175; IV. The 19th century. *Caries Res* 1976;10:401–414.

Morris RD, Audet AM, Angelillo IF, Chalmers TC, Mosteller F. Chlorination, chlorination by-products, and cancer: a meta-analysis. *Am J Public Health* 1992 Jul;82(7):955–963.

Morris SC, Lee TH. The toxicity and teratogenicity of Solanaceae glycoalkaloids, particularly those of the potato (*Solanum tuberosum*): a review. *Food Technol Aust* 36 1984;no. 3:118–124.

Morrow WJ, Yang YW, Sheikh NA. Immunobiology of the Tomatine adjuvant. *Vaccine* 2004 Jun 23;22(19):2380–2384.

Morrow-Brown H. Clinical experience with allergy and intolerance to potato (*Solanum tuberosum*). *Immunol Allergy Practice* 1993;15:41–47.

Moseson M, Koenig KL, Shore RE, Pasternack BS. The influence of medical conditions and associated hormones on the risk of breast cancer. *Int J Epidemiol* 1993;22:1000–1009.

Moss M, Freed D. The cow and the coronary: epidemiology, biochemistry, and immunology. *Int J Cardiol* 2003 Feb;87(2–3):203–216.

Movius HL. A wooden spear of third interglacial age from lower Saxony. *Southwest J Anthropol* 1950;6:139–142.

Mowat AM. Dendritic cells and immune responses to orally administered antigens. *Vaccine* 2005;23:1797–1799.

Moyal DD, Fourtanier AM. Broad-spectrum sunscreens provide better protection from solar ultraviolet-simulated radiation and natural sunlight-induced immunosuppression in human beings. *J Am Acad Dermatol* 2008 May;58(5 Suppl 2):S149–S154.

Mozaffarian D, Ludwig DS. Dietary guidelines in the 21st century—a time for food. *JAMA* 2010 Aug 11;304(6):681–682.

Mozaffarian D, Micha R, Wallace S. Effects on coronary heart disease of increasing polyunsaturated fat in place of saturated fat: a systematic review and meta-analysis of randomized controlled trials. *PLoS Med* 2010 Mar 23;7(3):e1000252.

Mullenix PJ, Denbesten PK, Schunior A, Kernan WJ. Neurotoxicity of sodium fluoride in rats. *Neurotoxicol Teratol* 1995 Mar–Apr;17(2):169–177.

Munger RG, Cerhan JR, Chiu BC. Prospective study of dietary protein intake and risk of hip fracture in postmenopausal women. *Am J Clin Nutr* 1999;69:147–152.

Munro JM, van der Walt JD, Munro CS, Chalmers JA, Cox EL. An immunolohistochemical analysis of human aortic fatty streaks. *Hum Pathol* 1987;18:375–380.

Muraille E, Pajak B, Urbain J, Leo O. Carbohydrate-bearing cell surface receptors involved in innate immunity: interleukin-12 induction by mitogenic and nonmitogenic lectins. *Cell Immunol* 1999 Jan 10;191(1):1–9.

Muscari A, Volta U, Bonazzi C, Puddu GM, Bozzoli C, Gerratana C, Bianchi FB, Puddu P. Association of serum IgA antibodies to milk antigens with severe atherosclerosis. *Atherosclerosis* 1989;77:251–256.

Muslimov GF. Role of epidermal growth factor gene in the development of pancreatic cancer and efficiency of inhibitors of this gene in the treatment of pancreatic carcinoma. *Bull Exp Biol Med* 2008 Apr;145(4):535–538.

Must A, Spadano J, Coakley EH, Field AE, Colditz G, Dietz WH. The disease burden associated with overweight and obesity. *JAMA* 1999;282:1523–1529.

Mutti DO, Zadnik K, Adams AJ. Myopia. The nature vs. nurture debate goes on. *Invest Ophthalmol Vis Sci* 1996;37:952–957.

Nachbar MS, Oppenheim JD, Thomas JO. Lectins in the US Diet. Isolation and characterization of a lectin from the tomato (*Lycopersicon esculentum*). *J Biol Chem* 1980 Mar 10;255(95):2056–2061.

Nadler JL, Buchanan T, Natarajan R, Antonipillai I, Bergman R, Rude R. Magnesium deficiency produces insulin resistance and increased thromboxane synthesis. *Hypertension* 1993;21:1024–1029.

Naisbett B, Woodley J. The potential use of tomato lectin for oral drug delivery: 4. Immunological consequences. *Int J Pharm* 1995;120:247–254.

Nam SY, Lee EJ, Kim KR, Cha BS, Song YD, Lim SK, Lee HC, Huh KB. Effect of obesity on total and free insulin-like growth factor (IGF)-1, and their relationship to IGF-binding protein (BP)-1, IGFBP-2, IGFBP-3, insulin, and growth hormone. *Int J Obes Relat Metab Disord* 1997;21:355–359.

Nanda R. Targeting the human epidermal growth factor receptor 2 (HER2) in the treatment of breast cancer: recent advances and future directions. *Rev Recent Clin Trials* 2007 May;2(2):111–116.

Napoli C, Ambrosio G, Palumbo G, Elia PP, Chiariello M. Human low density lipoproteins are peroxidized by free radicals via chain reactions triggered by the superoxide radical. *Cardiologica* 1991;36:527–532.

Naruszewicz M, Zapolska-Downar D, Kos´mider A, Nowicka G, Kozłowska-Wojciechowska M, Vikström AS, Törnqvist M. Chronic intake of potato chips in humans increases the production of reactive oxygen radicals by leukocytes and increases plasma C-reactive protein: a pilot study. *Am J Clin Nutr* 2009 Mar;89(3):773–777.

National Academy of Sciences, Institute of Medicine. Letter Report on Dietary Reference Intakes for Trans Fatty Acids, 2002 uic.edu/depts/mcam/nutrition/pdf/IOMTransFatsummary.pdf

National Center for Health Statistics. *The Third National Health and Nutrition Survey, 1988–94.* Washington, DC: US Department of Health and Human Services, 2000.

National Institute of Allergy and Infectious Diseases (July 2004). "NIH Publication No. 04–5518: Food Allergy: An Overview."

Neel JV. Health and disease in unacculturated Amerindian populations. *Ciba Found Symp* 1977;49:155–177.

Nelson GJ. Dietary fat, trans fatty acids, and risk of coronary heart disease. *Nutr Rev* 1998 Aug;56(8):250–252.

Nelson GJ, Schmidt PC, Kelley DS. Low-fat diets do not lower plasma cholesterol levels in healthy men compared to high-fat diets with similar fatty acid composition at constant caloric intake. *Lipids* 1995;30:969–976.

Nerbass FB, Feltrim MI, Souza SA, Ykeda DS, Lorenzi-Filho G. Effects of massage therapy on sleep quality after coronary artery bypass graft surgery. *Clinics (Sao Paulo)* 2010;65(11):1105–1110.

Nesse RM, Stearns SC, Omenn GS. Medicine needs evolution. *Science* 2006;311:1071.

Nesse RM, Williams GC. *Why We Get Sick: The New Science of Darwinian Medicine.* New York: Times Books, 1994.

Nestler JE. Insulin regulation of human ovarian androgens. *Hum Reprod* 1997;12(suppl 1):53–62.

Neuhausen SL, Steele L, Ryan S, Mousavi M, Pinto M, Osann KE, Flodman P, Zone JJ. Co-occurrence of celiac disease and other autoimmune diseases in celiacs and their first-degree relatives. *J Autoimmun* 2008 Sep;31(2):160–165.

Newman LC, Lipton RB. Migraine MLT-down: an unusual presentation of migraine in patients with aspartame-triggered headaches. *Headache* 2001 Oct;41(9):899–901.

Niederhofer H, Pittschieler K. A preliminary investigation of ADHD symptoms in persons with celiac disease. *J Atten Disord* 2006 Nov;10(2):200–2004.

Nieman DC. *Exercise Testing and Prescription. A Health Related Approach.* London: Mayfield Publishing, 1999.

Nieman, DC, Cayea, EJ, Austin, MD, Henson, DA, McAnulty SR, Jin F. Chia seed does not promote weight loss or alter disease risk factors in overweight adults. *Nutrition Research* 2009;(29):414–418.

Nin JW, Jorsal A, Ferreira I, Schalkwijk CG, Prins MH, Parving HH, Tarnow L, Rossing P, Stehouwer CD. Higher plasma levels of advanced glycation end products are associated with incident cardiovascular disease and all-cause mortality in type 1 diabetes: a 12-year follow-up study. *Diabetes Care* 2011 Feb;34(2):442–447.

Nnoaham KE, Clarke A. Low serum vitamin D levels and tuberculosis: a systematic review and meta-analysis. *Int J Epidemiol* 2008 Feb;37(1):113–119.

Noah ND, Bender AE, Reaidi GB, Gilbert RJ. Food poisoning from raw red kidney beans. *Br Med J* 1980 Jul 19;281(6234):236–237.

Noakes M, Keogh JB, Foster PR, Clifton PM. Effect of an energy-restricted, high-protein, low-fat diet relative to a conventional high-carbohydrate, low-fat diet on weight loss, body composition, nutritional status, and markers of cardiovascular health in obese women. *Am J Clin Nutr* 2005 Jun;81(6):1298–1306.

Noli D, Avery G. Protein poisoning and coastal subsistence. *J Archaeological Sci* 1988;15:395–401.

Noma T, Yoshizawa I, Ogawa N, Ito M, Aoki K, Kawano Y. Fatal buckwheat dependent exercised-induced anaphylaxis. *Asian Pac J Allergy Immunol* 2001 Dec;19(4);283–286.

Norris JM, Yin X, Lamb MM, Barriga K, Seifert J, Hoffman M, Orton HD, Barón AE, Clare-Salzler M, Chase HP, Szabo NJ, Erlich H, Eisenbarth GS, Rewers M. Omega-3 polyunsaturated fatty acid intake and islet autoimmunity in children at increased risk for type 1 diabetes. *JAMA* 2007 Sep 26;298(12):1420–1428.

Norrish AE, Skeaff CM, Arribas GL, Sharpe SJ, Jackson RT. Prostate cancer risk and consumption of fish oils: a dietary biomarker-based case-control study. *Br J Cancer* 1999;81(7):1238–1242.

Nuttall FQ, Gannon MC. Plasma glucose and insulin response to macronutrients in nondiabetic and NIDDM subjects. *Diabetes Care* 1991;14:824–838.

O'Bryne DJ, O'Keefe SF, Shireman RB. Low-fat monounsaturated-rich diets reduce susceptibility of low density lipoproteins to peroxidation ex vivo. *Lipids* 1998;33:149–157.

O'Dea K. Marked improvement in carbohydrate and lipid metabolism in diabetic Australian aborigines after temporary reversion to traditional lifestyle. *Diabetes* 1984;33(6):596–603.

O'Dea K, Traianedes K, Chisholm K, Leyden H, Sinclair AJ. Cholesterol-lowering effect of a low-fat diet containing lean beef is reversed by the addition of beef fat. *Am J Clin Nutr* 1990 Sep;52(3):491–494.

O'Dea K, Traianedes K, Ireland P, Niall M, Sadler J, Hopper J, De Luise M. The effects of diet differing in fat, carbohydrate, and fiber on carbohydrate and lipid metabolism in type 2 diabetes. *J Am Diet Assoc* 1989;89:1076–1086.

O'Hara AM, Shanahan F. The gut flora as a forgotten organ. *EMBO Rep* 2006 Jul;7(7): 688–693.

O'Keefe JH, Jr, Cordain L. Cardiovascular disease resulting from a diet and lifestyle at odds with our Paleolithic genome: how to become a 21st-century hunter-gatherer. *Mayo Clin Proc* 2004;79(1):101–108.

O'Keefe JH, Vogel R, Lavie CJ, Cordain L. Achieving hunter-gatherer fitness in the 21(st) century: back to the future. *Am J Med* 2010 Dec;123(12):1082–1086.

———. Organic fitness: physical activity consistent with our hunter-gatherer heritage. *Phys Sportsmed* 2010 Dec;38(4):11–8.

Obarzanek E, Velletri PA, Cutler JA. Dietary protein and blood pressure. *JAMA* 1996;275: 1598–1603.

Obeid OA, Mannan N, Perry G, Iles RA, Boucher BJ. Homocysteine and folate in healthy east London Bangladeshis. *Lancet* 1998;352:1829–1830.

Odeleye OE, de Courten M, Pettitt DJ, Ravussin E. Fasting hyperinsulinemia is a predictor of increased body weight gain and obesity in Pima Indian children. *Diabetes* 1997;46(8):1341–1345.

Oh SY, Ryue J, Hsieh CH, Bell DE. Eggs enriched in omega-3 fatty acids and alterations in lipid concentrations in plasma lipoproteins and in blood pressure. *Am J Clin Nutr* 1991;54:689–695.

Ohara N, Naito Y, Kasama K, Shindo T, Yoshida H, Nagata T, Okuyama H. Similar changes in clinical and pathological parameters in Wistar Kyoto rats after a 13-week dietary intake of canola oil or a fatty acid composition– based interesterified canola oil mimic. *Food Chem Toxicol* 2009; 47(1):157–162.

Ohara N, Naito Y, Nagata T, Tachibana S, Okimoto M, Okuyama H. Dietary intake of rapeseed oil as the sole fat nutrient in Wistar rats—lack of increase in plasma lipids and renal lesions. *J Toxicol Sci* 2008; 33(5):641–645.

Ohara N, Naito Y, Nagata T, Tatematsu K, Fuma SY, Tachibana S, Okuyama H. Exploration for unknown substances in rapeseed oil that shorten survival time of stroke-prone spontaneously hypertensive rats. Effects of super critical gas extraction fractions. *Food Chem Toxicol* 2006; 44(7):952–963.

Oleszek W, Junkuszew M, Stochmal A. Determination and toxicity of saponins from Amaranthus cruentus seeds. *J Agric Food Chem* 1999 Sep;47(9):3685–3687.

Oliver WJ, Cohen EL, Neel JV. Blood pressure, sodium intake, and sodium related hormones in the Yanomamo Indians, a "no-salt" culture. *Circulation* 1975;52:146–151.

Omenn GS, Goodman GE, Thornquist MD, Balmes J, Cullen MR, Glass A, Keogh JP, Meyskens FL, Valanis B, Williams JH, Barnhart S, Hammar S. Effects of a combination of beta carotene and vitamin A on lung cancer and cardiovascular disease. *N Engl J Med* 1996 May 2;334(10):1150–1155.

Orengo IF, Black HS, Wolf JE. Influence of fish oil supplementation on the minimal erytherma dose in humans. *Arch Dermatol Res* 1992;284:219–221.

Osendarp SJ, Murray-Kolb LE, Black MM. Case study on iron in mental development—in memory of John Beard (1947–2009). *Nutr Rev* 2010 Nov;68 Suppl 1:S48–52. doi: 10.1111/j.1753–4887.2010.00331.x.

Osgood C. *Ingalik Social Culture.* New Haven: Yale University Press, 1958, 166.

Oshida Y, Yamanouchi K, Hayamizu S, Nagasawa J, Ohsawa I, Sato Y. Effects of training and training cessation on insulin action. *Int J Sports Med* 1991;12:484–486.

Oski, FA. *Don't Drink Your Milk!: The Frightening New Medical Facts About the World's Most Overrated Nutrient.* New York: Wyden Books, 1977.

Osterdahl M, Kocturk T, Koochek A, Wandell PE. Effects of a short-term intervention with a Paleolithic diet in healthy volunteers. *Eur J Clin Nutr* 2008;62(5):682–685.

Ostman EM, Liljeberg Elmståhl HG, Björck IM. Inconsistency between glycemic and insulinemic responses to regular and fermented milk products. *Am J Clin Nutr* 2001;74:96–100.

Packard RR, Lichtman AH, Libby P. Innate and adaptive immunity in atherosclerosis. *Semin Immunopathol* 2009;31(1):5–22.

Paimela L, Kurki P, Leirisalo-Repo M, Piirainen H. Gliadin immune reactivity in patients with rheumatoid arthritis. *Clin Exp Rheumatol* 1995 Sep–Oct;13(5):603–607.

Palayekar MJ, Herzog TJ. The emerging role of epidermal growth factor receptor inhibitors in ovarian cancer. *Int J Gynecol Cancer* 2008 Sep–Oct;18(5):879–890.

Papadaki A, Linardakis M, Larsen TM, van Baak MA, Lindroos AK, Pfeiffer AF, Martinez JA, Handjieva-Darlenska T, Kunesová M, Holst C, Astrup A, Saris WH, Kafatos A,

DiOGenes Study Group. The effect of protein and glycemic index on children's body composition: the DiOGenes randomized study. *Pediatrics* 2010 Nov;126(5):e1143–1152.

Park M, Ross GW, Petrovitch H, White LR, Masaki KH, Nelson JS, Tanner CM, Curb JD, Blanchette PL, Abbott RD. Consumption of milk and calcium in midlife and the future risk of Parkinson disease. *Neurology* 2005 Mar 22;64(6):1047–1051.

Pasquali R, Casimirri F, Vicennati V. Weight control and its beneficial effect on fertility in women with obesity and polycystic ovary syndrome. *Hum Reprod* 1997;12(suppl 1):82–87.

Patel B, Schutte R, Sporns P, Doyle J, Jewel L, Fedorak RN. Potato glycoalkaloids adversely affect intestinal permeability and aggravate inflammatory bowel disease. *Inflamm Bowel Dis* 2002 Sep;8(5):340–346.

Peiretti PB, Meineri G. Effects on growth performance, carcass characteristics, and the fat and meat fatty acid profile of rabbits fed diets with chia (*Salvia hispanica L.*) seed supplements. *Meat Science* 2008;(80):1116–1121.

Pengiran Tengah CD, Lock RJ, Unsworth DJ, Wills AJ. Multiple sclerosis and occult gluten sensitivity. *Neurology* 2004 Jun 22;62(12):2326–2327.

Penny D, Steel M, Waddell PJ, Hendy MD. Improved analyses of human mtDNA sequences support a recent African origin for *Homo sapiens*. *Mol Biol Evol* 1995;12:863–882.

Phelan N, O'Connor A, Kyaw Tun T, Correia N, Boran G, Roche HM, Gibney J. Hormonal and metabolic effects of polyunsaturated fatty acids in young women with polycystic ovary syndrome: results from a cross-sectional analysis and a randomized, placebo-controlled, crossover trial. *Am J Clin Nutr* 2011 Mar;93(3):652–662.

Phinney SD, Bistrian BR, Evans WJ, Gervino E, Blackburn GL. The human metabolic response to chronic ketosis without caloric restriction: physical and biochemical adaptations. *Metabolism* 1983;32:757–768.

Piatti PM, Monti F, Fermo I, Baruffaldi L, Nasser R, Santambrogio G, Librenti MC, Galli-Kienle M, Pontiroli AE, Pozza G. Hypocaloric high-protein diet improves glucose oxidation and spares lean body mass: comparison to hypocaloric high-carbohydrate diet. *Metabolism* 1994;43:1481–1487.

Pili R, Kruszewski MP, Hager BW, Lantz J, Carducci MA. Combination of phenylbutyrate and 13-cis retinoic acid inhibits prostate tumor growth and angiogenesis. *Cancer Res* 2001;61:1477–1485.

Pinhasi R, Gasparian B, Areshian G, Zardaryan D, Smith A, Bar-Oz G, Higham T. First direct evidence of Chalcolithic footwear from the near eastern highlands. *PLoS One* 2010 Jun 9;5(6):e10984.

Pittman Fe, Holub Da. Sjögren's Syndrome and Adult Celiac Disease. *Gastroenterology* 1965 Jun;48:869–876.

Pitts GC, Bullard TR. Some interspecific aspects of body composition in mammals. In *Body Composition in Animals and Man* (Publication 1598). Washington, DC: National Academy of Sciences, 1968, 45–70.

Pizzo G, Piscopo MR, Pizzo I, Giuliana G. Community water fluoridation and caries prevention: a critical review. *Clin Oral Investig* 2007 Sep;11(3):189–193.

Playford RJ, Macdonald CE, Johnson WS. Colostrum and milk-derived peptide growth factors for the treatment of gastrointestinal disorders. *Am J Clin Nutr* 2000 Jul;72(1): 5–14.

Plourde M, Cunnane SC. Extremely limited synthesis of long chain polyunsaturates in adults: implications for their dietary essentiality and use as supplements. *Appl Physiol Nutr Metab* 2007 Aug;32(4):619–634.

Plum LA, DeLuca HF. Vitamin D, disease, and therapeutic opportunities. *Nat Rev Drug Discov* 2010 Dec;9(12):941–955.

Poikonen S, Puumalainen TJ, Kautiainen H, Burri P, Palosuo T, Reunala T, Turjanmaa K. Turnip rape and oilseed rape are new potential food allergens in children with atopic dermatitis. *Allergy* 2006;61(1):124–127.

Poikonen S, Rancé F, Puumalainen TJ, Le Manach G, Reunala T, Turjanmaa K. Sensitization and allergy to turnip rape: a comparison between the Finnish and French children with atopic dermatitis. *Acta Paediatr* 2009;98(2):310–315.

Pols H, Yazdanpanah N, van Meurs J. Homocysteine, the vitamin B complex family, and bone. In Burckhardt P, Heaney R, Dawson-Hughes B. *Proceedings of the International Symposium on Nutritional Aspects of Osteoporosis, 4–6 May 2006, Lausanne, Switzerland.* Elsevier, 2007, 151–157.

Popkin BM. Where's the fat? Trends in US Diets 1965–1996. *Prev Med* 2001;32:245–254.

Porrini M, Crovetti R, Riso P, Santangelo A, Testolin G. Effects of physical and chemical characteristics of food on specific and general satiety. *Physiol Behav* 1995;57:461–468.

Porrini M, Santangelo A, Crovetti R, Riso P, Testolin G, Blundell JE. Weight, protein, fat, and timing of preloads affect food intake. *Physiol Behav* 1997;62:563–570.

Potischman N, Weed DL. Causal criteria in nutritional epidemiology. *Am J Clin Nutr* 1999 Jun;69(6):1309S–1314S.

Pramod SN, Venkatesh YP, Mahesh PA. Potato lectin activates basophils and mast cells of atopic subjects by its interaction with core chitobiose of cell-bound non-specific immunoglobulin E. *Clin Exp Immunol* 2007 Jun;148(3):391–401.

Precetti AS, Oria MP, Nielsen SS. Presence in bovine milk of two protease inhibitors of the plasmin system. *J Dairy Sci* 1997;80:1490–1496.

Prentice AM. Manipulation of dietary fat and energy density and subsequent effects on substrate flux and food intake. *Am J Clin Nutr* 1998; 67(suppl 3):535S–541S.

Price TD, Petersen EB. A Mesolithic camp in Denmark. *Sci Am* 1987;256:113–121.

Price WA. *Nutrition and Physical Degeneration: A Comparison of Primitive and Modern Diets and Their Effects.* New York: P B, Hoeber, Inc., 1939.

Prinz JC. Psoriasis vulgaris—a sterile antibacterial skin reaction mediated by cross-reactive T cells? An immunological view of the pathophysiology of psoriasis. *Clin Exp Dermatol* 2001;26:326–332.

Prior IA, Davidson F, Salmond CE, Czochanska Z. Cholesterol, coconuts, and diet on Polynesian atolls: a natural experiment: the Pukapuka and Tokelau island studies. *Am J Clin Nutr* 1981;34(8):1552–1561.

Pritchard JK. How we are evolving. *Sci Am.* 2010 Oct;303(4):40–47.

Proctor CA, Proctor TB, Proctor B. Etiology and treatment of fluid retention (hydrops) in Meniere's syndrome. *Ear Nose Throat J* 1992;71:631–635.

Progress in Autoimmune Disease Research. The Autoimmune Disease Coordinating Committee Report to Congress. US Department of Health and Human Services, National Institutes of Health, National Institute of Allergy and Infectious Diseases. Bethesda (MD), 2005.

Pront R, Margalioth EJ, Green R, Eldar-Geva T, Maimoni Z, Zimran A, Elstein D. Prevalence of low serum cobalamin in infertile couples. *Andrologia* 2009 Feb;41(1):46–50.

Proud VK, Rizzo WB, Patterson JW, Meard GS, Wolf B. Fatty acid alterations and carboxylase deficiencies in the skin of biotin-deficient rats. *Am J Clin Nutr* 1990;51:853–858.

Proudman SM, Cleland LG, James MJ. Dietary omega-3 fats for treatment of inflammatory joint disease: efficacy and utility. *Rheum Dis Clin North Am* 2008 May;34(2):469–479.

Pruthi JS. Spices and Condiments. In *Advances in Food Research*, Chichester EM, Stewart GF (eds). New York: Academic Press, 1980, 13.

Prystupa J. Fluorine—a current literature review. An NRC and ATSDR based review of safety standards for exposure to fluorine and fluorides. *Toxicol Mech Methods* 2011 Feb;21(2):103–170.

Pusztai A. Dietary lectins are metabolic signals for the gut and modulate immune and hormone functions. *European Journal of Clinical Nutrition* 1993;47:691–699.

Pusztai A, Clarke EM, Grant G, King TP. The toxicity of Phaseolus vulgaris lectins. Nitrogen balance and immunochemical studies. *J Sci Food Agric* 1981 Oct;32(10):1037–1046.

Pusztai A, Ewen SW, Grant G, Brown DS, Stewart JC, Peumans WJ, Van Damme EJ, Bardocz S. Antinutritive effects of wheat-germ agglutinin and other N-acetylglucosamine-specific lectins. *Br J Nutr* 1993 Jul;70(1):313–321.

Pusztai A, Ewen SW, Grant G, Peumans WJ, van Damme EJ, Rubio L, Bardocz S. Relationship between survival and binding of plant lectins during small intestinal passage and their effectiveness as growth factors. *Digestion* 1990;46 Suppl 2:308–316.

———. Plant (food) lectins as signal molecules: effects on the morphology and bacterial ecology of the small intestine. In *Lectin Reviews*, Volume I, Kilpatrick, DC, Van Driessche E, Bog-Hansen TC (eds). St. Louis: Sigma, 1991, 1–15.

Pusztai A, Grant G. Assessment of lectin inactivation by heat and digestion. In *Methods in Molecular Medicine: Vol. 9: Lectin methods and protocols*, Rhodes JM, Milton JD (eds). Totowa, NJ: Humana Press Inc., 1998.

Pusztai A, Grant G, Spencer RJ, Duguid TJ, Brown DS, Ewen SWB, Peumans WJ, Van Damme EJM, Bardocz S. Kidney bean lectin-induced Escherichia coli overgrowth in the small intestine is blocked by GNA, a mannose-specific lectin. *Journal of Applied Bacteriology* 1993;75:360–368.

Pusztai A, Greer F, Grant G. Specific uptake of dietary lectins into the systemic circulation of rats. *Biochemical Society Transactions* 1989;17:527–528.

Puumalainen TJ, Poikonen S, Kotovuori A, Vaali K, Kalkkinen N, Reunala T, Turjanmaa K, Palosuo T. Napins, 2S albumins, are major allergens in oilseed rape and turnip rape. *J Allergy Clin Immunol*. 2006;117(2):426–432.

Pynnönen PA, Isometsä ET, Aronen ET, Verkasalo MA, Savilahti E, Aalberg VA. Mental disorders in adolescents with celiac disease. *Psychosomatics* 2004 Jul–Aug;45(4):325–335.

Pynnönen PA, Isometsä ET, Verkasalo MA, Kähkönen SA, Sipilä I, Savilahti E, Aalberg VA. Gluten-free diet may alleviate depressive and behavioural symptoms in adolescents with coeliac disease: a prospective follow-up case-series study. *BMC Psychiatry* 2005 Mar 17;5:14.

Qaddoumi M, Lee VH. Lectins as endocytic ligands: an assessment of lectin binding and uptake to rabbit conjunctival epithelial cells. *Pharm Res* 2004 Jul;21(7):1160–1166.

Qin LQ, He K, Xu JY. Milk consumption and circulating insulin-like growth factor-I level: a systematic literature review. *Int J Food Sci Nutr* 2009;60 Suppl 7:330–340.

Qin LQ, Wang PY, Kaneko T, Hoshi K, Sato A. Estrogen: one of the risk factors in milk for prostate cancer. *Med Hypotheses* 2004;62(1):133–142.

Qin LQ, Xu JY, Wang PY, Kaneko T, Hoshi K, Sato A. Milk consumption is a risk factor for prostate cancer: meta-analysis of case-control studies. *Nutr Cancer* 2004;48(1):22–27.

Qin LQ, Xu JY, Wang PY, Tong J, Hoshi K. Milk consumption is a risk factor for prostate cancer in Western countries: evidence from cohort studies. *Asia Pac J Clin Nutr* 2007;16(3):467–476.

Rabago D, Guerard E, Bukstein D. Nasal irrigation for chronic sinus symptoms in patients with allergic rhinitis, asthma, and nasal polyposis: a hypothesis generating study. *WMJ* 2008 Apr;107(2):69–75.

Rabinowitch IM. Clinical and other observations on Canadian Eskimos in the Eastern Arctic. *Can Med Assoc J* 1936;34:487–501.

Rahman MB, Driscoll T, Cowie C, Armstrong BK. Disinfection by-products in drinking water and colorectal cancer: a meta-analysis. *Int J Epidemiol* 2010 Jun;39(3):733–745.

Raj SD. Bottled water: how safe is it? *Water Environ Res* 2005 Nov–Dec;77(7):3013–3018.

Rajah R, Valentinis B, Cohen P. Insulin-like growth factor (IGF)-binding protein-3 induces apoptosis and mediates the effects of transforming growth factor-beta 1 on programmed cell death through a p53- and IGF-independent mechanism. *J Biol Chem* 1997;272:12181–12188.

Ramsden CE, Faurot KR, Carrera-Bastos P, Cordain L, De Lorgeril M, Sperling LS. Dietary fat quality and coronary heart disease prevention: a unified theory based on evolutionary, historical, global, and modern perspectives. *Curr Treat Options Cardiovasc Med* 2009;11(4):289–301.

Rana SK, Sanders TA. Taurine concentrations in the diet, plasma, urine, and breast milk of vegans compared with omnivores. *Br J Nutr* 1986 Jul;56(1):17–27.

Rao RK, Baker RD, Baker SS. Bovine milk inhibits proteolytic degradation of epidermal growth factor in human gastric and duodenal lumen. *Peptides* 1998;19(3):495–504.

Rasmussen HS et al. Influence of magnesium substitution therapy on blood lipid composition in patients with ischemic heart disease. *Arch Int Med* 1989;149:1050–1053.

Ratel S. High-intensity and resistance training and elite young athletes. *Med Sport Sci* 2011;56:84–96.

Ratnakar KS. Interaction of galactose and dietary protein deficiency on rat lens. *Opthalmic Res* 1985;17:344–348.

Ratner A. Interview of Dr. Alessio Fasano. *Gluten Free Living Magazine*, Dec 2010: 40–48, 54.

Rattray EAS, Palmer R, Pusztai A. Toxicity of kidney beans (*Phaseolus vulgaris L.*) to conventional and gnotobiotic rats. *Journal of the Science of Food and Agriculture* 1974;25:1035–1040.

Rauchhaus M, Coats AJ, Anker SD. The endotoxin-lipoprotein hypothesis. *Lancet* 2000 Sep 9;356(9233):930–933.

Ravnskov U, Allen C, Atrens D, Enig MG, Groves B, Kauffman JM, Kroneld R, Rosch PJ, Rosenman R, Werkö L, Nielsen JV, Wilske J, Worm N. Studies of dietary fat and heart disease. *Science* 2002 Feb 22;295(5559):1464–1466.

Ravnskov U. The fallacies of the lipid hypothesis. *Scand Cardiovasc J* 2008 Aug;42(4):236–239.

———. The questionable role of saturated and polyunsaturated fatty acids in cardiovascular disease. *J Clin Epidemiol* 1998 Jun;51(6):443–460.

Rayssiguier Y, Gueux E. Magnesium and lipids in cardiovascular disease. *J Am Coll Nutr* 1986;5:507–519.

Reaven GM. Syndrome X: 6 years later. *J Intern Med* 1994;236 (suppl 736):13–22.

———. Pathophysiology of insulin resistance in human disease. *Physiol Rev* 1995;75:473–486.

Reaven GM, Chen YD, Jeppesen J, Maheux P, Krauss RM. Insulin resistance and hyperinsulinemia in individuals with small, dense low density lipoprotein particles. *J Clin Invest* 1993;92:141–146.

Refsum H, Smith AD. Are we ready for mandatory fortification with vitamin B-12? *Am J Clin Nutr* 2008 Aug;88(2):253–254.

Refsum H, Yajnik CS, Gadkari M, Schneede J, Vollset SE, Orning L, Guttormsen AB, Joglekar A, Sayyad MG, Ulvik A, Ueland PM. Hyperhomocysteinemia and elevated methylmalonic acid indicate a high prevalence of cobalamin deficiency in Asian Indians. *Am J Clin Nutr* 2001 Aug;74(2):233–241.

Reichelt KL, Seim AR, Reichelt WH. Could schizophrenia be reasonably explained by Dohan's hypothesis on genetic interaction with a dietary peptide overload? *Prog Neuropsychopharmacol Biol Psychiatry* 1996 Oct;20(7):1083–1114.

Reid IR, Bolland MJ, Grey A. Does calcium supplementation increase cardiovascular risk? *Clin Endocrinol (Oxf)* 2010 Dec;73(6):689–695.

Reinhold JG. High phytate content of rural Iranian bread: a possible cause of human zinc deficiency. *Am J Clin Nutr* 1971;24:1204–1206.

Reinhold JG, Lahimgarzadeh A, Nasr K, Hedayati H. Effects of purified phytate and phytate rich bread upon metabolism of zinc, calcium, phosphorus, and nitrogen in man. *Lancet* 1973;1:283–288.

Remer T, Manz F. Potential renal acid load of foods and its influence on urine ph. *J Am Diet Assoc* 1995;95:791–797.

Remer T, Neubert A, Manz F. Increased risk of iodine deficiency with vegetarian nutrition. *Br J Nutr* 1999 Jan;81(1):45–49.

Renaud S et al. Dietary lipids and their relation to ischaemic heart disease: from epidemiology to prevention. *J Int Med* 1989;225(supp 1):39–46.

Renner W. The spread of cancer among the descendants of the liberated Africans or Creoles of Sierre Leone. *Brit Med J* 1910 Sept 3;587–589.

Reynolds RD. Bioavailability of vitamin B-6 from plant foods. *Am J Clin Nutr* 1988;48:863–867.

Rhodes ET, Pawlak DB, Takoudes TC, Ebbeling CB, Feldman HA, Lovesky MM, Cooke EA, Leidig MM, Ludwig DS. Effects of a low-glycemic load diet in overweight and obese pregnant women: a pilot randomized controlled trial. *Am J Clin Nutr* 2010 Dec;92(6):1306–1315.

Riboli E, Norat T. Epidemiologic evidence of the protective effect of fruit and vegetables on cancer risk. *Am J Clin Nutr* 2003 Sep;78(3 Suppl):559S–569S.

Rice C, Nicholas J, Baio J, Pettygrove S, Lee LC et al. Changes in autism spectrum disorder prevalence in 4 areas of the United States. *Disabil Health J* 2010 Jul;3(3):186–201.

Richards MP, Hedges REM, Jacobi R, Current, A, Stringer C. Focus: Gough's Cave and Sun Hole Cave human stable isotope values indicate a high animal protein diet in the British Upper Palaeolithic. *J Archaeol Sci* 2000;27:1–3.

Richards MP, Pettitt PB, Trinkaus E, Smith FH, Paunovic M, Karavanic I. Neanderthal diet at Vindija and Neanderthal predation: the evidence from stable isotopes. *Proc Natl Acad Sci USA* 2000;97:7663–7666.

Richardson SD, Plewa MJ, Wagner ED, Schoeny R, Demarini DM. Occurrence, genotoxicity, and carcinogenicity of regulated and emerging disinfection by-products in drinking water: a review and roadmap for research. *Mutat Res* 2007 Nov–Dec;636 (1–3):178–242.

Richter CP, Duke JR. Cataracts produced in rats by yogurt. *Science* 1970;168:1372–1374.

Rifkin J. *Beyond Beef.* London: Thorsons, 1994.

Rinaldi E, Albini L, Costagliola C, De Rosa G, Auricchio G, De Vizia B, Auricchio S. High frequency of lactose absorbers among adults with idiopathic senile and presenile cataract in a population with a high prevalence of primary adult lactose malabsorption. *Lancet* 1984 Feb 18;1(8373):355–357.

Ristow M, Zarse K, Oberbach A, Klöting N, Birringer M, Kiehntopf M et al. Antioxidants prevent health-promoting effects of physical exercise in humans. *Proc Natl Acad Sci* 2009;106(21):8665–8670.

Riveros M. First observation of cancer among the Pampidos (Chulupi) Indians of the Paraguayan Chaco. *Int Surg* 1970;53:51–55.

Robertson I, Ford JA, McIntosh WB, Dunnigan MG. The role of cereals in the aetiology of nutritional rickets: the lesson of the Irish national nutritional survey 1943–8. *Brit J Nutr* 1981;45:17–22.

Robinson J. *Why Grassfed Is Best.* Vashon, WA: Vashon Island Press, 2000.

Robinson SM, Jaccard C, Persaud C, Jackson AA, Jequier E, Schutz Y. Protein turnover and thermogenesis in response to high-protein and high carbohydrate feeding in men. *Am J Clin Nutr* 1990;52:72–80.

Roche HM. Dietary carbohydrates and triacylglycerol metabolism. *Proc Nutr Soc* 1999;58: 201–206.

Rode A, Shephard RJ. Physiological consequences of acculturation: a 20 year study of fitness in an Inuit community. *Eur J Appl Physiol* 1994;69:516–524.

Rodhouse JC, Haugh CA, Roberts D, Gilbert RJ. Red kidney bean poisoning in the UK: an analysis of 50 suspected incidents between 1976 and 1989. *Epidemiol Infect* 1990 Dec;105(3):485–491.

Rodríguez-Cabezas ME, Gálvez J, Camuesco D, Lorente MD, Concha A, Martinez-Augustin O, Redondo L, Zarzuelo A. Intestinal anti-inflammatory activity of dietary fiber (*Plantago ovata seeds*) in HLA-B27 transgenic rats. *Clin Nutr* 2003 Oct;22(5):463–471.

Roe DA. *A Plague of Corn.* Ithaca, NY: Cornell University Press, 1973.

———. History of promotion of vegetable cereal diets. *J Nutr* 1986;116:1355–1363.

Roed C, Skovby F, Lund AM. Severe vitamin B12 deficiency in infants breastfed by vegans. *Ugeskr Laeger* 2009 Oct 19;171(43):3099–3101.

Rogers EJ. Has enhanced folate status during pregnancy altered natural selection and possibly Autism prevalence? A closer look at a possible link. *Med Hypotheses* 2008 Sep;71(3):406–410.

Rohrmann S, Platz EA, Kavanaugh CJ et al. Meat and dairy consumption and subsequent risk of prostate cancer in a US cohort study. *Cancer Causes Control* 2007 Feb;18(1):41–50.

Róka R, Demaude J, Cenac N, Ferrier L, Salvador-Cartier C, Garcia-Villar R, Fioramonti J, Bueno L. Colonic luminal proteases activate colonocyte proteinase-activated receptor-2 and regulate paracellular permeability in mice. *Neurogastroenterol Motil* 2007 Jan;19(1):57–65.

Román GC. Autism: transient in utero hypothyroxinemia related to maternal flavonoid ingestion during pregnancy and to other environmental antithyroid agents. *J Neurol Sci* 2007 Nov 15;262(1–2):15–26.

Roman SD, Clarke CL, Hall RE, Ian EA, Sutherland RL. Expression and regulation of retinoic acid receptors in human breast cancer cells. *Cancer Res* 1992;52:2236–2242.

Rose NR, Mackay IR. *The Auto-Immune Diseases.* New York: Academic Press, 2006.

Rosell MS, Lloyd-Wright Z, Appleby PN, Sanders TA, Allen NE, Key TJ, Long-chain n-3 polyunsaturated fatty acids in plasma in British meat-eating, vegetarian, and vegan men. *Am J Clin Nutr* 2005 Aug;82(2):327–334.

Rosenberg IH. Science-based micronutrient fortification: which nutrients, how much, and how to know? *Am J Clin Nutr* 2005 Aug;82(2):279–280.

Rostow WW. *The Great Population Spike and After.* New York: Oxford University Press, 1998.

Rowlands MA, Gunnell D, Harris R, Vatten LJ, Holly JM, Martin RM. Circulating insulin-like growth factor peptides and prostate cancer risk: a systematic review and meta-analysis. *Int J Cancer* 2009 May 15;124(10):2416–2429.

Rudman D, DiFulco TJ, Galambos JT, Smith RB III, Salam AA, Warren WD. Maximal rates of excretion and synthesis of urea in normal and cirrhotic subjects. *J Clin Invest* 1973;52:2241–2249.

Ruff CB, Larsen CS, Hayes WC. Structural changes in the femur with the transition to agriculture on the Georgia coast. *Am J Phys Anthropol* 1984;64:125–136.

Rui T, Hongyu Z, Ruiqi W. Seven Chinese patients with buckwheat allergy. *Am J Med Sci* 2010 Jan;339(1):22–24.

Ruiz RG, Price KR, Arthur AE, Rose ME, Rhodes MJ, Fenwick RG. Effect of soaking and cooking on saponin content and composition of chickpeas (*Cicer arietinum*) and lentils (*Lens culinaris*). *J Agric Food Chem* 1996;44:1526–1530.

Rush EC, Chhichhia P, Hinckson E, Nabiryo C. Dietary patterns and vitamin B(12) status of migrant Indian preadolescent girls. *Eur J Clin Nutr* 2009 Apr;63(4):585–587.

Rustan AC, Nenseter MS, Drevon CA. Omega-3 and omega-6 fatty acids in the insulin resistance syndrome. Lipid and lipoprotein metabolism and atherosclerosis. *Ann NY Acad Sci* 1997;827:310–326.

Ruuskanen A, Kaukinen K, Collin P, Huhtala H, Valve R, Mäki M, Luostarinen L. Positive serum antigliadin antibodies without celiac disease in the elderly population: does it matter? *Scand J Gastroenterol.* 2010 Oct;45(10):1197–1202.

Ryan CA, Hass GM. Structural, evolutionary, and nutritional properties of proteinase inhibitors from potatoes. In *Antinutrients and natural toxicants in foods*, Ory RL (ed). Westport, CT: Food and Nutrition Press Inc., 1981.

Ryder SD, Smith JA, Rhodes JM. Peanut lectin: a mitogen for normal human colonic epithelium and human HT29 colorectal cancer cells. *Journal of the National Cancer Institute* 1992;84:1410–1416.

Saadatian-Elahi M, Norat T, Goudable J, Riboli E. Biomarkers of dietary fatty acid intake and the risk of breast cancer: a meta-analysis. *Int J Cancer* 2004 Sep 10;111(4):584–591.

Sabate J, Fraser GE, Burke K, Knutsen SF, Bennett H, Lindsted KD. Effects of walnuts on serum lipid levels and blood pressure in normal men. *N Engl J Med* 1993;328:603–607.

Sandberg AS. Bioavailability of minerals in legumes. *Br J Nutr* 2002 Dec;88 Suppl 3:S281–S285.

Sander GR, Cummins AG, Henshall T, Powell BC. Rapid disruption of intestinal barrier function by gliadin involves altered expression of apical junctional proteins. *FEBS Lett* 2005 Aug 29;579(21):4851–4855.

Sanders TA. DHA status of vegetarians. *Prostaglandins Leukot Essent Fatty Acids* 2009 Aug–Sep;81(2–3):137–141.

———. Growth and development of British vegan children. *Am J Clin Nutr* 1988;48:822–825.

Sanders TA, Roshanai F. Platelet phospholipid fatty acid composition and function in vegans compared with age- and sex-matched omnivore controls. *Eur J Clin Nutr* 1992 Nov;46(11):823–831.

Sanford GL, Harris-Hooker S. Stimulation of vascular proliferation by beta-galactoside specific lectins. *FASEB J* 1990;4:2912–2918.

Santayana G. *The Life of Reason or, The phases of Human Progress.* New York: C. Scribner's Sons, 1905.

Sargent JR, Tacon AG. Development of farmed fish: a nutritionally necessary alternative to meat. *Proc Nutr Soc* 1999;58:377–383.

Sato Y, Honda Y, Iwamoto J, Kanoko T, Satoh K. Effect of folate and mecobalamin on hip fractures in patients with stroke: a randomized controlled trial. *JAMA* 2005 Mar 2;293(9):1082–1088.

Satoh R, Koyano S, Takagi K, Nakamura R, Teshima R, Sawada J. Immunological characterization and mutational analysis of the recombinant protein BWp16, a major allergen in buckwheat. *Biol Pharm Bull* 2008 Jun;31(6):1079–1085.

Sauer J, Mason JB, Choi SW. Too much folate: a risk factor for cancer and cardiovascular disease? *Curr Opin Clin Nutr Metab Care* 2009 Jan;12(1):30–36.

Schaefer O. When the Eskimo comes to town. *Nutr Today* 1971;6:8–16.

Schairer C, Hill D, Sturgeon SR, Fears T, Mies C, Ziegler RG, Hoover RN, Sherman ME. Serum concentrations of estrogens, sex hormone binding globulin, and androgens and risk of breast hyperplasia in postmenopausal women. *Cancer Epidemiol Biomarkers Prev* 2005 Jul;14(7):1660–1665.

Schalkwijk CG, Stehouwer CD, van Hinsbergh VW. Fructose-mediated non-enzymatic glycation: sweet coupling or bad modification. *Diabetes Metab Res Rev* 2004 Sep–Oct;20(5):369–382.

Schaller GB, Lowther GR. The relevance of carnivore behavior to the study of early hominids. *Southwest J Anthropol* 1969;25:307–341.

Schecter A, Malik N, Haffner D, Smith S, Harris TR, Paepke O, Birnbaum L. Bisphenol A (BPA) in US food. *Environ Sci Technol* 2010 Dec 15;44(24):9425–9430.

Schettler T. Human exposure to phthalates via consumer products. *Int J Androl* 2006 Feb;29(1):134–139; discussion 181–185.

Schlundt DG, Hill JO, Sbrocco T, Pope-Cordle J, Sharp T. The role of breakfast in the treatment of obesity: a randomized clinical trial. *Am J Clin Nutr* 1992 Mar;55(3):645–651.

Schmid S, Koczwara K, Schwinghammer S, Lampasona V, Ziegler AG, Bonifacio E. Delayed exposure to wheat and barley proteins reduces diabetes incidence in non-obese diabetic mice. *Clin Immunol* 2004 Apr;111(1):108–118.

Schneede J, Ueland PM. Novel and established markers of cobalamin deficiency: complementary or exclusive diagnostic strategies. *Semin Vasc Med* 2005 May;5(2):140–155.

Scholz D. Relations between myopia and school achievements, growth, and social factors. *Offentl Gesundheitswes* 1970;32:530–535.

Schürks M, Glynn RJ, Rist PM, Tzourio C, Kurth T. Effects of vitamin E on stroke subtypes: meta-analysis of randomised controlled trials. *BMJ* 2010 Nov 4;341:c5702. doi: 10.1136/bmj.c5702.

Scott FW. Food-induced type 1 diabetes in the BB rat. *Diabetes Metab Rev* 1996;12:341–359.

Scott MJ, Scott AM. Effects of anabolic-androgenic steroids on the pilosebaceous unit. *Cutis* 1992;50:113–116.

Sebastian A. Dietary protein content and the diet's net acid load: opposing effects on bone health. *Am J Clin Nutr* 2005 Nov;82(5):921–922.

Sebastian A, Harris ST, Ottaway JH, Todd KM, Morris RC Jr. Improved mineral balance and skeletal metabolism in postmenopausal women treated with potassium bicarbonate. *N Engl J Med* 1994;330:1776–1781.

Sedman RM, Beaumont J, McDonald TA, Reynolds S, Krowech G, Howd R. Review of the evidence regarding the carcinogenicity of hexavalent chromium in drinking water. *J Environ Sci Health C Environ Carcinog Ecotoxicol Rev* 2006 Apr;24(1):155–182.

Seelig MS. Increased need for magnesium with the use of combined oestrogen and calcium for osteoporosis treatment. *Magnes Res* 1990 Sep;3(3):197–215.

Segall JJ. Dietary lactose as a possible risk factor for ischemic heart disease: review of epidemiology. *Int J Cardiol* 1994;46:197–207.

———. Plausibility of dietary lactose as a coronary risk factor. *J Nutr Environ Med* 2002:12:217–229.

Seino Y, Seino S, Ikeda M, Matsukura S, Imura H. Beneficial effects of high protein diet in treatment of mild diabetes. *Hum Nutr Appl Nutr* 1983;37A:226–230.

Seiwert TY, Cohen E. The emerging role of EGFR and VEGF inhibition in the treatment of head and neck squamous cell carcinoma. *Angiogenesis Oncol* 2005;1:7–10.

Selhub J, Morris MS, Jacques PF. In vitamin B12 deficiency, higher serum folate is associated with increased total homocysteine and methylmalonic acid concentrations. *Proc Natl Acad Sci USA* 2007 Dec 11;104(50):19995–20000.

Semaw S, Renne P, Harris JW, Feibel CS, Bernor RL, Fesseha N, Mowbray K. 2.5-million-year-old stone tools from Gona, Ethiopia. *Nature* 1997;385:333–336.

Semba RD, Nicklett EJ, Ferrucci L. Does accumulation of advanced glycation end products contribute to the aging phenotype? *J Gerontol A Biol Sci Med Sci* 2010 Sep;65(9):963–975.

Sempos CT, Liu K, Ernst ND. Food and nutrient exposures: what to consider when evaluating epidemiologic evidence. *Am J Clin Nutr* 1999 Jun;69(6):1330S–1338S.

Séverin S, Wenshui X. Milk biologically active components as nutraceuticals: review. *Crit Rev Food Sci Nutr* 2005;45(7–8):645–656.

Shahid SK, Schneider SH. Effects of exercise on insulin resistance syndrome. *Coronary Artery Dis* 2000;11:103–109.

Shakeri R, Zamani F, Sotoudehmanesh R, Amiri A, Mohamadnejad M, Davatchi F, Karakani AM, Malekzadeh R, Shahram F. Gluten sensitivity enteropathy in patients with recurrent aphthous stomatitis. *BMC Gastroenterol* 2009 Jun 17;9:44.

Shapin S. Vegetable love: the history of vegetarianism. *New Yorker* 2007 Jan 22:80–84.

Sharief S, Jariwala S, Kumar J, Muntner P, Melamed ML. Vitamin D levels and food and environmental allergies in the United States: results from the National Health and Nutrition Examination Survey 2005–2006. *J Allergy Clin Immunol* 2011 May;127(5)1195–1202.

Shatin R. Man and his cultigens. *Scientific Australian* 1964;1:34–39.

———. Preliminary report of the treatment of rheumatoid arthritis with high protein gluten free diet and supplementation. *Medical Journal of Australia* 1964;2:169–172.

———. The transition from food-gathering to food-production in evolution and disease. *Vitalstoffe Zivilisationskrankheitein* 1967;12:104–107.

Sheard C, Caylor HD, Schlotthauer C. Photosensitization of animals after the ingestion of buckwheat. *J Exp Med* 1928 May 31;47(6):1013–1028.

Shipman P. Scavenging or hunting in early hominids: theoretical framework and tests. *Am Anthropol* 1986;88:27–43.

Shiue HJ, Sather C, Layman DK. Reduced carbohydrate/protein ratio enhances metabolic changes associated with weight loss diet. *FASEB J* 2001;15(4 Pt 1):A301.

Sidossis LS, Mittendorfer B, Chinkes D, Walser E, Wolfe RR. Effect of hyperglycemia-hyperinsulinemia on whole body and regional fatty acid metabolism. *Am J Physiol* 1999;276(3 Pt 1):E427–E434.

Sidossis LS, Stuart CA, Shulman GI, Lopaschuk GD, Wolfe RR. Glucose plus insulin regulate fat oxidation by controlling the rate of fatty acid entry into the mitochondria. *J Clin Invest* 1996;98:2244–2250.

Sigal RJ, El-Hashimy M, Martin BC, Soeldner JS, Krolewski AS, Warram JH. Acute postchallenge hyperinsulinemia predicts weight gain: a prospective study. *Diabetes* 1997;46:1025–1029.

Simms SR. Behavioral Ecology and Hunter-Gatherer Foraging. An Example from the Great Basin. Oxford: BAR International Series 381, 1987:47.

Simonelli C et al. (July 2006). *ICSI Health Care Guideline: Diagnosis and Treatment of Osteoporosis, 5th edition (PDF)*. Institute for Clinical Systems Improvement.

Simoons FJ. Celiac disease as a geographic problem. In Walcher DN, Kretchmer N (eds.), *Food, Nutrition and Evolution*. New York: Masson Publishing, 1981, 179–199.

———. The geographic hypothesis and lactose malabsorption. A weighing of the evidence. *Dig Dis* 1978;23:963–980.

Simopoulos AP. Omega-3 fatty acids in the prevention-management of cardiovascular disease. *Can J Physiol Pharmacol* 1997;75:234–239.

Simpson SR, Rozeneck R, Garhammer J, Lacourse M, Storer T. Comparison of one repetition maximums between free weight and universal machine exercises. *J Strength Cond Res* 1997;11:103–106.

Sinclair DA. Toward a unified theory of caloric restriction and longevity regulation. *Mech Ageing Dev* 2005 Sep;126(9):987–1002.

Singer P, Berger I, Luck K, Taube C, Naumann E, Godicke W. Long-term effect of mackerel diet on blood pressure, serum lipids, and thromboxane formation in patients with mild essential hypertension. *Atherosclerosis* 1986;62:259–265.

Singh K, Singh SK, Sah R, Singh I, Raman R. Mutation C677T in the methylenetetrahydrofolate reductase gene is associated with male infertility in an Indian population. *Int J Androl* 2005 Apr;28(2):115–119.

Singleton VL. Naturally occurring food toxicants: phenolic substances of plant origin. *Adv Food Res* 1981;27:149–242.

Sippy BW. Gastric and duodenal ulcer. Medical cure by an efficient removal of gastric juice corrosion. *JAMA* 1915;64:1625–1630.

Siri-Tarino PW, Sun Q, Hu FB, Krauss RM. Meta-analysis of prospective cohort studies evaluating the association of saturated fat with cardiovascular disease. *Am J Clin Nutr* 2010 Mar;91(3):535–546.

———. Saturated fat, carbohydrate, and cardiovascular disease. *Am J Clin Nutr* 2010 Mar;91(3):502–509.

———. Saturated fatty acids and risk of coronary heart disease: modulation by replacement nutrients. *Curr Atheroscler Rep* 2010 Nov;12(6):384–390.

Sjolander A, Magnusson KE, Latkovic S. The effect of concanavalin A and wheat germ agglutinin on the ultrastructure and permeability of rat intestine. *Int Arch Allergy Appl Immunol* 1984;75:230–236.

Skov AR, Toubro S, Bulow J, Krabbe K, Parving HH, Astrup AI. Changes in renal function during weight loss induced by high vs. low-protein low-fat diets in overweight subjects. *Int J Obes Relat Metab Disord* 1999 23:1170–1177.

Skov AR, Toubro S, Ronn B, Holm L, Astrup A. Randomized trial on protein vs. carbohydrate in ad libitum fat reduced diet for the treatment of obesity. *Int J Obes* 1999;23:528–536.

Sly MR, van der Walt WH, Du Bruyn DB, Pettifor JM, Marie PJ. Exacerbation of rickets and osteomalacia by maize: a study of bone histomorphometry and composition in young baboons. *Calcif Tissue Int* 1984;36:370–379.

Smith AD, Kim YI, Refsum H. Is folic acid good for everyone? *Am J Clin Nutr* 2008 Mar;87(3):517–533.

Smith DB, Roddick JG, Jones JL. Potato glycoalkaloids: some unanswered questions. *Trends Food Sci Technol* 1996;7:126–131.

Smith MD, Gibson RA, Brooks PM. Abnormal bowel permeability in ankylosing spondylitis and rheumatoid arthritis. *Journal of Rheumatology* 1985;12:299–305.

Smith RN, Braue A, Varigos GA, Mann NJ. The effect of a low glycemic load diet on acne vulgaris and the fatty acid composition of skin surface triglycerides. *J Dermatol Sci* 2008;50(1):41–52.

Smith RN, Mann NJ, Braue A, Mäkeläinen H, Varigos GA. A low-glycemic-load diet improves symptoms in acne vulgaris patients: a randomized controlled trial. *Am J Clin Nutr* 2007 Jul;86(1):107–115.

———. The effect of a high-protein, low glycemic–load diet versus a conventional, high glycemic–load diet on biochemical parameters associated with acne vulgaris: a randomized, investigator-masked, controlled trial. *J Am Acad Dermatol* 2007;57(2):247–256.

Smulders YM, Blom HJ. The homocysteine controversy. *J Inherit Metab Dis* 2011 Feb;34(1):93–99.

Soedamah-Muthu SS, Ding EL, Al-Delaimy WK, Hu FB, Engberink MF, Willett WC, Geleijnse JM. Milk and dairy consumption and incidence of cardiovascular diseases and all-cause mortality: dose-response meta-analysis of prospective cohort studies. *Am J Clin Nutr* 2011 Jan;93(1):158–171.

Soffritti M, Belpoggi F, Tibaldi E, Esposti DD, Lauriola M. Life-span exposure to low doses of aspartame beginning during prenatal life increases cancer effects in rats. *Environ Health Perspect* 2007 Sep;115(9):1293–1297.

Sojka JE, Weaver CM. Magnesium supplementation and osteoporosis. *Nutr Rev* 1995 Mar;53(3):71–74.

Solomon CG. The epidemiology of polycystic ovary syndrome. Prevalence and associated disease risks. *Endocrinol Metab Clin North Am* 1999;28:247–263.

Song WO, Chun OK, Obayashi S, Cho S, Chung CE. Is consumption of breakfast associated with body mass index in US adults? *J Am Diet Assoc* 2005 Sep;105(9):1373–1382.

Soni MG, Thurmond TS, Miller ER 3rd, Spriggs T, Bendich A, Omaye ST. Safety of vitamins and minerals: controversies and perspective. *Toxicol Sci* 2010 Dec;118(2):348–355.

Soto AM, Sonnenschein C. Environmental causes of cancer: endocrine disruptors as carcinogens. *Nat Rev Endocrinol* 2010 Jul;6(7):363–370.

Spadaccino AC, Basso D, Chiarelli S, Albergoni MP, D'Odorico A, Plebani M, Pedini B, Lazzarotto F, Betterle C. Celiac disease in North Italian patients with autoimmune thyroid diseases. *Autoimmunity* 2008 Feb;41(1):116–121.

Sparks DL, Friedland R, Petanceska S, Schreurs BG, Shi J, Perry G, Smith MA, Sharma A, Derosa S, Ziolkowski C, Stankovic G. Trace copper levels in the drinking water, but not zinc or aluminum influence CNS Alzheimer-like pathology. *J Nutr Health Aging* 2006 Jul-Aug;10(4):247–254.

Speechly DP, Buffenstein R. Appetite dysfunction in obese males: evidence for role of hyperinsulinaemia in passive overconsumption with a high fat diet. *Eur J Clin Nutr* 2000;54:225–233.

Speth JD. Early hominid hunting and scavenging: the role of meat as an energy source. *J Hum Evol* 1989;18:329–343.

———. Protein selection and avoidance strategies of contemporary and ancestral foragers: unresolved issues. *Philos Trans R Soc Lond B Biol Sci* 1991 Nov 29;334(1270):265–269; discussion 269–270.

Speth JD, Spielmann KA. Energy source, protein metabolism, and hunter-gatherer subsistence strategies. *J Anthropol Archaeol* 1983;2:1–31.

Spindler SR. Rapid and reversible induction of the longevity, anticancer, and genomic effects of caloric restriction. *Mech Ageing Dev* 2005 Sep;126(9):960–966.

Sponheimer M, Lee-Thorp JA. Isotopic evidence for the diet of an early hominid *Australopithecus africanus*. *Science* 1999;283:368–370.

Squadrone R, Gallozzi C. Biomechanical and physiological comparison of barefoot and two shod conditions in experienced barefoot runners. *J Sports Med Phys Fitness* 2009;49(1):6–13.

Srikumar TS, Johansson GK, Ockerman PA, Gustafsson JA, Akesson B. Trace element status in healthy subjects switching from a mixed to a lactovegetarian diet for 12 mo. *Am J Clin Nutr* 1992 Apr;55(4):885–890.

St Jeor ST, Howard BV, Prewitt TE, Bovee V, Bazzarre T, Eckel RH et al. Dietary protein and weight reduction: a statement for healthcare professionals from the Nutrition Committee of the Council on Nutrition, Physical Activity, and Metabolism of the American Heart Association. *Circulation* 2001 Oct 9;104(15):1869–1874.

Stabler SP, Allen RH. Vitamin B12 deficiency as a worldwide problem. *Annu Rev Nutr* 2004;24:299–326.

Stamler J. Diet-heart: a problematic revisit. *Am J Clin Nutr* 2010;91:497–499.

Stamler J, Caggiula A, Grandits GA, Kjelsberg M, Cutler JA. Relationship to blood pressure of combinations of dietary macronutrients. Findings of the multiple risk factor intervention trial. (MRFIT). *Circulation* 1996;94:2417–2423.

Stampfer MJ, Krauss RM, Ma J, Blanche PJ, Holl LG, Sacks FM, Hennekens CH. A prospective study of triglyceride level, low-density lipoprotein particle diameter, and risk of myocardial infarction. *JAMA* 1996;276:882–888.

Stampfer MJ, Sacks FM, Salvini S, Willett WC, Hennekens CH. A prospective study of cholesterol, apolipoproteins, and the risk of myocardial infarction. *N Engl J Med* 1991;325:373–381.

Stanford CB, Wallis J, Mpongo E, Goodall J. Hunting decisions in wild chimpanzees. *Behaviour* 1994;131:1–18.

Steegers EP, Eskes TB, Jongsma HW, Hein PR. Dietary sodium restriction during pregnancy: a historical review. *Eur J Obstet Gynecol Reprod Biol* 1991;40:83–90.

Stefansson V. *Cancer: Disease of Civilization?* New York: Hill and Wang, 1960.

———. *The Fat of the Land.* New York: Macmillan Company, 1960.

Stein MD, Friedmann PD. Disturbed sleep and its relationship to alcohol use. *Subst Abus* 2005 Mar;26(1):1–13.

Steiner PE. Necropsies on Okinawans. Anatomic and pathologic observations. *Arch Pathol* 1946;42:359–380.

Stephen EH, Chandra A. Declining estimates of infertility in the United States: 1982–2002. *Fertil Steril* 2006 Sep;86(3):516–523.

Stephens WP, Berry JL, Klimiuk PS, Mawer EB. Annual high dose vitamin D prophylaxis in Asian immigrants. *Lancet* 1981;2:1199–1201.

Stetler RA, Gan Y, Zhang W, Liou AK, Gao Y, Cao G, Chen J. Heat shock proteins: cellular and molecular mechanisms in the central nervous system. *Prog Neurobiol* 2010 Oct;92(2):184–211.

Stevens VL, McCullough ML, Sun J, Gapstur SM. Folate and other one-carbon metabolism-related nutrients and risk of postmenopausal breast cancer in the Cancer Prevention Study II Nutrition Cohort. *Am J Clin Nutr* 2010 Jun;91(6):1708–1715.

Stewart P, Darvill T, Lonky E, Reihman J, Pagano J, Bush B. Assessment of prenatal exposure to PCBs from maternal consumption of Great Lakes fish: an analysis of PCB pattern and concentration. *Environ Res* 1999;80(2 Pt 2):S87–S96.

Stoll AL, Severus WE, Freeman MP, Reuter S, Zboyan HA, Diamond E, Cress KK, Marangell LB. Omega 3 fatty acids in bipolar disorder: a preliminary double-blind, placebo-controlled trial. *Arch Gen Psychiatry* 1999;56:407–412.

Stoll BA. Western diet, early puberty, and breast cancer risk. *Breast Cancer Res Treat* 1998;49:187–193.

Stoll LL, Denning GM, Weintraub NL. Endotoxin, TLR4 signaling and vascular inflammation: potential therapeutic targets in cardiovascular disease. *Curr Pharm Des* 2006;12(32):4229–4245.

Stolzenberg-Solomon RZ, Chang SC, Leitzmann MF, Johnson KA, Johnson C, Buys SS, Hoover RN, Ziegler RG. Folate intake, alcohol use, and postmenopausal breast cancer risk in the Prostate, Lung, Colorectal, and Ovarian Cancer Screening Trial. *Am J Clin Nutr* 2006 Apr;83(4):895–904.

Story JA, LePage SL, Petro MS, West LG, Cassidy MM, Lightfoot FG, Vahouny GV. Interactions of alfalfa plant and sprout saponins with cholesterol in vitro and in cholesterol-fed rats. *Am J Clin Nutr* 1984 Jun;39(6):917–929.

Streltsov VA, Titmuss SJ, Epa VC, Barnham KJ, Masters CL, Varghese JN. The structure of the amyloid-beta peptide high-affinity copper II binding site in Alzheimer disease. *Biophys J* 2008 Oct;95(7):3447–3456.

Strobel S, Mowat MA. Oral tolerance and allergic responses to food proteins. *Curr Opin Allergy Clin Immunol* 2006 Jun;6(3):207–213.

Stuart AJ. Mammalian extinctions in the late Pleistocene of northern Eurasia and North America. *Biol Rev* 1991;66:453–562.

Stubbs RJ, van Wyk MC, Johnstone AM, Harbron CG. Breakfasts high in protein, fat, or carbohydrate: effect on within-day appetite and energy balance. *Eur J Clin Nutr* 1996;50:409–417.

Su HY, Hickford JG, Bickerstaffe R, Palmer BR. Insulin-like growth factor 1 and hair growth. *Dermatol Online J* 1999;(2):1.

Sugumar A, Liu YC, Xia Q, Koh YS, Matsuo K. Insulin-like growth factor (IGF)-I and IGF-binding protein 3 and the risk of premenopausal breast cancer: a meta-analysis of literature. *Int J Cancer* 2004 Aug 20;111(2):293–297.

Surh YJ, Lee SS. Capsaicin in hot chili pepper: carcinogen, co-carcinogen, or anticarcinogen? *Fd Chem Toxic* 1996;34:313–316.

Swallow DM. Genetics of lactase persistence and lactose intolerance. *Annual Review of Genetics* 2003 37:197–219.

Swan SH, Waller K, Hopkins B, Windham G, Fenster L, Schaefer C, Neutra RR. A prospective study of spontaneous abortion: relation to amount and source of drinking water consumed in early pregnancy. *Epidemiology* 1998 Mar;9(2):126–133.

Sweet MJ, Hume DA. Endotoxin signal transduction in macrophages. *J Leukoc Biol* 1996;60:8–26.

Sweeten MK, Cross HR, Smith GC, Savell JW, Smith SB. Lean beef: impetus for lipid modifications. *J Am Diet Assoc* 1990;90:87–92.

Sweeten MK, Cross HR, Smith GC, Smith SB. Subcellular distribution and composition of lipids in muscle and adipose tissues. *J Food Sci* 1990;43–45.

Sweileh N, Schnitzler A, Hunter GR, Davis B. Body composition and energy metabolism in resting and exercising Muslims during Ramadan fast. *J Sports Med Phys Fitness* 1992 Jun;32(2):156–163.

Swithers SE, Baker CR, Davidson TL. General and persistent effects of high-intensity sweeteners on body weight gain and caloric compensation in rats. *Behav Neurosci* 2009 Aug;123(4):772–780.

Swithers SE, Davidson TL. A role for sweet taste: calorie predictive relations in energy regulation by rats. *Behav Neurosci* 2008 Feb;122(1):161–173.

Swithers SE, Martin AA, Clark KM, Laboy AF, Davidson TL. Body weight gain in rats consuming sweetened liquids. Effects of caffeine and diet composition. *Appetite* 2010 Dec;55(3):528–533.

Swithers SE, Martin AA, Davidson TL. High-intensity sweeteners and energy balance. *Physiol Behav* 2010 Apr 26;100(1):55–62.

Szodoray P, Barta Z, Lakos G, Szakáll S, Zeher M. Coeliac disease in Sjögren's syndrome—a study of 111 Hungarian patients. *Rheumatol Int* 2004 Sep;24(5):278–282.

Szymanski KM, Wheeler DC, Mucci LA. Fish consumption and prostate cancer risk: a review and meta-analysis. *Am J Clin Nutr* 2010 Nov;92(5):1223–1233.

Takács T, Rakonczay Z Jr, Varga IS, Iványi B, Mándi Y, Boros I, Lonovics J. Comparative effects of water immersion pretreatment on three different acute pancreatitis models in rats. *Biochem Cell Biol* 2002;80(2):241–251.

Takeuchi M, Iwaki M, Takino J, Shirai H, Kawakami M, Bucala R, Yamagishi S. Immunological detection of fructose-derived advanced glycation end-products. *Lab Invest* 2010 Jul;90(7):1117–1127.

Talat N, Perry S, Parsonnet J, Dawood G, Hussain R. Vitamin D deficiency and tuberculosis progression. *Emerg Infect Dis* 2010 May;16(5):853–855.

Taneja S, Bhandari N, Strand TA, Sommerfelt H, Refsum H, Ueland PM, Schneede J, Bahl R, Bhan MK. Cobalamin and folate status in infants and young children in a low-to-middle income community in India. *Am J Clin Nutr* 2007 Nov;86(5):1302–1309.

Tang QQ, Du J, Ma HH, Jiang SJ, Zhou XJ. Fluoride and children's intelligence: a meta-analysis. *Biol Trace Elem Res* 2008 Winter;126(1–3):115–120.

Tanskanen A, Hibbeln JR, Tuomilehto J, Uutela A, Haukkala A, Viinamaki H, Lehtonen J, Vartiainen E. Fish consumption and depressive symptoms in the general population in Finland. *Psychiatr Serv* 2001;52:529–531.

Taubes G. Nutrition: The soft science of dietary fat. *Science* 2001 Mar 30;291(5513):2536–2545.

Taylor CB, Peng SK, Werthessen NT, Tham P, Lee KT. Spontaneously occurring angiotoxic derivatives of cholesterol. *Am J Clin Nutr* 1979;32:40–57.

te Velde E, Burdorf A, Nieschlag E, Eijkemans R, Kremer JA, Roeleveld N, Habbema D. Is human fecundity declining in Western countries? *Hum Reprod* 2010 Jun;25(6):1348–1353.

Teikari JM. Myopia and stature. *Acta Ophthalmol* 1987;65:673–676.

Teleki G. The omnivorous chimpanzee. *Sci Am* 1973;228:33–42.

Teppo AM, Maury CP. Antibodies to gliadin, gluten, and reticulin glycoprotein in rheumatic diseases: elevated levels in Sjögren's syndrome. *Clin Exp Immunol* 1984 Jul;57(1):73–78.

Testart A. The significance of food storage among hunter-gatherers: residence patterns, population densities, and social inequalities. *Curr Anthropol* 1982;23:523–537.

Teuteberg HJ. Periods and turning points in the history of European diet: a preliminary outline of problems and methods. In Fenton A, Kisban E (eds.), *Food in Change. Eating Habits from the Middle Ages to the Present Day.* Atlantic Highlands, NJ: Humanities Press, 1986, 11–23.

Thapa B, Skalko-Basnet N, Takano A, Masuda K, Basnet P. High-performance liquid chromatography analysis of capsaicin content in 16 Capsicum fruits from Nepal. *J Med Food* 2009;12:908–913.

Thiboutot DM. An overview of acne and its treatment. *Cutis* 1996;57:8–12.

Thieme H. Lower palaeolithic hunting spears from Germany. *Nature* 1997;385:807–810.

Thierry van Dessel HJ, Lee PD, Faessen G, Fauser BC, Giudice LC. Elevated serum levels of free insulin-like growth factor I in polycystic ovary syndrome. *J Clin Endocrinol Metab* 1999;84:3030–3035.

Thomas BH, Steenbock H. Cereals and rickets. The comparative rickets-producing properties of different cereals. *Biochemistry Journal* 1936;30:177–188.

Thomas DE, Elliott EJ, Baur L. Low glycaemic index or low glycaemic load diets for overweight and obesity. *Cochrane Database Syst Rev* 2007 Jul 18;(3):CD005105.

Thresher JS, Podolin DA, Wei Y, Mazzeo RS, Pagliassotti MJ. Comparison of the effects of sucrose and fructose on insulin action and glucose tolerance. *Am J Physiol Regul Integr Comp Physiol* 2000;279:R1334–R1340.

Tikkiwal M, Ajmera RL, Mathur NK. Effect of zinc administration on seminal zinc and fertility of oligospermic males. *Indian J Physiol Pharmacol* 1987 Jan-Mar;31(1):30–34.

Tobian L. High-potassium diets markedly protect against stroke deaths and kidney disease in hypertensive rats, an echo from prehistoric days. *J Hypertens* 1986;4(suppl):S67–S76.

———. Potassium and sodium in hypertension. *J Hypertens* 1988;6(suppl 4): S12–S24.

———. Salt and hypertension. *Hypertension* 1991;17(suppl I):I-52–I-58.

Tobian L, Hanlon S. High sodium chloride diets injure arteries and raise mortality without changing blood pressure. *Hypertension* 1990;15:900–903.

Tolson JK, Roberts SM. Manipulating heat shock protein expression in laboratory animals. *Methods* 2005 Feb;35(2):149–157.

Tong WM, Hofer H, Ellinger A, Peterlik M, Cross HS. Mechanism of antimitogenic action of vitamin D in human colon carcinoma cells: relevance for suppression of epidermal growth factor-stimulated cell growth. *Oncol Res* 1999;11:77–84.

Torre M, Rodriguez AR, Saura-Calixto F. Effects of dietary fiber and phytic acid on mineral availability. *Crit Rev Food Sci Nutr* 1991;1:1–22.

Torrey JC, Montu E. The influence of an exclusive meat diet on the flora of the human colon. *J Infect Dis* 1931;49:141–176.

Toumi D, Mankai A, Belhadj R, Ghedira-Besbes L, Jeddi M, Ghedira I. Thyroid-related autoantibodies in Tunisian patients with coeliac disease. *Clin Chem Lab Med* 2008;46(3):350–353.

Travers SH, Labarta JI, Gargosky SE, Rosenfeld RG, Jeffers BW, Eckel RH. Insulin-like growth factor binding protein-I levels are strongly associated with insulin sensitivity and obesity in early pubertal children. *J Clin Endocrinol Metab* 1998;83:1935–1939.

Trinkaus, E. Anatomical evidence for the antiquity of human footwear use. *J Archaeol Sci* 2005;32(10):1515–1526.

Trinkaus E, Shang H. Anatomical evidence for the antiquity of human footwear: Tianyuan and Sunghir. *J Archaeol Sci* 2008;35(7):1928–1933.

Tripoli E, Giammanco M, Tabacchi G, Di Majo D, Giammanco S, La Guardia M. The phenolic compounds of olive oil: structure, biological activity, and beneficial effects on human health. *Nutr Res Rev* 2005;18(1):98–112.

Trowell H. Dietary fibre: a paradigm. In Trowell H, Burkitt D, Heaton K, Doll R (eds.), *Dietary Fibre, Fibre-Depleted Foods and Disease*. New York: Academic Press, 1985, 1–20.

Truswell AS. Diet and nutrition of hunter-gatherers. In *Health and disease in tribal societies*. New York: Elsevier, 1977, 213–221.

———. Human Nutritional Problems at Four Stages of Technical Development. Reprint. Queen Elizabeth College (University of London), Inaugural Lecture, May, 1972.

Tsukura Y, Mori M, Hirotani Y, Ikeda K, Amano F, Kato R, Ijiri Y, Tanaka K. Effects of capsaicin on cellular damage and monolayer permeability in human intestinal Caco-2 cells. *Biol Pharm Bull* 2007 Oct;30(10):1982–1986.

Tucker KL, Hannan MT, Chen H, Cupples LA, Wilson PW, Kiel DP. Potassium, magnesium, and fruit and vegetable intakes are associated with greater bone mineral density in elderly men and women. *Am J Clin Nutr* 1999;69:727–736.

Turner CG. Dental anthropological indicators of agriculture among the Jomon people of central Japan. *Am J Phys Anthropol* 1979;51:619–636.

Turner JC. Adaptive strategies of selective fatty acid deposition in the bone marrow of desert bighorn sheep. *Comp Biochem Physiol* 1979;62A:599–604.

Tuxen MK, Nielsen HV, Birgens H. Poisoning by kidney beans (*Phaseolus vulgaris*). *Ugeskr Laeger* 1991 Dec 16;153(51):3628–3629.

Tuyns A. Salt and gastrointestinal cancer. *Nutr Cancer* 1988;11:229–232.

Ulrich CM, Potter JD. Folate and cancer—timing is everything. *JAMA* 2007 Jun 6;297(21):2408–2409.

Umemura T, Slinger SJ, Bhatnagar MK, Yamashiro S. Histopathology of the heart from rats fed rapeseed oils. *Res Vet Sci* 1978;25(3):318–322.

United States Census Bureau. Historical Estimates of World Population. census.gov/ftp/pub /ipc/www/worldhis.html.

United States Department of Agriculture. Economic Research Service. Sugar and Sweeteners Yearbook Tables.

Uribarri J, Woodruff S, Goodman S, Cai W, Chen X, Pyzik R, Yong A, Striker GE, Vlassara H. Advanced glycation end products in foods and a practical guide to their reduction in the diet. *J Am Diet Assoc* 2010 Jun;110(6):911–916.

Urquhart JA. The most northerly practice in Canada. *Can Med Assoc J* 1935;33:193–196.

USDA MyPlate. choosemyplate.gov.

Vaarala O, Knip M, Paronen J et al. Cow's milk formula feeding induces primary immunization to insulin in infants at genetic risk for type 1 diabetes. *Diabetes* 1999;48:1389–1394.

Vaarala O, Paronen J, Otonkoski T, Akerblom HK. Cow milk feeding induces antibodies to insulin in children—a link between cow milk and insulin-dependent diabetes mellitus? *Scand J Immunol* 1998;47:131–135.

van den Bourne BE, Kijkmans BA, de Rooij HH, le Cessie S, Verweij CL. Chloroquine and hydroxychloroquine equally affect tumor necrosis factor-alpha, interleukin 6, and interferon-gamma production by peripheral blood mononuclear cells. *Journal of Rheumatology* 1997;24:55–60.

van der Merwe NJ, Thackeray JF, Lee-Thorp JA, Luyt J. The carbon isotope ecology and diet of Australopithecus africanus at Sterkfontein, South Africa. *J Hum Evol* 2003;44: 581–597.

van Meurs JB, Dhonukshe-Rutten RA, Pluijm SM, van der Klift M, de Jonge R, Lindemans J, de Groot LC, Hofman A, Witteman JC, van Leeuwen JP, Breteler MM, Lips P, Pols HA, Uitterlinden AG. Homocysteine levels and the risk of osteoporotic fracture. *N Engl J Med* 2004 May 13;350(20):2033–2041.

van Mil NH, Oosterbaan AM, Steegers-Theunissen RP. Teratogenicity and underlying mechanisms of homocysteine in animal models: a review. *Reprod Toxicol* 2010 Dec;30(4):520–531.

Varner JA, Jensen KF, Horvath W, Isaacson RL. Chronic administration of aluminum-fluoride or sodium-fluoride to rats in drinking water: alterations in neuronal and cerebrovascular integrity. *Brain Res* 1998 Feb 16;784(1–2):284–298.

Varo P. Mineral element balance and coronary heart disease. *Internat J Vit Nutr Res* 1974;44:267–273.

Vasconcelos IM, Oliveira JT. Antinutritional properties of plant lectins. *Toxicon* 2004 Sep 15;44(4):385–403.

Vegetarianism in America. *Vegetarian Times Magazine*, 2008. vegetariantimes.com/features /archive_of_editorial/667.

Venter FS, Thiel PG. Red kidney beans—to eat or not to eat? *S Afr Med J* 1995 Apr;85(4):250–252.

Verkleij-Hagoort AC, Verlinde M, Ursem NT, Lindemans J, Helbing WA, Ottenkamp J, Siebel FM, Gittenberger-de Groot AC, de Jonge R, Bartelings MM, Steegers EA, Steegers-Theunissen RP. Maternal hyperhomocysteinaemia is a risk factor for congenital heart disease. *BJOG* 2006 Dec;113(12):1412–1418.

Vetter J. Plant cyanogenic glycosides. *Toxicon* 2000;38:11–36.

Vieth R. Why the optimal requirement for vitamin D3 is probably much higher than what is officially recommended for adults. *J Steroid Biochem Mol Biol* 2004;89–90:575–579.

Vieth R, Bischoff-Ferrari H, Boucher BJ, Dawson-Hughes B, Garland CF, Heaney RP et al. The urgent need to recommend an intake of vitamin D that is effective. *Am J Clin Nutr* 2007;85:649–650.

Vigers AJ, Roberts WK, Selitrennikoff CP. A new family of plant antifungal proteins. *Mol Plant Microbe Interact* 1991 Jul-Aug;4(4):315–323.

Villanueva CM, Fernández F, Malats N, Grimalt JO, Kogevinas M. Meta-analysis of studies on individual consumption of chlorinated drinking water and bladder cancer. *J Epidemiol Community Health* 2003 Mar;57(3):166–173.

Virtanen SM, Räsänen L, Ylönen K, Aro A, Clayton D, Langholz B, Pitkäniemi J, Savilahti E, Lounamaa R, Tuomilehto J et al. Early introduction of dairy products associated with increased risk of IDDM in Finnish children. The Childhood in Diabetes in Finland Study Group. *Diabetes* 1993 Dec;42(12):1786–1790.

Voegtlin WL. *The Stone Age Diet*. New York: Vantage Press, 1975.

Vogel T, Dali-Youcef N, Kaltenbach G, Andrès E. Homocysteine, vitamin B12, folate, and cognitive functions: a systematic and critical review of the literature. *Int J Clin Pract* 2009 Jul;63(7):1061–1067.

Vojdani A, O'Bryan T, Green JA, Mccandless J, Woeller KN, Vojdani E, Nourian AA, Cooper EL. Immune response to dietary proteins, gliadin, and cerebellar peptides in children with autism. *Nutr Neurosci* 2004 Jun;7(3):151–161.

Vojdani A, Pangborn JB, Vojdani E, Cooper EL. Infections, toxic chemicals, and dietary peptides binding to lymphocyte receptors and tissue enzymes are major instigators of autoimmunity in autism. *Int J Immunopathol Pharmacol* 2003 Sep–Dec;16(3):189–199.

Wagner M, Oehlmann J. Endocrine disruptors in bottled mineral water: estrogenic activity in the E-Screen. *J Steroid Biochem Mol Biol* 2011 Oct;127(1–2):128–135.

————. Endocrine disruptors in bottled mineral water: total estrogenic burden and migration from plastic bottles. *Environ Sci Pollut Res Int* 2009 May;16(3):278–286.

Wald DS, Law M, Morris JK. Homocysteine and cardiovascular disease: evidence on causality from a meta-analysis. *BMJ* 2002 Nov 23;325(7374):1202.

Waldmann A, Dörr B, Koschizke JW, Leitzmann C, Hahn A. Dietary intake of vitamin B6 and concentration of vitamin B6 in blood samples of German vegans. *Public Health Nutr* 2006 Sep;9(6):779–784.

Waller K, Swan SH, DeLorenze G, Hopkins B. Trihalomethanes in drinking water and spontaneous abortion. *Epidemiology* 1998 Mar;9(2):134–140.

Walsh SJ, Rau LM. Autoimmune diseases: a leading cause of death among young and middle-aged women in the United States. *Am J Public Health* 2000 Sep;90(9):1463–1466.

Walter PB, Knutson MD, Paler-Martinez A, Lee S, Xu Y, Viteri FE, Ames BN. Iron deficiency and iron excess damage mitochondria and mitochondrial DNA in rats. *Proc Natl Acad Sci USA* 2002 Feb 19;99(4):2264–2269.

Wang Q, Yu LG, Campbell BJ, Milton JD, Rhodes JM. Identification of intact peanut lectin in peripheral venous blood. *Lancet* 1998 Dec 5;352(9143):1831–1832.

Wang TK, Bolland MJ, van Pelt NC, Horne AM, Mason BH, Ames RW, Grey AB, Ruygrok PN, Gamble GD, Reid IR. Relationships between vascular calcification, calcium metabolism, bone density, and fractures. *J Bone Miner Res* 2010 Dec;25(12):2501–2509.

Ward MH, Mark SD, Cantor KP, Weisenburger DD, Correa-Villasenor A, Zahm SH. Drinking water nitrate and the risk of non-Hodgkin's lymphoma. *Epidemiology* 1996 Sep;7(5):465–471.

Watkins BA. Dietary biotin effects on desaturation and elongation of 14Clinoleic acid in the chicken. *Nutr Res* 1990;10:325–334.

Watkins BA, Li Y, Seifert MF. Dietary ratio of n-6/n-3 PUFAs and docosahexaenoic acid: actions on bone mineral and serum biomarkers in ovariectomized rats. *J Nutr Biochem* 2006; 17(4):282–289.

Webster D, Webster G. Optimal hunting and Pleistocene extinction. *Hum Ecol* 1984;12:275–289.

Weigle DS, Breen PA, Matthys CC, Callahan HS, Meeuws KE, Burden VR, Purnell JQ. A high-protein diet induces sustained reductions in appetite, ad libitum caloric intake, and body weight despite compensatory changes in diurnal plasma leptin and ghrelin concentrations. *Am J Clin Nutr* 2005 Jul;82(1):41–48.

Weiss LA, Barrett-Connor E, Von Muhlen D. Ratio of omega-6 to omega-3 fatty acids and bone mineral density in older adults: the Rancho Bernardo Study. *Am J Clin Nutr* 2005;81(4):934–938.

Weller O. The earliest rock salt exploitation in Europe. A salt mountain in Spanish Neolithic. *Antiquity* 2002;76:317–318.

Werder SF. Cobalamin deficiency, hyperhomocysteinemia, and dementia. *Neuropsychiatr Dis Treat* 2010 May 6;6:159–195.

Whitehouse CR, Boullata J, McCauley LA. The potential toxicity of artificial sweeteners. *AAOHN J* 2008 Jun;56(6):251–259.

Whorton JC. Historical development of vegetarianism. *Am J Clin Nutr* 1994;59 (suppl) 1103S-1109S.

Wiesenthal KE, McGuire MJ, Suffet IH. Characteristics of salt taste and free chlorine or chloramine in drinking water. *Water Sci Technol* 2007;55(5):293–300.

Wieslander G, Norbäck D, Wang Z, Zhang Z, Mi Y, Lin R. Buckwheat allergy and reports on asthma and atopic disorders in Taiyuan City, Northern China. *Asian Pac J Allergy Immunol* 2000 Sep;18(3):147–152.

Wilhelm KR, Yanamandra K, Gruden MA, Zamotin V, Malisauskas M, Casaite V, Darinskas A, Forsgren L, Morozova-Roche LA. Immune reactivity towards insulin, its amyloid, and protein S100B in blood sera of Parkinson's disease patients. *Eur J Neurol* 2007 Mar;14(3):327–334.

Willardson JM, Bressel E. Predicting a 10 repetition maximum for the free weight parallel squat using the 45 degrees angled leg press. *J Strength Cond Res* 2004;18:567–561.

Willett WC. Is dietary fat a major determinant of body fat? *Am J Clin Nutr* 1998;67(suppl): 556S–562S.

Willett WC, Ascherio A. Trans fatty acids: are the effects only marginal? *Am J Public Health* 1994;84:722–724.

Williams CM. Nutritional quality of organic food: shades of grey or shades of green? *Proc Nutr Soc* 2002;61:19–24.

Williams GC, Nesse RM. The dawn of Darwinian medicine. *Q Rev Biol* 1991 Mar;66(1):1–22.

Wilson AB, King TP, Clarke EMW, Pusztai A. Kidney bean (*Phaseolus vulgaris*) lectin-induced lesions in the small intestine. II. Microbiological studies. *Journal of Comparative Pathology* 1980;90:597–602.

Wilson AK, Ball MJ. Nutrient intake and iron status of Australian male vegetarians. *Eur J Clin Nutr* 1999 Mar;53(3):189–194.

Wilson ME. Premature elevation in serum insulin-like growth factor-I advances first ovulation in rhesus monkeys. *J Endocrinol* 1998 Aug;158(2):247-257.

Windham GC, Waller K, Anderson M, Fenster L, Mendola P, Swan S. Chlorination by-products in drinking water and menstrual cycle function. *Environ Health Perspect* 2003 Jun;111(7):935–941.

Wing RR. Physical activity in the treatment of the adulthood overweight and obesity: current evidence and research issues. *Med Sci Sports Exerc* 1999;31:S547–S552.

Winterhalder B, Smith EA (eds). *Hunter-Gatherer Foraging Strategies. Ethnographic and Archaeological Analyses*. Chicago: University of Chicago Press, 1981, 1–268.

Woese K, Lange D, Boess C, Bogl KW. A comparison of organically and conventionally grown foods—results of a review of the relevant literature. *J Sci Food Agric* 1997;74:281–293.

Wolever TM, Bolognesi C. Prediction of glucose and insulin responses of normal subjects after consuming mixed meals varying in energy, protein, fat, carbohydrate, and glycemic index. *J Nutr* 1996;126:2807–2812.

Wolfe BM. Potential role of raising dietary protein intake for reducing risk of atherosclerosis. *Can J Cardiol* 1995;11(suppl G):127G –131G.

Wolfe BM, Giovannetti PM. Short-term effects of substituting protein for carbohydrate in the diets of moderately hypercholesterolemic human subjects. *Metabolism* 1991;40:338–343.

Wolfe BMJ, Piche LA. Replacement of carbohydrate by protein in a conventional-fat diet reduces cholesterol and triglyceride concentrations in healthy normolipidemic subjects. *Clin Invest Med* 1999;22:140–148.

Wolmarans P, Benade AJ, Kotze TJ, Daubitzer AK, Marais MP, Laubscher R. Plasma lipoprotein response to substituting fish for red meat in the diet. *Am J Clin Nutr* 1991;53:1171–1176.

Wong WW, Copeland KC, Hergenroeder AC, Hill RB, Stuff JE, Ellis KJ. Serum concentrations of insulin, insulin-like growth factor-I, and insulin-like growth factor binding proteins are different between white and African American girls. *J Pediatr* 1999;135:296–300.

Wong WY, Merkus HM, Thomas CM, Menkveld R, Zielhuis GA, Steegers-Theunissen RP. Effects of folic acid and zinc sulfate on male factor subfertility: a double-blind, randomized, placebo-controlled trial. *Fertil Steril* 2002 Mar;77(3):491–498.

Wood B, Collard M. The human genus. *Science* 1999;284:65–71.

Wormuth M, Scheringer M, Vollenweider M, Hungerbühler K. What are the sources of exposure to eight frequently used phthalic acid esters in Europeans? *Risk Anal* 2006 Jun;26(3):803–824.

Worthington V. Effect of agricultural methods on nutritional quality: a comparison of organic with conventional crops. *Alternative Therapies* 1998;4:58–68.

———. Nutritional quality of organic versus conventional fruits, vegetables, and grains. *J Altern Complement Med* 2001;2:161–173.

Wrensch M, Swan SH, Lipscomb J, Epstein DM, Neutra RR, Fenster L. Spontaneous abortions and birth defects related to tap and bottled water use, San Jose, California, 1980–1985. *Epidemiology* 1992 Mar;3(2):98–103.

Wright JD, Kennedy-Stephenson J, Wang CY, McDowell MA, Johnson CL, National Center for Health Statistics, CDC. Trends in intake of energy and macronutrients—United States, 1971–2000. *JAMA* 2004;291:1193–1194.

Wu J, Lyons GH, Graham RD, Fenech MF. The effect of selenium, as selenomethionine, on genome stability and cytotoxicity in human lymphocytes measured using the cytokinesis-block micronucleus cytome assay. *Mutagenesis* 2009 May;24(3):225–232.

Xavier D, Pais P, Devereaux PJ, Xie C, Prabhakaran D, Reddy KS, Gupta R, Joshi P, Kerkar P, Thanikachalam S, Haridas KK, Jaison TM, Naik S, Maity AK, Yusuf S, CREATE registry investigators. Treatment and outcomes of acute coronary syndromes in India (CREATE): a prospective analysis of registry data. *Lancet* 2008 Apr 26;371(9622):1435–1442.

Xu Q, Yin X, Wang M, Wang H, Zhang N, Shen Y, Xu S, Zhang L, Gu Z. Analysis of phthalate migration from plastic containers to packaged cooking oil and mineral water. *J Agric Food Chem* 2010 Nov 10;58(21):11311–11317.

Yamshchikov AV, Kurbatova EV, Kumari M, Blumberg HM, Ziegler TR, Ray SM, Tangpricha V. Vitamin D status and antimicrobial peptide cathelicidin (LL-37) concentrations in patients with active pulmonary tuberculosis. *Am J Clin Nutr* 2010 Sep;92(3):603–611.

Yan SF, Ramasamy R, Schmidt AM. The RAGE axis: a fundamental mechanism signaling danger to the vulnerable vasculature. *Circ Res* 2010 Mar 19;106(5):842–853.

Yang Q. Gain weight by "going diet?" Artificial sweeteners and the neurobiology of sugar cravings. Neuroscience 2010. *Yale J Biol Med* 2010 Jun;83(2):101–108.

Yang Q, Mori I, Shan L, Nakamura M, Nakamura Y, Utsunomiya H, Yoshimura G, Suzuma T, Tamaki T, Umemura T, Sakurai T, Kakudo K. Biallelic inactivation of retinoic acid receptor B2 gene by epigenetic change in breast cancer. *Am J Pathol* 2001;158:299–303.

Yang YW, Sheikh NA, Morrow WJ. The ultrastructure of tomatine adjuvant. *Biomaterials* 2002;23(23):4677–4686.

Yang YW, Wu CA, Morrow WJ. The apoptotic and necrotic effects of tomatine adjuvant. *Vaccine* 2004 Jun 2;22(17–18):2316–2327.

Yee LD, Lester JL, Cole RM, Richardson JR, Hsu JC, Li Y, Lehman A, Belury MA, Clinton SK. Omega-3 fatty acid supplements in women at high risk of breast cancer have dose-dependent effects on breast adipose tissue fatty acid composition. *Am J Clin Nutr* 2010 May;91(5):1185–1194.

Yu LG, Milton JD, Fernig DG, Rhodes JM. Opposite effects on human colon cancer cell proliferation of two dietary Thomsen-Friedenreich antigen-binding lectins. *J Cell Physiol* 2001 Feb;186(2):282–287.

Yudkin AM, Arnold CH. Cataracts produced in albino rats on a ration containing a high proportion of lactose or galactose. *Trans Am Opthalmol Soc* 1935;33:281–290.

Yudkin J. Archaeology and the nutritionist. In *The Domestication and Exploitation of Plants and Animals*, PJ Ucko, GW Dimbleby (eds.), Chicago: Aldine Publishing Co., 1969, 547–552.

Zahm SH, Ward MH. Pesticides and childhood cancer. *Environ Health Perspect* 1998 Jun;106 Suppl 3:893–908.

Zambon D, Sabate J, Munoz S, Campero B, Casals E, Merlos M, Laguna JC, Ros E. Substituting walnuts for monounsaturated fat improves the serum lipid profile of hypercholesterolemic men and women. A randomized crossover trial. *Ann Intern Med* 2000;132:538–546.

Zender R, Bachand AM, Reif JS. Exposure to tap water during pregnancy. *J Expo Anal Environ Epidemiol* 2001 May–Jun;11(3):224–230.

Zhang CX, Ho SC, Chen YM, Fu JH, Cheng SZ, Lin FY. Greater vegetable and fruit intake is associated with a lower risk of breast cancer among Chinese women. *Int J Cancer* 2009 Jul 1;125(1):181–188.

Zhang J, Kesteloot H. Milk consumption in relation to incidence of prostate, breast, colon, and rectal cancers: is there an independent effect? *Nutr Cancer* 2005;53(1):65–72.

Zhang J, Temme EH, Kesteloot H. Fish consumption is inversely associated with male lung cancer mortality in countries with high levels of cigarette smoking or animal fat consumption. *Int J Epidemiol* 2000;29:615–621.

Zhang R, Naughton DP. Vitamin D in health and disease: Current perspectives. *Nutr J* 2010 Dec 8;9:65.

Zhao JH, Sun SJ, Horiguchi H, Arao Y, Kanamori N, Kikuchi A, Oguma E, Kayama F. A soy diet accelerates renal damage in autoimmune MRL/Mp-lpr/lpr mice. *Int Immunopharmacol* 2005 Oct;5(11):1601–1610.

Zhao YT, Chen Q, Sun YX, Li XB, Zhang P, Xu Y, Guo JH. Prevention of sudden cardiac death with omega-3 fatty acids in patients with coronary heart disease: a meta-analysis of randomized controlled trials. *Ann Med* 2009;41(4):301–310.

Zhu X, Wallman J. Opposite effects of glucagon and insulin on compensation for spectacle lenses in chicks. *Invest Ophthalmol Vis Sci* 2009;50(1):24–36.

Zimmerman MR. The paleopathology of the cardiovascular system. *Texas Heart Inst J* 1993;20252–20257.

Zimmermann MB. Iodine deficiency. *Endocr Rev* 2009 Jun;30(4):376–408.

———. The adverse effects of mild-to-moderate iodine deficiency during pregnancy and childhood: a review. *Thyroid* 2007 Sep;17(9):829–835.

Zohary D. The progenitors of wheat and barley in relation to domestication and agricultural dispersal in the Old World. In Ucko PJ, Dimbleby GW (eds.), *The Domestication and Exploitation of Plants and Animals.* Chicago: Aldine Publishing, 1969, 45–65.

Zoppi G, Gobio-Casali L, Deganello A, Astolfi R, Saccomani F, Cecchettin M. Potential complications in the use of wheat bran for constipation in infancy. *J Pediatr Gastroenterol Nutr* 1982;1(1):91–95.

Zouboulis CC, Xia L, Akamatsu H, Seltmann H, Fritsch M, Hornemann S, Ruhl R, Chen W, Nau H, Orfanos CE. The human sebocyte culture model provides new insights into development and management of seborrhoea and acne. *Dermatology* 1998;196:21–31.

Zucker GM, Clayman CB. Landmark perspective: Bertram W. Sippy and ulcer disease therapy. *JAMA* 1983 Oct 28;250(16):2198–2202.

Zvelebil M. Postglacial foraging in the forests of Europe. *Sci Am* 1986;254:104–115.

Index

Underscored references indicate boxed text, tables, or graphs.